INVESTING IN

MORTGAGE
SECURITIES

INVESTING IN

MORTGAGE SECURITIES

Laurence G. Taff, M.S., Ph.D.

St. Lucie Press

Boca Raton   London   New York   Washington, D.C.

AMACOM
American Management Association

New York • Atlanta • Brussels • Buenos Aires
Chicago • London • Mexico City • San Francisco • Shanghai
Tokyo • Toronto • Washington, D.C.

Library of Congress Cataloging-in-Publication Data

Taff, Laurence G., 1947-
    Investing in mortgage securities / by Laurence G. Taff.
        p. cm.
    Includes bibliographical references.
    ISBN 1-57444-338-0 (alk. paper)
    1. Mortgage-backed securities—United States. I. Title.

HG4655 .T34 2002
332.63'23—dc21
                                          2002069848
                                            CIP

Visit the CRC Press Web site at www.crcpress.com

© 2003 by CRC Press LLC
St. Lucie Press is an imprint of CRC Press LLC

No claim to original U.S. Government works
International Standard Book Number 1-57444-338-0
Library of Congress Card Number 2002069848
Printed in the United States of America 1 2 3 4 5 6 7 8 9 0
Printed on acid-free paper

Dedication

———

To My Wife, Lois, Who Has Made Every One
of Our Houses a Home

Preface

This is a book about residential mortgage-backed securities and investing in them. Mortgages are financial instruments whose main features are their face amounts and their associated interest rates. In the good old days, the 1950s to 1960s, interest rates were stable and mortgage-backed securities did not exist because there was no need for them. Over the last 30 years interest rates have gone from about 5%/year to roughly 18%/year and back down. The volatility associated with interest rates — that is, a measure of the amplitude of their changes — has gone from a quiet 2% to a raucous 25% at times. This has made all fixed-income instruments, including mortgages and the securities based on them, much more electrifying investment vehicles. Adding further importance, the U.S. housing debt market is now the largest nongovernmental market in the world. Indeed, it is second only to the U.S. federal debt. Today it stands at over four trillion dollars (that is, $4,000,000,000,000.00 plus). It is far larger than the combination of all the American stock markets. Mortgages and mortgage-backed securities play a very large role in today's investment mix.

This text is more numerical and mathematical than most books on the subject. Mortgages are fixed-income securities that are priced based on their note rates and their cash flows. The latter need to be predicted —or at least understood. These and other market-related factors depend in a quantitative fashion on the other parameters of mortgages and the securities derived from them. When mortgages are packaged together to form a pool of assets backing a mortgage-backed security, the numerical and financial complications only increase and become even more subtle and intricate. To truly understand the nature of the individual whole loan and its many financially engineered investment vehicles, and to truly understand the ways and wherefores of how and why their prices can change, one must become proficient at the basic arithmetical components or elements of fixed-income securities.

The first four chapters of this book allow you the opportunity to master these arithmetical aspects. Many numerical examples are worked through and many more exercises and problems, always with answers, are incorporated. All of the problems can be solved with a standard business calculator. If your interest is not in the quantitative subtleties of these securities, then the material surrounding the mathematical parts of the text is mandatory for understanding fixed- and floating-rate securities, alternative investment possibilities (to evaluate competing places for your funds), how to evaluate what others are telling you about mortgages and mortgage-backed securities, and how and why you should partition your monies among them.

The material covered in the first four chapters includes simple, compound, and continuous interest, the time value of money in the context of present and future value, annuities, and the composition of a nominal interest rate. Also discussed are various types of short- and long-term fixed-income securities and their pricing, fixed- and adjustable-rate mortgages and their properties (and their less obvious value-related aspects), other common types of mortgages found in the U.S., and a thorough verbal, pictorial, and mathematical exploration of Macaulay duration, modified duration, and convexity. These concepts are absolutely critical to understanding the price risk in mortgages and mortgage-backed securities and to managing a portfolio of mortgage-related securities successfully. Mathematical developments of duration beyond the norm are included at the end of Chapter 3. Finally, a brief overview of automated underwriting ends Chapter 4.

In addition to discussing the financial and numerical aspects of mortgages and mortgage-backed securities, I have tried to place them in their historical setting as the U.S. financial markets have evolved over the last 60 years. The major developments were the creation of government-affiliated institutions, from the FHA and Ginnie Mae to Fannie Mae and Freddie Mac. The special roles that these organizations play, and their overall success at it, have been crucial to the development and growth of the U.S. mortgage markets and their products.

Chapters 5 and 6 are devoted to exploring the types of mortgage-backed securities most frequently encountered. These include pass-through, mortgage-backed securities, stripped mortgage-backed securities, and REMICs (formerly CMOs). The more widespread REMIC tranches — classes such as sequential pay, residual interest, accrual or Z, planned amortization, targeted amortization, reverse TACs, support or companion, floating-rate, inverse floating-rate, and about a half-dozen others — are defined and their pricing vulnerabilities explained. Not only are interest rate sensitivity and its relationship to prepayments covered, but also price variability stemming from alterations in the shape of the yield curve. Naturally, option-adjusted spread methodology and other pricing algorithms for mortgages are covered too. Finally, nonconforming, private-label issuances, their credit enhancement mechanisms, and their risks and rewards are thoroughly dealt with relative to their conforming brethren. It becomes more difficult to perform meaningful numerical computations by hand between Chapters 1 to 4 and 5 to 6; therefore, the number of exercises and problems declines rapidly.

The book turns more mathematical in Chapters 7 and 8. These two chapters cover the term structure of interest rates, the yield curve, forward, spot, and short rates, the probabilistic and financial bases for interest rate modeling, binomial lattices, interest rate swaps, floors and caps and their theoretical pricing, portfolio construction and diversification, and the complete mathematics of mean-variance theory for a two-component portfolio. Chapter 7 also contains the only explanation I have ever seen of why an interest rate swap really works to the benefit of both counterparties. Chapter 8 concludes with a unique, concrete suggestion on how to increase profitability without relying on mostly statistical interest-rate prediction concepts. I am expert in the mathematical content of these two chapters; my feelings with regard to the success, or faults, of commonly used methods are plainly expressed. Because it is relatively easy simply to criticize, whenever I can I offer definite suggestions on how to do better with today's knowledge and technology.

Commercial mortgage-backed securities in our country and investment opportunities overseas are two other growing components to the mortgage-backed securities markets. The largest non-U.S. market is in Germany, but the British have made significant progress too. Commercial mortgage-backed securities, which really deserve their own book, and non-U.S. markets are briefly covered in Chapter 9.

For the mortgage professional, or aspiring mortgage professional, this book provides a solid grounding in the industry. Those of you with a mathematical bent can ponder some very nice examples and extensions of the usual material.

The Author

Laurence G. Taff has an M.S. in Finance from The Johns Hopkins University. He is employed by one of America's leading financial institutions. As an internal business consultant, Dr. Taff's primary expertise is in the mortgage markets, fixed-rate securities, and risk modeling. He has consulted and delivered papers on financial modeling, portfolio management, and interest rate and credit risk analyses nationally and internationally. Dr. Taff specializes in translating theoretical and abstract concepts into actionable, tangible, profitable results. This is his first business textbook.

Prior to his business career, Dr. Taff worked as a highly accomplished astrophysicist (Ph.D. Physics and Astronomy, University of Rochester; M.S., B.S. Physics and Mathematics, City College of New York). His academic appointments include being the principal research scientist at The Johns Hopkins University. Moreover, he worked for several years at both the Space Telescope Science Institute (where he was in charge of pointing the Hubble Space Telescope) and at M.I.T.'s Lincoln Laboratory.

Dr. Taff's computing experience includes decades of software design, development, and the implementation of procedural and object oriented language programs (e.g., FORTRAN, C, C++, Objective C, etc.) De novo, he conceived, coded, and implemented his discipline's first real-time calibration program. He also constructed the largest astrometric catalog (18 million data points), allowing its users a 300% increase in accuracy. Another project involved melding optimal search techniques, real-time analysis, and correlation resulting in an increased capability by 20-fold. His work typically includes the conceptualization, development, and implementation of unique mathematical "tools."

Dr. Taff has published three other books. Two are standards in classical astronomy, the third a text on scientific statistical data adjustment. In addition, he has published over 100 papers in scientific journals and conference proceedings.

Contents

1 Interest and the Time Value of Money

Mortgages in the U.S. are mostly *fixed-rate securities*. This chapter covers the basics of *simple*, *compound*, *and continuous interest* calculations and their usage in fixed-income securities with (mostly) constant cash flows. *Present value*, *future value*, and other aspects of fixed-income mathematics and definitions of key interest rate concepts are dealt with too. When we move on to mortgage-related derivatives, the importance of this and the next two chapters for valuation and portfolio management will become even more apparent. (The first time a financially important concept is mentioned it will appear in italics.)

I. BASIC INTEREST CONCEPTS

A. WHAT IS INTEREST?

"What is interest?" or, more properly put if you are a borrower, "what are *interest charges*?" is an important question. Interest charges are the cost to you of renting someone else's money. We are so used to being colloquial about it that we tend to refer only to the *interest rate,* or just the interest, as the cost of renting money. It should not surprise you that a cost is associated with *borrowing* (renting) money because a cost is associated with renting most things. Alternatively, you could be the lender. Then the question "What is interest?" means "What are the interest payments you will receive for *lending* out your funds?" Put differently, if you are making an *investment* by lending money, what will the *rate of return* on your venture be?

You have some money. You could spend it now on goods or services. Another option is that you could lend it out to someone. Hence, a more sophisticated interpretation for the interest rate you are willing to accept is that the interest you charge is the price for your deferment of immediate consumption. With many tens of thousands of participants in the financial markets, "the" interest rate is the consensus market rate for the suspension of consumption. In reality various interest rates exist, each appropriate to a diverse customer segment (primarily separated by *credit* or *default risk* and the time span of the loan).

When you make an investment, your intention is to give up immediate possession of those funds for a larger, future amount. The greater quantity of money will then be available for procurement of goods, use of services, or further investment. It is the expected growth in the amount of money, over time, that induces you to defer expenditures for future consumption, that is, to *invest*. Some rate of exchange must exist between current dollars and future dollars (just as there is some rate of exchange

1

between the U.S. dollar and the British pound). The *nominal rate of interest* is the markup factor between present and future dollars. This interest rate is the basis of the relationship between dollars now and the dollars you will have after your investment matures. This gives money a *time value*.

Any market rate of interest incorporates several elements designed to compensate the lender of the funds for their use and the many risks associated with the possibility of not receiving all those monies back in full or in a timely fashion (known as default or credit risk). The nominal interest rate includes three components: 1. the *pure* or *real rate of return*, which is the economic cost of lending, 2. the expected *inflation rate*, and 3. a variety of risk premia cast in the form of an interest rate cost. The details of how these factors become entangled will be described after discussing compound interest.

Because of our informal convention of describing the interest charges in terms of an interest rate, there is a great potential for ambiguity. For instance, is the interest charged annually or is it charged semiannually? Perhaps it is billed quarterly, monthly, weekly, daily, or even continuously? Are there 365 days in your year or 360 days broken into 12 months of 30 days each? If you borrow for a month does that mean the same numerical date to the same numerical date or for 30 days (what about February and leap years)? How would you handle due dates falling on weekends or business holidays? These questions concern what is known as the *day count convention*. Each niche of the financial markets has its own method of dealing with this issue. Other queries might revolve around how the interest is to be computed — as a function of the amount borrowed or the outstanding balance — or when the interest is paid — after the fact (that is, in *arrears*) or before the funds are proffered (that is, *discounted*).

1. Simple Interest and the Time Value of Money

Imagine that your sibling is to be married in 1 year. You decide to spend $1,000.00 for his wedding present. You take $1,000.00 in cash and place it under your mattress. One year later you take the money out from under the mattress and buy the gift. You had an alternative; you could have taken the cash and bought a 1-year *certificate of deposit*. Since the *effective annual interest rate* the bank quoted you was 6 3/8%, at the end of the year when your certificate of deposit matured, you would have received $1,063.75 from the bank. This quantity represents your initial $1,000.00 *principal* amount plus $63.75 as a simple interest payment, that is,

$$\$63.75 = 6\ 3/8\% \times \$1,000.00 = 0.06375 \times \$1,000.00.$$

(For clarity, in general "a × b" represents the product of a and b.)

Had you invested your money, instead of placing it under the mattress, you could have received more for your funds in the future than their current worth. There is a time value, going forward, to your funds. When your investment turns out for the better, the time value is positive. In the U.S. you can always invest in the debt obligations of the U.S. Government so, unless we are willing to assume risk, the time value of money can always be considered positive.

Conversely, if you knew you would need exactly $1,000.00 in a year and that you could earn an effective annual yield of 6.375%, then you would only need to allot $940.07 today toward the purchase of the present. Your $940.07 would earn $59.93 in simple interest after 1 year:

$$\$59.93 = 6.375\% \times \$940.07 \quad \text{and} \quad \$59.93 + \$940.07 = \$1,000.00.$$

The amount of money returned to you is equal to the initial *principal value*, P, plus the simple interest earned on the principal. A simple interest payment is calculated by multiplying the interest rate, denoted here by i, times the principal amount. If A is the final amount into which P grows, then

$$A = P \times (1 + i) \tag{1.1}$$

where, P is equal to $940.07, i is equal to 0.06375/year, and A is computed to be $1,000.00.

The terms used to describe the temporal dependence of money are future value and present value. The future value of P, after receiving interest at the rate i for one payment period, is A as computed from Equation 1.1. Conversely, if the amount to be received in the future is denoted by A, then A is described as the future value of P and is related to P and i by Equation 1.2. A has been discounted by the interest rate i:

$$P = A/(1 + i). \tag{1.2}$$

A is the future value of P when the interest rate is i; P is the present value of A with the interest rate i. These two formulas and concepts underlie the pricing of all fixed-income (and *floating-rate*) securities.

a. *Numerical Examples*

  1. Let P = $1,234.56 and i = 11.11%/year; compute from Equation 1.1 that A = $1,371.72.

  2. If A = $2,222.22 and i = 12.12%/year, then P must have been $1,982.00 from Equation 1.2.

  3. Solving for the i, find that i = A/P − 1. If P = $3,456.78 and A = $4,444.44, then i is 28.572%.

b. *Exercises*

  1. Find the future value, in 1 year, of $1,234.56, given an interest rate of 9.87%/year. ($1,356.41)

  2. Compute the present value of an amount that will be worth $2,345.67 1 year in the future if the effective annual discount rate is 8.76%. ($2,156.74)

  3. What annual interest rate turns $555.55 into $600.00 after 1 year? (8.001%)

2. Multiple Simple Interest Payments

In the case of multiple payment periods, with simple interest paid at the end of each interval, let $N \geq 1$ (the symbol means greater than or equal to) be the total number of periods over which interest at the rate I is earned. At the end of this time period, the initial investment amount of p dollars will have grown into a dollars. The latter is given by

$$a = p \times (1 + N \times I).$$

a. Exercises

1. If you received \$2,222.22 from a 2-year investment in which you invested \$1,678.90, what was the annual interest rate? (16.181%)
2. What was the annual interest rate in the preceding exercise if it lasted for 3.5 years? (9.246%)

3. Compound Interest

Rarely is an interest computation so elementary that you can use an effective annual yield over exactly 1 year. More general calculations require either a higher frequency of payment — for example, semiannually, quarterly, or monthly — or an extended period of time. A method of relating the interest rate paid once a payment period to the effective annual yield builds on the fact that the annual yield, or annual interest rate, is applied once per year and the *periodic interest rate* is applied m times per year. The periodic interest rate is computed from the effective annual yield by

$$\text{Periodic Interest Rate} = (1 + \text{Effective Annual Yield})^{1/m} - 1. \qquad (1.3)$$

The inverse formula is given by the expression:

$$\text{Effective Annual Yield} = (1 + \text{Periodic Interest Rate})^{m} - 1. \qquad (1.4)$$

a. Exercises

1. If the effective annual yield is 19.99% and interest is charged monthly, what is the periodic interest rate? (1.530%)
2. If the quarterly interest rate is 4%, then what is the effective annual interest rate? (16.986%)
3. If the effective annual yield is 25% and the periodic interest rate is 7.72%, what is the frequency of application? (m = 3 or three times per year)

How can Equations 1.3 and 1.4 be extended to allow for multiple payments of interest on a growing principal balance when the growth is a consequence of successive interest payments? To put it differently, if we reinvest the interest earned on the principal, it receives the same rate of interest, and all of this is occurring more frequently than once per year, how can we generalize the preceding formulas? Suppose the interest payments were made semiannually and r is the stated annual interest rate. At the end of 1 year there would have been two applications of interest, each at the rate of r/2 and 6 months apart. The first one was made on the original principal amount while the second would have been made on the original principal amount augmented by the first interest payment. The interest has been *compounded*; this is an example of compound interest.

For the numerical case considered earlier, namely r = 6 3/8%, P = $1,000.00, we would find that P had grown into $1,064.77 after 1 year with semiannual compounding. Comparing this to the simple interest amount of $1,063.75, the compounding of interest has increased the gain by $1.02 (= $1,064.77 – $1,063.75). This amount is also equal to the interest earned on the first interest payment or

$$\$1,000.00 \times (0.06375/2) \times (0.06375/2) = \$1,000.00 \times (0.06375/2)^2.$$

At the end of the first 6 months the balance would be equal to $1,031.88 because this is equal to the original principal amount plus the interest charge evaluated at half the annual rate for 6 months;

$$\$1,031.88 = \$1,000.00 + (0.06375/2) \times \$1,000.00 = \$1,000.00 + \$31.88.$$

At the end of the second 6 months' time interval, the balance is $1,064.77 because this is equal to $1,031.88 (the new starting balance) plus interest on it evaluated at half the annual rate for 6 months:

$$\$1,064.77 = \$1,031.88 + (0.06375/2) \times \$1,031.88 = \$1,031.88 + \$32.89$$

$$= \$1,000.00 + \$63.75 + \$1.02.$$

The ending amount is equal to the original principal plus 1 year's simple interest plus one increment of interest on interest. (The effective annual yield is now 6.477% because $1,000.00 \times 0.06477 = $64.77.)

The first application of interest was to the original investment of P resulting in $P \times (1 + r/2)$ dollars at the end of the first payment period. The second increment of interest payment would have been computed on this larger amount, yielding a total, at the end of the second compounding period, of

$$A = [P \times (1 + r/2)] \times (1 + r/2) = P \times (1 + r/2)^2 = P \times (1 + r + r \times r/4)$$

$$= P \times (1 + r) + P \times (r \times r/4)$$

$$= \text{Principal} + \text{Simple interest for one year} + \text{Interest on interest}$$

$$\text{(or compounding).}$$

Therefore, with semiannual compounding, the future value A of an original principal amount P with annual interest rate r at the end of 1 year would be

$$A = P \times (1 + r/2)^2.$$

Conversely, the present value of A dollars to be received 1 year in the future, with respect to annual interest rate r and semiannual compounding, would be P with P given by the inverse expression

$$P = A/(1 + r/2)^2 = A \times (1 + r/2)^{-2}.$$

b. Exercises

1. With an annual interest rate of 6 3/32 (this notation means 6 and 3/32nds or 6.09375%; it is sometimes written as 6–3, or even worse 6.3, when the unit of a 32nd is understood), compute the future value of $1500 if the interest charges are paid semiannually. ($1,592.80)
2. The discount rate is 11 17/64 and the value, going 1 year forward, of P dollars will be worth $3,456.78. If the discounting is executed semiannually, how much is P worth today? ($3,097.95)
3. If the future value of $345.67 is $456.78 after 2 years with quarterly compounding, what was the annual interest rate? (14.181%)

If we extend the compounding problem to monthly payments — because mortgages usually are paid monthly — then, at the end of 1 year, we will have a total amount A equal to the result of paying interest at the monthly rate r/12, where r is the annual interest rate on the original principal P, given by

$$A = P \times (1 + r/12) \times (1 + r/12) \times \bullet\bullet\bullet \times (1 + r/12) = P \times (1 + r/12)^{12}$$

(a total of 12 interest rate factors in the product).

First note that the ellipsis, i.e., the three dots above, indicates that more terms of the same form have not been explicitly written out. Second, keeping the same numerical values that we have been using (i.e., P = $1,000.00 and r = 6 3/8%), in this instance, the initial principal amount will have grown to

$$\$1,065.65 = \$1,000.00 \times (1 + 0.06375/12)^{12}.$$

This reflects that 1 year has elapsed with monthly compounding. Conversely, the present value of A dollars to be received in 1 year, with annual discount rate r and monthly compounding, would be P:

$$P = A/(1 + r/12)^{12} = A \times (1 + r/12)^{-12}.$$

c. Exercises

1. Using the same notation, write down the present and future value formulas for fortnightly, weekly, and daily compounding. Use a 364-day $(= 52 \times 7)$ year. $[A = P \times (1 + r/26)^{26}$ and $P = A/(1 + r/26)^{26}$; $A = P \times (1 + r/52)^{52}$ and $P = A/(1 + r/52)^{52}$; $A = P \times (1 + r/364)^{364}$ and $P = A/(1 + r/364)^{364}]$

2. What will the future value of \$1,122.33 be after 5 years of monthly compounding at an annual interest rate of 12.34%? (\$2,073.54)

3. What annual interest rate, compounded weekly, would be comparable to an annual interest rate of 12.12% compounded monthly? (12.073%)

4. At an annual growth rate of 6, 8, and 10%, with interest paid monthly, how long will it take for an investment to treble in value? (approximately 220, 165, and 132 months, respectively)

The general formulas for present and future value for interest paid at one frequency and compounded at a multiple of it, using P, A, and r as above, m for the frequency of payment (e.g., annual m = 1, if monthly m = 12, and so on), and N for the total number of payment periods (N = 1,2,…) are

$$A = P \times (1 + r/m)^N, \tag{1.5}$$

and

$$P = A/(1 + r/m)^N = A \times (1 + r/m)^{-N}, \tag{1.6}$$

plus

$$r = m \times [(A/P)^{(1/N)} - 1]. \tag{1.7}$$

You would need to multiply the end result by 100 in Equation 1.7 to change it into a percentage value.

d. Exercises

1. Compute the future value of \$5,432.10 if the annual interest rate is 8.76%, the compounding frequency is monthly, and the investment interval is 23 months. (\$6,421.27)

2. How much money would you have to invest to accumulate \$12,345.67 after 42 months, if the annual interest rate was 5.55% and interest was paid semiannually? (\$10,193.01)

3. Your original principal amount of \$123.45 grew to \$234.56 after 32 months with quarterly compounding of interest. What was the annual interest rate? (33.416%)

4. Continuous Compounding

Continuous compounding is a convenient mathematical fiction that allows you to compute certain interest-related quantities very quickly. Do not misunderstand; even with continuous compounding, you cannot drive the interest charges to infinity. Consider the following:

1. You borrow $10,000.00 at a 10% annual interest rate. At the end of 1 year (364 days long in this example) you owe $11,000.00.
2. You borrow the same amount at the same rate, but must pay compound interest semiannually. In this instance you would owe $11,025.00.
3. In the same scenario but with monthly compounding, you would now be obliged to pay back $11,047.13.
4. The interest is compounded weekly (364/7 = 52). You would be indebted for another $3.52 for a new total of $11,050.65.
5. The lender is greedy and demands daily compounding. In this case you would owe less than one dollar more; the amount due is $11,051.56.
6. The lender forces you to accept hourly compounding. In this instance the amount to be repaid has grown by just 14¢ and you now owe $11,051.70.

Even though the compounding frequency dramatically escalated (by a factor of $364 \times 24{:}1 = 8{,}736{:}1$), the interest charge barely gained at all (from $1,000.00 to just $1,051.70 or about 5%).

a. Exercise

1. Repeat the preceding six different compounding exercises to compute a future value when the present value is $11,223.34 and the annual interest rate is 15 19/32. ($12,973.48; $13,041.71; $13,104.14; $13,114.25; $13,116.88; $13,117.30)

By extension you should be willing to believe that, even at the limit of continuous compounding, the total interest charges will be finite and not very different from a considerably slower compounding frequency. We can express the relationship of equivalence between a continuously compounded annual rate of interest, r_c, and a discontinuously compounded annual rate of interest, r, compounded with a frequency of m times per year, by using the exponential function. This function is normally abbreviated by *exp* (or just the letter *e* whose numerical value is 2.7182818...). The formula is

$$\exp(r_c) = (1 + r/m)^m. \tag{1.8}$$

The future value of one dollar, whether continuously compounded at the rate r_c or compounded m times a year at the annual rate r, must be the same. Solving for r_c in terms of r produces the inverse formula

$$r_c = m \times ln(1 + r/m) \tag{1.9}$$

where ln means the natural, or Naperian, logarithm. The solution for r in terms of r_c is given by

$$r = m \times [\exp(r_c/m) - 1]. \qquad (1.10)$$

b. *Exercises*

1. Show that an annual interest rate of 12.34%, compounded quarterly for 1 year, is equivalent to a continuously compounded rate of 12.153%.
2. If the continuously compounded rate is 18.18%, is the equivalent annual rate, for bimonthly compounding, given by 18.25%? (Yes)

The formulas for the future and present value with continuous compounding at the rate r_c with t measured in years are

$$A = P \times \exp(r_c t) \text{ and } P = A \times \exp(-r_c t) = A/\exp(r_c t). \qquad (1.11)$$

c. *Exercises*

1. If the annual continuously compounded rate is 3.21%, and the value of an amount P will be $1,000,000.00 41 months in the future, what is it worth today? What reasonable assumption did you need to make? ($896,125.33 and 12 equal months/year)
2. If $55,555.55 grew into $66,666.66 after 1.35 years, what was the annual continuously compounding interest rate? (13.505%)

5. Discounted Interest

Suppose that you borrow A dollars from the bank but instead of allowing you to pay the interest charges at the end of the term of the loan (i.e., in arrears), the bank requires you to pay the interest at the beginning of the term of the loan (i.e., discounted). Then you would only receive $P = A/(1 + i)$ dollars to use. Clearly the effective interest rate is greater than i in this case because the true interest rate is computed from

True Interest Rate $=$ Interest Charged/(Amount Received)

$=$ Interest Charged/(Borrowed Amount $-$ Interest Charged)

$= P \times i/(P - P \times i).$

As a numerical example, suppose that you were borrowing $500,000 at 7.89%. Then you would actually receive $460,550 = $500,000 - $39,450 (the latter amount being 0.0789 × $500,000) and the true interest rate would be about 8.57%. This is referred to as *discounted interest*.

6. Holding Period Return

A standard topic in most finance books is the *holding period return*. The idea is to evaluate the net value of the percentage increase (or, if you are unlucky, the percentage decrease) in your assets and use that measure to gauge your economic progress. This is converted into a *yield*, known as the *holding period yield*. The final value of the investment includes *capital gains* (increases in value of the asset *per se*) and any dividends or interest income received. If you were investing in real estate, then your final value would include the selling price of the buildings or land plus any rents received while you owned it minus any taxes, repairs, or real estate commissions. The holding period return is the ratio of the terminal value of an investment to its initial value,

Holding Period Return = Final Net Value of Investment/Initial Value of Investment.

If $234.56 grew into $345.67 over 2 years — referred to as the *holding period* — then the holding period return would be 1.47 or 147% (= $345.67/$234.56). Even if your investment lost money, the holding period return would always be nonnegative (i.e., at least zero).

The holding period yield is not a very meaningful concept because of the lack of a time frame associated with it. Moreover, it averages returns on shorter time intervals disguising variability. As an alternative, investors in the U.S. will frequently evaluate one investment opportunity with respect to another by comparing their (semiannual) rates of return. Semiannual yields are used because bonds in the U.S. normally pay interest semiannually. This allows a comparison among different investment possibilities via the concept of *bond-equivalent yield* explained later.

B. Fixed-Income Mathematics

1. An Example

Suppose that you invested $1,000.00 starting today for 2 years. If this investment earns a 6.78% rate of return for the first year and an 11.22% rate of return for the second year, then what is the average rate of return? The answer hinges on the connotation of the word "average." In the financial context this means asking for the average rate of return on an investment: what is the *constant* rate of return that can be applied to the initial investment, over the same time period with the same payment frequency, that makes the result identical to what was actually obtained?

For the stated problem the answer is the *geometric average* (8.977% in this case). To understand why, start with how much money there was at the beginning of the investment — $1,000.00. At the end of the first year these funds earned, at an annual rate of 6.78%, $67.80 (= 6.78% × $1,000.00 = 0.0678 × $1,000.00). After 1 year the quantity of money to be further invested was $1,067.80; this returned 11.22% over the second year. Those gains amounted to 11.22% × $1,067.80 = $119.81 and the initial $1,000.00 has turned into a total of $1,187.61 (= $1,067.80 + $119.81).

After earning a constant rate of return r on an initial principal amount P, the new gross value will be equal to an amount A, where A = initial amount plus interest = P + r × P = P × (1 + r). After 2 years of increase at the same rate of return r, the gross amount would equal [P × (1 + r)] × (1 + r) = P × (1 + r)². Thus, it is the mean value of 1 + r that we wanted. Hence, we should find that value of r such that

$$(1 + r)^2 = (1 + 0.0678) \times (1 + 0.1122).$$

Solving this equation for r, we will be assured that the correct total amount of funds will be reproduced:

$$r = [(1 + 0.0678) \times (1 + 0.1122)]^{1/2} - 1 = 8.977\%. \qquad (1.12)$$

The value of an equivalent investment using this rate of return, for 1 year, would be worth $1,089.77 [= $1,000.00 × (1 + 0.08977)]. At the end of the second year, its value will be $1,187.60 (= 1.08977 × $1,089.77). This result is within 1¢ of the quantity we were trying to reproduce (the difference stems from round-off error).

a. *Exercises*

1. If the annual rates of return on a 3-year investment are 5.55%, –6.66%, and 9.99%, then what is the average rate of return? {2.713% = [(1 + 0.0555) × (1 – 0.0666) × (1 + 0.0999)]$^{(1/3)}$ – 1}
2. If the average return on a 5-year investment was 11.11% and the annual returns for four of the years were 7.77, 9.99, 13.33, and 15.55%, then what was the return for the fifth year? (9.094%)

2. The Geometric Mean

Why take the square root in Equation 1.12 of a 2-year investment? Why would the cube root be appropriate for a 3-year investment? The mathematical basis for these computations involves the concept of the *geometric mean*, which is the type of average commonly found in financial applications. The reason is that compounding interest payments or discounting a series of cash flows involves the multiplication or division of quantities. (The addition of quantities would introduce the *arithmetic mean* or *arithmetic average value*.) First, let us review some material from algebra.

To raise a number to an integral power means to multiply that number by itself as many times as the value of the power. To raise the number 6.54 to the third power means to multiply 6.54 times itself a total of three times; 6.54 × 6.54 × 6.54 = 279.726264. To raise a number to the second power or multiply it by itself is to square it; the customary description for raising a number to the third power is to say that one has cubed it. The cube of 3.45 is 41.063625.

One writes z raised to the Nth power, N a positive integer, as z^N. This notation really means

$$z^N = z \times z \times z \times z \times z \times \bullet\bullet\bullet \times z \times z$$

where there are a total of N factors in the product. If N is a negative integer, then one uses the notation z^{-N} to indicate that what is really desired is the reciprocal of z^N;

$$z^{-N} \equiv 1/z^N.$$

The three-lined equal sign means "is defined to be." Hence, $1.23^{-8} \equiv 1/1.23^8 \cong 1/5.238909 \cong 0.190879$. The symbol $\cong$ means "approximately equal to." Any quantity, including zero, raised to the zeroth power is defined to be unity, so $z^0 \equiv 1$ for all values of z.

a. Exercises

    1. Show that 2^{12} is equal to 4096.
    2. Show that 5.9499018×10^{-5} is approximately equal to 7^{-5}.

The inverse operation of raising a number to a power is to extract a root — to evaluate what quantity, when raised to a power whose reciprocal is equal to the root, will reproduce the given number. So, we speak of obtaining the eighth root of 5.238909 and would write this as $5.238909^{1/8}$. The notation means that we are asking for the value of that number, when raised to the eighth power (one-eighth = 1/8) will be equal to 5.238909. The answer is 1.230000 (approximately). Similarly, the cube root (or one-third and note that 1/one-third = 3) of 27 is 3, the square root of 64 is 8. One can always raise a number to an integral power by the method of multiplication. Extracting a root is a more complicated operation except in the rare instances when the number is a perfect square (i.e., $4 = 2^2$ so $4^{1/2} = 2$), or a perfect cube (i.e., $216 = 6^3$ so $216^{1/3} = 6$), or so on.

b. Exercises

    1. Show that the cube root of ten is approximately equal to 2.154435.
    2. If the reciprocal of the fifth root of a number is equal to 0.933033, what is the number? ($\sqrt{2}$)

The geometric mean of two numbers, e.g., 36 and 49, is obtained by multiplying them together and then taking the square root of the product:

$$\text{geometric mean} = (36 \times 49)^{1/2} = (1{,}764)^{1/2} = 42.$$

The geometric mean of any two quantities a and b is given by the expression

$$\text{geometric mean} = (a \times b)^{1/2}.$$

The geometric mean of the three quantities — a, b, and c — is given by the cube root of their product,

$$\text{geometric mean} = (a \times b \times c)^{1/3}.$$

(A geometric mean with one or more of the quantities being negative has mathematical, but not financial, sense.) The geometric mean is always computed with equal *weights*. The reason that the geometric mean is preferred over the arithmetic mean when evaluating multiperiod investment performance is because it more truly reflects the compounding effect of the individual year's gains (losses). The arithmetic average does not accurately mirror the time value of money.

c. Exercises

1. Compute the geometric mean of 8, 27, and 64. (24)
2. Suppose that the geometric mean of four quantities is roughly 5.544443 and that three of the quantities are 3, 5, and 7. What is the fourth one? (9)

There is a short-hand used for representing the product of many connected terms. This form is useful whenever an amount is compounded or discounted. In this case the upper-case Greek letter pi, Π, is used to symbolize a product. The upper limit is written above pi (and is usually an upper-case Latin letter) and the lower limit is written below pi (usually a lower-case Latin letter):

$$\prod_{n=1}^{N} a_n = a_1 \times a_2 \times \cdots \times a_{N-1} \times a_N = \prod_{m=1}^{N} a_m. \tag{1.13}$$

The meaning of the product sign is explicitly indicated in Equation 1.13. The notation a_n implies a rule or formula for obtaining the nth value of the variable a. The symbolism literally is an abbreviation for writing out the individual terms. The variable n represents a dummy summation index; any letter, from any alphabet, will do; hence, the far right-hand side version of Equation 1.13.

The geometric mean of the set of N, positive, quantities $\{b_n\}$, and the curly bracket is standard notation used to indicate that the entire set of the b_n, n = 1,2,..., N is meant, is given by

$$\left[\prod_{n=1}^{N} b_n \right]^{(1/N)} = (b_1 \times b_2 \times \cdots \times b_{N-1} \times b_N)^{1/N}. \tag{1.14}$$

d. Exercise

1. Compute the average annual rate of return for a security that lasts 5 years and has annual rates of return of 3.45, 4.56, 5.67, 6.78, and −7.89%. (2.369% — disappointing, is it not?)

3. The Arithmetic Average Value or Mean

The utility of an average value is its ability to quickly summarize or locate the center of a distribution of values in one quantity. The main defect of an average value is that it is only one statistic, or one number, used to characterize many amounts. (In general, a statistic is a function of the numerical values of a set of quantities.) Such a brief summarization has its dangers. Consider two sets of bank account balances. The first one contains $0 in account 1 and $100 in account 2. The second has $50.01 and $49.99, respectively. The average values of the accounts are both $50.00, but the spread of the balances around this mean is considerable for the first duo and nearly zero for the second set. One can never tell from the average value which situation obtains (or if account 1 had $25 and account 2 had $75).

The type of average value most people are familiar with is the one just used. It is known as the arithmetic mean or as the average value. The average value of the two quantities, for example, 5.43 and 6.78, is found by adding them together and dividing the tally by two:

$$\text{average value} = (5.43 + 6.78)/2 = 6.105.$$

The formula for the average value of two quantities denoted by a and b would be written as

$$\text{arithmetic mean value} = \text{average} = (a + b)/2. \tag{1.15}$$

The formula for computing the mean value of the three quantities a, b, and c is given by the expression

$$\text{arithmetic mean value} = (a + b + c)/3.$$

Note that each quantity is weighed by unity. When forming the simple average the weights are uniform — that is, they are all equal to each other — and no entry has more importance than any other.

a.   Exercises

1. Compute the average value of 10.5, 14.5, and 20. (15.0)
2. If the average value of four quantities is 17.25, and three of the quantities are equal to 15.75, 19.35, and 11.85, what is the fourth one equal to? (22.05)
3. If you used your credit card to buy $50 worth of goods on even-numbered days and $35 worth of goods on odd-numbered days and your average daily balance was $42.24, what month was it? (February in a leap year)

The expression *weighted mean* or *weighted average* implies that a nonuniform weighing scheme was used. If we were averaging 11.22, 22.33, and 33.44 and they had weights in the proportions 3:2:1, then the weighted mean value is created by adding thrice 11.22 to twice 22.33 to once 33.44 and then dividing the result by 6 (= the sum of the weights). Translating this into an equation, we would write

$$\text{weighted mean value} = (3 \times 11.22 + 2 \times 22.33 + 1 \times 33.44)/(3 + 2 + 1) \cong 18.627.$$

The sum of the weights [i.e., 6 = 3 + 2 + 1 in this instance and 2 = 1 + 1 in Equation (1.15)] appears in the denominator of the expression so that the proper normalization occurs. The symbolic version for the weighted average value of the three quantities a, b, and c whose weights are in the proportions 3:2:1 is

weighted arithmetic mean value = $(3 \times a + 2 \times b + 1 \times c)/(3 + 2 + 1)$.

b. *Exercises*

1. If the weighted average value of two numbers is exactly 10, the weights are in the proportion 1:5, and the quantity with the lesser weight is equal to 11, what is the other quantity equal to? (9.8)
2. What was the weight of the fourth component of an unequally weighted average whose mean value was 17.35, if the four quantities being averaged were 10, 14, 19, and 25 and the weights for the first three were 1.2, 2.3, and 3.4? (1.427)

Observe that there truly are weights in the formulas for the average of two and three quantities given above; however, they are all equal, whereas those in the preceding equation were unequal. If we rewrote Equation 1.15 to show the weights explicitly, then it would have the appearance:

equally weighted arithmetic mean value = $(1 \times a + 1 \times b)/(1 + 1)$.

Conceptually, no difference exists between an average value formed with equal weights and the unequally-weighted version, but some people seem to think that the calculation of an unequally weighted mean requires stronger assumptions than the computation of an unweighted average (or, more properly, an equally-weighted mean). This allegedly more powerful knowledge is required to justify the nonequality of the weights. The real statistical point is that there is no such thing as an unweighted average — all determinations of a mean value require the explicit assignment of weights to each element comprising the statistic. Making the assumption that the weights are uniform (i.e., equal) is just as strong a supposition as that the weights are not uniform (and follow some particular scheme or pattern).

The upper-case Greek letter sigma (Σ) can be used to represent the computation of the average value of many related terms compactly. An example would be

$$\sum_{n=1}^{N} a_n = a_1 + a_2 + \cdots + a_{N-1} + a_N. \tag{1.16}$$

This sum contains exactly N terms $[= (N) - (1) + 1$; that is (the value of the upper summation limit) minus (the value of the lower summation limit) plus (one)]. Since n is set equal to unity underneath Σ, it is understood that the summation commences with a_1. The utility of this notation will become clear later.

c. Exercise

1. Write out the explicit meaning of

$$\sum_{n=3}^{N} a_n$$

where $a_n = 1/(1 + i)^n$, i is an interest rate of 10%, N = 6, and numerically compute the result. $[1/(1.1)^3 + 1/(1.1)^4 + 1/(1.1)^5 + 1/(1.1)^6 \cong 2.619724]$

The (equally weighted) average value of set of N > 1 quantities a_1, a_2,..., a_N can be compactly written, where the angular brackets are used to indicate the mean value, as,

$$<a> = \sum_{n=1}^{N} a_n / N = (a_1 + a_2 + \bullet\bullet\bullet + a_{N-1} + a_N)/N. \qquad (1.17)$$

Note that this is just a straightforward extension of Equation 1.15. Each item enters once, with a weight of unity, and the sum is normalized by the total number of elements in the summation.

d. Exercises

1. Suppose that there are five outcomes to your most recent fling in which you invested $100.00. The first one has an ending value of –$111.00, the second terminal value of –$22.22, the third value of $33.33, the fourth a value of $444.44 at completion, and the least likely end result value of $5,555.55. The probabilities (i.e., the weights) for these prospects are 21.21, 12.12, 13.13, 45.45, and 8.09%, respectively. What is the average result of your investment? ($629.58)
2. If your retirement funds are distributed in three different types of invest-ments in the proportions 1:2:0.5, and the expected annual rates of return on the three are 4.5, 10.5, and 15%, respectively, then what is your expected average rate of return? (9.43%)

Consider a set of properly normalized weights $\{w_n\}$. Properly normalized means that each weight is between zero and one (inclusive) and that their sum is unity. For the set of N > 1 values $w_1, w_2,..., w_N$, the average value of a is given by

$$<a> = \sum_{n=1}^{N} w_n a_n = (w_1 \times a_1 + w_2 \times a_2 + \bullet\bullet\bullet + w_N \times a_N). \qquad (1.18)$$

e.   Exercises

1. Compute the mean value of b if $b_j = 1/j$ and $w_j = j$ for $j = 1,2,3,..., M$ terms in the sum. (M)
2. Acme Co. expects its sales next year to be $999,000 if the economy continues to grow strongly but only $666,000 if the economy maintains its current level of performance and $345,000 if the economy weakens. The firm's treasurer believes that the probabilities of these three events are 20, 55, and 25%, respectively. What is Acme's expected level of sales next year? ($652,350)

C. INFLATION AND INTEREST RATES

1.   The Risk-Free Rate

The interest rate usually quoted to you is a nominal interest rate. However, a dollar is not necessarily worth the same today as it might be a year from now. Its purchasing power may change owing to deflation or *inflation.* Inflation is a general rise in the prices of goods and services. It has been common in the U.S. for the last 50 years. As a consequence, investors have built this expectation into their financial life. Thus, a financier might be satisfied with a real or pure (that is, with inflation taken out) rental cost of 2 to 3% (the historical range of real returns on fixed-income securities in the U.S.), but, because of the expectation of inflation, may charge more. The *risk-free rate* R_f includes a real rate of return, r, and an expected inflation premium, expressed as an interest rate, i. The rigorous relationship among the three rates, all expressed as decimals, is obtained by compounding the factors:

$$R_f = (1 + r) \times (1 + i) - 1.$$

When the real rate of return and the anticipated inflation rate are not too large, the approximation

$$R_f \cong r + i$$

for the risk-free rate of return is frequently used. The real rate of return does vary; during the inflationary 1980s it reached 4 to 6% while immediately prior to that it was slightly negative.

2.   The Nominal Interest Rate

The nominal interest rate includes risk factors beyond those associated with inflation such as credit or default risk, *political risk*, *market* or *interest rate risk*, *foreign currency exchange risk*, an extra premium for long-term lending (known as the *liquidity premium*), and so on. Were they to be included, then the nominal interest rate I would be written, where R represents the risk premia expressed as an annual percentage rate, as

$$I = (1 + r) \times (1 + i) \times (1 + R) - 1 = (1 + R_f) \times (1 + R) - 1. \qquad (1.19)$$

When none of these quantities are too large, then the approximation

$$I \cong r + i + R = R_f + R$$

is convenient. This deconvolution of the nominal interest rate for the effect of inflation is called the *Fisher Effect* after Irving Fisher, who first wrote on many fixed-income subjects in an organized fashion.

D. ANNUITIES

The future and present value examples we have been considering are relatively simple because there is only a single initial principal amount or one terminal payment. Consider a more complicated problem: the annual interest rate is known and you want to save a given number of dollars per year for a certain number of years to reach a total saved amount that is also specified (and that includes the compounded interest). What is the relationship among these four variables and how can it be determined? This kind of financial instrument is called an *annuity* because it is defined as a series of equal annual payments. It is a popular insurance and mutual fund investment and bears an important relationship to a fixed-rate, *fully amortizing*, level-payment mortgage.

1. The Formula for the Future Value

As a retirement vehicle, *regular* or deferred annuities are commonly structured so that they make payments at the end of the year. When the first payment comes at the beginning of the annuity's term, instead of at the end, the annuity is referred to as an *annuity due*. The formula for the future value of a regular annuity, FV_a, whose annual dollar deposit amount is denoted by a, when the fixed annual interest rate is symbolized by i with a total of N years to compound, is obtained by computing the future value of each individual annual payment and then adding them up. For a regular annuity,

$$
\begin{aligned}
FV_a ={}& \text{Future Value of the 1st contribution after } N-1 \text{ years of compounding} \\
& + \text{Future Value of the 2nd contribution after } N-2 \text{ years of compounding} \\
& + \cdots + \text{Future Value of the last contribution after 0 years of compounding} \\
={}& a \times (1 + i)^{N-1} + a \times (1 + i)^{N-2} + a \times (1 + i)^{N-3} + \cdots + a \times (1 + i)^0 \\
={}& a \times \sum_{n=0}^{N-1} (1 + i)^n = a \times [(1 + i)^N - 1]/i. \qquad (1.20)
\end{aligned}
$$

The next section will explain how the last form was obtained.

a. *Exercises*

1. You are planning to save for your newborn son's college education. You can afford to invest $2,950/year for this purpose, starting on his first birthday. You assume that, in 17 years, you will need $65,000 to pay for his education. How much must your rate of return be? (3.146%)
2. How much must you put away every year for 15 years, if the interest rate is 9.99%, to yield $10,000 at the end of that time period? (only $314.99)
3. How long would you need to save $750 per month, if it earns 13.13% per year (compounded monthly), to acquire at least $22,222.22? (25 months)

2. The Geometric Series

Many of the simpler evaluation problems of fixed-income securities can be expressed in terms of compounding an initial amount with a fixed rate of interest or discounting a series of constant cash flows with a fixed rate of demanded return. Both of these can be cast into the form of a *geometric series*. It is the time value of money and the act of compounding that bring geometric series to the fore in fixed-income mathematics. Thus, an understanding of, and facility with, geometric series is important for a full discussion of the mathematics of fixed-income securities. Other fixed-income analytical concepts, such as *duration* and *convexity*, can be represented as geometric series too (as always, only when the *term structure of interest rates* is *flat* — that is, interest rates are not changing with time or over time).

A geometric series is a sequence of terms wherein the next entry is a constant multiplicative factor times the previous element in the series. Let the third term of a geometric series be 9. Let the ratio of successive pairs of terms be 3. Then the next term, the fourth, in this series would be $27 = 3 \times 9$ and the preceding one, the second, was 3 because $9/3 = 3$. The seventh term will be equal to 729, which is the same as 3 times itself 6 times (e.g., the fifth term is $3 \times 27 = 81 = 3^4$ and the sixth term is $3 \times 81 = 243 = 3^5$ so the seventh term is equal to $3 \times 243 = 729 = 3 \times 3 \times 3 \times 3 \times 3 \times 3 = 3^6 = 3^{7-1}$). This particular series commenced with $1 = 3^0$ but that is not required.

a. *Exercise*
1. If the initial value of a geometric series was 0.7 and the multiplicative factor was 5/3, then write down the 11th term of the series and evaluate it. $[0.7 \times (5/3)^{11} \cong 192.945336]$

If the constant multiplicative factor is denoted by the lower-case Greek letter rho, ρ, then for a geometric series with starting value s_1, the rule for computing the nth term is

$$s_n = s_1 \times \rho^{n-1}, \quad n = 1, 2,\ldots, N.$$

The sum of this geometric series, starting at summation index equal to unity, would be written as

$$s_1 \times \sum_{n=1}^{N} \rho^{n-1} = s_1 \times (1 + \rho + \rho^2 + \cdots + \rho^{N-2} + \rho^{N-1}).$$

s_1 can be taken out from the summation symbol because s_1 does not depend on the summation index n; it represents an overall multiplicative factor.

One can evaluate such a sum by computing the values of the individual summands and adding them up; after all, that is exactly what the upper-case Greek letter sigma notation implies. It would be much more convenient to find a closed form expression for a geometric series. If we had such a version — a formula not requiring for its evaluation the labor involved in the explicit summation of N terms — then we could calculate using the latter instead of reckoning the individual terms in the sum and then adding them up. For the typical 30-year mortgage, N would be 360 and the savings in computational effort of a closed form expression would be considerable.

Consider the following geometric series:

$$S_N \equiv \sum_{n=0}^{N} \rho^n = 1 + \rho + \rho^2 + \cdots + \rho^{N-1} + \rho^N = (1 - \rho^{N+1})/(1 - \rho). \quad (1.21)$$

(The symbol S_N will be reserved to always mean the sum of an N-term geometric series beginning at summation index zero.) This result can be proved in several ways; one method is by long division, that is, by explicitly dividing $\rho^{N+1} - 1$ by $\rho - 1$ and seeing that the result is $S_N = \rho^N + \rho^{N-1} + \cdots + \rho^2 + \rho + 1$.

b. Exercises

1. Find the sum of the 20-term geometric series, first term equal to 5, ratio = 1/3. (7.500)
2. If the first term of a geometric series is unity and the sum of 25 terms is 4/3, find the ratio. (1/4)

A demonstration of Equation 1.21 can be had by algebraic means. Multiply it by ρ to obtain

$$\rho \times S_N = \rho \times \sum_{n=0}^{N} \rho^n = \rho + \rho^2 + \rho^3 + \cdots + \rho^N + \rho^{N+1}$$

$$= 1 + \rho + \rho^2 + \cdots + \rho^N + (\rho^{N+1} - 1) = S_N + (\rho^{N+1} - 1).$$

The intermediate form was obtained by adding and subtracting unity. After rearrangement, this is

$$S_N = (1 - \rho^{N+1})/(1 - \rho),$$

or Equation 1.21. Note that in most fixed-income applications the ratio of successive terms will be a discount factor, of the form $1/(1 + i)$, where i is an interest rate or a required rate of return. These formulas can be found next.

c.   Exercise

1. Compute the value of a geometric series commencing with the zeroth term, with a multiplicative factor equal to $1/2$, and unit overall factor. Assume that the series has eight terms in it. Repeat this for a series with 16 terms and one with 32 terms. Do you notice a trend? (1.99609375, 1.99998474, 2.00000000)

Because interest is paid in arrears, the summation occurring in the fixed-income context is

$$S_N - 1 = \sum_{n=1}^{N} \rho^n = \rho + \rho^2 + \cdots + \rho^N = (1 - \rho^{N+1})/(1 - \rho) - 1 \tag{1.22}$$

$$= \rho \times (1 - \rho^N)/(1 - \rho).$$

Another commonly occurring sum used for duration computations is:

$$T_N \equiv \sum_{n=0}^{N} n \times \rho^n = \rho \times [1 - (N+1) \times \rho^N + N \times \rho^{N+1}]/(1-\rho)^2. \tag{1.23}$$

3.   The Fixed-Income Form for Geometric Series

In most fixed-income applications, the ratio of successive terms ρ will be equal to the reciprocal of 1 plus an interest rate (e.g., i),

$$\rho = 1/(1 + i). \tag{1.24}$$

Since, generally, i will be positive, ρ will be in the semiclosed interval 0,1 or, in mathematical terms $\rho \in$ (belongs to) $[0,1]$ where ρ could be zero (the ultimate in hyperinflation because the interest rate would then be infinite), but must be strictly less than unity, that is $1 > \rho \geq 0$. Restating S_N in terms of i,

$$S_N - 1 = \sum_{n=1}^{N} \rho^n = \sum_{n=1}^{N} 1/(1+i)^n = [1 - (1 + i)^{-N}]/i. \tag{1.25}$$

4. The Present Value of an Annuity

Having defined an annuity, how do we compute the value of its payouts (at the rate of a dollars per year) over a predetermined time scale (N years), if it was already funded? Conversely, given the payment amount we desire to receive over a number of years (a dollars again over N years), how could we compute the value of the lump sum deposit (e.g., P dollars) we would need to fund it fully for a given interest rate i? As phrased, these are present value computations whose solution is given by the inverse of Equation 1.20, namely the present value of an annuity, PV_a, is given by discounting each cash flow and adding them all up:

$$PV_a = a/(1 + i)^1 + a/(1 + i)^2 + \bullet\bullet\bullet + a/(1 + i)^N = a \times [1 - (1 + i)^{-N}]/i. \qquad (1.26)$$

This formula is also appropriate for computing the fixed-rate, fully amortizing, level-payment mortgage payment. Suppose that your mortgage was the 1998 *conforming* loan limit ceiling of $227,150 at the rate of 5.875% for 15 years (N = 180 = 15 years × 12 months/year). From Equation 1.26, with PV_a equal to the face value of the mortgage, your monthly payment (= a) would be $1,901.51 (= $227,150/119.4574).

a.   Exercises

1. You have just taken out a 20-year, fixed-rate, fully amortizing, level-payment mortgage in the amount of $155,000. The annual interest rate is 6.50%. What will your monthly payment be? ($1,155.64)
2. For how many years will a lump sum of $12,345.67 last, paying out $1,122.33 per year, if the interest rate is 4.15%? (15)
3. You have just won the lottery. They are promising to pay you $75,000 per year, for 20 years. The lottery commission claimed that this was a million dollar prize. What interest rate are they using? (4.217%)

b.   Adding in Inflation

If you had an annuity to draw from for your retirement, the level-payment aspect would not be desirable because of inflation. Retrieving a constant dollar amount every year, when inflation is eroding the buying power of that dollar, implies that your standard of living must decrease as time goes on. To compensate for this diminishment in purchasing power you would want the withdrawal amount to increase at a constant growth rate, equal to the average expected inflation rate. Then, Equation 1.26 would become, with g symbolizing the growth rate needed to redress the deleterious effects of inflation,

$$PV_a = a \times (1 + g)/(1 + i) + a \times (1 + g)^2/(1 + i)^2 + \bullet\bullet\bullet + a \times (1 + g)^N/(1 + i)^N$$

$$= a \times [(1 + g)/(i - g)] \times [1 - (1 + g)^N(1 + i)^{-N}].$$

c. Exercise

1. If the assumed inflation rate will be 3.33%, you can earn an annual rate of 7.77% on your savings, and you expect to live for 27 more years, what sum must you put aside today to be able to start withdrawing $65,432 per year this and every year going forward? ($1,033,773)

II. NET PRESENT VALUE

A. THE CONCEPT

Net present value is the term used for determining the net value today of an investment you are contemplating making, taking into account its funding costs, the rate of return that you will demand from it, and its cash flows. This present value is computed as all present values are — by discounting an income stream over time, by a particular rate of return, to the present. The net aspect includes adjusting for the investment cost. Let the latter, the initial cash outflow, be denoted by CF_0. For the cash inflow at the nth payment period, use the symbol CF_n ($n > 1$). Let the constant required rate of return be denoted by r. Then, the net present value of this investment, over N discounting periods, is given by

$$NPV = \sum_{n=1}^{N} CF_n / (1 + r)^n - CF_0. \qquad (1.27)$$

a. Exercise

1. You desire an annual rate of return of 15% per year. An opportunity is presented to you that has a purchase price of $345.67, will last 7 months, and will return $77.77 the first month, $66.66 the second month, $55.55 the third month, and so on until $11.11 comes back in the last month. Should you invest in this project? (No, the NPV is –$45.90)

If the net present value is positive, or at least non-negative, then one would consider investing in this project. If the net present value were zero, then that would imply that the earnings from the initial cash outflow were just sufficient to pay back the purchase price at the demanded rate of return. The pricing of fixed-income securities is based on the assumption that the price is a fair one if the net present value of the investment is exactly zero. (This is equally true for floating-rate investments.)

1. Arbitrage-Free Pricing

It is impossible to overstress that the pricing of fixed-income securities is performed on the assumption that the fair market price is the one that makes the present value of its cash flows just balance the cost, i.e., has a net present value of exactly zero. Why should this be so? Because if it were not, then you could make infinite amounts of money without any risk or investment (i.e., the true meaning of *arbitrage*). To see how, suppose that, ignoring the usual *transaction costs* (i.e., taxes, broker's fees, commissions, margin accounts, and so forth), XYZ Company was offering a $1,000.00, 1-year investment at an interest of 8% per year. Further imagine that you can obtain financing at 7% per year. So, what do you do? You borrow $1,000.00 for 1 year at 7% and buy the XYZ Company investment. There is no net expenditure by you at the initial time; $1,000.00 came in from your loan and $1,000.00 went out to purchase the 1-year security.

At the end of the year the investment matures and pays you $1,080.00. You take $1,070.00 of that amount and pay off your loan leaving you $10 ahead with no net investment (i.e., none of your funds were ever at risk, barring default) because the final outcome was certain at the beginning of the transaction. As your greed overcomes you and you try to borrow more and more, to make your risk-free $10/$1000 off of XYZ Company debt, you drive up the cost of borrowing through the mechanism of supply and demand. Simultaneously, your buying pressure on Company XYZ 1-year securities acts to drive their price up (that is, their yield down), eventually bringing the borrowing and lending rates back into equilibrium.

Suppose the XYZ Company was issuing 1-year, 8% debt but you could earn 9% elsewhere. Now what do you do? You let someone else purchase the XYZ Company issue, you borrow it from them promising to return it — or its equivalent (that is, $1080) — at its maturity date, sell the debt at its market price of $1,000, and take the $1,000 proceeds and invest it into whatever was offering you 9%. At the end of 1 year, the higher-paying security matures and pays you $1,090. You take $1,080 of the proceeds and return it to the party from which you borrowed the XYZ security. Once more you are ahead $10/$1000! However, if you try to repeatedly replicate this strategy, to maximize your gains, your desire to *short-sell* XYZ Company debt will drive its price down (i.e., its yield will go up) while, simultaneously, your eagerness to participate in the higher-paying investment will lower its yield through the supply and demand mechanism. Soon, equilibrium will be restored and the borrowing and lending rates will be equal.

So, if the net present value of a fixed-income investment were not zero, someone could make arbitrarily large, risk-free profits. Even if this opportunity remained hidden from the rest of us, one's own activities to benefit from it would force equilibrium via the supply and demand mechanism. When you do discover it, your actions will only increase the rate at which a balance is restored. This kind of no-arbitrage argument is a very powerful one in finance.

B. The Term Structure of Interest Rates: An Introduction

We have been making the assumption that the interest rate or the discount rate for one time period is identical to the interest rate or discount rate for all other time periods. We have also been assuming that tomorrow's rates will be the same as today's. These are economically simplistic but allow a more straightforward presentation of many financial concepts and the use of the geometric series to present neat, compact, analytical results. With these it is relatively easy to test your arithmetic facility with the formulas. More generally, the interest rate you would be quoted today for borrowing money for 1 year is different than the interest rate you would be quoted today, for borrowing money for two years, and different yet again from the interest rate you be would be quoted today for borrowing money for 30 years (another example of the liquidity premium). Moreover, tomorrow's rates for the same times to maturity would all be different too. (These are called *spot rates* because they refer to borrowing commencing now, on the spot.)

This dependence of interest rates on the length of time of the loan is captured by saying that there is a term structure of interest rates. In the parlance of fixed-income securities, we have been assuming that the term structure is flat; that is, there is no time dependence (in either sense) to the term structure. In this particular circumstance the interest rate for lending over one time span is the same as for lending over any time span and at any date in time. In Chapter 7 this issue will be more thoroughly discussed and formulas will be generalized to account for this effect. Also, when we speak of changes in the market rate of interest this alteration will be assumed to be constant across the entire term structure. For obvious graphic reasons, this is referred to as a *parallel shift* in the term structure.

There is one last point to make: *the yield curve* and the term structure of interest rates are not synonymous. Technically, the yield curve refers to the time projection of interest rates into the future for coupon-paying instruments whereas the term structure of interest rates refers to the temporal dependence of interest rates for *zero coupon bonds*. The difference is generally small but does not vanish and is, of course, a function of the coupon rates.

PROBLEMS

1. Find the future value, in 1 year, of $1,111 given an interest rate of 5.43%/year. ($1,171.33)
2. How much money will your savings account contain after 5 years of 8% growth if interest is paid annually, semiannually, quarterly, and monthly. Assume an initial deposit of $3,333. ($4,897.27, $4,933.65, $4,952.66, and $4,965.66, respectively)
3. What must have been the annual discount rate if $5,566.77 were worth $4,455.66 today, three years earlier, using a quarterly payment frequency? (7.491%)
4. Determine if both sides of the 7/10 rule-of-thumb are approximately true; namely, that with compound interest your money will double in 10 years if the annual interest rate is 7% or that with compound interest your money will double in 7 years if the annual interest rate is 10%. Which is the better approximation? (1.967 vs. 1.949; so the first)
5. Denote the doubling time by T and the interest rate in percent by r. Making a hasty generalization about the preceding, it appears as if the product of T and r is approximately equal to 70. Explain why. ($100 \times ln\ 2 \cong 70$)

6. If the annual continuously compounded rate is 4.32%, how much will $1,000,000 be worth in 1.5 years? ($1,066,946)

7. If a class has five students and their test scores on the final exam were 85, 90, 95, 80, and 70, what was the average score? (84)

8. Let a be 10, b be 15, and c be 30. Compute the "unweighted" average and the weighted average using the 3:2:1 weights. Recompute with 1:2:3 weights. (18.33, 15, and 21.67, respectively).

9. Write out the explicit meaning of

$$\sum_{n=1}^{N} a_n$$

where $a_n = 2n^2$ and $N = 5$ and numerically compute the result. ($2 \times 1^2 + 2 \times 2^2 + 2 \times 3^2 + 2 \times 4^2 + 2 \times 5^2$; 110)

10. If the real rate of return is 2.5% and the anticipated inflation rate is 11.5%, what will the nominal interest rate be? (14.29%)

11. If the nominal interest rate is 22.22% and the real rate of return is a high value of 4.44%, then what is the expected inflation rate? (17.02%)

12. If the market interest rate is 12.34%, the real rate of return is 3.45%, the anticipated inflation rate is −1.23% (i.e., a general lowering of prices is expected), then what interest rate corresponds to the remaining risk factors? (9.95%)

13. My son started a paper route on February 1, 1986. He was paid quarterly and made $35/quarter. He deposited his money in a money market account which paid 7.5% annually, compounded quarterly. After three years of deposits he withdrew his money and placed all of it in a 5-year CD paying 12.5% annually. How much was all this worth when the CD matured? ($840.00; he withdrew $466.14 from the money market account)

14. What must the annual interest rate be for an annuity payment of $1,000 per year to grow to at least $50,000 after 25 years? (5.336%)

15. You can participate in an investment club that requires quarterly payments of $650, a minimum membership of 7.5 years, and expects to generate capital gains equivalent to 14.14% per year (compounded quarterly). If you want to have a total of $35,000 at the end of the minimum membership period should you join? (No, total value = $33,748.67)

16. Find the sum of the geometric series consisting of 100 terms, ratio = 0.952381 = 1/1.05 (i.e., discounting for a 5% interest rate) whose first term is equal to unity. (20.847910)

17. Show that the present value of an annuity due is 1 + i times that of a regular annuity.

18. Show that the future value of an annuity, with A dollars deposited at the end of each period, earning simple interest at the periodic rate I, is worth, after N deposits, $(N + 1) \times A \times (1 + N \times i/2)$.

19. Show that the present value of N annual deposits of A dollars with a simple annual interest rate I is worth

$$\sum_{n=1}^{N} A/(1 + n \times I)$$

if the deposits occur at the end of the year, but only

$$\sum_{n=0}^{N-1} A/(1 + n \times I)$$

if they are made at the beginning of the year.

2 Money and Bond Market Overview

Money is fungible, which means that it can be used in a variety of ways. For instance, it can be invested in *U.S. Treasury Bills*, *bonds* issued by *government-sponsored enterprises* such as *Fannie Mae, Freddie Mac*, or the TVA, *commercial paper, corporate bonds*, certificates of deposit, *interest rate swaps*, mortgages, or placed under your mattress. Hence, one needs to understand at least the basics of these many opportunities as short- and long-term alternatives, or complements, to mortgage investments. This chapter is a brief overview of these common selections to mortgage-related ventures. The mathematics underlying the basic pricing for these certificates is also included and serves as a prelude to pricing and valuing mortgages.

I. INTRODUCTION

There are many varieties of fixed-income securities. What distinguishes a fixed-income security is that everything about it is contractually predetermined: the *par* or *face value*, the *redemption amount*, the interest rate, the frequency and amount of interest payments, and the *maturity date*. The legal document specifying how much will be paid, to whom, and when is known as an *indenture* or *deed of trust*. *Short-term* securities are those with a lifetime less than 1 year from their date of issuance, while *long-term* financial instruments, or bonds, are those with a maturity date greater than 1 year from their date of issuance. Frequently the category of *intermediate-term* is made, usually meaning 2 to 10 years. (The definitions of the first two are standard; that of intermediate-term is context-dependent.)

Fixed-income securities differ among themselves by the extent to which they are secured by *collateral*; corporate bonds are unsecured by any specific physical property or *assets*. The bond holder must rely on the credit worthiness of the issuer for complete and timely repayment of the amounts owed to him. A *debenture* (a bond whose credit rating is solely based on the reputation and financial state of the issuer) that happened to be a poor credit risk is referred to as a *junk bond* or *speculative bond*. The term *high yield bond* might also be used. The high *coupon*, or interest payment, associated with junk bonds arises because of the high risk of default and the typical investor's aversion to risk. Bonds above the standard credit rating threshold are termed *investment grade* and those below this threshold are known as noninvestment grade. Many mutual funds, pension funds, life insurance companies, banks, and so forth are only allowed to purchase investment grade issues.

(Investment grade has a stricter meaning in the U.K.; only the top three ratings qualify there whereas in the U.S. the top four do.)

Money market instruments — including commercial paper and *negotiable certificates of deposit*, *interest rate futures*, U.S. Treasury Bills, *federal funds*, *repurchase agreements*, *bankers acceptances*, and *call money loans* — *municipal bonds* (that is, nonfederal but governmental), *U.S. Treasury Notes* and *Bonds*, and money and bond mutual funds round out the more common types of fixed-income investment vehicles. Finally, fixed-income securities are generally purchased because someone values the *fixed-income* aspect, or its certainty, as opposed to the capital gain potential of common stock or the variability of a floating-rate security.

The definite stream of income is frequently sought because it will balance, in amount and timing, the cash flows of a liability. However, fixed-income instruments can have appreciable price changes in response to varying market rates. Some investors purchase long-term bonds and mortgages to attempt to benefit from this effect. Other investors actively trade in fixed-income securities of different maturities because they are exploiting perceived mispricing opportunities along the yield curve. (The yield curve illustrates the time dependence of interest rates for coupon paying bonds.) However, one does not have to sell and take the capital gain (or loss); one can always hold the security until maturity, collecting the agreed-upon cash flows from the bonds, mortgages, or other fixed-rate instruments.

The best macroeconomic scenario for fixed-income investors is one of falling market rates because then they have the option of selling their security for a capital gain or holding onto it for its now relatively high stream of income. However, if rates rise, then the market value of a fixed-income security will decrease. If the rise in interest rates is because of anticipated inflation, then the fixed-income investor will be doubly disadvantaged: the cash flow will be devalued by inflation and the sale price of the security will have diminished because of the rise in interest rates.

II. SHORT-TERM SECURITIES

A. NOTES

A *promissory note* is a promise to pay a certain amount of money at a definite date. Sometimes it may be an obligation to pay a given sum of money on demand. Notes are usually used for very short-term borrowing, typically 60 days or less, and for relatively large amounts of money, in the millions. The note is payable to the payee and the promise to pay is made by the maker. The note is due on the maturity date or *due date*; the amount owed on that date is known as the par or face value or principal amount. (Almost everything in finance has at least two, and frequently three, different names.)

Notes are not explicitly interest-bearing. Instead of buying a million-dollar, 3-month note for $1,000,000 cash and receiving a million dollars plus an interest payment, the million dollar note would be sold to you at a *discount*. This means that when you purchase it you pay less than the face value. When you receive your redemption amount (i.e., the million dollars) on the note's maturity date (3 months from the purchase date), the difference between the face amount and the sum you actually paid is an implied interest payment. Hence, the term *discount notes.*

No single convention is used to measure the time interval between the date of issuance and the maturity date to calculate interest; both the actual number of days in between the dates and the number of 30-day months between them are common. Consider a 90-day note issued on February 16 of a leap year. It would be due on May 16. (Count the days!) In contrast, a 3-month note issued on February 16 would be due on May 16, leap year or not. Sometimes multimonth notes are issued on days (i.e., the 31st) for which there is no corresponding date in the month due; they automatically become due on the last day of that month. Banks usually charge interest based on the exact number of days, while the commercial practice is to use a 12-month, 30 days/month, year.

The most liquid financial instruments in the world are U.S. Treasury Bills. Hundreds of billions of dollars of them are outstanding. One can buy or sell tens of millions of dollars of *T-Bills* with very narrow bid–ask price spreads in seconds. The formula for pricing U.S. Treasury Bills, in terms of face value, price, yield, and number of days to redemption, is

$$\text{Price} = \text{Face Value} \times (1 - \text{Yield} \times \text{Number of Days}/360). \qquad (2.1)$$

If we wanted to know the yield in percent, then we would invert this to obtain

$$\text{Yield} = 100 \times (1 - \text{Price}/\text{Face Value}) \times (360/\text{Number of Days}). \qquad (2.2)$$

If an actual day count for a year were used, then 365 would replace 360. In some markets, namely the U.S. Treasury 1-year Bill, a year consists of 52 weeks of 364 days. (This Treasury Bill is no longer issued having been recently replaced by a 1-month Bill that actually has 4 weeks to maturity.)

a. Exercises

1. Suppose you purchased a million-dollar, 3-month T-Bill for $975,000 on March 1. What was the implied annual interest rate using an actual/actual day count convention? On a 12-month/year convention? (9.918%, 92 days out of a 365 day year; 10%)
2. What would a 6-month (180-day) million-dollar note cost if the annual interest rate is 10.10%? ($949,500)
3. How many days remain to maturity on a 7.77% ten-million dollar note if its current price is $9,611,500? (180)

B. OTHER SHORT-TERM SECURITIES

The buying and selling of short-term (i.e., less than 1 year in maturity) instruments is performed in the money markets. These include securities of the Federal Home Loan Banks, the Farm Credit Banks, and the Federal Land Bank; negotiable certificates of deposit; commercial paper; repurchase agreements; bankers acceptances;

interest rate futures; call money; the federal funds that member banks of the Federal Reserve System trade among themselves; and so forth. The rate on federal funds, the *fed funds rate*, is the headline rate that is discussed after the Federal Reserve's Open Market Committee meets every 5 to 6 weeks. The Federal Reserve Bank actually only controls the *discount rate*, which is the interest rate member banks are charged for short-term borrowing at the Discount Window of the Federal Reserve Bank of New York. The discount rate is not actually computed in a discount fashion anymore; now it is computed as an add-on (i.e., simple interest) rate. (See Stigum, 1990; references are collected at the end of the book).

1. Repurchase Agreements

A repurchase (*repo*) agreement is the overnight simultaneous selling and buying back of the identical securities, for fixed prices on both sides of the transaction. It can be a method of financing an inventory of government securities or a short-term, collateralized loan. In the former case a dealer will use government securities he purchased as collateral for borrowing. The counterparty lends the dealer cash. At the end of the repurchase agreement — a *term repo* would be one for a longer period of time than overnight — the dealer pays the other party the amount borrowed plus *accrued interest* and the same collateral is returned to the dealer.

Let the collateral be $10 million of liquid securities. The repurchase agreement rate is 6.5% per year. The dealer will loan out $9,998,194. The $1,806 difference is equal to the interest i.e.,

$ Interest = ($ Amount of Principal) × (Annual Repo Rate) × (Repo Term)/360.

Even less than this would be actually lent because the market price of the collateral is subject to interest rate risk. If the lender of the securities fails to redeem them the next day, and if market interest rates rise overnight, then the securities could not be sold for $10 million. Hence, in case the borrower defaults on the repurchase agreement — known as a *fail* — the lender might lend 1 to 3% less (known as the *haircut*) to protect himself. (After destruction of communication cables underneath the World Trade Center towers on September 11, 2001, there were half a billion dollars of fails that continued for weeks on end. The reason was that parts of the computer systems of the The Bank of New York, a major trustee for these transactions, could not communicate with each other because their lines underneath the World Trade Center towers had been severed. Since no one believed that these failures were real, as opposed to a communication problem, no major disruption of the market occurred.)

a.   Reverse Repurchase Agreements

A *reverse repurchase agreement* is a repo as seen from the other side of the transaction. Suppose that the dealer, instead of owning the government security, is short the security. This means that the dealer has borrowed it from a third party and sold it because he expects interest rates to rise, allowing him to buy back the same instrument at a lower price in the future. Concurrently, the dealer lends funds to the counterparty, who returns them plus interest.

The repurchase agreement market can be dominated by securities that are *on special*. This means that there is an excess of demand, or lack of supply, of a particular U.S. Treasury Bill or Note, for example. This too occurred after September 11, 2001. Many investors sold their fixed-income securities and purchased 10-year U.S. Treasury Notes in a *flight-to-quality*. Unfamiliar with the role that this note played in the repo market, they did not participate in it nor would they let their dealers do so on their behalf. The U.S. Treasury had to hold a special sale of 10-year Notes to alleviate the unbalanced supply and demand pressures and restore equilibrium to the repurchase agreement market.

If the rate on an ordinary repo is R_r while that for the security on special is R_s, then over N days the additional cost of shorting the special collateral will be $P \times (R_r - R_s) \times N/360$ where P is the price of the securities being sold short. The present value of this would be given by

$$[P \times (R_r - R_s) \times N/360]/(1 + R_r \times N/360)$$

where the repo rate for general collateral is used as the discount rate.

III. LONG-TERM SECURITIES AND THEIR VALUATION

A. DEFINITIONS

A bond is a long-term promissory note. Bonds are backed by the general credit worthiness of the issuer; they have no claim to specific assets as a guarantee. In contrast, a mortgage is a pledge of designated property, usually real, as collateral for a loan. Homeowners pledge their land and the buildings on it. Businesses will also issue mortgage bonds on their land and buildings, but these are not the type of securities considered in this chapter.

Bonds have several key features:

1. Their *issue amount* or the total dollar quantity of the securities sold is not generally purchased by one entity (but might be so in a private placement).
2. Their principal amount, face or par value: $5,000 and $10,000 are the minimum retail denominations commonly available, although one may be able to purchase units as small as $1,000.
3. Their maturity date, *term-to-maturity,* or due date; maturity date and due date concern when, in the future, the redemption value of the bond will be repaid. Normally this is 10 to 20 years from the date of issue (though the Walt Disney Corp. issued a 100-year bond in 1993).
4. Bonds usually pay interest, at half the stated annual rate, on a semiannual basis, starting 6 months from the issue date. The rate is known as the *coupon rate.* This interest income is sometimes referred to as *coupon income* or the *nominal yield.*
5. The redemption amount, barring default, will be repaid in full on the maturity date. Another name for the standard corporate bond is a *bullet bond* because the repayment of the relatively large principal amount (compared to a coupon payment) comes all at once.

Bonds were once issued on fine paper handsomely engraved. The origin of the terms coupon rate and *coupon payment* (the latter meaning the dollar amount of each of the semiannual payments, the former referring to the annual interest rate) stems from this earlier era when bonds were physical paper documents instead of just *book entries* in a computerized ledger. The paper bond had tear-off portions, i.e., the coupons, which the bond holder presented at a payment station (typically a commercial bank) to receive his semiannual interest payments in cash.

The phrases *term* and term-to-maturity indicate the number of years until the redemption date of the bond whereas maturity only signifies that date. Some bonds are retired serially which means that a particular debt issue is broken up into different pieces — each with its own maturity date such as 20, 21,..., and 25 years. Such *serial bonds* are usually issued by municipalities. One rarely sees a *perpetual bond*, whose principal is never meant to be retired; they are illegal in the U.S.

Sometimes a corporate bond is issued with a *call option*. *Callable debt* may be called in, or forcefully redeemed, by the issuer once a certain date, the *call date*, has passed. The issuer may have to pay a *call premium* to the holder of the loan for this privilege. Highly leveraged corporations — that is, they issue relatively large amounts of debt compared to their amount of owner's equity — are heavy users of callable debt. They can protect themselves against a decline in interest rates, with a call date, for example, 3 years in the future. If market rates drop, then by calling in the outstanding liability the firm can save itself millions of dollars by issuing new debt at the then current, lower interest rate. This savings should more than offset the issuance costs of the new flotation as well as any call premium. (This process is exactly analogous to homeowners *refinancing* their mortgages.) Sometimes different elements of a bond offering will have different call dates: one subset with a 5-year call date, another with a 10-year call date, and so on.

1.   Simple Bond Evaluation and Pricing

Why does a 30-year, $10,000,000 bond cost exactly $10,000,000 at the time of issuance?: 1. The market interest rate, for this corporation's credit worthiness and for loans of 30 years term, is equal to the bond's stated coupon rate of, for example, 12.25%, and 2. the present value of all the cash flows, discounted by the stated coupon rate, sum to precisely $10,000,000. These cash flows consist of 60 semiannual coupon payments, over the next 30 years every 6 months, of $612,500 [$= (0.1225/2) \times \$10,000,000$], and a single lump sum payment of $10,000,000 thirty years from now.

a.   Numerical Example

Let us examine, in detail, why a face amount F = $10,000, i_c = 5%/year coupon rate, 3-year, semiannually paying corporate bond is worth $10,000. The cash flows are a payment of $C = i_c \times F/2 = 0.05 \times \$10,000/2 = \$250$ every 6 months, commencing 6 months from now and a repayment of the face amount 3 years from now. How much are each of these cash flows worth today? Using 5% as the discount rate, you can construct the following table from Equation 1.6:

Payment Number	Nominal Value	PV(Cash Flow)		
1	$250	$250/(1 + 0.05/2)^1	=	$243.90
2	$250	$250/(1 + 0.05/2)^2	=	$237.95
3	$250	$250/(1 + 0.05/2)^3	=	$232.15
4	$250	$250/(1 + 0.05/2)^4	=	$226.49
5	$250	$250/(1 + 0.05/2)^5	=	$220.96
6	$10,250	($250 + $10K)/(1 + 0.05/2)^6	=	$8,838.54

The sum of the present value of the cash flows comes to $9,999.99 (a penny has been lost in the rounding) and that is why one is willing to pay $10,000 for this particular bond. All fixed- and floating-rate instruments are valued in essentially the same fashion.

The general formula for the market value, MV, of the cash flows of a bond, with a constant discount rate i, is given in Equation 2.3 below. It expresses the fact that the fair market value of (any option-free) fixed-income security is equal to the present value of the discounted cash flows arising from the instrument (i.e., the total investment has a net present value of zero from Equation 1.27). The investor's desired annual rate of return is denoted by i, Par stands for the par value of the instrument, the symbol C is used for the semiannual coupon payment (i.e., C = coupon rate × Par/2 = i_c × Par/2), and N is the number of semiannual interest payment periods (so the bond's maturity date is N/2 years from now). Note that the norm outside the U.S. is to pay interest annually, not semiannually, and that there are all sorts of variations (e.g., quarterly paying, monthly paying, amortizing, floating, and so forth). Thus, the market value MV is given by the expression

$$MV = \sum_{n=1}^{N} C/(1+i/2)^n + Par/(1+i/2)^N. \qquad (2.3)$$

b. Exercises

1. Compute the market value of a 3-year bond, face amount $10,000, coupon rate 10.56%, issued today, paying interest semiannually, if the current market interest rate for this type of security is really 9.56%. Repeat the computation for a market rate of 11.56%. (C = $528, $10,255.58; $9,752.43)
2. If the market value of a bond, face amount $25,000, issued today, maturity date 2 years in the future, when current interest rates are 9.63%, is $25,905.46, then what was the coupon rate? Assume semiannual coupon payments. (C = $1,458.00, i_c = 11.664%/year)

3. For a fixed-income security, valued with a constant discount factor, the valuation problem can be cast in the form of a geometric series. In terms of the notation introduced in Equation 1.22, with $\rho = 1/(1 + I)$, where I is the periodic interest rate, show that the market value, MV, is given by

$$MV = C \times (S_N - 1) + \text{Par} \times \rho^N. \tag{2.4a}$$

C is the amount of the cash flow per payment period and, from Equation 1.25,

$$S_N - 1 = [1 - (1 + I)^{-N}]/I. \tag{2.4b}$$

Consider the valuation of a bond with 13 years to maturity, coupon rate 13.13%/year, face value of $75,000, paying interest semiannually. Suppose rates drop to 10.10%. How much is the bond worth? [First, $C = (0.1313/2) \times \$75,000 = \$4,923.75$. Second, $\rho = 1/(1 + 0.1010/2) \cong 0.951928$. Third N is equal to 26 and fourth, $S_N - 1$ comes to about 14.3014. Hence, the market value MV is given by

$$MV = \$4,923.75 \times 14.3014 + \$75,000 \times 0.277778$$
$$= \$70,416.35 + \$20,833.57 = \$91,249.92.$$

Or you can discount the cash flows one by one. Note that with an uneven term structure of interest rates or a nonconstant coupon payment, this is what you (or your computer), must do.]

c. *Exercises*

1. Compute the value of a corporate bond if it has a coupon rate of 11.11%, 20 years to maturity, pays interest semiannually, has a face value of $15,000, and you require an annual rate of return of 15.15%. ($C = \$833.25$, $11,215.58$)
2. Suppose that 1-, 2-, and 3-year interest rates, for borrowing commencing now, are 6.75, 7.25, and 8.00%, respectively. Further suppose that the cash flows from a $10,000 investment are $1,000, $1,200, and $1,500 plus the repayment of principal. How much is this worth today? ($11,109.08)

When the interest is paid m times per year the value of the periodic interest rate is i/m where i is the annual interest rate. The new formula for MV is, with N still the total number of payment periods,

$$MV = \sum_{n=1}^{N} C/(1 + i/m)^n + \text{Par}/(1 + i/m)^N. \tag{2.5}$$

d. Exercise

1. What must have been the coupon rate of a 30-year, $45,000 par value, quarterly paying, bond if its market value is $39,876 and current interest rates are 8.88%? (C = $876.46, i_c = 7.791%)

It is important to realize that the market price of a bond (any option-free, fixed-income security) is inversely related to market interest rates. For those who remember calculus, the simplest method of proving this is to compute the partial derivative of the market price in Equation 2.3 with respect to the discount rate and show that it is negative; i.e.,

$$-2 \times \partial(MV)/\partial i = \sum_{n=1}^{N} n \times C/(1+i/2)^{n+1} + N \times Par/(1+i/2)^{N+1} > 0.$$

A strictly algebraic demonstration of this fact is presented next.

e. Algebraic Proof

Consider a corporate bond with face amount F, N payment periods remaining, coupon payment $C = I_c \times F$ where I_c is the periodic interest rate and not the annual interest rate (i.e., $I_c = i_c/m$ where m is the number of payment periods per year). Let I be the current periodic market interest rate at the same payment frequency. We have the constraints $1/m \geq I$, $I_c \geq 0$. Then if we use Equations 2.3 and 1.25 to compute the market value, MV, of the bond and rearrange the result, we obtain

$$MV/F = I_c/I + (1 + I)^{-N} \times (1 - I_c/I). \tag{2.6}$$

This version of the formula makes the dependence on the ratio of the coupon and market interest rates more transparent. For instance, if $I_c = I$ then it is clear that MV must be equal to F. On the one hand, if the current interest rate exceeds the coupon rate, $I > I_c$, then the second term on the right-hand side of Equation 2.6 is positive. Therefore,

$$MV/F < I_c/I < 1$$

so the market value is less than the face value when the market interest rate exceeds the coupon rate. On the other hand, if $I_c > I$, then $1 < I_c/I$ and the last term on the right-hand side of Equation 2.6 is negative. In this case

$$MV/F > I_c/I > 1$$

so the market value exceeds the face value when the market interest rate is less than the coupon rate.

2. More on Yields

A key concept in valuing fixed-income securities (or floating-rate ones for that matter) is yield, which is not the same as the coupon rate. The coupon rate determines the coupon payments via, for bonds, $C = i_c \times F/m$, where i_c is the stated annual interest rate expressed as a decimal fraction, F is the face value of the bond, and m is the frequency of interest payments per year.

a. The Yield-to-Maturity

The inversion of Equation 2.5, i.e., determining the yield of a bond given its characteristics and market value, is often necessary. This particular quantity is known by the misnomer *yield-to-maturity*. It is a good term for bond salesmen but a poor one for investors. If we clear the fractions in this formula, then we have an Nth order polynomial to deal with. Once N is beyond four, this problem cannot be solved (in general) analytically. The simplest, fastest converging numerical approximation scheme to use is Newton's method, although linear interpolation will work surprisingly well because of a very good way to estimate this quantity. (See Equation 2.7 below.)

b. Exercise

1. One of the (few) exceptions to being able to compute the yield-to-maturity is a zero coupon bond because then C in Equation 2.5 vanishes. Show that the annual yield-to-maturity is given by

$$Y = 2 \times [(Par/MV)^{1/N} - 1],$$

where MV is the market price of the bond, the time to maturity is N/2 years, and semiannual interest payments have been assumed. For a 30-year, $1,000,000, zero coupon bond currently selling for $111,111.11, what is the corresponding market interest rate? (7.460%)

An analytical approximation, difficult to improve on, for computing the yield-to-maturity can be had by calculating the straight line amortization of the capital gain (or loss), and dividing that, plus the amount of the coupon payment, by the weighted average investment:

$$Y \cong y' = m \times [C + (Par - MV)/N]/(0.6 \times MV + 0.4 \times Par). \qquad (2.7)$$

where MV, N, C, m, and Par retain their previous meanings. Moreover, it turns out to be a relatively good guess for the true answer.

For a fixed-income security other than a zero coupon bond, the owner of the debt instrument receives non-zero cash flows during its life. What is he to do with them? If the phrase yield-to-maturity is to have the meaning implied by its mathematical computation, then these cash flows must be reinvested at that rate of return until the maturity date of that security. Thus, locking in a high yield because the yield-to-maturity is 15% is only locking in an illusion. To actually reap 15% from all the initial investment, all the bond's cash flows would need to be reinvested at 15% also until the bond matured. Finally, the yield-to-maturity is sometimes referred to as the *internal rate of return* of the investment. It is this quantity that is listed for U.S. government bonds.

c. *Exercise*

1. What would you estimate the annual yield-to-maturity of a 30-year bond, paying interest quarterly at a 8.50% rate, with a face amount of $100,000 would be if the bond were 10 years old and priced at $111,111.11? (N = 80, C = $2,125, y' = 7.45%)

d. *Current Yield*

The stated coupon rate is rarely the most meaningful measure of the yield of a bond. If there is a call provision — or other embedded option — or if market rates have changed, then the coupon rate can be very misleading with respect to the yield an investor will earn. A better measure is the *current yield*, shown in the corporate bond listings in *The Wall Street Journal*. The current yield is computed by dividing the annual interest payment by the market price of the bond and converting the result to a percentage. Thus, a bond with the following parameters — coupon rate = 11.56%/year, par value = $5,000, market price = $5,123.45 — has a current yield of 11.28% = 100 × 0.1156 × $5,000/$5,123.45. Note that the calculation of the current yield ignores the maturity date of the bond. To partially correct for this, bond investors normally use the yield-to-maturity.

B. THE REINVESTMENT ISSUE AND ZERO COUPON BONDS

The issue of *reinvestment risk*, or the computation of the true *total return* or terminal wealth from an investment, is an important point for any fixed-income security except zero coupon bonds. As we have seen, a zero coupon bond is one that pays no interest (explicitly). Zero coupon bonds are discount instruments except that they are long-term in nature. The market valuation problem of a zero coupon bond is just the calculation of the present value of the redemption, or face, amount;

$$MV = Par/(1 + i/m).^N$$

A 25-year, $100,000 face amount, zero coupon bond, paying an implied annual interest rate of 8.88%, paid annually, would sell for just $11,920.57 ($11,393.49 semiannually and $11,127.88 quarterly). Clearly, for a zero coupon bond, the true yield and the yield-to-maturity are always identical precisely because there is no reinvestment problem.

a. *Exercises*

1. Compute the par value of zero coupon bond, with 15 years to maturity, currently priced at $15,662.53 if its annual interest rate is 7.89% and the implied coupons are paid semiannually. ($50,000)

2. What must be the coupon rate on a zero coupon bond, 20 years to maturity, paying the implied interest quarterly, if its face value is $100,000 and it sells for $37,016.68? (5%)
3. What is the maturity of a zero coupon bond, face value $30,000, implied annual interest rate 5.55%, if it costs $7,774.37? (25 years)

1. An Alternative Interpretation of a Standard Bond

Equation 2.5 could just be regarded as the sum of the present value of N+1 zero coupon bonds. The first zero coupon bond has dollar value C and comes 1/m years from now. The second one has value C too and comes 2/m years from now... and the Nth one has value C also and comes N/m years from now. Finally, the N+1st one has value F and arrives N/m years from now as well. Certainly, from the mathematical point of view, this interpretation is entirely consistent. However, it is not in harmony with the economic or the financial characteristics of the instrument and should be discarded because it provides little true explanatory value. A separate market exists for zero coupon and bullet bonds. Zero coupon bonds are usually bought to satisfy a specific funding requirement or because of their financial leverage. Bullet bonds are customarily purchased, or sold, to match a liability with a similar cash flow.

Another difficulty with this interpretation of any series of cash flows as a collection of zero coupon bonds (albeit of possibly different face amounts) is the reinvestment risk issue. Specifically, reinvestment risk refers to the hazard associated with having to reinvest any intermediary cash flows, until the time to maturity of the underlying instrument, at the same rate of return. Otherwise, the concept of yield-to-maturity is misleading, as we have seen. If market interest rates decrease, then any intermediary cash flows will be reinvested at the lower rate of return thereby decreasing the effective yield.

2. More on the Yield-to-Maturity

Look again at Equation 2.5. What does the market price MV really represent? It is the present value of the discounted cash flows because the fair price for this security is the one that makes the net present value of a stake in it exactly zero. What will the amount MV be worth at maturity? Put differently, what is the future value of the present value? It will be worth exactly

$$FV = MV \times (1 + i/m)^N.$$

Now multiply Equation 2.5 through by the future value factor for MV to obtain the following identity

$$FV = MV \times (1 + i/m)^N = \sum_{n=1}^{N} C \times (1 + i/m)^{N-n} + Par$$

$$= C \times (1 + i/m)^{N-1} + C \times (1 + i/m)^{N-2} + \cdots + C \times (1 + i/m)^{1} + C + Par.$$

The future value of the market value is equal to the future value of the first cash flow —assuming that it was reinvested at the discount rate, interest paid m times per year, for a total of N – 1 payment periods — plus the future value of the second cash flow — assuming that it was reinvested at the discount rate, interest paid m times per year, for a total of N – 2 payment periods — plus…, and so on, plus the last cash flow (i.e., the last coupon payment plus the principal repayment). However, this is just another way of saying what was written earlier.

Purchasing a bond, whose face value is F dollars, for F′ dollars is especially relevant to portfolio management. If the bond were selling at a *premium*, then F′ would be greater than F. If the bond were selling at a discount, then F′ would be less than F; if the bond were selling at par, then F′ would be equal to F. Suppose you keep this bond, which pays coupons in the amount of C dollars m times per year, for N payment periods. You (possibly) invest these coupons in various other financial instruments with sundry rates of return. Then you sell the bond (or it matures) and receive F″ dollars for it as well as cashing in all the investments generated by the intermediate cash flows. These total C″ dollars. How much has your money actually earned on an annual basis? The total return is obtained by retrospectively viewing your portfolio of investments stemming from this bond — the bond itself including any capital loss or gain plus all those additional ventures spawned by the coupon payments — as an "annuity" which returned F″ + C″, over N payment periods occurring at a frequency of m per year, stemming from F′ dollars.

a. Numerical Example

You have a 30-year bond, paying 7.65% semiannually, face value $15,000. What is the total return? It consists of 60 coupon payments of $573.75 [= (0.0765/2) × $15,000], total value 60 × $573.75 = $34,425, the principal repayment of $15,000, plus the interest earned on the coupons assumed to be reinvested at 7.65% until maturity. The valuation of the latter is similar to that of an annuity. From Equation 1.20, N = 60, a = $573.75, and i = 3.825% (= 7.65%/2). The result for the future value of the reinvested coupon payments is $127,629. Hence, the total return is given by $34,425 + $15,000 + $127,629 = $177,054. The interest on interest represents 72% (= $127,629/$177,054) of the *total wealth*.

Now halve the time to maturity of the same bond. The value of the coupons comes to $17,212.50. This time the annuity formed from the reinvestment of the coupon payments comes to only $31,254.02. The total return has been reduced to $63,466.52, with the interest on interest comprising 49%.

b. Exercise

1. Compute the total, or terminal, wealth of a $45,000 investment paying interest quarterly at a rate of 7.89% for 25 years if the coupons are reinvested in a similar fashion. Repeat the computation for reinvestment rates 1.5 percentage points higher and lower than the coupon rate. (C = $887.63, terminal wealth = $45,000 + $88,763 + $272,337.42 = $406,100.42; at 9.39%, $45,000 + $88,763 + $347,090.36 = $480,853.36 and at 6.39%, $45,000 + $88,763 + $215,513.67 = $349,276.67)

3. Perpetual or Consol Bonds

After the Napoleonic Wars of the early 19th century, England sold a huge bond issue to pay off its war debts. The main purpose of this flotation was to *consol*idate a variety of smaller issues made during the fighting. The intention was never to pay off the principal but only to pay interest. With annual interest rate i, face value F pounds, then C = i × F. The present value of the never-ending stream of the coupon payments from a *consol bond* or *perpetuity* is

$$PV = C/(1 + i)^1 + C/(1 + i)^2 + \bullet\bullet\bullet + C/(1 + i)^n + \bullet\bullet\bullet = C/i = i \times F/i = F.$$

This is not a very surprising result once you think about it. (If you paid F pounds for it, then it had better be worth F pounds.) If the discount rate changed from i to I, then the present value would become

$$PV' = C/I = i \times F/I.$$

Such financial instruments still exist. Finally, some kinds of *preferred stock* can be valued in this fashion too. Preferred stock pays a specified dividend, usually expressed as a percentage of the par value of the certificate, and some forms are never meant to be retired.

a. Exercise

1. A consol bond, face value £1,000,000, was issued with a coupon rate of 5%. If its present value is £1,234,567, what is the current market rate for this type of investment? (4.050%)

IV. U.S. GOVERNMENT BILLS, NOTES, AND BONDS

A. T-Bills

Government, or *sovereign* debt is not new. In the 13th century the Venetian city-state was selling long-term loans known as *prestiti*. In the U.S., the New York Stock Exchange traded government bonds under the proverbial buttonwood tree as far back as 1792. The Continental Congress, in June 1775, issued the first U.S. debt, worth £6,000,000. The Treasury's first issuances were at 3 and 6%/year with interest paid quarterly. Today the U.S. Treasury Bill, or T-Bill, is the name for the negotiable, short-term, debt security issued by the U.S. government. Treasury Bills are sold at auction by the Department of the Treasury; maturities are 1 year or less. Treasury Bills used to come in maturities of 3 months, 6 months, and 1 year. (Of 364 days; 3 months can mean 89, 90, 91, or 92 days and 6 months can mean 181 or 182 days.) Recently the 1-year Bill was discontinued and a 1-month (i.e., 4-week) Bill introduced. These instruments are sold at a discount from the face value. The size of the discount and the time to the due date imply the interest rate. The yield on a Treasury Bill is referred to as the *T-Bill yield*. The formula was given earlier in Equation 2.2.

1. Bond-Equivalent Yield

Because the universe of short-term, fixed-income investment opportunities is large, it helps to be able to compare the yield of one type of security to another, if there is a common basis for doing so. The standard procedure is to convert the yield of whatever instrument you are considering into that of a bond. One imagines that the certificate of interest (no pun intended, honest) pays on a semiannual basis. The bond-equivalent yield (or *BEY*) of a half-year or shorter T-Bill is given by (with F the face amount, MP the market price, and N the number of days to maturity),

$$BEY = (F - MP)/MP \times (365/N), \qquad (2.8)$$

For instance, a 90-day, $1 million, T-Bill with a quoted (annual) yield of 5.35% would cost

$$MP = \$1,000,000 \times [1 - (90/360) \times 0.0535] = \$986,625.$$

The bond-equivalent yield is

$$BEY = [(\$1,000,000 - \$986,625)/\$986,625] \times (365/90) = 1.35563\% \times (365/90)$$
$$= 5.498\% \text{ after conversion to an annual yield.}$$

a. Exercises

1. What is the market price of a million-dollar, 6-month T-Bill whose bond-equivalent yield is 6.54%? Use N = 182. (MP = $967,390)
2. Show that the relationship between the BEY and discount yield Y is given by $BEY = 365 \times Y/(365 - Y \times N)$ where N is the number of days between purchase (i.e., *settlement date*) and expiration.

For a Treasury Bill with more than a year to maturity, the BEY would be modified on the assumption that the instrument is paying interest semiannually. Hence, there should be the opportunity to reinvest the 6 month's interest payment. Therefore, the BEY must be calculated from the quadratic equation based on Equation 1.5 with m = 2,

$$P \times (1 + BEY/2) \times [1 + (BEY/365) \times (N - 365/2)] = \text{Face Amount.}$$

This example points out one of the subtle problems of converting from a periodic interest rate to one paid yearly. If a particular security has a semiannual interest rate of 8.90%, then what is its effective annual rate? What annual rate of interest would return to you the identical amount as the quoted semiannual rate does over two compounding periods? The answer is not to double the semiannual rate, for $10,000 will grow to $11,859.21 after two annual compoundings at 8.90%. However,

$2 \times 8.90\% = 0.178$, and 17.8% interest on $\$10,000$ will return only $\$11,780$, or $\$79.21$ less. Thus, the necessity of Equations 1.3 and 1.4.

Nonetheless, the convention in the bond market is to double the semiannual yield and refer to that quantity as the bond-equivalent yield. This is true for other types of securities as well. A residential consumer mortgage, on which payments are received monthly ($m = 12$), would have its BEY computed by first converting the monthly interest rate to a semiannual rate via

$$BEY = (1 + \text{Monthly Interest Rate})^6 - 1$$

and then doubling the BEY.

b.　Exercises

1. Verify that, if the monthly rate of interest on a home mortgage was 1.23%, then the bond-equivalent yield would be 15.22%.
2. If you are told that the BEY of a mortgage you are considering purchasing is 12.00%, what is the monthly interest rate? (1.907%)

2.　When-Issued Trading

There are three kinds of Treasury instruments, of each maturity, at all times: *off-the-run, on-the-run,* and *when-issued.* The difference is the issue date of the security relative to the next auction for that kind of instrument. The one most recently auctioned is referred to as on-the-run, the collateral sold at the previously occurring auction is referred to as off-the-run, and the security about to be sold at the next auction is referred to as the when-issued form. Huge differences in liquidity exist among them, with the when-issued version the most liquid, the on-the-run variety reasonably liquid, and the off-the-run issue frequently relatively illiquid. (A similar phenomenon exists in the mortgage markets for the future trading of generic *agency mortgage-backed securities.*)

B.　Treasury Notes and Bonds

Treasury Notes and Bonds are the intermediate- and long-term debt securities issued by the U.S. government via the Department of the Treasury. Bonds have maturities beyond 10 years, Notes have maturities of 2 to 10 years inclusive. Both have a stated coupon rate and pay semiannually. The only real difference between Treasury Notes and Bonds is their time to maturity. The interest rate on the 30-year Treasury Bond, introduced in 1973, was an important measure of the expected inflation rate. Now the 10-year Note plays this role because the 30-year Bond (the *long bond*) is no longer sold. Residential mortgage rates have always been tied to the 10-year Note.

Because the U.S. government once led the world as its biggest debtor (Japan has taken over this dubious distinction), the secondary market for Treasury securities is huge. Hence, these instruments are extremely liquid and the settlement of a T-Note or T-Bond trade is normally the next business day. The timing is important because of the large face value of these securities and the accrual of interest payments. In contrast, corporate bonds are normally settled on the third business day following a sale (referred to as a *regular way sale*).

1. Pricing Formula

The market price MP of a T-Bond with an annual yield-to-maturity y, semiannual coupon payment C dollars, N semiannual payment periods remaining, and face value F dollars is given by

$$MP = \sum_{n=1}^{N} C / (1 + y / 2)^{[(n-1) + (t/T)]} + F / (1 + y / 2)^{[(N-1) + (t/T)]}. \tag{2.9}$$

A close reading of Equation 2.9 reveals two additional terms in each exponent, a −1 and a t/T. T is the total number of days between the two coupon payment dates bracketing the time of settlement and t is the number of days from the settlement date until the next coupon payment is owed. Immediately after a coupon payment has been made, t will be equal to T and $n - 1 + t/T$ will be just n. Compare with Equation 2.5.

2. Day Count

The day count convention refers to the number of days in the year, quarter, or month used to compute simple interest. The standard commercial bank practice is to use a year of 360 days. For computational purposes leap years may have 365 or 366 days. You must know the day count convention in the specific sector of the fixed-income security market in which you are working. The possibilities for the appropriate day count convention include, but are not limited to: 1. the ratio of the actual number of days involved to the actual number of days in a year (referred to as Actual/Actual); 2. the ratio of the actual number of days to 365 (Actual/365); 3. the ratio of the actual number of days to 366 or 365 if this year is (is not) a leap year (Actual/366 or 365); 4. the ratio of the actual number of days to 360 (Actual/360); and 5. various month counting conventions (i.e., 12 of 30 days or 30/360). Some financial companies smooth their interest revenues and expenses using 30.4167 (= 365/12) days per month because income will normally drop in February (i.e., 28 days in length) relative to the preceding January (31 days in length) by almost 10%. This helps Wall Street analysts immensely.

The market price MP in Equation 2.9 includes the present value of the remaining semiannual coupon payments and of the repayment of the face value. The quoted price one finds in a newspaper such as *The Wall Street Journal* is less than this by the accrued interest. In terms of t and T just defined, the accrued interest is equal to C × (T − t)/T, which is the same as C × (Number of Days since the Last Coupon)/(Number of Days between Adjacent Coupon Payment Dates). Hence,

$$MP = \text{Quoted Price} + C \times (T - t)/T. \tag{2.10}$$

In the bond market one speaks of *clean* and *dirty prices*; the difference is the value of the accrued interest. The seller must be compensated for the interest he would otherwise lose since the next coupon payment will go to the holder of record, the buyer in this case. Thus, the quoted, or clean, price, must be increased by the accrued interest to obtain the dirty price, the actual sales price.

C. OTHER RELATED TOPICS

1. Municipal Bonds

A municipal bond is a bond issued by any domestic governmental authority or agency not part of the federal government. Sometimes a municipal bond will be called a *revenue bond* (or an *income bond*) as opposed to a *general obligation bond*. The former means that the toll income from a particular bridge or section of highway is dedicated to paying the bond's cash flows. A general obligation bond is one whose interest and principal payments will be provided from general tax revenues that the issuing municipality expects to collect. A common type of revenue bond is a *mortgage revenue bond* (see Chapter 4). These are issued by municipalities to finance single- and multifamily housing projects. Because all these securities are issued by a local government, the interest income received from them is exempt from state and federal taxes. If the interest rate is i and the tax rate is τ (the lower-case Greek letter tau), then the after-tax yield is magnified to be $i/(1 - \tau)$ from i. A tax rate of 33.3% increases the yield by 50% [i.e., $3/2 = 1/(1 - 1/3)$].

State and local authorities sometimes issue notes, usually to provide a short-term solution to a funding gap. A state that expects to realize a tax payment at the end of the current fiscal year but needs money now might issue a *tax anticipation note*. A *revenue anticipation note* might be issued by a turnpike or bridge authority in similar circumstances or a city expecting federal funds for a housing project. There are also *bond anticipation notes,* notes issued in the face amount of a long-term securities issue which will be forthcoming (and retired when the bonds are sold).

2. Bond Ratings

A *bond rating* refers to an attempt to evaluate the credit worthiness of the issuing company, municipality, or foreign country, and to evaluate the probability that the coupon payments and the terminal principal repayment will occur in a full and timely fashion. The issuer pays for the bond rating. (The credit worthiness of the U.S. government is not rated; by assumption it is higher than any other organization's and its debt is risk-free.)

Moody's Investor Service and the Standard and Poor's Corporation rate bonds. Moody's is the older of the two, founded in 1909, and lists many more bonds than does Standard and Poor's, especially in the municipal bond arena. Duff and Phelps Credit Rating Company and the Fitch Investors Service are two other well-known rating agencies. Originally Moody's used Aaa, Aa, A, Baa, Ba, B, Caa, Ca, and C for its ratings. In 1982, they added numerical subgroups to produce a finer, and no doubt more meaningful, mesh. Aa1 is higher than Aa2, which is higher than Aa3, which is higher than A1, etc. A high quality rating implies a low default risk with investors expected to be satisfied with a lower rate of return. Over the last half-century the spread in yields from Treasuries to Aaa corporate bonds has been about 50 *basis points*, or 0.5 percentage points, with the spread from there to Baa another 100 basis points. (These are rough numbers. A basis point is one-hundredth of a percentage point; its abbreviation is bp).

Standard and Poor's rating system is similar, although it uses only capital letters (e.g., BB instead of Ba or AAA instead of Aaa), and with plus and minus signs to denote subcategories. Standard and Poor's also includes a D rating to denote bonds in default. The Fitch Investor Service and Duff and Phelps ratings are identical, in letter format, with Standard and Poor's until one reaches issues in default. In the U.S. bonds in the top four categories are defined to be investment grade.

a. Bond Indices

A *bond index* is a measure of return from a portfolio of bonds. Most bond indices and other fixed-income model portfolios have been created in the last two decades and usually include the total return: capital gains or losses, accrued interest, and an assumed coupon reinvestment rate. Bond indices are value-weighted, meaning that they are based on market prices for the bonds. Best known are the Lehman Brothers Indices, the Merrill Lynch Bond Indices, the Ryan Index, the Salomon Brothers Bond Indices, the Merrill Lynch Convertible Securities Indices, the Merrill Lynch International Bond Indices (mostly Eurobond), the Salomon Brothers International Bond and Money Market Indices, and the J. P. Morgan International Government Bond Indices.

To effectively use one of these indices as a standard for your investment performance, you should carefully match the type, quality, and maturity of the bonds comprising the chosen index with those in your portfolio. Ten-year studies of correlation among the monthly bond indices shows a relatively high positive linear correlation. Finally, it is much easier to construct an equity index than it is to build a fixed-income index because of the huge diversity among bonds; a corporation usually has one type of common stock but might issue dozens of bonds that differ by coupon, maturity date, call features, and so on. In addition, bonds are traded (often thinly) in the over-the-counter market, making it difficult to obtain consistent market prices.

V. BOND PRICING MAXIMS

The basic maxims of option-free, fixed-income, pricing follow.

When the instrument's coupon rate is equal to the market rate, then the price equals the par value. This is a restatement of the fact that an investment in a debenture has a zero net present value. See Equation 1.27. Conversely, when the market price equals the par value, then the coupon rate must be equal to the market rate. This is merely the other side of Equation 2.5, but more difficult to prove formally.

If the coupon rate is less than the market rate, then the market price is greater than its face value. The converse is true too: if the coupon rate on the bond is greater than the market rate, then the market price of the bond is less than its face (or par) value.

Alternatively, the market price of a bond changes in the opposite direction to the change in market interest rates. Why is this true? No one would pay par value for a bond with a coupon rate of 5% if he could pay par value for another, otherwise equivalent, bond with a coupon rate of 7%. (Equivalent is an important phrase referring to credit rating, liquidity, time remaining, and so forth.) To entice the purchaser to accept less in the form of coupon payments, the price of the bond must be reduced (thereby increasing the current yield). Conversely, when the coupon rate is greater than the market rate, then the price of the bond will be greater than the par value. This is true because an investor would prefer to pay par for a bond with a coupon rate of 8% rather than buy a similar bond at the market rate of 6%. Because you are not foolish, you demand to be renumerated for giving up the extra compensation your 8% bond provides.

When market rates rise or fall, the decrease or increase in the price of a bond will not be symmetric. Consider a $40,000, 10%, 20-years-to-maturity bond, paying coupons semiannually. Let interest rates for this type of security drop to 8%. Then, from Equation 2.3, the market value of the bond will be equal to (C = $2,000) $47,917.11. Now imagine that market rates rise by two percentage points to 12%. The market value of the instrument will now be $33,981.48. The increase in value was $7,917.11 because of a 200-basis-point drop in rates, yet the decrease in value, because of a 200-basis-point rise in rates, was only $6,018.52.

The mathematical explanation for this is that the Taylor series bond/interest rate function alternates in sign. The linear term in a small change Δi in interest rates is inherently negative. (The upper case Greek letter delta is used to indicate a small change in mathematics.) Why? As rates increase, prices decrease and vice versa. The next term, the one quadratic in Δi is intrinsically positive (the convexity term) so, for small changes in rates, the second-order term is always positive. Hence, interest rates dropping (i.e., $\Delta i < 0$ — so that the first-order term is positive too and these terms add together) will cause a greater gain in prices than the drop in value that will occur when interest rates increase (i.e., $\Delta i > 0$ so that the linear term is negative and there is a partial numerical offset).

There is another asymmetry in bond prices in that they are more responsive to a decrease in market rates than they are to an increase in market rates. The reason is that bond prices are always positive or one-sided; the least any bond can be worth is zero while its upper limit is $N \times C + F$ (for a zero discount rate). Since prices move inversely with changes in rates, there is much more room for a price to increase when rates fall than there is room for a price to decrease when rates rise. Also, bond prices will react more strongly to changes in rates of return when they are lower than when they are higher.

The lower the bond's coupon rate, the more sensitive its percentage price change is to varying market interest rates. Note that the lowest coupon payment bond is a zero coupon bond and that it has the highest price sensitivity. The basis for this statement is the standard bond pricing formula. The lower the coupon rate, the more the market value of the bond consists of the discounted value of the principal amount because the market price of the bond is always the sum of two components: 1. the value of the discounted coupon payments and 2. the value of the discounted principal repayment. These two always add up to the price, so if the coupon component is lower because the coupon rate itself is low, then the principal repayment must be higher to maintain the equality.

Consider a $30,000, 30-year bond, paying interest semiannually, at a coupon rate of 3.33%. It is worth $30,000 because this is the sum of the discounted value of its coupon payments (= $18,861.33, C = $499.50) plus the value of its principal repayment (= $11,138.67). If the coupon rate were 13.33% instead, then it would still be worth $30,000 because that is the sum of the discounted value of its coupon payments (= $29,375.11, C = $1,999.50) and of its principal repayment (= $624.89). When the coupon rate was lower, the principal repayment amounted to more than one-third of the market value of the instrument (= $11,138.67/$30,000 = 37%), whereas for the higher coupon rate it was a negligible 1/50 (2.1%).

The longer the time to maturity of a bond, the greater the effect of a change in interest rates on its price. Consider two bonds, each paying interest semiannually at 9.99%/year and each with a face amount of $50,000. However, one has a maturity date 10 years from now, the other a maturity date 20 years from now. Let market rates be 13.13%. What would their prices be? The shorter-term instrument would be worth (C = $2,497.50) $41,394.95; the longer term one would sell for $38,982.48. Decompose the two prices into the value of the discounted coupon payments plus the present value of the principal repayment. For the shorter term debt they are $27,377.21 and $14,017.75, while for the longer term version they are $35,052.54 and only $3,929.94. Note the dramatic diminishment of the present value of the return of the face amount. (When priced at par the 10-year certificate's worth was composed of coupon and principal present values of $31,137.57 and $18,862.43, whereas the 20-year loan's value was made up of $42,884.17 + $7,115.83.)

To see that this is true when market rates of return drop, suppose that 5.67% is the appropriate annual yield-to-maturity. Now the 10-year instrument would be valued at $37,729.71 (present value of the coupons) + $28,585.84 (present value of the face amount) = $66,315.55 and the 20-year security would come to $59,300.42 + $16,343.00 = $75,643.42. The longer-term bond increased more in value, for the same change in interest rates, but this time it was because of the increased contribution of the coupon payments. Hence, an investor trying to reap a capital gain from a fixed-income instrument, when he expects interest rates to decline, would preferentially purchase longer-term securities than not. This effect does begin to wear off as the maturity increases; in other words, had the above computations been performed for 20- and 30-year investments instead of 10- and 20-year certificates, the results would not have been as striking. So, another general rule is that bond price sensitivity increases at a decreasing rate as the time to maturity lengthens.

a. Exercise

1. Recompute all the figures obtained in the preceding paragraph for a 25-year and a 50-year bond. (The ratio of two between maturities has been kept to keep the comparison fair.) (At par, for the 25-year bond, the present value of the coupons, C = $2,497.50, plus principal = $45,629.42 + $4,370.58 = $50,000.00, while for the 50-year bond they are $49,617.96 + $382.04 = $50,000.00. At 13.13% these figures become

$36,459.43 + $2,080.85 = $38,540.28 for the 25-year security and $37,976.76 + $86.60 = $38,063.36 for the 50-year instrument — hardly different at all. At 5.67%, the corresponding numbers are $66,322.91 + $12,357.27 = $78,680.18 and $82,714.31 + $3,054.04 = $85,768.35.)

The longer the time to maturity of a bond, the greater the amount of compound interest in the total return compared to amount of coupon interest (for a fixed coupon rate and yield-to-maturity). The key phrase is total return. It means the future value of the coupon payments, the future value obtained by reinvesting them, and the value of the redemption amount.

If a bond were sold at a discount, then as the maturity date approaches, its price will approach its redemption value from below; that is, its price will increase. If a bond were sold at a premium, then as the maturity date approaches, its price will approach its redemption value from above or its price will decrease.

PROBLEMS

1. What is the yield on a million-dollar, 6-month note 2 months from maturity if its current price is $985,000? (4.500%)
2. If a 3-month (91 day), million-dollar note has a yield of 8.88% and a price of $977,800, how many days in the year are being used? (364)
3. What is the yield on a million-dollar T-Bill with 37 days to maturity if the price is $994,861.11? (5.000%)
4. How many days to maturity does a million-dollar T-Bill have if the price is $925,000 and the yield is 7.759%? (348)
5. Compute the market value of a 2-year bond, face amount $25,000, coupon rate 9.99%, issued today, paying interest quarterly, if the current market interest rate for this type of security is 8.88%. Repeat the computation for a market interest rate of 11.11%. (C = $624.38, $25,503.46, $24,504.01)
6. Compute the value to you of a 15-year, $85,000 par value bond paying interest quarterly at an annual rate of 12.34%, if your required rate of return is only 10.34%. (C = $2,622.25, MV = $97,885.54)
7. You are considering two different investment alternatives. Your annual required rate of return is 10.10%. The first is a 5-year-old, 30-year corporate bond paying semiannual interest at a coupon rate of 9.55%. The second is a new issue 25-year corporate bond paying interest every 4 months at an annual rate of 9.25%. They have the same face value. What is their relative value to you? (The first bond has a coupon of $47.75/$1,000 face value and an MV of $950.18/$1,000 of face value. The second bond has a coupon of $30.83/$1,000 of face value and an MV of $922.78/$1,000 of face value.)
8. Compute the market value of a $35,000, 25-year bond, paying interest semiannually with a coupon rate of 10.86%, if the annual market rate is 8.64% (12.99%). [C = $1,900.50, MV = $42,907.81 ($29,507.79)]

9. Think about a $5,000,000 zero coupon bond with an annual interest rate of 10% and a semiannual frequency of imputed interest payments. Suppose it has 10 years left until its due date (N = 20). Consider two price scenarios: a market value of $2,281,934.73 and a market value of $1,559,023.63. What are the corresponding yields? (8% and 12%)

10. If I wanted to sell you a $10,000 zero coupon bond with 20 years to maturity and a coupon rate of 6.66% for the first 10 years — paying semiannually — and a coupon rate of 9.99% for the second 10 years — paying quarterly — what would a fair price be? ($1,936.16)

11. You are offered a choice of two investments: A $30,000 face value corporate bond paying interest semiannually at 11.99% for 30 years with the coupons to be reinvested at 9.99% or a $30,000 face value corporate bond paying interest semiannually at 9.99% for 30 years with the coupons to be reinvested at 10.99%. Which would you choose and why? (First alternative C = $1,798.50, terminal wealth = $772,547.96; second alternative C = $1,498.50, terminal wealth = $768,102.87)

12. What is the market value of a three million par amount consol bond issued at 5.55% annual interest if the current market rate for such an instrument is 6.66% ($2.5 million)

13. Show that the present value of a perpetuity whose payments are made at the beginning of a period is 1 + i times that of one whose payments are made at the end.

14. Consider withdrawing an amount of A dollars per year from an initial deposit of P dollars that earns compound interest at the rate i. Show that the number of years required to exhaust the account is given by $N = -ln (1 - P \times i/A)/ln(1 + i)$ if $A > P \times i$ and infinite otherwise.

15. Suppose you bought an $11,000 bond, time to maturity 30 years, when the market interest rate for this type of instrument was 9.87%. Compute the coupon payment. (C = $542.85) All in all you will receive 60 of these periodic cash flows and then you will receive a complete return of your $11,000 principal amount. The bond is worth exactly $11,000 to you today because the sum of the discounted cash flows, discounted by the coupon rate of 9.87%, is equal to $11,000. Show this in detail. (the present value of the 60 interest payments comes to $10,388.82 and the present value of the principal comes to $611.18).

16. Turn the preceding cash flow around in time. From the reverse temporal perspective, the process of reinvesting the stream of semiannual interest payments amounts to a form of annuity. Show that the future value of this annuity is worth $186,976.98 if paid semiannually at the coupon rate of 9.87%/year. Compute the total return, or terminal wealth, of your investment when it matures. ($186,976.98 + $32,571 + $11,000 = $230,547.98) Determine the percentage of the ending value or terminal value of your investment that came from reinvestment interest received on the coupon payments (81%)

17. Consider a bond, face value $35,000, paying interest quarterly, over 15 years, at a rate of 12.12%. Determine the coupon payment ($1,060.50). Suppose rates of return instantaneously increase to 14.14%. With the full time to maturity remaining, what would the bond now trade for? ($30,621.93) What is the percentage decrease in price? (−12.5%) Next imagine a similar bond except that its coupon rate is 6.12% and rates have increased by 2.02 percentage points too. What would it then be worth? (C = $535.50, MV = $28,907.75). What is this percentage change? (−17.4%) Note that this shift in price is almost 150% more for the lower coupon rate certificate.

3 More Advanced Fixed-Income Topics

Some of the major mathematical tools, including duration and convexity, used in fixed-income portfolio management are developed in this chapter. Duration and convexity can materially aid in managing interest rate-sensitive revenue and expense cash flows over time. They also play a major role in maintaining the price balance between assets and liabilities. Next *negative convexity*, which leads to *price compression*, is explained and its consequences outlined. Debt with an embedded call option is also treated in this chapter because almost all residential mortgages have one.

I. DURATION

A variety of time periods are associated with fixed-income instruments. The most obvious one is maturity, the date upon which the instrument repays its redemption amount. The next one is the term-to-maturity — the amount of time remaining until maturity is reached. A temporal concept frequently utilized in the mortgage industry is the *weighted average maturity*. It measures the average time to receive each dollar of principal (see Chapter 5). The first part of this chapter is concerned with two other measures of time associated with the cash flows from fixed-income securities: *Macaulay duration* and *modified duration* and their accidental relationship in some special financial circumstances. (A third kind of duration, *effective duration*, was invented to accommodate contingent cash flows.)

A. MACAULAY DURATION

1. Duration and Portfolio Management

Macaulay duration has an important role to play in fixed-income portfolio management. Suppose that you were managing a bond fund. Then you would have cash flows in — namely interest earnings from your assets — and cash flows out — the income stream expected by the fund's owners. The assets are the investments originally made by you, the bond fund manager, and any reinvestments of additional cash flows and excess earnings. You, the manager of the bond fund, have two very different problems: 1. you must invest the monies initially received and coming in over time in financial instruments that, with a high degree of certainty, provide an appropriate level of return so that the promised disbursements to the fund holders will be met; and 2. you must be able to do so relatively independently of the market rate of return between now and when the cash outflows will occur (essentially forever).

To deal with the first constraint, you confine yourself (mostly) to fixed-income securities at an appropriate level of return. It is much more difficult to keep the two cash flows in balance over long periods of time as market interest rates change. This is what you need to accomplish to stay in business as an on-going concern. If the Macaulay durations of the two sets of cash flows, as well as their dollar amounts, are roughly equal, then both objectives will be met. Note that the assets and liabilities of the fund can match in dollar value (so that the fund is technically solvent) without the value of their discounted cash flows being in near-equilibrium over time. *Duration-matching*, because of its time-weighted nature, allows you to go to the next step and aids you in fulfilling your fiduciary responsibilities.

2. Definitions

There are two commonly used types of duration: Macaulay duration, named after the man who popularized the concept in the 1930s, and modified duration. Macaulay duration plays the foremost role in balancing the present value of the cash flows of an interest rate-sensitive portfolio of assets and liabilities over time. Modified duration is the quantity to use when discussing the alterations in price of an interest-rate sensitive mixture of securities (see Equation 3.6).

Macaulay duration is the name for the time-weighted average value of the cash flows from a security discounted by the required rate of return. It is the weighted average time to complete the recovery of the present value of the discounted cash flows and of the repayment of the principal amount. Duration is measured in units of time, typically years. It is a useful quantity to utilize to assess the mean period over which the discounted cash flows from a fixed- or a floating-income security will arrive. (When balancing a portfolio of assets and liabilities whose durations should approximately match, months are the more appropriate unit of time for the difference between the Macaulay duration of the assets and that of the liabilities. This quantity is known as the *duration gap*; the term has a slightly different definition in the savings bank industry, but its purpose is very similar.)

a.   Formula for the Macaulay Duration

The formula for the market value, MV, of a security that has cash flow CF_n at payment period n, n = 1,2,..., N — (CF_n includes any possible repayment of principal as, for example, with a mortgage or amortizing bond), interest compounded with a frequency of m times per year, annual discount rate i, and total number of remaining payment periods equal to N, is

$$MV = \sum_{n=1}^{N} CF_n / (1 + i / m)^n .$$ (3.1)

The formula for the Macaulay duration of this instrument (on a coupon payment date) is given by

$$D = \sum_{n=1}^{N} [n \times CF_n / (1+i/m)^n] / (m \times MV).$$ (3.2)

The factor of m in the denominator converts the result into years. Note that in the numerator each cash flow, $\{CF_n\}$, is multiplied by the time of arrival (i.e., n) of that cash flow. (The unit of time is implicitly 1/m years.) If it were not a coupon date, then the exponent n would need to include the number of days to the next coupon. This will be made explicit for U.S. Treasury Bonds; see Equation 3.7b.

The pricing and Macaulay duration formulas for a standard corporate bond, in particular, with face amount F and all the other symbols having their usual meaning, are

$$MV = \sum_{n=1}^{N} C / (1+i/2)^n + F / (1+i/2)^N$$ (3.3)

and

$$D = [\sum_{n=1}^{N} n \times C / (1+i/2)^n + N \times F / (1+i/2)^N] / (2 \times MV)$$

$$= [C \times T_N + N \times F \times (1+i/2)^{-N}] / [C \times (S_N - 1) + F \times (1+i/2)^{-N}]$$ (3.4)

in terms of the symbols introduced in Equations 1.22 and 1.24 with $\rho = 1/(1 + i/2)$.

b. Numerical Example

Consider again the F = $10,000, $i_c = 5\%$, 3 years to maturity, semiannually (m = 2, N = 6) paying bond. Here its Macaulay duration is computed. The cash flows are a payment of $C = i_c \times F/2 = 0.05 \times \$10,000/2 = \$250$ every 6 months commencing 6 months from now and a repayment of the face amount 3 years from now. The table illustrates the duration calculation details:

Payment Number	Nominal Value	$n \times$ PV(Cash Flow)		
1	$250	$1 \times \$250/(1 + 0.05/2)^1 = 1 \times \$243.90$	=	$243.90
2	$250	$2 \times \$250/(1 + 0.05/2)^2 = 2 \times \$237.95$	=	$475.90
3	$250	$3 \times \$250/(1 + 0.05/2)^3 = 3 \times \$232.15$	=	$696.45
4	$250	$4 \times \$250/(1 + 0.05/2)^4 = 4 \times \$226.49$	=	$905.96
5	$250	$5 \times \$250/(1 + 0.05/2)^5 = 5 \times \$220.96$	=	$1,104.80
6	$10,250	$6 \times (\$250 + \$10K)/(1 + 0.05/2)^6 = 6 \times \$8,838.54$	=	$53,031.24

The sum of the present value of the cash flows comes to $9,999.99. The sum of the far right-hand column is $56,458.25, so the Macaulay duration is D = 2.823 years.

c. Exercises

1. Compute the market value and Macaulay duration of a 15-year, semiannually paying bond with a face value of $75,000, coupon of 5 $^1/_2$ when
   interest rates are 6 7/8. (C = $2,062.50, MV = $65,441.90, and D = 10.037
   years)
2. Repeat the preceding exercise for a 20-year, quarterly paying bond with
   a face value of $30,000, coupon 11 $^1/_2$ if market rates are 13 $^{11}/_{16}$.
   (C = $862.50, MV = $25,530.38, and D = 7.029 years)

3.   What Duration-Matching Does for You

The normal appearance of a balance sheet is in the *account form*; assets are on the
left-hand side and liabilities and owner's equity are on the right-hand side. (The
report form of the balance sheet is usually seen on one page with a downward flow
from assets to liabilities to owner's equity.) A different presentation, more appropriate
for financial institutions likely to invest heavily in mortgages or manage portfolios
of fixed-income investments, is illustrated in Figure 3.1. The owner's equity is shown
at the bottom of the inverted triangle. This is also the risk-based capital of the firm.
The upper portion has been divided into two, almost equal, halves: assets and
liabilities.

   Think of this inverted triangle as a child's swimming pool toy. It is supposed to
float in a stable fashion no matter how rough the waves (= market changes of interest
rates) are. The owner's equity (= risk-based capital) serves as the ballast for holding
the toy upright. Each of the upper two compartments — assets and liabilities — has
the independent capability of accepting airflow (i.e., cash flow) in or out. Pumping
air into the asset side represents the receipt of interest-related income revenue on,
for example, your mortgage-related assets. Air leaking out of the liability side
represents the payment of interest expense on the debt instruments you issued to
purchase the assets. Some of these may be short-term but most of them are inter-
mediate- and long-term to more closely match the duration of the assets. A significant
percentage of the latter should be in the form of callable debt or *callable bonds*.
(These instruments are discussed, in detail, later. They allow for refinancing one's
debt.) There is also a safety valve between the upper two sections from which profits
can be bled off. This is a one-way valve.

   Initially this model is set up to be in balance in the accountant's sense of the
term. (We can ignore the owner's equity at this point because it represents a small
correction to the overall balance, i.e., the leverage is so high.) Under historical
generally accepted accounting principles (*GAAP*), barring defaults, once the balance
has been set up it is relatively easy to maintain. When mortgages on the asset side
of the float toy mature or are prepaid, those funds are used to purchase newly
originated home loans. When the debt instruments on the liability side of the toy
come due, they are paid off and more debentures are issued to support the outstanding
mortgage assets.

   If there is a big downward change in market rates — the trough of a wave across
the pool — then the *prepayment rate* will dramatically increase as consumers take

BALANCE SHEET

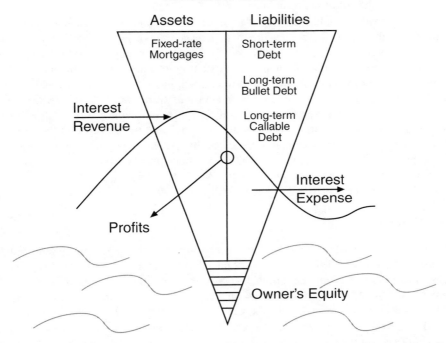

FIGURE 3.1 The float toy model of a Balance Sheet. Balance is represented by A(ssets) = L(iabilities) + O(wner's)E(quity). However, since A,L >> OE, A ≅ L. The Macaulay durations are roughly equal for cash flow stability; $D_A \cong D_L$. The modified durations also match for price stability under FASB SFAS #133. The wave represents changes in interest rates.

advantage of their refinancing opportunities. (A *prepayment* is the complete pay-off of the outstanding mortgage balance before the maturity date. When you refinance you obtain a new mortgage, normally at a lower rate, to replace the outstanding one, thereby prepaying the extant mortgage. Of course just moving and selling your house will result in a prepayment too.) The funds paid into the buy-and-hold mortgage portfolio are used to purchase new liens. Their coupon rates will be lower than those on the ones they replaced. To keep the discounted time average of the interest revenue cash flow inward stabilized with respect to the discounted time average of the interest expense cash flow outward, some of the outstanding callable debt is called and then reissued as new, lower coupon rate debt.

Thus, the same way homeowners take advantage of their opportunity to refinance their mortgage debt, you, the manager of the buy-and-hold investment portfolio, take advantage of the chance to refinance your intermediate- and long-term debt. Thus, in the context of the float toy, when the trough of an interest rate changing wave sweeps by, and we speak of a fixed-income portfolio being *immunized*, or duration-matched, we mean that the time averaged rate of air inflow into the asset compartment balances the time averaged rate of air outflow from the liability compartment. If a positive net interest margin, or spread, is between the two, then it is bled off through the profitability valve.

Alternatively, should the crest of an interest rate changing wave go by and the float toy rock, then you must be sure that a substantial portion of your liabilities are not about to come due. If too many debt issues are near their maturity dates, then you must issue new debt, to support the extant assets, at a time of higher interest rates. This would unbalance the cash flows and diminish (or eliminate) your profits. At the worst you might be forced to remove funds from your ballast — your risk-based capital — further endangering your prospects of keeping the toy afloat in a stable fashion into the future. Thus, neither do you want to be exposed to acquiring lower paying assets without having the capability of reissuing your debt nor do you want to be exposed to premature debt replacement. In other words, you want the duration gap, the difference between the Macaulay duration of your assets and liabilities, to be near zero. (The price sensitivity of this toy is described later.)

4.   Duration Maxims

Duration is always less than the time to maturity except for a zero coupon bond when the two are equal. The reason is simple: a zero coupon bond has no intermediate cash flows. Hence, from Equation 3.3, only the term involving the face value F enters into the Macaulay duration computation with a non-zero value; but in this case $F = MV$ and N is just twice the time to maturity, thus D = time to maturity.

For a fixed-income security, the lower or higher the market interest rate is, the longer or shorter the duration. Also, the lower the coupon rate, the larger the duration and vice versa. The reason for this stems from the time-weighting in the computation of duration; large coupons coming early in the life of the instrument contribute little to the overall calculation. Thus, the Macaulay duration moves inversely with both the required rate of return and the coupon rate. Duration changes more when interest rates drop than when they rise (by the same absolute amount). This was true of bond prices for the same reasons.

The longer the time to maturity of the instrument, the longer the duration. This aspect also originates in the time-weighted aspect of the definition of duration; the greater the time to maturity the higher the potential values of the temporal weights in the numerator of Equation 3.2 and the larger their cumulative effect. Though a major determinant of duration is the term-to-maturity, all the other elements of the bond pricing formula, Equation 3.2, enter into its computation. Hence, it is possible to have two bonds of significantly different maturities with durations in the opposite relationship; namely, the bond with a shorter term-to-maturity has the longer duration and thus has a price more sensitive to interest rate changes than the bond with the larger term to maturity. Duration does not increase one-to-one with maturity; indeed, duration augments at a decreasing rate with increasing maturity.

Suppose you have a corporate bond with a maturity of N years. Imagine extending the due date 1 year. What will happen to the Macaulay duration? Because two more semiannual coupon payments are made, the duration must increase. However, the discounting associated with these two new payments, and the discounting of the par value, are at most equal to the discounting of the 1-year-shorter bond. They are multiplied by larger time values though. Think about a further extension of the maturity to N + 2 years; the same type of thing will happen. However, as the discounting factors become smaller and smaller, the increase in the duration slows down, although the duration increases. Eventually, this process will result in a perpetuity whose duration is

$$D_{per} = (1 + I)/I$$

where I is the periodic interest rate.

This discussion really only applies to par bonds and those sold at a premium. For discount bonds it is possible that the duration approaches that of a perpetuity from above instead of from below. For these bonds duration can decrease with an increasing maturity — just the opposite of the usual case.

Finally, the larger the duration, the more sensitive the price of a fixed-income security is to changes in market rates.

a. Exercises

1. To see that the lower the interest rate the greater the duration, consider an $80,000 par 10-year bond, paying interest quarterly, with a coupon of 12.48%. Compute the market value and the duration if it has 8 years until maturity, for market rates of return of 9.63% and 6.39%. (C = $2,496; for 9.63%, MV = $92,617.62, and D = 5.389 years, while for 6.39%, MV = $110,329.64, and D = 5.628 years)

2. To see that the longer the time to maturity the longer the duration, consider an $80,000 par fixed-income security, paying interest quarterly, with a coupon of 13.57%. Compute the market value and the Macaulay duration if it has 8 years and 18 years to maturity for a market rate of return of 8.64%. (C = $2,714; for 8 years until maturity, MV = $102,610.67 and D = 5.376 years, while for 18 years, MV = $115,848.75 and D = 8.549 years)

3. Suppose that you own a corporate bond paying interest semiannually at 7.53%, face amount $85,000, due in 17 years. Compute its market price and duration if interest rates increase (decrease) by 200 basis points. (C = $3,200.25, D = 9.858 years. If i = 9.53%, MV = $70,826.01, and D = 9.163 years; if i = 5.53%, MV = $103,579.94, and D = 10.554 years. So, when rates dropped, the duration changed by –0.695 years and when they rose it changed by a nearly symmetrical amount of +0.696 years.)

B. MODIFIED DURATION

The primary usage of modified duration is to compute the approximate percentage change in price of a fixed-income security when the discount rate is altered. If we are managing a portfolio of interest–rate-sensitive assets and liabilities, then the requirement to be in balance in the *mark-to-market* age of FASB #133 means that the price sensitivity of the two sides of the balance sheet need to be roughly equal.

(To mark-to-market a security means to value it based on current prices rather than at its historical cost.) If this is not true, then larger reserves of risk-based capital will need to held to insure solvency. This will decrease potential profits. Modified duration can be defined as the Macaulay duration divided by $1 + i/m$, using the symbols of Equation 3.2, and if certain restrictive financial and mathematical conditions are met. The correct definition of modified duration is given in Equation 3.5.

1. The Formula for Modified Duration

If you do not know or remember calculus, then skip down to the sentence above Equation 3.6. The reason modified duration can play the role of estimating fixed-income price sensitivity to interest rate alterations is that its proper definition is as the negative of the first partial derivative of the natural logarithm of the market value, MV, of a security with respect to the discount rate. For the usual bond with coupon payment C, a redemption value of F dollars, and with i and m having their previous meanings,

$$D_{mod} \equiv -\partial ln(MV)/\partial i = -(1/MV) \times \partial(MV)/\partial i$$

$$= (1+i/m)^{-1} \times [\sum_{n=1}^{N} n \times C/(1+i/m)^n + N \times F/(1+i/m)^N]/(m \times MV)$$

$$= D/(1+i/m) \tag{3.5}$$

where D is the Macaulay duration of this instrument. For the more general instrument with cash flow CF_n at the nth payment period, the formula for the modified duration, on a cash flow receipt date, is

$$D_{mod} = (1+i/m)^{-1} \times \left[\sum_{n=1}^{N} n \times CF_n /(1+i/m)^n\right]/(m \times MV).$$

The derivative in Equation 3.5 is intrinsically negative for an option-free, fixed-income security so, in practice, the negative of it is used in the definition of modified duration. From Equation 3.5, the approximate percentage change in the market value owing to a change in market rates Δi is given by

$$\Delta(MV)/MV = -D_{mod} \times \Delta i. \tag{3.6}$$

Δi represents a signed absolute amount (not a percentage alteration). Suppose that interest rates were 5%, they increased by 20% to 6% (i.e., a signed absolute amount of +1.00 or 100 basis points), and that the duration of the security was 6.66 years. Then the percentage change in market value would be

$$\Delta(MV)/MV = -6.66 \times 1.00\% \cong -6.7\%.$$

The market price will drop by about 6.7% (the extra decimal places are meaningless, if not misleading).

2. The Relationship between the Two Durations

There are three requirements for a simple relationship between Macaulay and modified duration:

1. The underlying term structure of interest rates is flat. This is necessary so that the price is sensitive to only one discount rate (unlike the real case in which different spot rates are associated with each cash flow).
2. The shift in the term structure is a parallel one. This is required so that the apparatus of the ordinary differential calculus can be used as opposed to partial differentiation. (Otherwise one would need to compute the gradient of the market value with respect to the collection of important interest rates. The result would be a vector duration. So-called key-rate durations are an example of this.)
3. The cash flows are interest-rate independent (e.g., no embedded options). This is mandatory so that no other terms are introduced when interest rates are varied. For mortgages or callable bonds, this would not be true.

Under these circumstances,

$$D_{mod} = D/(1 + i/m)$$

is a mathematical accident from the reader's perspective. There is no particular reason why the price sensitivity of an option-free, fixed-income instrument (modified duration) should have any relationship to its average time to recover cash flows (Macaulay duration).

Written using more words, Equation 3.6 would read

$$\% \text{ change in MV} = -D_{mod} \times \text{change in interest rates.}$$

A bond with a duration of 5.678 years, when interest rates increase by 2.25 percentage points (i.e., +225 basis points) will decrease in market value by approximately 13% (= −5.678 × 2.25).

a. Exercises

1. You own a 40-year corporate bond coupon rate of 10% paying interest quarterly with a face value of $100,000. It has 22.25 years left to its maturity date. You want to know, approximately, how much the price will change if interest rates change by ±175 bp. The answers are? (C = $2,500, D = 9.112 years, D_{mod} = 8.889 years, for i = 8.25%, MV = $117,764.72, Δ(MV)/MV = +15.6% vs. 17.8% actually; for i = 11.75%, MV = $86,238.65, Δ(MV)/MV = −15.6 vs. −13.8% actually)

2. You are considering purchasing a $125,000 zero coupon bond that pays interest semiannually with 15 years to maturity and for $21,397.42. Compute its approximate value for market interest rate changes of −150 bp and +225 bp. (i_c = 12.12%, D = 15 years, D_{mod} = 14.143 years; for i = 10.62%, MV = $26,474.13, Δ(MV)/MV = +21.2 vs. 23.7%; for i = 14.37%, MV = $15,591.56, Δ(MV)/MV = −31.8 vs. −27.1%)

b. Incorporating Day Count

The duration of a U.S. Treasury Note or Bond is similarly computed with due allowance for the actual settlement date and accrued interest. Repeating Equation 2.9 for the market value (MV) of a U.S. Treasury Bond, and remembering that t stood for the time from the last coupon payment and T stood for the time between the two coupon payments surrounding the settlement date,

$$MV = \sum_{n=1}^{N} C / (1 + y/2)^{[(n-1)+(t/T)]} + F / (1 + y/2)^{[(N-1)+(t/T)]}. \qquad (3.7a)$$

The Macaulay duration, D, of this security is given by

$$D = \left\{ \sum_{n=1}^{N} [(n-1)+(t/T)] \, C / (1+y/2)^{[(n-1)+(t/T)]} \right.$$

$$\left. +[(N-1)+(t/T)] \, F / (1+y/2)^{[(N-1)+(t/T)]} \right\} / (2 \times MV). \qquad (3.7b)$$

3. Modified Duration and the Float Toy

So far we have only considered time-averaged, discounted, cash flows and historical pricing for the stability of the float toy in Figure 3.1. Now we must face the fact that the Financial Accounting Standards Board, in Statement of Financial Accounting Standards #133, is forcing financial firms to report many items on the balance sheet for the first time and to report some securities in a mark-to-market fashion as income.

We know that the price of a fixed-income security goes up or down if interest rates go down or up. Modified duration measures this (approximately). Therefore, as an interest rate wave crosses the swimming pool, not only must the time-averaged, discounted cash flows be kept in balance in the mean, but the absolute levels of the assets and liabilities must also be kept near balance on average. As air goes in or out of each of the upper compartments of the inverted triangle representing the float toy because an interest wave trough or crest sweeps over it — thereby changing the mark-to-market prices via Equation 3.6 — the only place to make up a short-fall is from the ballast: the owner's equity. However, comparatively little owner's equity exists with regard to liabilities because the most profitable method of running this type of business is to be highly leveraged (see immediately below). Thus, the modified durations of both sides of the balance sheet must be nearly the same as well.

Fortunately for portfolio managers, we know that in the simplest case (e.g., a flat yield curve, no dependence of cash flows on interest rates, and a parallel shift in the yield curve) there is an inflexible relationship between modified and Macaulay duration. It was given on the far right-hand side of Equation 3.5. Being duration-matched in one sense automatically means being duration-matched in the other sense (in this simplest of instances). Thus, if air flows into the asset side (mark-to-market price levels are increasing), then roughly the same amount of air must be nearly simultaneously going into the liability side. Conversely if air is being removed from the asset side (mark-to-market price levels are decreasing), then it is equally rapidly being removed from the liability side in the same gross amount.

Hence, being immunized, or being duration-matched, is required to keep the float toy up and stable. Reverting to our financial portfolio management problem, we can say that being duration-matched serves two purposes concurrently: 1. we have a time-averaged, discounted, cash flow balance between interest income and interest revenue which will preserve our net, positive, interest margin (i.e., profits) and 2. we have a price sensitivity correspondence between the assets and the liabilities that will preserve the equilibrium of the balance sheet. The toy stays upright and afloat even in choppy waters and the firm stays profitably out of bankruptcy even with relatively large interest rate volatility and a high degree of financial leverage.

a. Why a Highly Leveraged Portfolio Needs to Have a Small Duration Gap

There is a straightforward way to see that a highly leveraged firm must have a small duration gap if it is to remain a going concern. From the fundamental equation of accounting, the assets (A) equal the sum of the liabilities (L) and the owner's equity (OE). Differentiate both sides of this equality, with respect to the market interest rate i, and divide through by A to obtain

$$D_A = (\partial A/\partial i)/A = (\partial L/\partial i)/A + [\partial(OE)/\partial i]/A$$

where D_A is the Macaulay duration of the assets. Replace A by L + OE on the right and rearrange it:

$$D_A = (\partial L/\partial i)/(L + OE) + [\partial(OE)/\partial i]/A = D_L/(1 + OE/L) + [\partial(OE)/\partial i]/A.$$

If the firm is highly leveraged, then the *debt-to-equity ratio* is very high or L >> OE, so, approximately

$$D_A \cong D_L \times (1 - OE/L) + [\partial(OE)/\partial i]/A.$$

Therefore, by subtraction,

$$D_A - D_L \cong - (OE/L) \times D_L + [\partial(OE)/\partial i]/A,$$

or

$$(D_A - D_L)/D_L \cong -OE/L + [\partial(OE)/\partial i]/(A \times D_L).$$

However, if the owner's equity is really retained earnings, then it is not interest rate-sensitive and $|\partial(OE)/\partial i|$ is small in magnitude. Thus, after taking the absolute value of both sides, we are left with

$$|D_A - D_L|/D_L \cong OE/L,$$

which is what we set out to demonstrate.

4. The Duration of a Floating-Rate Security

One frequently hears that the duration of a floating-rate security is zero (or almost zero). (A floating-rate security is one whose coupon rate changes with time in some well-defined, but not necessarily known in advance, fashion.) What can this mean? Clearly whoever said this cannot be referring to the Macaulay duration. This floating-rate instrument has cash flows arriving over time; when they are multiplied by their time of arrival, discounted by an interest rate (albeit unknown as yet but certainly not unpredicted), and summed, then the result will clearly be non-zero and could be quite large for a long-term security. So perhaps it is the modified duration that was meant. This could make sense if one really meant that the price of a floating-rate security is always near par because its coupon rate floats. As its interest rate is always adjusting to the market rate, although with a delay, then its price should always be near par.

Perhaps what is really meant is that its modified duration will be relatively small because its price never varies much. However, modified duration is the negative of the rate of change of the logarithm of the price with respect to interest rates. Which interest rate? Not the new floating-rate because it does not exist yet. Not a posited *forward rate* structure because that would mean that multiple interest rates are under consideration and we should be using partial differentiation to denote the dependence of the market value on them. (Forward rates are interest rates for borrowing or lending starting some time in the future instead of immediately.) Thus, this is a poor usage to convey a real fact of life in the trading room that has another, better description.

5. Portfolio Duration

There are two simple ways to compute the duration of a portfolio of securities. One is to use the dollar-weighted average value of the durations $\{D_k\}$ of each of the certificates or

$$D = \sum_{k=1}^{N} f_k \times D_k,$$

where

$$\sum_{j=1}^{N} f_j = 1,$$

and the fractional weights $\{f_i\}$ are given by

f_i = market value of instrument #i/market value of the portfolio.

The other method is to use the total portfolio cash flow (Equations 3.1 and 3.2). The cash flow at payment time #n now means the sum of all the cash flows from the mix of securities that you own. The discount rate i must be reinterpreted to be the yield-to-maturity of the portfolio as a whole based on the entire set of cash flows. The weighted average definition is more commonly used because of its computational simplicity. The latter is preferable. It turns out to be possible to salvage a formula of the form

$$\Delta(MV)/MV = -d_{mod} \times \Delta r,$$

even when the term structure of interest rates is not flat and does not shift in a parallel fashion. This offers a method in between the alternatives just discussed. The process also reveals something noteworthy about the way forward rates affect the computation of the present value of the cash flows. See the last section of this chapter for the details.

a.   Dollar Duration

Modified duration relates a change in the discount rate to a percentage change in price. In some applications the absolute change in the price (i.e., as measured in dollars) is more important than knowledge of the percentage change. This is called *dollar duration*. Equation 3.6 is rearranged to read

$$\Delta(MV) = -D_{mod} \times \Delta i \times MV.$$

Since the market value MV is in dollars, so is the change in market value $\Delta(MV)$. Therefore, two bonds with the same modified duration of 10 years, one with a market price of par and one selling at a 10% premium, will have changes in market value, because of a 50 basis point decrease in interest rates of $5.00 per $1,000 of face value and $5.50 per $1,000 of face value, respectively.

Dollar duration is also the name given to 1% of the modified duration times the price:

$$D_\$ = 0.01 \times D_{mod} \times Price.$$

It represents the approximate change of a $100 bond if the market yield alters by 100 basis points.

b.   Value of a Basis Point

Another measure sometimes encountered in the world of bond traders is the *price value of a basis point* or the *dollar value of a basis point*. These are the same and represent the change in price of a bond if the yield changes by one basis point. This measure is a dollar-based alteration, not a percentage-based one.

II. CONVEXITY

If you do not know calculus, then skip Section B. With the widespread availability of high speed computers and fixed-income pricing software, there is no longer any reason to rely on rough methods for computing changes in price owing to changes in discount rate. In order to go one step better one needs to work out and retain higher derivatives in the abbreviated Taylor series approximation to the debt's price dependence on interest rates. The version of the second derivative used in this context in financial circles is known as convexity. By including higher-order derivatives one can do a better job at matching curvilinear functions. (No Taylor series can do a really good job in approximating a series of discounted cash flows because the Laurent series for such a function exists, converges absolutely, and contains no positive powers.) Having said that, understanding convexity and the role it plays in fixed-income (especially mortgage) portfolio management is even more important today than it was before we had electronic computers to calculate it.

Duration was defined by Macaulay in an attempt to explain and interpret a more meaningful time for the receipt of the discounted cash flows from a fixed-income instrument than the time-to-maturity. Because a simple relationship exists between the change of the present value of a fixed-income security and Macaulay duration when the term structure of interest rates used to discount the cash flows is flat or constant and so on, there is a material usage for duration. Given the connection between modified and Macaulay duration, a natural question to ask is "How good is this approximation?" A second logical query is "How can we make it better (and by how much)?"

The answers require a digression into the mathematical methods available to approximate any function. The short answer is that it is possible — under suitable conditions that the present value as a function of the discount rate satisfies — to estimate the alterations in the present value owing to shifts in the (flat term structure) discount rate via modified duration. Moreover, an extremely accurate upper bound to the error in this approximation can be simply obtained. More important is the generalization contained in the last section of this chapter.

The response to the second question is to evaluate the error term and add it on. One reason to do this is that modified duration provides a systematically biased estimate of the change in the present value with discount rate because the convexity for any option-free, fixed-income security is positive. Hence, when the discount rate increases, the estimate for the change in the present value via the modified duration always overestimates its magnitude because the duration is negative, so the product of the modified duration and the increase in the discount rate is negative, and a positive component — the convexity — is left out. Similarly, when the discount rate decreases, the estimate for the change in the present value via the modified duration always underestimates its magnitude because the modified duration is negative, so the product of the modified duration and the decrease in the discount rate is positive, and a positive contribution — the convexity — is still left out. By adding the error term, we will come much closer to the true change in the present value.

A. WORD EXAMPLES OF DURATION AND CONVEXITY

When teaching this material I use two word examples to try to intuitively convey the meaning of duration and convexity for option-free, fixed-income securities.

1. The U-Haul® Example

Your family is moving from your current house to your new home. The trip will take several hours by automobile. You and your brother have identical cars; one is named Assets and the other is called Liabilities. The two automobiles are equally filled up with gas, clothing, linen, dishes, books, and other similar belongings. The family's valuables — the china, the nice silverware, your mother's jewelry, and all your stock and bond certificates — were placed into a small U-Haul trailer called Owner's Equity. You and your brother are going to tie the trailer to both cars, with ropes of equal length and strength, and pull the trailer down the road from your old to your new house. When you commence the trip the two of you are lined up as shown in Figure 3.2.

At the beginning of the journey the extensions of the ropes from the cars to the trailer should be equal; in other words your family's accounts should be in balance. It is now time to depart and you both start to speed up to 30 mph. Once you simultaneously reach cruising speed you both must remain aligned (i.e., balanced) and traveling at nearly the same speed (i.e., duration-matched); otherwise the U-Haul (= owner's equity = risk-based capital) will tip over. One of you can pull slightly ahead of the other or drop a bit behind (temporarily being out of strict balance), but soon a correction will be necessary to prevent excess tension on one or the other rope connecting the trailer to a vehicle.

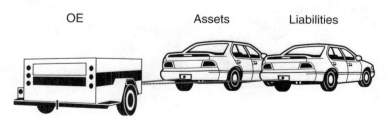

FIGURE 3.2 Two identical cars (labeled Assets and Liabilities) pulling the Owner's Equity in the U Haul with equal length and strength ropes. They must stay together (i.e., in balance), at the same average rate of speed (Macaulay duration-matched), and accelerate or decelerate at the same rates (be convexity-matched).

For the whole trip to be successful — that is, the U-Haul does not tip over (into bankruptcy) — you must be matched in speed as well as in position on average throughout the course of your journey. More than this, neither one of you can suddenly brake nor accelerate for any length of time without the other one rapidly compensating. Therefore, you must be *convexity-matched*, too, if you want to keep the trailer in tow and upright in a stable fashion. You will maintain this configuration until you arrive at your new house. Then you will both brake, starting at essentially the same instant of time, at the same rate of deceleration, for the same period of time, bringing the cars to a complete stop aligned and parallel.

Small deviations in positioning, speed, and acceleration or deceleration are allowed throughout the trip, but it is critical that no large discrepancies are permitted to develop. Steering the convoy down the road is a combination of many minute adjustments, some to the left and some to the right. So too is the maintenance of keeping the cars parallel, at roughly equal speeds, and at more or less equal acceleration or deceleration patterns. If this example does not work for you, then try the next one.

2. The Airplane Fuel Tank Example

The main fuel tanks of a big airplane are in the wings. Your airplane has one in each wing. The one on the left (as seen from the pilot's seat in the cockpit) is called Assets and the one on the right is called Liabilities. In addition, a small fuselage-centered tank is known as Owner's Equity. Each fuel tank can separately supply gasoline (jet fuel) to either of the two engines (see Figure 3.3). The airplane can also be refueled in flight. You, the pilot, have the job of taking off on January 1, 2002, and landing on the same field 1 year later. So, would you taxi down the takeoff runway with

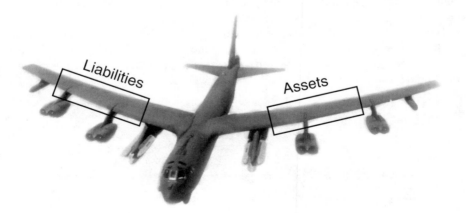

FIGURE 3.3 Airplane fuel tanks in the wings of a large plane. One is labeled Assets, the other Liabilities. Each fuel tank can supply the engines on either side of the wings. Both must be drawn down (filled up) at roughly equal rates. This maintains balance and duration-matching.

your asset and liability fuel tanks unequally filled? Not likely —you do not want to fight for control (or balance) as you leave the ground. A similar scenario holds for landing the plane a fiscal year later. Hence, your fuel tanks (accounts) will be in balance at the beginning and at the end of the journey. (Notice that the tanks need not be filled up so much as they be roughly equally filled.)

As you are flying around you must choose one or the other fuel tank from which to expend gasoline. Would you drain one of Assets or Liabilities completely before starting to empty the other one? The answer is "no" again because of the equilibrium issue. Why try to fight the potential unstable weight distribution of an unbalanced plane? Over time you drain the two tanks roughly equally to minimize your difficulties in handling the aircraft. In other words, you stay duration-matched. When both of your wing tanks are just about empty it is time for an inflight refueling. Would you let one wing's tank be completely filled up before starting refueling flow into the other one or would a more or less equal filling of the two fuel tanks be better? Obviously the latter is better. In different words, you would want to stay duration-matched during refueling too. Thus, whether fuel is being expended or taken on board, you want to be in a stable configuration.

So, how does convexity enter into the discussion? Real fuel tanks are not large monolithic structures but are divided into subunits for safety reasons. So the assets and liabilities fuel tanks actually have three subcompartments as shown in Figure 3.4. After take-off, you choose to drain the outermost one from the asset side first. To remain duration-matched you now need to switch to the liability side of the plane. Which sub-compartment would you drain first? You (should) want to answer, "The symmetrically placed one on the liability side." Why? Doing so preserves balance, duration-matching, and convexity-matching. Draining them in any but the most symmetric fashion would maintain a rough balance and duration-match, but only by emptying the symmetrically placed subcompartment can convexity-matching be maintained too.

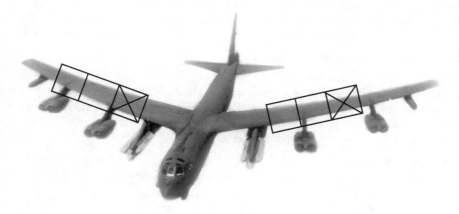

FIGURE 3.4 The fuel tanks have been subdivided. One can use up a sub-compartment on one side and a non-symmetrically placed one on the other side and still stay roughly balanced and duration-matched. You would not be convexity-matched, however.

a. Revisiting the Float Toy

In the context of the float toy, being convexity-matched means that the rate of change of the rate of change in air pressure (the rate of the rate of change of cash flow) of the two compartments is equal.

3. What Positive Convexity Really Means

Positive convexity is a desirable trait for a fixed-income security; it means that price depreciation will be slower with rising market interest rates and that price appreciation will be faster with lowering market interest rates. See Figure 3.5. Hence, positive convexity has value and you must pay for it.

a. Mathematics and Finance

Nothing in mathematics is called positive convexity. Curves that have the shape of the price/yield curve for option-free fixed-income, as seen in Figure 3.6, are known as convex; curves that bend the other way are called concave. One of these is shown as the dotted line. Somehow these concepts were mistranslated as positive and negative convexity instead of convexity and concavity.

B. The Formal Definition of Convexity

The name given in the finance literature to the rate of change of the modified duration with respect to the discount rate is convexity. Convexity is defined, using the usual symbols, by the following formula (the lower-case Greek letter gamma, γ, is routinely used to designate convexity)

$$\gamma = \frac{\sum_{n=1}^{N} n \times (n+1) \times C / (1+i/m)^n + N \times (N+1) \times F / (1+i/m)^N}{m^2 \times (1+i/m)^2 \times MV} \tag{3.8}$$

when the interest is paid m times annually. Note that the modification to alter the Macaulay duration is already included in the definition of convexity, i.e., the $(1+i/m)^2$ term in the denominator. Equation 3.8 tells us convexity in units of (payment periods)^2.

a. Numerical Example

Consider again the face amount F = $10,000, i_c = 5%, 3-year, semiannually paying corporate bond. Here we compute its convexity. The cash flows are a coupon payment of $C = i_c \times F/2 = 0.05 \times \$10,000/2 = \$250$ every 6 months commencing 6 months from now and a repayment of the face amount 3 years from now. The following table shows the convexity computation details:

Payment Number	Nominal Value	$n \times (n + 1) \times PV(\text{Cash Flow})$		
1	$250	$1 \times 2 \times \$250/(1 + 0.05/2)^1 = 1 \times 2 \times \$243.90$	=	$487.80
2	$250	$2 \times 3 \times \$250/(1 + 0.05/2)^2 = 2 \times 3 \times \$237.95$	=	$1,427.70
3	$250	$3 \times 4 \times \$250/(1 + 0.05/2)^3 = 3 \times 4 \times \$232.15$	=	$2,785.80
4	$250	$4 \times 5 \times \$250/(1 + 0.05/2)^4 = 4 \times 5 \times \$226.49$	=	$4,529.80
5	$250	$5 \times 6 \times \$250/(1 + 0.05/2)^5 = 5 \times 6 \times \$220.96$	=	$6,628.80
6	$10,250	$6 \times 7 \times (\$250 + \$10K)/(1 + 0.05/2)^6 = 6 \times 7 \times \$8,838.54$ =		$371,218.68

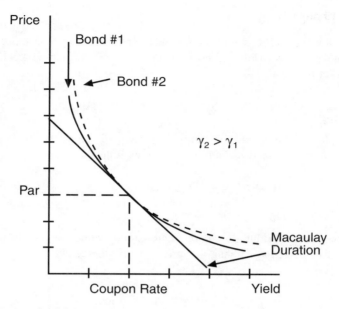

FIGURE 3.5 Two bonds, labeled 1 and 2, with identical prices at their equal coupon rates and the same Macaulay duration at that interest rate. They have, however, different convexities γ.

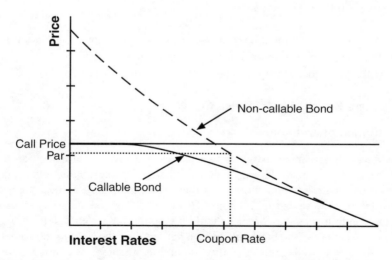

FIGURE 3.6 The price/yield curve for a callable bond and a noncallable bond. The latter is said to have negative convexity because it turns over as interest rates move below its coupon rate. The maximum price for it will be the Call Price = Par + Call Premium.

The sum of the present value of the cash flows comes to $9,999.99. The sum of the far right-hand column is $387,079, so the convexity is 9.21. Convexity has no unit associated with it.

1. Price Change Usage

Equation 3.8 is a consequence of the fact that, mathematically, convexity is defined as the second partial derivative of the market price of a fixed-income security divided by the market price,

$$\text{Convexity} = \gamma = \partial^2(MV)/\partial i^2/MV.$$

Convexity plus modified duration can be used to provide a pretty good estimate for the price change in a fixed-income instrument as follows:

$$\Delta(MV)/MV \cong -D_{mod} \times \Delta i + {}^1\!/_2 \times \gamma \times (\Delta i)^2.$$

a. Dollar Convexity

Just as there is a dollar duration, *dollar convexity* is defined as the change in price (as opposed to percentage change in price) owing to second order alterations in interest rates:

$$\gamma_\$ = {}^1\!/_2 \times \gamma \times (\Delta i)^2 \times \text{Price}.$$

2. Convexity Maxims

Some general rules about convexity:

- If the coupon payment goes up, the convexity goes down and vice versa.
- The longer the time to maturity, the greater the convexity.
- If the yield-to-maturity decreases, the convexity increases.

C. CALLABLE BONDS AND NEGATIVE CONVEXITY

1. Definition of an Option

An *option* is an agreement between two parties that gives one of the parties, the option buyer, the right to demand that the other party, the option seller, perform some service or deliver something of value. The option buyer does not need to exercise his option; he can let it expire. However, the option seller is obligated to fulfill the conditions of the contract should the option holder choose to exercise it. A *call option* is the right to buy something; a *put option* is the right to sell something. For obtaining this privilege of flexibility the option purchaser pays a fee, known as the *option premium*, to the option seller. An option has several features associated with it:

1. A date in the future, known as the *exercise date, expiration date,* or maturity date, when the privilege granted runs out.
2. An *exercise price* or *strike price*: the level of some quantity (e.g., the price of shares of common stock, a 10-year U.S. Treasury Note interest rate,

the price of an ounce of gold, and so on) that determines whether or not the option is *in-the-money* (profitable for the holder of the option to exercise it), *out-of-the-money*, (not profitable for the holder of the option to exercise it), or *at-the-money* (neutral with respect to execution).

3. The option premium is the cost of entering into the agreement and is paid at the time the option is sold.

A housing-related example of a call option is the practice of renting a house with the option to buy it in 6 months (the exercise date) for a specified price, $235,000 (the exercise price). The rent paid would be above the current market rate; the difference represents the option premium. The option buyer lives in the house, gets to know the building's properties, the nature of the neighborhood, and so forth. If the renter likes what he sees, then he exercises his option at the end of 6 months and purchases the house at the agreed upon price of $235,000. The landlord must honor his agreement with the renter if the renter chooses to exercise the option. If the renter does not like something about the situation, then he chooses not to exercise his option to buy and loses the option premium (e.g., the spread between the market rent and the higher amount of rent actually paid over the 6 months of tenancy).

a. The Main Types of Option Exercise

Because the option just discussed had one particular exercise date, it is known as a *European option* or European-style option. Had the renter been able to exercise his option to buy at any time during the 6 months of renting, then the option would be called an *American option* or an American-style option. Almost all home loans in the U.S. give the homeowner the option to pay off part or all of the outstanding principal balance, at any time, for any reason. The originator of the mortgage grants this American-style option as part of the loan commitment. The cost of this option is reflected in the coupon rate of the loan (about 50 basis points). Another type of temporal exercise between American- and European-style options is known as a *Bermudan option* (for obvious geographic reasons). In the rental example considered previously, the exercise dates might be the first of every month when the rental payment would be due.

2. Callable Bonds

Bonds that provide the issuer with the right, but not the obligation, to redeem the debt prior to its stated maturity are known as callable bonds. (Noncallable bonds are also known as bullet bonds.) Most callable debt is issued with a *no-call* or *lock-out* period that ends on a coupon payment date. This is designed to ensure that the purchaser of the debt has some guaranteed time during which he will receive interest payments. The abbreviation used to refer to callable bonds is to write, for example, 10NC6. The notation means that the bond has a maturity of 10 years with a lock-out period lasting for the first 6 years during which it is noncallable. One might see a 1NC6m, meaning that it was a 1-year instrument callable after 6 months had elapsed. (Bonds with an embedded put option are known as *puttable bonds*. Puttable bonds are relatively rare, although the basic U.S. savings bond is puttable.)

A 12NC8E (E for European) bond is callable only on the date of the coupon payment that begins the eighth year of the security's 12-year life. A Bermudan option for a 12NC8 debt issue would entitle the bond's issuer to call the instrument on coupon dates starting with the eighth anniversary of the bond's existence. Finally, an American-style option in a 12NC8 would come into effect on the eighth year anniversary date of the bond and thereafter could be called any time until the bond's maturity date. Because the American-style option in bonds most closely matches the American-style option in residential mortgages, mortgage portfolio managers greatly prefer this type of optionality. Freddie Mac, for instance, has almost 80% of its long-term debt in callable form; for Fannie Mae it is about 50%. (The difference stems from dissimilar methods used to manage interest rate risk.)

a. What a Buyer Loses If His Bond Is Called

Let us review exactly what you lose should a callable bond be called. Suppose that it is a 10NC2E, 10%/year, $1 million face bond. You would expect $50,000 every 6 months for 10 years plus the repayment of the principal amount at the end of 10 years. If the bond was called on its second-year anniversary, as the notation indicates is possible, then you would forego 8 years of semiannual interest payments of $50,000 each. That amounts to $800,000, more nominally than the present value of the coupon payments contributed to the original bond's price. One can assume that the issuer of the bond would only exercise the option if it made economic sense to do so. That means that interest rates must have dropped between the time of issuance and the call date. Hence, you lose 8 years worth of interest cash flow, your principal is returned to you in a lower interest rate environment, and, therefore, you can only reinvest it in a similar security at a lower coupon.

b. The Forms of Compensation

As a buyer of a callable bond you would demand to be compensated for the additional risk you are accepting. There are three common types of reimbursement used:

1. Increasing the coupon rate over the otherwise equivalent non-callable instrument.
2. Selling the callable bond at a discount without changing the coupon rate.
3. Paying a call premium on the exercise date (if the bond is, in fact, redeemed).

Increasing the coupon rate is a straightforward method of providing the purchaser with additional compensation over time for the risk he is accepting by purchasing the callable version of the instrument instead of the equivalent noncallable version. (To compare them meaningfully, they are assumed to have the same maturities, issue amounts, secondary market liquidity, and credit ratings. In most of the bond market an equivalent, noncallable version does not exist. See the end of the next paragraph.) The investor knows at the moment of purchase that he will earn a higher yield than on the bullet bond as long as the bond is not redeemed.

This extra yield, over and above the underlying, noncallable, equivalent security's coupon rate, is properly referred to as the *option-adjusted spread*. By construction, the only difference between the alternatives is the call option (same issuer, same amounts, same maturity, same issuance date, and so on). In the mortgage market and most of the bond market, the concept of option-adjusted spread is broadened and no longer reflects only the optionality component. The market practice is to fall back to the comparable duration U.S. Treasury instrument and refer to the option-adjusted spread as the difference between the coupon rate on the callable instrument and this yield.

If the bond had been sold at a discount without adjusting the coupon rate upwards, then the purchaser of the callable security would have been compensated at settlement for accepting the risk of a call. The bond owner could immediately invest the amount discounted and earn additional funds, thereby increasing his effective yield. The third frequently utilized method of compensating the callable bond purchaser is to sell the bond at par, with a coupon rate equal to the equivalent noncallable instrument; the issuer pays an extra amount over par to the bond owner should early redemption occur. This is referred to as the call premium. Bonds sold this way come with a table of call premiums specifying the amount to pay over time. In the case of a 5NC2, the call premium might be 12% for a call at the lock-out date, decreasing by two percentage points a coupon interval and reaching zero at maturity.

3. Calculating the Yield-to-Call

The investor wants to compute the *yield-to-call* — the interest rate associated with the security that actually represents the rate of return. There are several ways of looking at this. The simplest assumption to make is that the bond will be called at the first opportunity. Then we have a straight discounting problem with the end of the lock-out period replacing the maturity date. Just as there is an approximate formula for the yield-to-maturity of a noncallable bond, there is one for the yield-to-call. The conventional approximation to the yield-to-call, y_c, is based on the call price CP (which may include a call premium) and the number of coupon payment periods left until the earliest possible call date (N_c):

$$y_c \cong y_c{}' = m \times [C + (CP - MV)/N_c]/(0.6 \times MV + 0.4 \times CP).$$

a. Calculating the Yield-to-Worst

For any callable bond one can also compute what is known as the *yield-to-worst*. Suppose, for simplicity, that the option was Bermudan style. Then, for each possible call date, with its associated call premium, one could calculate the yield-to-maturity. The lowest of these is known as the yield-to-worst.

4. Negative Convexity

Look again at Figure 3.6, which shows the price/yield relationship for a noncallable, fixed-income security; if interest rates increase prices decrease and vice versa. For the callable instrument this is not true. When interest rates rise significantly above the coupon rate on the callable bond, then it acts much like a bullet bond. No rational issuer will recall the callable bond to reissue it at a higher interest rate. However, when interest rates drop through the coupon level of the callable bond, the situation is different. Eventually market rates will be so much lower than the coupon rate that it will make economic sense to exercise the embedded call option, pay any call premium, new flotation costs, and so on and benefit from the now lower interest rate environment. Hence, a callable bond can have a maximum value. The negative convexity induced into the bond's price/yield relationship has caused a price cap or the bond to suffer from price compression. It is even possible for the callable instrument's price to drop as interest rates further decrease because of the increased probability of the call option being exercised.

D. The Option-Adjusted Spread

1. Callable Bond Pricing

Think of callable bond in the following terms: when one is *long*, or owns, a callable bond, one has effectively purchased the noncallable equivalent and sold, or is short, the call option:

Long a Callable Bond = Long a Noncallable Bond + Short a Call Option.

Thus, the price of a callable bond, in terms of the equivalent noncallable version of the instrument, is

Callable Bond Price = Noncallable Bond Price − Call Option Price.   (3.9)

Designate the price of the callable security as p, the price of the equivalent, underlying, noncallable security as P, and that of the option premium as ΔP; then Equation 3.9 is the same as

$$p = P - \Delta P.$$

The price of a fixed-income instrument can be translated into a yield. Hence, we can also view the value of the option in terms of the difference between yields. The yield of a callable bond is composed of the return of the equivalent underlying bullet bond plus the option premium, expressed as a yield, for the call privilege. We speak of the interest rate of the underlying noncallable bond plus the interest rate equivalent of the option premium because the prices of fixed-income instruments move inversely with yields and the option premium is subtracted from the price of the noncallable version of the underlying instrument. Denoting the yield of the callable security as y, that of the equivalent, noncallable security as Y, and that of the option premium viewed as a yield as ΔY, this thought can expressed as

$$y = Y + \Delta Y.$$

Since the prices, or yields, of many securities are frequently compared to U.S. Treasury instruments, where comparable means equal time-to-maturity (preferably Macaulay duration) and equal frequency of coupon payment, one can speak of the spread between the security under discussion and that of the similar Treasury certificate. The option-adjusted spread is then the difference between the option-adjusted yield just computed (i.e., Y in the above formula) and the yield on the matching U.S. Treasury Bill, Note, or Bond. Note that credit issues, liquidity concerns, and all sorts of other real-life pricing fears are now buried in one all-purpose, and misleading, phrase.

The option-adjusted spread, or OAS, is the amount that must be added to the coupon rate i of the duration-matching Treasury instrument, over the entire life of the callable security, to make the net present value vanish. That is, the option-adjusted spread is the solution to Equation 3.10, given the bond's parameters C, F, and N and its market value MV:

$$MV = \sum_{n=1}^{N} C / (1 + i / 2 + OAS / 2)^n + F / (1 + i / 2 + OAS / 2)^N. \qquad (3.10)$$

This formulation of the problem explicitly shows that: 1. a flat term structure of interest rates has been assumed because the annual discount rate is equal to (i + OAS)/2 and 2. only one scenario of possible interest rates and cash flows has been considered. (A bond sold at a discount would send F to F − ΔF where ΔF was the amount of the discount. If there were a call premium, then it would send F to F + CP.) This process will be made much more complicated once we consider interest rate modeling.

III. A PORTFOLIO VERSION OF DURATION

A. INTRODUCTION

The simple relationship between Macaulay and modified duration holds only if the cash flows are interest-rate independent, if the shift in the term structure is a parallel one, and, most importantly, if the underlying term structure was constant or flat to begin with. The purposes of this section are:

1. To demonstrate a way to extend the familiar modified duration/price change relationship to initially nonflat term structures.
2. To similarly illustrate, with the same technique, how to handle nonparallel adjustments of the term structure of interest rates in the conventional formalism. While, as a bonus
3. To simultaneously provide a mathematically simple way to appreciate the sensitivity of one's portfolio to the combination of its cash flows and the posited term structure when it is time to rebalance the mixture of securities.

These three goals can be satisfactorily accomplished while maintaining the uncomplicated aspects of the familiar duration formulas. Hence, portfolio managers and fixed-income security analysts have a simple device to assist them in their sophisticated, real-world work of portfolio immunization.

This analysis is based on forward rates instead of spot rates. Why forward rates? Remember that a spot rate is the interest rate for borrowing or lending commencing immediately, while a forward rate is an interest rate, agreed to today, for borrowing or lending beginning some time in the future. The algebra of this section is easier to see through if forward rates are used to discount cash flows. Also, forward rates are frequently used as estimates for what future spot rates will be, so the effect of this common assumption can be explicitly visualized if the analysis is based on them rather than spot rates.

B. THE AVERAGE DISCOUNT RATE FOR A MORTGAGE

1. Mathematical Preliminaries

First consider a fixed-rate, fully amortizing, level-payment, *monthly paying* mortgage. (Mortgages are amortizing instruments, so the principal is paid off over the life of the instrument; the redemption value is zero.) Let its monthly payment be $1; the calculations will scale with this quantity. Suppose that the forward rates of return you want to use are denoted by r_1, r_2, ..., r_N for the N payment periods (N = 360 for a 30-year mortgage) remaining on the lien. Let PV_m stand for the present value of the mortgage. Then

$$PV_m \equiv 1/(1 + r_1) + 1/[(1 + r_1) \times (1 + r_2)] + \bullet\bullet\bullet +$$
$$1/[(1 + r_1) \times (1 + r_2) \times (1 + r_3) \times \bullet\bullet\bullet \times (1 + r_N)]$$

where there are N multiplicands in the last inverse product. Our first problem is to find a formula for a single discount rate (symbolized by r) that will make the set of cash flows have the same present value. In mathematical terms, we want to find the value of r which is the solution of

$$PV_m = 1/(1+r) + 1/(1+r)^2 + \bullet\bullet\bullet + 1/(1+r)^N = \sum_{n=1}^{N} 1/(1+r)^n. \quad (3.11)$$

This value of r will be some sort of unequally weighted average discount rate. These weights will provide the insight into how our posited forward rate structure influences the present value.

The first thing to do is to make a change of variables from r to ρ (the lower-case Greek letter rho);

$$\rho = 1/(1 + r). \quad (3.12)$$

For consistency, also do something comparable for each of the forward discount rates $\{r_n\}$. Define $\{\rho_n\}$ as

$$\rho_n \equiv 1/(1 + r_n), \; n = 1,2,..., N. \quad (3.13)$$

This substitution allows us to transform the nonlinear Equation 3.11 into a more familiar-looking Nth order polynomial equation, which, after rearranging the terms a bit, takes the form

$$F(\rho) = \sum_{n=1}^{N} \rho^n - (\rho_1 + \rho_1\rho_2 + \rho_1\rho_2\rho_3 + \cdots + \rho_1\rho_2 \cdots \rho_N) = 0. \qquad (3.14)$$

All the factors of rho, with or without a subscript, are multiplied by unity because we started out considering the equivalent of a monthly annuity with a one-dollar cash flow per payment period. Generalizations of this scenario to the standard corporate bond and beyond will be presented later.

Let us convert the constant term in two steps. First notice that the nth term in the constant has the form

$$\rho_1\rho_2\rho_3 \cdots \rho_n$$

which, using the standard product notation introduced earlier, can be rewritten as

$$\rho_1\rho_2\rho_3 \cdots \rho_n = \prod_{m=1}^{n} \rho_m$$

The entire constant term, which consists of the sum of N terms of this form, can be concisely depicted as

$$\sum_{n=1}^{N} \left(\prod_{m=1}^{n} \rho_m \right)$$

With the aid of the last expression, the function $F(\rho)$ in Equation 3.14 takes the form

$$F(\rho) = \sum_{n=1}^{N} \rho^n - \sum_{n=1}^{N} \left(\prod_{m=1}^{N} \rho_m \right) = 0. \qquad (3.15)$$

Since interest rates are usually positive, it follows from Equation 3.13 that every ρ_n, $n = 1,2,\ldots, N$ is less than unity and positive; $0 < \rho_n < 1$ with $\rho_n = 1$ if and only if $r_n = 0$. Since the product of any two positive numbers less than unity is also less than unity (and positive), it follows that every product in the last summation in Equation 3.15 is less than unity (and positive) in value. With exactly N terms in the sum, the value of the sum is bounded below by zero and above by N. Thus,

$$F(0) < 0.$$

Reexamine Equation 3.15 and observe exactly N powers of ρ in the definition of $F(\rho)$. Hence, combining this fact with the previous argument, we can declare that, at $\rho = 1$,

$$F(1) = N - \sum_{n=1}^{N} \left(\prod_{m=1}^{N} \rho_m \right) > 0. \tag{3.16}$$

Thus, we know that F (which is obviously continuous because it is a polynomial function of rho) changes sign for $\rho \in [0,1]$. Therefore, there must be at least one root of F for $\rho \in (0,1)$. This should not be a surprise; however, if the $\{r_n\}$ are not too large (i.e., $r_n \cong 0.1$), then each of the N values of $\{\rho_m\}$ is just slightly less than unity. Each of the products in the constant term is not much less than unity, so the sum of N terms of this form is close to, but still less than, N. Hence, the root of F must lie much closer to unity than to zero; this is another, possibly convoluted, way of saying that the value of r sought is not too large if all the $\{r_n\}$ are not either. Rather than attack the general problem initially, first consider some special, and educational, cases for small values of N.

a.   *Some Special Cases*

The simplest instance is that N is 1. Then $\rho = \rho_1$ and $r = r_1$. Because it is trivial, this is not a very interesting case. Instead, suppose that N is equal to 2. Equation 3.15 becomes a quadratic equation in the unknown ρ. Solve this exactly to find that

$$\rho = \{-1 + [1 + 4\rho_1 \times (1 + \rho_2)]^{1/2}\}/2.$$

(The other root of the quadratic equation can be discarded because we know the magnitude of rho.)

This becomes a little more intriguing if we make the approximation that products and squares of forward rates can be neglected. Now we can write rho, and each $\{\rho_m\}$, as one minus a small quantity. To this level of approximation, they are just the forward rates $\{r_m\}$. That is,

if $r_m \ll 1$, then $\rho_m = 1/(1 + r_m) \cong 1 - r_m$ for m = 1,2,..., N,

where

$$\rho \equiv 1 - R_2 \cong 1 - r \text{ where } 0 < R_2 \ll 1.$$

The solution for ρ is roughly given by

$$\rho = 1 - R_2 \cong 1 - (2r_1 + r_2)/3 \text{ or } r \cong (2r_1 + r_2)/3.$$

Step back from the analytical work and look at the last expression. It tells us that the (approximate) formula for the average discount rate r, which makes the cash flows have the same present value as the actual one PV_m in Equation 3.11, is one that weighs the forward rate for the first period twice as heavily as the forward rate for the second period. We also see that the correct normalization for computing a temporally weighted average has automatically fallen out. One suspects that the forward rate for the first payment period has twice the weight of the forward rate for the second because it is used to discount the first and the second periods' cash flows. Can this type of result be generalized? Next in complexity would be a third-order version of the problem.

If we suppose three payment periods, then F would take the form

$$F(\rho) = \rho^3 + \rho^2 + \rho - (\rho_1 + \rho_1\rho_2 + \rho_1\rho_2\rho_3) = 0.$$

Using the standard procedure for finding the roots of cubic equations, we can show that this cubic has exactly one real root and that it is approximately given by

$$\rho \cong [44/27 + (8/3)^{1/2}]^{(1/3)} \times (1 - \{3 + [(11/6) \times (8/3)^{1/2}]\} \ (R_3/3) \ )/[44/27 + (8/3)^{1/2}]$$

$$+ [44/27 - (8/3)^{1/2}]^{(1/3)} \times (1 - \{3 - [(11/6) \times (8/3)^{1/2}]\} \ (R_3/3) \ )/[44/27 - (8/3)^{1/2}] - 1/3.$$

The only assumption used to derive this was that it was permissible to neglect products and squares of forward rates. In the process the quantity R_3 was defined to be equal to

$$R_3 \equiv (3r_1 + 2r_2 + r_3)/6,$$

or the average of the forward rates weighted according to the number of times they appear in the present value formula. Had R_3 been defined via $\rho \equiv 1 - R_3 \cong 1 - r$, then the result just obtained would have been both its and r's first-order approximation.

Working through the algebra, you may convince yourself that the expression is identically equal to

$$\rho \equiv 1 - R_3 \cong 1 - (3r_1 + 2r_2 + r_3)/6$$

and the pattern of the two-component forward curve has been repeated. This coincidence arouses suspicion and, since the quartic equation is exactly soluble in closed form, too, makes us wonder whether or not we could explicitly show, when N is equal to 4, that

$$\rho \equiv 1 - R_4 \cong 1 - (4r_1 + 3r_2 + 2r_3 + r_4)/24.$$

The answer is affirmative but, rather than explicitly demonstrating this, let us turn to proving that this generalization is true for all values of N > 1.

2. The General Solution for a Mortgage

To make the case, use Newton's method to provide an approximate magnitude for the value of rho that makes $F(\rho)$ in Equation 3.15 vanish. Use unity as the starting point in the iteration scheme and carry it through one more level. We know what $F(1)$ is from Equation 3.16. Next we need to compute the derivative of $F(\rho)$ with respect to rho and evaluate it at $\rho = 1$; the result is

$$dF(\rho)/d\rho = N \times \rho^{N-1} + (N-1) \times \rho^{N-2} + \bullet\bullet\bullet + 2\rho + 1 = \sum_{n=1}^{N} n = N \times (N+1)/2$$

where the middle equality obtains if rho is equal to unity. Hence, the next estimate for the root of F is

$$\rho' \cong 1 - F(\rho=1)/[dF(\rho=1)/d\rho] = \left[N - \sum_{n=1}^{N} \left(\prod_{m=1}^{N} \rho_m \right) \right] / [N \times (N+1)/2].$$

Make the substitution for the $\{\rho_n\}$ in terms of the $\{r_n\}$ defined in Equation 3.13. Also, observe that, to first order in the small quantities $\{r_n\}$, the product becomes a summation:

$$\prod_{m=1}^{N} \rho_m \cong \prod_{m=1}^{N} (1 - r_m) \cong 1 - \sum_{m=1}^{N} r_m.$$

Hence, the new estimate for the root of F can be written as

$$\rho' \cong 1 - \left[N - \sum_{n=1}^{N} \left(1 - \sum_{m=1}^{n} r_m \right) \right] / [N \times (N+1)/2].$$

The first summation on the right-hand side of this formula is the sum of unity N times and perfectly cancels the first factor of N, allowing the reduction of the previous expression to

$$\rho' \cong 1 - \sum_{n=1}^{N} \left(\sum_{m=1}^{n} r_m \right) / [N \times (N+1)/2].$$

By writing out the double sum, you will see that it can be cast into the form of a single summation, i.e.,

$$\rho' \equiv 1 - R_N \cong 1 - \sum_{n=1}^{N} (N-n+1) \times r_n / [N \times (N+1)/2].$$

So, the approximate formula for $r \equiv R_N$ is given by

$$r \cong \sum_{n=1}^{N} (N-n+1)r_n / [N \times (N+1)/2] \qquad (3.17)$$

$$= [Nr_1 + (N-1)r_2 + \bullet\bullet\bullet + r_N] / [N \times (N+1)/2].$$

This is just the symbolic version of what was found for the $N = 1$, 2, and 3 special cases. R_N, or r, at this level of estimation, is the weighted average of the individual one-period forward rates with the weights equal to the number of times that that particular forward rate appears in the discounted cash flow evaluation. Using the forward rates to discount the cash flows, instead of the spot rates, more clearly illustrates their relative contribution to the present value. Remembering that forward rates are frequently used as estimates for future spot rates, you can now quantify the effect of any errors going into the future that this presumption will entail in the portfolio average discount rate. After solving a similar problem for a corporate bond, we will see how to use the same results in computing duration and price sensitivity.

C. THE AVERAGE DISCOUNT RATE FOR A BULLET BOND

The case of a mortgage was straightforward because all the numerators were the same. The instance of a bullet bond is only mildly more complicated. So, restating the formula for the present value of a bullet bond with equal *annual* coupon payments of C dollars, par amount P dollars, and with annual forward rates $\{r_n\}$, over N coupon payment periods,

$$PV_b = C/(1+r_1) + C/[(1+r_1) \times (1+r_2)]$$

$$+ \bullet\bullet\bullet + (C+P)/[(1+r_1) \times (1+r_2) \times \bullet\bullet\bullet \times (1+r_N)]. \qquad (3.18)$$

(If you prefer to think in terms of a series of semiannual cash flows, then none of the analytical work changes; only the meaning of $\{r_n\}$ and C do in the obvious fashion.) Using the nomenclature of an equivalent average, annual, constant discount rate, r, the last formula would be rewritten as

$$PV_b = C/(1+r) + C/(1+r)^2 + \bullet\bullet\bullet + (C+P)/(1+r)^N$$

$$= \sum_{n=1}^{N} C/(1+r)^n + P/(1+r)^N. \qquad (3.19)$$

With the same changes of variables as in Equations 3.12 and 3.13, the new expression for determining the average discount factor rho becomes

$$F(\rho) = C \times \sum_{n=1}^{N} \rho^n + P \times \rho^N - C \times \sum_{n=1}^{N} \left(\prod_{m=1}^{n} \rho_m \right) - P \times \prod_{m=1}^{N} \rho_m.$$

The estimation of the solution to $F(\rho) = 0$ is very similar to the mortgage version of the problem so I will just pass right to the answer. It is, under the same set of approximations mentioned above (namely neglecting the squares and products of forward rates), once again for $r \equiv R_N \cong 1 - \rho$,

$$r \cong R_N \cong [C \times \sum_{m=1}^{N} (N - m + 1)r_m$$
$$+ N \times P \times <r>] / [C \times N \times (N + 1) / 2 + N \times P] \tag{3.20}$$

where $<r>$ is the arithmetic average of the forward rates $\{r_m\}$ in the posited forward curve,

$$<r> = \sum_{m=1}^{N} r_m / N.$$

Equation 3.20 complements Equation 3.17 and is an even more interesting and potentially informative result. The individual forward rates now appear in the formula for $r \cong R_N$ twice — once unequally weighted with the same temporal weighing scheme as for a mortgage and once weighted uniformly — by the amount of the par value. We can understand the first part of this result because Equation 3.20 reduces to Equation 3.17 when there is no terminal principal repayment. (The coupon payment C is just a scale factor now.) The appearance of the arithmetic mean in conjunction with the par value is a consequence of the latter's occurrence with only one (albeit compound) discount factor in the present value formula, Equation 3.18, in which the full set of discount factors appear equally frequently. In contrast, the coupons appear discounted N separate times, and differently in each instance, in Equation 3.18.

D. Extending the Usefulness of Modified Duration

Now we come to the second key point: extending the usefulness of modified duration to fixed-income pricing and portfolio management when neither the discounting term structure was flat nor the changes in it constant. The market price of a fixed-income security was equally computed with the forward curve $\{r_n\}$ or the average discount rate $r = 1/\rho - 1$. The constraint induced was that the results be identical; that defined r. Now suppose that the posited forward curve changes with $\{r_n\} \rightarrow \{r_n + \delta r_n\}$. (The lower-case Greek letter delta, δ, is also commonly used to indicate a small change and, by allowing each forward rate to alter independently, nonparallel shifts in the yield curve can be accommodated.) Can one use, with some degree of numerical confidence, something like

$$\delta(PV)/PV = - d_{mod} \times \delta r, \tag{3.21}$$

to approximate the relative price change in the instrument? The definition of the r-based modified duration d_{mod}, in terms of the r-based Macaulay duration d, is given by

$$d_{mod} = d / (1+r) = \rho \times d = \rho \times (C \times \sum_{n=1}^{N} n \times \rho^n + P \times N \times \rho^N) / PV_b$$

$$= (1+r)^{-1} \times [C \times \sum_{n=1}^{N} n / (1+r)^n + N \times P / (1+r)^N] / PV_b \qquad (3.22)$$

$$= -\partial ln(PV_b) / \partial r = -(1 / PV_b) \times \partial(PV_b) / \partial r$$

where the equivalence with the negative of the logarithmic derivative of the present value follows because, through the use of r, once more there is a flat (pseudo-) term structure of interest rates. Building upon the bullet bond result,

$$\delta r = [C \times \sum_{m=1}^{N} (N-m+1)\, \delta r_m + N \times P \times < \delta r >] / [C \times N \times (N+1) / 2 + N \times P]$$

with $<\delta r>$ defined by

$$< \delta r > = \sum_{m=1}^{N} \delta r_m / N.$$

This works well enough, quantitatively, to be a useful approximation. Equations 3.21 and 3.22 will allow a quick estimate of the dependence of the value of an interest-rate sensitive portfolio of assets and liabilities on cash flow and the forward rate structure when a component of the mix of securities is about to come due or the yield curve alters the forward rates.

1. Arbitrary Cash Flows

We can generalize one step further to an arbitrary series of cash flows. The present value (PV) of a general fixed-income portfolio whose stream of cash flows $\{CF_n\}$ is discounted by a term structure with forward rates $\{r_n\}$ is

$$PV = \sum_{n=1}^{N} CF_n \times \left[\prod_{m=1}^{n} (1 + r_m)^{-1} \right]$$

Define an average discount rate $r = 1/\rho - 1$ such that equality in market price is maintained:

$$PV = \sum_{n=1}^{N} CF_n \times \rho^n = \sum_{n=1}^{N} CF_n \times \left[\prod_{m=1}^{n} (1 + r_m)^{-1} \right] = \sum_{n=1}^{N} CF_n \times \left(\prod_{m=1}^{n} \rho_m \right)$$

As before, analytically approximate the value of rho that makes the above formula an equality by Newton's method. The result is

$$\rho' \cong 1 - \sum_{n=1}^{N} CF_n \times \left[\prod_{m=1}^{n} (1 - \rho_m) \right] / \sum_{k=1}^{N} k \times CF_k$$

PROBLEMS

1. Compute the present value of an unequal set of cash flows at a constant discount rate r = 18.577%/year. The cash flows are $CF_1 = \$111.11$, $CF_2 = \$222.22$, and $CF_3 = \$333.33$, m = 4 per year, and N = 3 (i.e., 9 months). Show that the result is

   $PV = CF_1/(1 + r/m)^1 + CF_2/(1 + r/m)^2 + CF_3/(1 + r/m)^3$

   $\quad = \$111.11/(1 + 0.18577/4)^1 + \$222.22/(1 + 0.18577/4)^2$

   $\quad\quad + \$333.33/(1 + 0.18577/4)^3$

   $\quad = \$600.00.$

2. Spot rates are interest rates quoted today for borrowing commencing today for a specified time into the future. If we were using 3-month rates, then r_1 would be the interest rate for borrowing for 3 months starting today, r_2 would be the interest rate for borrowing for 6 months starting today, r_3 would be the interest rate for borrowing for 9 months starting today, and so forth. Consider a bond with the following parameters and spot curve, C = \$123.45 (i.e., i_c = 1.646% per year and m = 2), F = \$15,000, N = 4, and $\{r_n\}$ = {0.0555, 0.0666, 0.0777, 0.0888}. Explain why the present value PV is correctly given by

   $PV = C/(1 + r_1)^1 + C/(1 + r_2)^2 + C/(1 + r_3)^3 + (C + F)/(1 + r_4)^4$

   $\quad = \$123.45/(1 + 0.0555)^1 + \$123.45/(1 + 0.0666)^2$

   $\quad\quad + \$123.45/(1 + 0.0777)^3 + (\$123.45 + \$15,000)/(1 + 0.0888)^4$

   $\quad = \$11,085.24.$

3. Consider two bonds, with face amount \$30,000 each, one with a 10-year time to maturity and the other with 20 years to retirement. Each pays interest semiannually. Let the coupon interest rate on the shorter-term debt be 15% and that on the longer one be 5%. Compute their durations at a market interest rate of 10%. (For the 10-year bond, C = \$2,250, MV = \$39,346.66, and D = 6.046 years while for the 20-year bond, C = \$750, MV = \$17,130.69, and D = 10.376 years)

4. Consider a 30-year, face value F = \$5,000,000 bond with i_c = 12.34%/year. The semiannual coupon payment C = i_c × F/2 = \$308,500. Suppose that

the interest rate increases to 15%/year immediately after the bond is priced. Show that its market value, MV, will decrease to $4,124,901.18 and that its Macaulay duration will be equal to D = 7.137 years.

5. Consider two bonds with face amount $60,000 each, one with a 10-year time to maturity and the other with 15 years to retirement. Each pays interest semiannually. Let the coupon interest rate on the shorter-term debt be 18% and that on the longer one be 4%. Compute their durations at a market interest rate of 12%. (For the 10-year bond, C = $5,400, MV = $80,645.86, and D = 5.624 years, while for the 15-year bond, C = $1,200, MV = $26,964.41, and D = 9.285 years) Show that for continuous compounding, the Macaulay and modified durations are identical.

6. Compute the present value and the duration of a bond with an 11-year time to maturity, coupon interest rate of 8.34%, and a face value of $35,000. The current market interest rates have decreased to 6.78%. Also, use the modified duration to evaluate the current market price. Recompute the same triplet of quantities in the event that the market interest rate suddenly jumped to 9.01% instead of decreasing. Assume that interest is paid quarterly. (C = $729.75, MV = $39,209.12, D = 7.530 years, D_{mod} = 7.404 years, $\Delta(MV)/MV$ = +11.5% or MV = $39,025; MV = $33,374.04, D = 7.204 years, D_{mod} = 7.046 years, $\Delta(MV)/MV$ = –4.7% or MV = $33,360)

7. There is one aspect of duration that is fairly easy to demonstrate mathematically. Consider two fixed-income securities with the same maturity N, the same face amount, and the same frequency of interest payments per year m. Let the periodic discount rate be I = i/m where i is the annual discount rate. Then we can write the duration of either of them as in Equation 3.4. Now assume that one pays coupons in different amounts from the other, for example, C_1 and C_2 where C_2 is greater than C_1. Denote their corresponding durations by D_2 and D_1 and let us examine the consequences of assuming that D_2 exceeds D_1. Using Equation 3.4 for the two durations, enforcing the inequality, and after cross-multiplying to clear fractions and canceling common factors, one is left with the fact that $D_2 > D_1$ implies that

$$T_N > N \times (S_N - 1).$$

After some further manipulations, this turns out to be equivalent to the statement that [$\rho = 1/(1 + I)$]

$$(\rho^N - 1)/(\rho - 1) > N.$$

However, after the indicated long division is performed, the quotient on the left is equal to

$$\rho^{N-1} + \rho^{N-2} + \bullet\bullet\bullet + \rho^2 + \rho + 1$$

and there are $N - 1$ terms involving rho in the above expression. Since i and $I \in [0,1)$, it follows that $\rho = 1/(1 + I) \in [1/2,1]$ so that an upper bound to the $N - 1$ ρ-dependent terms is just $N - 1$. [A slightly better upper bound is given by $(N - 1)\rho + 1$.] As $N - 1 + 1 = N$, and N cannot be less than itself, it follows that the assumption that D_2 is greater than D_1, when C_2 is greater than C_1, is false. Interestingly, a proof based on calculus, i.e., that $\partial D/\partial C < 0$, hinges on the same inequality. Prove this.

4 Overview of Common U.S. Mortgage Types

This chapter concentrates on the American residential mortgage market, presenting its history and its current structure. The standard fixed-rate, fully amortizing, level-payment lien and its mathematics is examined in full detail. Other types of common mortgages, especially *adjustable-rate mortgages,* are also discussed. The last section of the chapter contains a brief overview of *automated underwriting.*

I. THE U.S. MORTGAGE MARKETS TODAY

A. THE COMPONENTS

The residential housing finance system in the U.S. has evolved dramatically since the end of World War II. Today it has several components whose functions and purposes are described below:

A *primary residential mortgage market* for the retail origination of single-family loans whose collateral is real property (that is, the land and the buildings on it). This is the meeting place between consumers purchasing homes and the institutions that provide funds for home buying via liens on the property, i.e., mortgages. Utilizing the balances of their depositors, savings banks and savings and loan (or thrift) institutions were the main sources of funds for this purpose in the past. Today the international capital markets provide most of the monies for housing loans. In addition, the government-sponsored enterprises Fannie Mae and Freddie Mac play a significant role in providing capital to those who perform the loan origination function. In the case of mortgage brokers and others who do not have access to their own base for monies, this is the place where *warehouse banks* and other temporary sources of finance operate. However, the U.S. still basically has a two-component primary market:

1. One led by the depository-based system of savings banks, savings and loan institutions, credit unions, life insurance companies, and commercial banks in cooperation with the *Federal Home Loan Banks.*
2. One that is more complicated, involving banks, mortgage bankers and brokers, and the federally sponsored *conduits Ginnie Mae,* Fannie Mae, and Freddie Mac (the *Government National Mortgage Association* or *GNMA*, the *Federal National Mortgage Association* or *FNMA*, and the *Federal Home Loan Mortgage Corporation* or *FHLMC*, respectively).

The part of the *secondary residential mortgage market* that provides the link between the primary residential mortgage market and the capital markets. These

89

participants facilitate the flow of funds from investors in mortgage-*derivative* securities to the primary housing market. (In finance, a derivative is any security that derives its value from some other, underlying, instrument. Mortgage-backed securities, *REMICs*, and so on all fall into this class. However, the bad publicity surrounding derivative instruments in the past causes dealers and creators of these instruments to shy away from labeling them as such.) This encompasses buying and selling mortgage assets among lenders, conduits (especially the Freddie Mac and Fannie Mae investment portfolios but also other private firms), and fixed-income investors: life insurance companies, pension funds, bank mortgage portfolios, hedge funds, and so on. Here liquidity is provided for financing the construction and sale of residential housing. (Fannie Mae and Freddie Mac also help to ensure the availability of funds at competitive interest rates across the U.S. Ginnie Mae only insures mortgage-backed securities; it does not fund nor purchase them.)

Another part of the secondary market is chiefly devoted to *whole loan* sales. (Whole loans are mortgages whose cash flows have not been divided among multiple owners. It is possible to purchase a *participation interest* in a mortgage in which case one does not own the whole, or entire, loan.) The need for this market segment among mortgage brokers, bankers, dealers, and other secondary mortgage market participants also includes filling forward commitments in the event of *pipeline fallout* (i.e., *pairing-off*), to sell excess collateral from a deal bundled into mortgage-backed securities (*MBSs*), the buying and selling of nonconforming *conventional mortgages*, niche products, and so on.

There are several subcomponents determined by whether or not the loan is conventional or nonconventional (i.e., federal *government-insured* vs. nongovernment insured) and conforming or nonconforming (e.g., primarily nonjumbo vs. *jumbo loans*, which is determined by the maximum loan amount). Government agencies (including the Federal Housing Administration, the Veterans Administration, the Rural Housing Service, the Farmers Home Administration, and Ginnie Mae) and the government-sponsored enterprises (Fannie Mae and Freddie Mac) concentrate their operations in this section of the secondary market. Also included here are the large financial institutions — commercial banks, life insurance companies, pension funds, Wall Street dealers — who issue *whole-loan* and *private-label* MBSs, structure REMIC deals (more complicated mortgage-backed securities) and buy government-sponsored enterprise (*GSE*) issuances for investment purposes. (A whole-loan MBS is one whose underlying collateral are nonconforming, usually jumbo, mortgages. A private-label MBS is one whose underpinning consists of conforming liens; however, the issuer is not a government-sponsored enterprise.)

The GSEs purchase home loans from lenders, including state and local government agencies, resupplying their funds. They buy conventional *single-* and *multi-family mortgages*, *second mortgages*, and liens insured by the FHA or guaranteed by the VA. They buy whole loans for their own investment portfolios and they issue guaranteed securities backed by pools of conforming loans. Both federally created agencies also issue and manage multiple-class mortgage derivative securities known as REMICs.

The activities of dealers trading in the *TBA* market (meaning *to-be-announced*, because the exact composition of a mortgage pool to be used to support a mortgage-backed security about to be issued has not been completely identified), those utilizing *dollar rolls* for funding or hedging purposes (the mortgage market's version of a repurchase agreement), *pipeline hedging* (a *mortgage pipeline* refers to the retail loans in process at an originator from application through closing), and so forth also take place here.

Finally, a part of the secondary market deals with non-A-credit rated loans, *home equity loans* or second mortgages, liens on *manufactured housing* (i.e., trailers on permanent foundations), and so forth. The credit worthiness of consumers is rated on an alphabetical scale with "A" the best. Approximately 70% of American consumers can achieve an A credit rating. In contrast, *Alternative-A* loans consist mainly of loans with documentation, *loan-to-value ratio* (e.g., a loan-to-value ratio in excess of 80%), occupancy status (e.g., not owner-occupied), and other underwriting variances from conforming loans and properties. (The loan-to-value ratio is the lesser of the appraised amount of the property and the sales price divided into the loan amount.) *Low documentation* liens also fall into this category. A low documentation loan means that one of the employment, income, or asset verifications required by the GSEs has not been supplied. Self-employed borrowers can easily fall into this group. The last section of this chapter briefly discusses the main underwriting factors used to determine eligibility for a home loan.

Loans labeled *A-*, on the other hand, are those for which the borrowers generally have lower *credit scores* than desirable (e.g., a *FICO* score between 575 and 620), high loan-to-value ratios, or high *front-* or *back-end debt-to-income ratios*. (The front-end debt-to-income ratio is the ratio of total housing-related monthly payments to gross monthly income and is preferably less than 28%. The back-end debt-to-income ratio is the total of all monthly debt-related payments to gross income and is preferably no greater than 36%.) Finally, there are lower credit quality borrowers who have B and C rated loans.

1. What the Secondary Market Does

The structure of the U.S. secondary residential mortgage market, especially the role of the government-sponsored enterprises Fannie Mae and Freddie Mac, helps to accomplish several important housing objectives:

1. It assists in smoothing out imbalances in the availability of mortgage funds across the country. This keeps the foremost expense of homeownership more or less uniform for low-, moderate-, and middle-income families. These income levels are precisely defined terms based on the median income of a metropolitan statistical area. Middle income equals median income, moderate income equals 80% of median income, and low income equals 60% of median income. Very-low income families, such as those eligible for FHA loans, have family incomes of 40% of the median income in their metropolitan statistical area.
2. It allows lenders to originate mortgages for sale rather than retain them for portfolio investment. This frees their capital and allows them to structure their balance sheets in risk-minimizing, profit-maximizing ways.

Also, by resupplying their funds, they can originate more mortgages, thus increasing their fee-related income.

3. It attracts investors to mortgage-related investments via standardized product definition and underwriting.
4. It provides greater liquidity by financially engineering security structures to meet the changing cash flow needs of investors. This reduces bid–ask spreads.
5. It increases the affordability of home owning because of a larger supply of less expensive funds.
6. It closely ties mortgage rates to other fixed-income interest rates (particularly the 10-year U.S. Treasury Note). They are also intimately tied to the interest rate swap markets.

2. Mortgage-Backed Bonds

Most states have a state-level agency to assist potential homeowners, as do many cities or counties in which they reside. Their efforts are usually directed at very low-, low-, and moderate-income families. The purposes may be for providing rental housing or home owning *per se*. The funds to support these efforts usually come from the issuance of tax-exempt mortgage revenue bonds. Though fairly common in Europe, true *mortgage-backed bonds* have been relatively rare in the U.S. (The first one was issued by a California savings and loan in 1975.) The collateral for these bonds are mortgages. There is no *pass-through* of the monthly mortgage cash flows; rather they are used to pay semiannual coupon payments on the bonds and to retire their principal. One purpose of this instrument was to provide a shorter-term security than the traditional mortgage in order to increase investor enthusiasm. Hence, the bonds had to be significantly *overcollateralized* to ensure sufficient cash flow to pay them off relatively quickly; a common minimum cushion was 50%.

Overcollateralization also provides protection against mark-to-market price drops in a rising interest rate environment. These instruments were restricted by the tax laws to be passively managed in a *grantor trust* —a one-class, debt-only device. A disadvantage to the lending institutions was that because mortgage-backed bonds could not be issued in a pass-through form, they could not serve to provide financing for the additional origination of new mortgages. Eventually, even large savings banks and thrifts started to run out of enough capital to support them (especially in their overcollateralized state). The *CMO* (*collateralized mortgage obligation*) replaced it relatively quickly.

a. Pay-Through Bonds

Pay-through bonds, also known as cash flow bonds, were introduced in 1981. The pay-through bond is structurally different from the mortgage-backed bond because a mortgage-backed bond has a stated maturity, but a pay-through bond does not. Its maturity is determined by the rate of its scheduled and unscheduled principal payments. The pay-through structure, first issued privately in 1976, enabled an issuer to realize the present value of its mortgage assets without selling the assets or significantly overcollateralizing the bonds. This was especially advantageous for those liens whose mark-to-market value had decreased because of rising interest rates. Without selling these below-market home loans and taking the loss, issuers could obtain nearly full financing of their now discounted mortgages. Finally, pay-through bonds were issued as debt.

B. SOME HISTORY

Before the growth of a significant town and city population in the U.S., homeown-ership was mostly a self-fulfilling activity. With the closing of the western frontier in the 1890s and the creation of an industrial economy, increasing numbers of people started to move into cities and towns in search of factory work (and many immigrants never left their ports of entry). Though many people lived in rental housing and apartments, urban single-family housing became more common. Such buildings and their land typically cost the equivalent of 3 to 7 years' gross income. Therefore, the purchase of housing had to be funded by loans. Originally the depository institutions — savings and loans, mutual savings banks, credit unions, and commercial banks — were responsible for the majority of lending for home purchases. Demand, savings, and other time deposits taken from the public were used to fund residential home buying via intermediate-term loans. The first savings and loan was opened in 1831 in Frankfort, Pennsylvania. Its first mortgagor went delinquent.

Before the Depression town or city homeownership was a challenge for most Americans. In addition to the price barrier, lending terms were very stringent with mortgages requiring a down payment of 40 or 50%. What is more, the most common type of loan available through the 1930s was the *balloon mortgage*. (This instrument was significantly different from today's *balloon re-set mortgage* in that only interest was paid over the life of the loan; no principal was retired nor *equity* built up.) The term of the mortgage was in the 3- to 7-year range and the lien required a complete payment of the original principal balance at the maturity date. The most frequently used method for paying off a balloon mortgage was to secure yet another one. This scheme led to many foreclosures during the Depression years.

To partially alleviate problems in the housing finance industry, the U.S. Congress created the Federal Housing Administration (FHA) as part of the passage of the National Housing Act of 1934. The FHA was authorized to provide programs to assist in all phases of homeownership; construction, acquisition (i.e., purchasing), and rehabilitation of both single- and multifamily housing. (After World War II its mandate was extended to include urban renewal projects, hospitals, nursing homes, and so on.) The main mechanism the FHA used was to offer investors in single-family mortgages insurance against default by the borrowers. However, only those mortgages (and borrowers) that conformed to the FHA's homogeneous underwriting standards could be eligible for such insurance. Thus, as a by-product, the FHA created the first uniform mortgage application and underwriting requirements.

This standardization dramatically increased the efficiency and liquidity of the secondary mortgage market. Today almost all mortgage originators use the govern-ment-sponsored enterprises' loan application forms, whether or not the lien is expected to conform to their underwriting standards. In addition, the FHA invented a replacement instrument for the balloon mortgage by developing and promoting the fixed-rate, fully amortizing, long-term, level-payment, monthly paying mortgage. The standard term of 30 years meant manageable monthly payments for the home buyer. The fixed-rate and level-payment aspects stabilized housing expense and made it easier for homeowners to budget. The complete amortization feature meant that the homeowner would (albeit slowly at first) build up equity in the property and eventually own it outright.

Who would invest in these new instruments (i.e., supply the funds)? To answer this query in 1938 Congress created the Federal National Mortgage Association, or FNMA, under Title III of the act that created the FHA. The FNMA was to be a private corporation regulated by the government and its chief purpose was to buy and sell mortgages insured by the FHA. This government-sponsored entity was to provide liquidity to the nation's secondary mortgage market. Fannie Mae's first VA-guaranteed transaction was in 1948. Its first secondary market transaction took place in 1949 and involved two savings and loans and a sale of approximately $1.5 million. The FNMA underwent a major restructuring in 1954, mixing ownership of the corporation with private stockholders and separating pre- and post-1954 lines of business. The sale of participation interests in mortgage loans was authorized a little later, in 1957, when the Federal Home Loan Bank Board issued the necessary regulations.

In 1968 Congress divided the FNMA into a quasi-private derivative now known as Fannie Mae (a federally chartered corporation owned by private shareholders) and the still wholly government-owned and controlled Government National Mortgage Association [usually referred to as the GNMA or Ginnie Mae and part of the Department of Housing and Urban Development (HUD)]. Ginnie Mae took over the old FNMA's responsibilities with respect to the government mortgage market, which now included loans insured by the FHA, the Veterans Administration (or VA, starting in 1944), the Farmers Home Administration (FmHA, serving farmers and others in rural areas), and the Farmers Home Loan Bank (recently renamed the Rural Housing Service).

The FHA's principal activity is to insure approved lending institutions against mortgagor defaults; the homeowner pays an insurance premium for this warranty. In return for the agency's guarantee, lending institutions must abide by FHA credit guidelines and restrictions. In the event of default, the VA guarantees the lender up to the first $60,000 of the loan, on a sliding scale. There is no true insurance *per se* as with the FHA. Ginnie Mae, in contrast, only guarantees securities backed by pools of mortgages issued by Ginnie Mae-approved private institutions. These instruments are called mortgage-backed securities. The agency provides a guarantee of the timely payment of interest and principal; the lenders are responsible for selling the securities. Ginnie Mae securities are backed by the full faith and credit of the U.S. government. The mortgages are separately insured by the FHA, by the VA, or guaranteed by the Rural Housing Service. Ginnie Mae has guaranteed more than $1.5 trillion in mortgage-backed securities. Historically, 95% of all FHA and VA mortgages have been bundled in this form.

The partially privatized Fannie Mae was made fully private by act of Congress in 1968 and authorized to purchase conventional loans (i.e., those not insured by the full faith and credit of the U.S. government). Fannie Mae purchased its first conventional mortgage, in 1972, in Birmingham, Alabama. Thus, a government agency supported government-insured loans and a government-sponsored enterprise supported nongovernment insured loans (up to mandated loan maximum amounts).

1. Further Developments

Ginnie Mae created the first publicly traded pass-through security (in 1970) that included undivided interests in pools of FHA and VA mortgages. This instrument enabled bankers to sell mortgages and their derivatives in larger volumes to new mortgage investors. It also brought greater liquidity and encouraged a wider group of investors to participate in owning residential mortgages. Separately in 1970 Congress created the Federal Home Loan Mortgage Corporation, or Freddie Mac, to provide further liquidity to the conventional secondary residential mortgage market. Initially Freddie Mac was a government-charted corporation owned by the 12 Federal Home Loan banks and was authorized to purchase conventional loans as well as FHA-insured and VA-guaranteed mortgages. It issued its first pass-through mortgage-backed security, known as a *Participation Certificate*, in 1971. A 1989 law (known as the FIRREA) changed Freddie Mac into a private corporation very similar in charter and structure to Fannie Mae.

a. Distinctions among Mortgage Underwriting Activities

When a lender makes a loan based on the credit worthiness of the borrower and the collateral for the lien, the mortgage is said to be a conventional mortgage. The borrower will usually be required to obtain *private mortgage insurance* to protect the lender against default if the loan-to-value ratio exceeds 80%. The cost of the insurance is paid by the borrower and the premium depends on the difference between the actual loan-to-value ratio and 80% and the borrower's credit rating. Private mortgage insurance can be purchased from half-a-dozen companies. The first (modern) private mortgage insurance company was MGIC, established in 1956. (Private mortgage insurance started in the 1870s, principally regulated by the state of New York; however, all of the extant mortgage insurance companies went bankrupt during the Depression.) A government-insured mortgage is one issued by the VA, FHA, or RHA, so the payments to the investor are backed by the full faith and credit of the U.S. government.

A mortgage is conforming if it conforms, or meets, the underwriting standards set by the GSEs. A subclass of nonconforming mortgages is known as jumbo loans. These are liens conforming in all other respects except that their loan amounts exceed the limits imposed on the agencies. (The 2001 limit was $275,000, up substantially in the last few years as a result of housing price inflation; it is $300,700 for 2002.) This limit may be adjusted annually, following a nation-wide survey of housing prices conducted in the first week of October, by the Federal Housing Finance Board.

2. The Federal Home Loan Bank System

The 12 independently operated (wholesale) regional banks of the Federal Home Loan Bank system were established in 1932 to support residential housing lending and related community investment. The Federal Home Loan Banks (FLHBanks) offer funds to members for the purpose of residential mortgage lending primarily directed toward low- and moderate-income people. The FHLBanks also make it possible for members to provide financing for mortgages that do not conform to agency guidelines. The regional banks are owned by their private member institutions and the FHLBank system operates completely on the private capital that they provide. The FHLBanks provide financing support to about 7900 institutions: 5750 commercial banks, 1500 thrifts, 550 credit unions, and 50 insurance companies.

The FHLBanks raise money by issuing corporate debt. These funds, known as *advances,* are lent to members at lower rates than those available in the commercial markets. FHLBanks raise the money they lend in three ways: 1. by issuing bonds or discount notes, known as *consolidated obligations*, 2. by accepting deposits from member institutions, and 3. by selling capital stock to members. As of mid-2001, the FHLBanks had about $665 billion in assets and $450 billion in advances.

Under the mortgage partnership finance program, the FHLBanks leverage the credit expertise of the local lender with the financial advantages of the regional Home Loan Bank to provide an attractive method of funding guaranteed mortgages. The FHLBanks purchase the home loans from its members and also provide a *credit enhancement* fee to the member bank for retaining the default risk of the lien. The FHLBank, as the owner of the asset, assumes the interest and prepayment risks of the asset.

3. More Recent History

The fixed-rate mortgage worked well until the mid-1970s. Its downfall was inflation and Regulation Q. (Regulation Q effectively capped interest rates on certain types of bank deposits.) High levels of inflation led to the disintermediation of funds, from thrift and savings banks to money market mutual funds and other higher, short-term interest rate alternatives. A solution to rapidly rising interest rates for the mortgagees was the creation of the adjustable-, or *floating-rate, mortgage.* By adjusting the interest rate on, for example, a yearly basis, the bulk of the interest-rate risk was passed to the homeowner from the investor or bank holding the loan in its portfolio. In the latter case, it was funded increasingly by expensive short-term deposits. The FHA was granted permission to deal in *variable-rate mortgages* in 1968. (Remember: everything in finance has two or three names.)

Until recently adjustable-rate mortgages (*ARMs*) and their *hybrid* variations comprised about 15 to 20% of new mortgage originations. ARMs are more attractive in high interest-rate environments or when the yield curve is sloping steeply upward. Because they simplify the asset and liability problem of mortgage portfolio managers, they are preferentially kept in the investment portfolios of banks. Recent low interest-rate levels have caused consumers to prefer the certainty of fixed-rate mortgages; therefore, the rate of issuance of adjustable-rate mortgages had diminished to about 10% of new originations by early 2002 but was up to 30% by mid-year.

The mortgage-backed security market continued to grow through the 1980s and 1990s for many reasons. First came the Resolution Trust Corporation's efforts to off-load salable assets of failed savings and loan institutions. New mortgage types proliferated, investor sophistication increased, more advanced computer technology was applied to loan underwriting (e.g., Freddie Mac's Loan Prospector® and Fannie Mae's Desktop Underwriter®) and cash flow modeling, advances were made in electronic marketing. There was also a dramatic rise in the supply of raw product because of rapidly rising rates of refinancing and a significant population growth.

Most mortgages in the U.S. are fixed-rate, fully amortizing, 30-year, level-paying, monthly payment instruments. This type of lien is referred to as the *traditional mortgage* in this book. (Both shorter- and longer-term types exist, as do *bi-weekly mortgages*.) In the case of the traditional mortgage, the monthly payment amount is determined so that, after 360 timely outlays by the mortgagor, the original unpaid mortgage balance is paid in full, along with monthly simple interest on the outstanding principal balance. This is what "fully amortizing" means. An amortized loan has an associated *amortization schedule*, the time history of the partial principal repayments. The fixed-rate aspect refers to the interest rate being constant (as opposed to floating, variable, or adjustable) for the life of the loan. The level-payment feature means the same dollar charge, typically paid monthly, is made for the entire term of the mortgage.

a. Numerical Example

The formula for computing the monthly payment (MP) for a fixed-rate, fully amortizing, level-paying, monthly payment mortgage is identical in form to that of an annuity, i.e., from Equation 1.26,

$$MP = r \times UPB/[1 - (1 + r)^{-N}].$$

In this version of the formula, UPB stands for the initial *unpaid principal balance* (i.e., the face amount of the loan), r is the monthly interest rate (= annual interest rate/12), and N is the total number of payments (e.g., N = 360 for a 30-year instrument). A traditional lien with an annual coupon rate of 7.5% and an initial balance of $275,000 has a monthly payment of $1,922.84 (scheduled principal plus interest).

4. More on Amortization

To better understand how the amortization proceeds, consider the previous example, month-by-month. Of what does the monthly payment of $1,922.84 consist? It depends on the month.

In the mortgage markets, the day count convention is that a year consists of 12 equal months of 30 days each. Mortgage payments are made in arrears, that is, the mortgagor has the use of the money for a full month before making a payment. Hence, the first month that the lien is outstanding the mortgagor has borrowed $275,000 at an annual rate of 7.5% (or a monthly rate of 0.625% = 7.5%/12). The (simple) interest due on this amount after 1 month is $275,000 × 0.075/12 = $1,718.75. The level monthly payment is $204.09 larger than this and the extra amount goes to amortizing, or partially reducing, the outstanding principal amount of the loan. The second month, the balance outstanding is $275,000 − $204.09 = $274,795.91. The interest owed on this amount at the end of the second month is

$274,795.91 \times 0.075/12 = \$1,717.47$, so a principal reduction occurs in the second month in the slightly larger amount of $205.37.

Some of the outstanding principal balance was paid off during the first month. Hence, the portion of interest in the second month's (equal) payment going to interest on the outstanding principal balance decreased relative to the first month. Therefore, the amount going toward principal reduction in the second month was increased relative to that of the first month (in this case by the munificent sum of $1.28!), resulting in a lower proportion devoted to interest in the third month,…. Ultimately, fairly late in the life of the mortgage (around year 21 or so), the balance shifts and most of the monthly payment is going to principal reduction, eventually leading to a complete amortization of the loan.

a. Numerical Example Continued

In the real world, a consumer mortgage would have a *servicing fee* and a *guarantee fee* built into the note rate. Nominally these are both 25 bp (and their purposes will be discussed later). Let us see how this changes the cash flows. The first month's interest payment is now $0.070 \times \$275,000/12 = \$1,604.17$ because the true interest rate on the borrowed money is $7.5\% - 0.25\% - 0.25\% = 7.0\%$, since the two fees (which the consumer pays, of course) are not-interest, that is, borrowing related. The level monthly payment is still $1,922.84. The combination of the fees comes to $0.005 \times \$275,000/12 = \$114.58$. The amount left to amortize the outstanding principal balance remains at $204.09 = \$1,922.84 - \$1,604.17 - \$144.58$. The next month, the net interest charge will be $0.070 \times (\$275,000 - \$204.09)/12 = \$1,602.98$. The total of servicing and guarantee fees comes to $0.005 \times (\$275,000 - \$204.09)/12 = \$114.50$, with $\$1,922.84 - \$1,602.98 - \$114.50 = \$205.36$ going toward principal reduction. (A penny has been lost in the rounding. Who gets it: the mortgagor or the mortgagee?) And so on…

b. Daily Simple Interest

Your mortgage payment is almost certainly due on the first of the month. You will not be charged a late fee until mid-month (the exact day depends on your deed of trust). Moreover, the amortization and interest computation of your mortgage will go forward as if you paid on time and the year consisted of 12 equal months of 30 days each. In mortgages where the interest is computed on a daily basis, this kind of float opportunity is lost. They are known as *daily simple interest mortgages.*

5. Default Generalities

Because default is one of the major risks associated with a consumer loan, this subsection briefly reviews the main factors pertaining to it in the mortgage markets. The likelihood of default by the homeowner is highly correlated with the amount of equity held in the real estate. This is by far the most important predictive variable of default. The borderline for the rapid increasing of default probability is at a loan-to-value ratio (*LTV*) of 80%. (Other characteristics do play a statistically measurable role and are discussed later.) Should default occur, then from the option theoretic perspective, the homeowner can sell the house for whatever it will bring in and satisfy the debt (the option is in-the-money) or abandon the property to the bank (the option is out-of-the-money). Since the homeowner typically does not want his credit rating destroyed and still needs a place to live, the exercise of the default option is usually not so clinical.

The fully documented, owner-occupied, detached, single- (in the true sense of the word) family house with a traditional, *purchase money mortgage* has the lowest probability of default. Every deviation from this conforming standard increases the probability of default. Though the LTV at origination is a key predictive variable of default, in regions of the country where house prices have changed considerably, the *current LTV* will be a much more accurate forecaster of the default probability. Rising house prices increase the effective amount of equity the homeowner has, thus lowering his current LTV and leaving sufficient funds to satisfy the mortgage debt in case of a job loss or some other unfortunate occurrence. Conversely, in an area of the country where housing prices have declined, the 80% current LTV threshold may be crossed the other way and dramatically increase the probability of default should some calamity (divorce, disease, disability) befall the homeowner. The slow amortization of the principal with the traditional instrument is also an important factor in the current LTV ratio computation.

Adjustable-rate mortgages are less favorably viewed by the mortgagee than are fixed-rate mortgages. The uncertainty of the level of future monthly payments and the possibility that they might increase too much for the homeowner to bear increases the default rate and its probability on this type of home loan. ARMs underwritten at the *teaser rate* are especially vulnerable to this occurrence. One should always make sure that an ARM or hybrid mortgage was underwritten on the assumption of the maximum increase at the first re-set date based on today's front- and back-end debt-to-income ratios.

Perception and level of risk associated with the purpose of a home loan also differ. A *cash-out refinancing*, meaning that the homeowner depleted some of the equity built up with the new lien, increases the probability of default. A current LTV threshold of 75% (instead of 80%) is frequently used as the break-point between higher and lower coupon rates on home loans of this nature. A *no-cash-out refinancing* would generally be viewed much more favorably.

In the 1990s, when lenders tried to maintain market share and servicing fee income, they made it very easy for a borrower to refinance. In particular, many of the agency-required documentation verifications were foregone. This lead to fraud, poorly underwritten loans, and high default rates. Such low-documentation loans are difficult to find now. The leading exception is a *no documentation loan* in which the loan is totally based on the property value. Such loans require very high down payments, typically 40%.

People planning to occupy the property, whether it is a true single-family house or a two- to four-family property with the other units to be rented out, are more likely to take care of and be responsible for their real estate than those merely purchasing it for investment purposes. Hence, second homes and rental property are viewed less favorably than are owner-occupied dwellings. Similarly, the detached single-family residence is preferred over attached town houses, condominiums, co-operatives, and so forth. The latter tend to be built (or converted) on a speculative basis by a developer, leading to an oversupply and causing price decreases.

II. FIXED-RATE MORTGAGES

A. Fixed-Rate Mortgage Mathematics

Payments on fixed-rate mortgages are typically due monthly, though bi-weekly forms have become common. A bi-weekly payment mortgage requires 26 payments per year at half the monthly rate, instead of 12 full monthly payments. This significantly reduces the total amount of interest paid over the life of the loan. For a traditional mortgage, paying half the monthly amount bi-weekly shortens the term of the mortgage to about 22 years. The nominal amount of interest reduction per hundred thousand dollars borrowed at 7.0%/year comes to about $43,200.

From the consumer's perspective, a monthly payment consists of two parts: 1. simple interest charges on the outstanding principal balance using 1/12 of the annual interest rate and 2. a repayment of a portion of the outstanding balance. The next month's payment has the same two components but, since the amount borrowed has been slightly reduced, the interest charges will be slightly reduced too, with more of the equal monthly payment lessening the outstanding principal, and so on. Use MP to indicate the constant monthly payment amount for a monthly interest rate r (= the annual interest rate/12), N for the total number of months over which the loan is amortized (i.e., $240 = 20 \times 12$ for a 20-year lien), and UPB_0 for time zero initial unpaid principal mortgage balance. Then, MP is given by the standard annuity formula

$$UPB_0 = MP \times [1 - (1 + r)^{-N}]/r. \tag{4.1}$$

The inverse formula can be written as

$$MP = UPB_0 \times r \times (1 + r)^N/[(1 + r)^N - 1]. \tag{4.2}$$

a. Exercises

1. The GSE maximum mortgage amount was $227,150 in 1998. For a mortgage of this face value and an annual interest rate of 7.77%, what is the monthly payment for a 25-year term? Note mortgage rates at the consumer level only exist in steps of one-eighth of a percentage point. (MP = $1,718.71)

2. If the monthly payment on a $155,000 traditional mortgage is $1550, what is the annual interest rate? (11.625%, actually 11.627%)

3. Determine how long it will take to fully amortize a level-payment mortgage in the amount of $235,000 if the interest rate is 7 7/8 and the monthly payment is $2,093.44. (17 years)

The monthly payment amount MP consists partly of scheduled principal repayment of amount P_n at the nth payment time and partly of interest payment of amount I_n, also at the nth payment time, on the unpaid principal balance. These quantities are given by the following formulas (r = the monthly interest rate):

$$P_n = UPB_0 \times r \times (1 + r)^{n-1}/[(1 + r)^N - 1], n = 1,2,\ldots, N \qquad (4.3)$$

and

$$I_n = UPB_0 \times r \times [(1 + r)^N - (1 + r)^{n-1}]/[(1 + r)^N - 1],$$
$$n = 1,2,\ldots, N. \qquad (4.4)$$

Of course, $I_n = r \times P_{n-1}$ and $I_n \times P_{n-1}$ and

$$MP = I_n + P_n \text{ for every value of } n = 1,2,\ldots, N.$$

Finally, the unpaid mortgage balance remaining after n monthly payments, UPB_n, is given by

$$UPB_n = UPB_0 \times [(1 + r)^N - (1 + r)^n]/[(1 + r)^N - 1], n = 1,2,\ldots, N. \qquad (4.5)$$

b. Exercises

1. Compute the interest amount and principal reduction in the 180th month of a 30-year, $225,000, 8.88% annual interest rate mortgage. (MP = $1,791.01, P_{180} = $471.57, I_{180} = $1,319.44)
2. Find the number of the month, for a 20-year, $133,500, 7.89% annual interest rate mortgage, when the interest payment will be half the monthly payment. (MP = $1,107.53, n = 135)

1. Derivation of the Formulas

Where did these formulas come from? Start with the stated characteristics of a fixed-rate, fully amortizing, level-payment mortgage with monthly interest rate r, for N payment periods. The level-payment aspect means that the homeowner makes the same dollar payment every month (MP). The interest rate is fixed and simple, computed at a constant (monthly) rate r on the unpaid principal balance. (The annual interest rate is equal to $12 \times r$ and this rate is stated in the loan documents.) We also know that payments are made in the month following the start of the mortgage (that is, interest and principal are paid in arrears). Finally, the initial scheduled principal payment, P_0, is zero (the amount due at closing).

In symbols, the first interest payment on the mortgage is equal to initial unpaid principal balance UPB_0, minus the initial scheduled principal payment P_0, times the monthly interest rate:

$$I_1 = r \times (UPB_0 - P_0) = r \times UPB_0. \qquad (4.6)$$

The principal amount for the first month, P_1, is the difference between MP and I_1,

$$P_1 = MP - I_1 = MP - r \times UPB_0, \qquad (4.7)$$

where Equation 4.6 has been used on the far right-hand side of Equation 4.7. The second month's interest, I_2, is computed on the unpaid principal balance at that time, UPB_0, minus P_0 and P_1,

$$I_2 = r \times (UPB_0 - P_0 - P_1) = r \times [UPB_0 - 0 - (MP - r \times UPB_0)]$$

$$= r \times UPB_0 \times (1 + r) - r \times MP = (r \times UPB_0 - MP) \times (1 + r) + MP.$$

The terms involving MP and UPB_0 have been rewritten after some simple rearrangements (it helps to know the answer in advance). For the second month, the partial principal repayment amount P_2 is the difference between the level monthly payment amount MP and the interest paid in the second month, I_2,

$$P_2 = MP - I_2 = (1 + r) \times (MP - r \times UPB_0).$$

The third month's interest, I_3, is calculated based on the unpaid principal amount at that time, which is UPB_0 minus the sum of P_0, P_1, and P_2. After some algebraic manipulation, this can be recast in the form

$$I_3 = r \times (UPB_0 - P_0 - P_1 - P_2) = (r \times UPB_0 - MP) \times (1 + r)^2 + MP.$$

(I am adding and subtracting MP to complete the power of $1 + r$ that appears. This results in a common factor multiplying $MP - r \times UPB_0$, which becomes immediately apparent in the monthly principal repayment formula.) Lastly, for the third month, the scheduled principal repayment amount, P_3, is given by

$$P_3 = MP - I_3 = (1 + r)^2 \times (MP - r \times UPB_0).$$

You should begin to see a pattern. Indeed, if we carry this one month further, then we would find that the equations describing the monthly interest and partial principal repayments take the form

$$I_4 = r \times (UPB_0 - P_0 - P_1 - P_2 - P_3) = (r \times UPB_0 - MP) \times (1 + r)^3 + MP,$$

and

$$P_4 = MP - I_4 = (1 + r)^3 \times (MP - r \times UPB_0).$$

The scheme seems clear and, at the risk of committing the fallacy of hasty generalization, we can guess that the general forms for the interest paid and partial principal repayment made at month #n are given by

$$I_n = r \times (UPB_0 - \sum_{m=0}^{n} P_m) = (r \times UPB_0 - MP) \times (1 + r)^{n-1} + MP, \; n = 1,2,\ldots$$

and

$$P_n = MP - I_n = (1 + r)^{n-1} \times (MP - r \times UPB_0), \; n = 1,2,\ldots.$$

Note that n has no terminal value because we do not yet know the number of payments until the principal is paid in full. We must use the formulas just derived in an implicit fashion to determine the time when the mortgage will be fully paid off. We want the value of N that makes the following true:

$$UPB_0 = \sum_{m=0}^{N} P_m.$$

Inserting the formula for the monthly principal repayment amount, this becomes (P_0 vanishes)

$$UPB_0 = \sum_{m=1}^{N} P_m = \sum_{m=1}^{N} (1 + r)^{m-1} \times (MP - r \times UPB_0).$$

This is a form of a geometric series. Reconfiguring the summand into the standard form (see Equation 1.21) leads to a formula that can be solved for UPB_0. The answer is identical in form to Equation 4.1. So, by translating the meaning of the adjectival phrase defining a traditional mortgage into equations, we have found out how to relate the monthly payment amount MP to the face amount UPB_0, the monthly interest rate r, and the number of payment periods N. (Actually, though I continually speak of a monthly payment, nothing is inherently "monthly" in what we have done. These equations are true for bi-weekly or even daily repayment schedules, given that r, MP, and N are consistently and appropriately redefined.)

Utilizing the last relationship, the principal amount paid in any month #m is given by Equation 4.3. Using UPB_m for the unpaid balance of the par value at the end of month #m and replacing MP again, we would find another distorted geometric series. After maneuvering the terms, it has the form given in Equation 4.5.

a. Exercises

1. For a 25-year, level-payment, fully amortizing, fixed-interest mortgage, compute the principal repayment and interest proportions of the 144th monthly payment if the coupon rate is 5 7/8 and the par amount was $125,500. (MP = $799.04; P_{144} = $371.16, I_{144} = $427.88, UPB_{144} = $87,024.61)
2. If the unpaid balance of a 20-year, level-payment, fully amortizing mortgage is equal to half the face amount after 15 years, what was the coupon rate? (12.25%)

2. Macaulay Duration for a Mortgage

The formula for the Macaulay duration for a mortgage looks just like that for a semiannual coupon paying bond. The coupon C is replaced by the monthly payment MP. The discount rate becomes the appropriate monthly required rate of return. The frequency of payment m becomes 12 instead of two and the redemption term is zero because the instrument is fully amortizing. The par or face amount is the initial unpaid principal balance or the total amount borrowed.

a. Exercises

1. Compute the market value and duration of a traditional mortgage with face amount $227,150, at issuance, if the discount rate is 5.55% but the coupon on the mortgage is 6.66%. (MP = $1,459.73, MV = $255,675.81, D = 11.068 years)
2. Consider a 20-year, $240,000 initial unpaid principal balance mortgage, with a coupon of 8 1/8%/year. Show that the monthly payment is $2,026.17. Also demonstrate that, if interest rates instantly declined to 7 3/8%/year after issuance of the debt, then the market value would be equal to $253,916.45 and its Macaulay duration would be D = 7.675 years.
3. Compute the market value and duration of a traditional mortgage whose face amount is $150,000 and coupon rate is 7.75%, if the investor's required rate of return is 9.00%. (MP = $1,074.62, MV = $133,555.58, D = 9.708 years)
4. Why is the Macaulay duration of a traditional mortgage less than that of a comparable 30-year bond where comparable means the same face amount, maturity, and interest rate? (It amortizes.)

b. Modified Duration and Price Changes

Just as the formula for the Macaulay duration of a bond easily transforms into that for a mortgage with the set of substitutions outlined previously, so does that for the modified duration. However, mortgages have a call option embedded in them so the assumption that the cash flows are interest rate-independent is no longer appropriate (nor is the assumption that the yield curve is flat; otherwise the option could never come into the-money). Hence, these two concepts are of limited value for mortgages (option-embedded instruments in general). Both the duration and convexity computations are altered to account for this. See Chapter 7 for a discussion of the effective duration and the *effective convexity*.

c. *Exercises*

1. You own a traditional mortgage with a coupon of 9 1/8 and face value of $165,000. Interest rates have dropped by 125 bp. Approximately how much has its market value increased? (MP = $1,342,49, D = 8.943 years; D_{mod} = 8.875 years, Δ(MV)/MV = +11.1%; actual new market value = $185,153.32, which is 12.2% higher)

2. Compute the approximate change in price of a 25-year, level-payment, fully amortizing, $155,000 mortgage with a coupon of 7.75% if interest rates decrease by 1.25 percentage points. Also, calculate the exact price change. (MP = $1,170.76, D_{mod} = 8.692 years, percentage change in price = +10.9%; new market value = $173,392.71 or +11.9%)

3. Compute the dollar decrease in the fair market value of a 20-year, $100,000 mortgage if the interest rate changes upward by 13 basis points from 7 7/8%. (D_{mod} = 7.478 years, –$972; actual amount = –$964.59)

3. The Negative Convexity of Mortgages

Fixed-income instruments without embedded options have positive convexity (see Figure 3.5). This means, among other things, that as market rates increase, the price decreases and conversely. This is not true for callable certificates such as callable bonds or mortgages (see Figure 3.6). If interest rates increase, the price of a callable bond or a mortgage will decrease but not as fast as that of the equivalent, underlying, noncallable version (even if we must imagine that it exists). Looking back at Equation 3.9, we remember that the price of a callable instrument is equal to the price of the equivalent, underlying, noncallable version minus the option price. Hence, the price of the callable instrument, when interest rates rise, stays below that of the equivalent, underlying, noncallable version. The difference represents the value of the option. In standard option pricing models, the more volatile interest rates are, the more valuable the option is thought to be (because of the mistaken belief that high volatility implies a chance of large interest rate decreases even if interest rates are already high). Hence, the higher the volatility, the bigger the spread in prices.

When interest rates drop, the price between the callable version and the equivalent, underlying, noncallable version diverge. The noncallable instrument rises in price increasingly rapidly because both its modified duration and its convexity are positive. The callable version's price will never exceed its call price, which may include a call premium because, once interest rates drop below the coupon rate, the probability of the call option being rationally exercised starts to approach unity. Hence, we will have the phenomenon of price compression, with the price rise capped by the call price. This is negative convexity in action.

4. 50% Tables

Table 4.1 shows (depressingly) the value of the month (denoted by t) such that the partial principal repayment is balanced by the interest charges for 15- and 30-year terms-to-maturity. It also contains the month at which the sum of the principal repayments reaches half the original face value. The equality is to be understood in the sense that the difference between P_t and I_t is least at that value of t and similarly that the difference between the sum of the principal repayments and half the par value is a minimum. More formally, the latter would be expressed as

$$\min_t \left| \sum_{n=1}^{t} P_n - UPB_0 / 2 \right|.$$

The computations use a \$100,000 initial principal amount. A study of the table shows that, as the interest rates become larger, the month in which the payment is 50% principal and 50% interest also approaches the month in which half the original amount is repaid.

a.   Exercise

1. Using Equations 4.3 and 4.5, analytically show the basis for the preceding observation.

B. BI-WEEKLY PAYMENT MORTGAGES

As mentioned earlier, with a bi-weekly payment mortgage one makes a payment every 2 weeks of half the amount of the equivalent monthly paying mortgage. Some people prefer this because it dramatically lowers the total interest cost associated with the mortgage without the higher payment an equivalent 15-year fixed-rate instrument would require.

1. The Mathematics

There are 26 bi-weekly periods per year, so if r still represents the monthly interest rate, then the bi-weekly interest rate is 6/13 of this [= (2 weeks/payment period) × (1 year/52 weeks) × (12 months/year)]. Let the lower-case Greek letter alpha, α, represent the constant 6/13. In this instance, the constant bi-weekly payment amount is MP/2, and not MP (where MP is computed as the level-payment amount for monthly paying liens over the specified term of the mortgage as opposed to how long the mortgage will really remain outstanding). Then the formula for the total number of payments is given by

$$N = - \ln\{1 - 2\alpha[1 - (1 + r)^{-M}]\}/\ln(1 + \alpha \times r).$$

Actually, one takes for N the integer obtained from rounding up N/26 because it is the number of bi-weekly payments we really want. Now we can derive the following table that shows how fast a bi-weekly payment mortgage pays back its principal for a variety of terms-to-maturity and interest rates.

a. Exercise

1. Fill in the remainder of Table 4.2.

C. MORTGAGE VALUATION TECHNIQUES

1. Twelve-Year Average Life

For a long time the standard pricing formula for a traditional mortgage rested on the assumption of no prepayments at all until the end of the 12th year. Then the entire remaining principal balance was repaid. In today's markets, with lower barriers to refinancing and more economic information available, a better approximation might be 8 years. Slightly better would be to incorporate a simple prepayment estimate coupled with an 8-year average life. This pricing model has advantages over more complicated ones in that it is easy to understand, easy to implement, simple to alter slightly, and not a bad approximation. The alternative frequently presented is to use the option-adjusted spread in a variety of more statistically (not financially) complicated forms.

2. Static OAS Computation

Consider what you know about a callable bond or any fixed-income security with an embedded option. You know its maturity, remaining time to maturity, coupon rate, interest payment frequency, par value, and market price. You want to adjust something in the standard fixed-income pricing relationship

$$\text{Par} = \sum_{n=1}^{N} CF_n/(1 + i/m)^n$$

to account for the fact that you might not receive cash flows $\{CF_n\}$ until time period N and that they might end earlier at $M < N$.

How many quantities can you adjust? You only have one additional piece of information, the market value MV. (Everything else you know has been buried in either i, m, CF_n, or N.) Thus, you can alter only one thing on the right-hand side of the equality, when Par is replaced by the market value MV, and the only place to do so legitimately is in the discount rate i. This is why there is only one option-adjusted spread.

So, in practice, because the market value is almost always less than instrument's par value, the one thing you can do is to discount the cash flows by a higher effective interest rate. You add the annual option-adjusted spread to the

TABLE 4.1
50% Values for Mortgages: Interest and Principal

Annual Interest Rate	MP for 15 Years on $100K	Month #t such that $P_t = I_t$	t such that $UPB_t = UPB_0/2$	MP for 30 Years on $100K	Month #t such that $P_t = I_t$	t such that $UPB_t = UPB_0/2$
5.00	790.74	14	106	536.82	194	242
5.25	803.88	22	107	552.20	202	244
5.50	817.08	29	108	567.79	209	247
5.75	830.41	36	109	583.57	216	249
6.00	843.86	42	110	599.55	222	252
6.25	857.42	48	110	615.72	228	254
6.50	871.11	53	111	632.07	233	256
6.75	884.91	57	112	648.60	237	259
7.00	898.83	62	113	665.30	242	261
7.25	912.86	66	113	682.18	246	263
7.50	927.01	70	114	699.22	250	265
7.75	941.28	73	115	716.41	253	267
8.00	955.65	77	115	733.77	257	269
8.25	970.14	80	116	751.27	260	271
8.50	984.74	83	117	768.91	263	273
8.75	999.45	86	118	786.70	266	274
9.00	1014.27	88	118	804.62	268	276
9.25	1029.19	91	119	822.68	271	278

9.50	1044.23	93	120	840.85	273	279
9.75	1059.36	95	120	859.15	275	281
10.00	1074.61	97	121	877.57	277	282
10.25	1089.95	100	122	896.10	279	284
10.50	1105.40	101	122	914.74	281	285
10.75	1120.95	103	123	933.48	283	287
11.00	1136.60	105	123	952.32	285	288
11.25	1152.35	107	124	971.26	287	289
11.50	1168.19	108	125	990.29	288	291
11.75	1184.13	110	125	1009.41	290	292
12.00	1200.17	111	126	1028.61	291	293
12.25	1216.30	113	126	1047.90	293	294
12.50	1232.52	114	127	1067.26	294	295
12.75	1248.84	115	128	1086.69	295	296
13.00	1265.24	117	128	1106.20	297	298
13.25	1281.74	118	129	1125.77	298	299
13.50	1298.32	119	129	1145.41	299	300
13.75	1314.99	120	130	1165.11	300	301
14.00	1331.47	121	130	1184.87	301	302
14.25	1348.58	122	131	1204.69	302	302
14.50	1365.50	123	131	1224.56	303	303
14.75	1382.54	124	132	1244.48	304	304
15.00	1399.59	125	132	1264.44	305	305

TABLE 4.2
Pay-Off Times for Bi-Weekly Payment Mortgages

N =	360 months	300 months	240 months	180 months
$12 \times I = 10\%$	21.0 yrs	18.8 yrs	16.0 yrs	12.6 yrs
$12 \times I = 9\%$				
$12 \times I = 8\%$	22.8	20.0	16.7	12.9
$12 \times I = 7\%$				
$12 \times I = 6\%$	24.5	21.0	17.2	13.2
$12 \times I = 5\%$				

annual discount rate i, call it the OAS, and write a new version of the net present value zero pricing formula

$$MV = \sum_{n=1}^{N} CF_n/[1 + (i + OAS)/m]^n. \qquad (4.8)$$

The simple interpretation of Equation 4.8 is that the higher the OAS, the riskier the cash flows.

Instead of the note rate on the lien, one might use for the interest rate i the coupon rate on the equivalent duration U.S. Treasury instrument; namely the 10-year U.S. Note. Since we priced off one point of the true yield curve, the spread would be referred to as static — hence the phrase *static spread*. Even if we replaced i by a full spot rate structure and kept the OAS constant, the same terminology would be used. This technique also implies that the optionality component has an equal probability of coming into-the-money at any point in the instrument's life. Such a pricing formula would look like

$$MV = \sum_{n=1}^{N} CF_n/(1 + s_n + OAS/m)^n \qquad (4.9)$$

where $\{s_n\}$ are the set of the monthly spot rates.

a.   Pricing with No Interest Rate Volatility

In Equation 4.8 we did not allow for interest rate changes — again begging the question of how the embedded call option can come into-the-money. At least in Equation 4.9 we used monthly spot rates so we could compare the coupon rate on the home loan in order to decide this issue. Performing the computations in this fashion is known as using a *zero volatility spread*. In Chapter 7 all these approximations will be relaxed. In particular, with a nonflat yield curve, cash flows when each coupon payment is due may depend upon current economic circumstances. So, one should really be:

1. Constructing a financially meaningful model for the yield curve between today and the maturity date of the security.
2. Evaluating, based on the "monieness" of the call (the phrase used to indicate whether or not an option is in- or out-of-the money) the cash flows for each time period of the yield curve.
3. Guessing a value for the OAS and computing the present value of the predicted cash flows using the yield curve time history.
4. Repeating the second and third steps a large number of times and then calculating the average present value.
5. Verifying that the mean just computed is, in fact, equal to the market price.

If it is not equal to the market price, then the assumed OAS value was wrong and the second through fifth steps need to be repeated. If the desired market price is obtained, then this was the value of the option-adjusted spread.

b. Option-Adjusted Duration and Convexity

If we are going to change the discount rate for a mortgage by adding an option-adjusted spread, then we must rethink what we meant earlier by duration and convexity. What was intended before clearly does not include the possibility of altering the OAS in describing average time to recoup the discounted cash flows, price sensitivity, or convexity. This is especially true for the latter because an option-free, fixed-income instrument always has positive convexity, whereas certificates with embedded call options have negative convexity. This means that they suffer from price compression as interest rates drop and the call option comes into-the-money. Because the option-adjusted spread will be computed in a numerical fashion, it makes sense to revert to the difference approximation for derivatives when computing the option-adjusted duration or the option-adjusted convexity (sometimes known as the effective duration and effective convexity, respectively).

Let P_0 be the price before we adjust the OAS. Let it change to P_- (P_+) when we decrease (increase) the discount rate by Δy. (This is clearly a static alteration in that the same change must be made across the entire yield curve). Then we can define the option-adjusted duration, OAD, as

$$OAD = (P_- - P_+)/(2 \times P_0 \times \Delta y).$$

Similarly, for the option-adjusted convexity, OAC, we would have the difference formula

$$OAC = (P_+ + P_- - 2 \times P_0)/[2 \times P_0 \times (\Delta y)^2].$$

The unresolved numerical question is how large Δy should be. Although a recommendation for much higher values can be found, 25 basis points seems sufficient to me. Higher values distort the intent of the differentiation process.

III. OTHER TYPES OF COMMON MORTGAGES

A. BACKGROUND

In 1978 the single-family mortgage was redefined to mean one- to four-family occupancy housing. Conventional multifamily loans were approved for purchase by government-sponsored enterprises in 1983. In addition, several other forms of common mortgage forms in the U.S. are defined next. First, the most customary nontraditional variant, the adjustable-rate mortgage (ARM) and its parameters are treated.

1. Adjustable-Rate Mortgages

The consumer's acceptance of variable-rate mortgages was not immediate. The floating-rate product slowly gained in popularity following its mid-1970s introduction and standardization as consumer understanding of the instrument, and its many variations increased. Demand for ARM mortgages rose relative to the fixed-rate mortgage as a consequence of double-digit interest rates in the mid-1980s. ARMs were almost 65% of new mortgage originations then because they were less expensive than fixed-rate mortgages, especially through their earlier years. Floating-rate mortgages were 20% of the single-family mortgage market in 1993 and rose to more than 40% the next year. Subsequently, ARM output dropped to about 15% of new liens and has slowed since the mid-1990s to just over 10% in early 2002. They are back up to 30% by mid-2002. Stable and lower long-term interest rates have decreased the attractiveness of variable-rate mortgages' temporary savings.

In 1981 approval for origination of ARMs by national banks and federally chartered savings institutions was granted. Fannie Mae began purchasing floating-rate mortgages in 1983 and in 1984 issued its first mortgage-backed securities whose underlying collateral was ARMs. Managers of savings bank mortgage portfolios prefer the interest rate risk protection offered by floating-rate liens because variable-rate MBSs have comparable interest rate sensitivities (as assets) to match short-term or floating-rate liabilities. Hence, banks tended to keep them in their own portfolios. This slowed the development of the ARM-backed MBS market. In addition, investors required the standardization of ARM structures and features before they would become willing purchasers and a secondary market could develop. Lastly, the lesser capitalization requirements set by the Federal Reserve have made ARM-backed MBSs a lower risk-based capital investment opportunity.

2. Definitions

To induce borrowers to accept an ARM, and to compensate them partially for future payment uncertainty, lenders offer ARMs at coupon rates substantially lower than their fixed-rate counterparts. This initial lower rate is known as a teaser rate and is typically 50 to 100 bp or more below the market rate for a traditional mortgage. The interest rate on a variable-rate mortgage is determined by adding a *spread* or *gross margin* to a (reference) *index*. The coupon rate on the adjustable-rate lien (index plus margin) is re-set at uniform intervals specified in the loan documents.

The sum of the index plus the margin is the *fully indexed rate*. (Because contractual features limit the amplitude of interest rate changes, the interest rate paid on a *seasoned* ARM may not equal the fully indexed rate. To be seasoned means to be a few years past origination; see immediately below.)

An ARM mortgage-backed security is typically supported by a pool of adjustable-rate mortgages that share the same index and other aspects (e.g., similar coupon rates, the same re-set frequency and re-set date, the same amortization term, the same *periodic* and *lifetime interest rate caps and floors,* and so forth.). The *pass-through rate,* the interest rate actually received by the investor, will equal the index plus the *net margin* or *security margin*. The difference between the gross margin and the security margin is referred to as the *servicing spread*, which includes the cost of mortgage servicing and the cost of the guarantee fees paid to the GSEs in the case of conforming loans.

The *margin* of a floating-rate security is the extra yield of the instrument over a comparable U.S. Treasury instrument. The higher the margin, the higher the price is. For example, a margin of 200 bp might translate into one point more in price than a margin 50 bp lower. The higher margin also represents a higher interest rate to the borrower. Therefore, loans with higher margins have a greater tendency to prepay faster, thereby shortening the life of the security. To make a higher margin loan more alluring to the borrower, it may need to be offset by lower periodic or lifetime interest rate caps. The lower caps would decrease the likelihood that the security would attain its fully indexed rate, counteracting the value of the higher security margin.

Periodic interest rate caps and floors limit the amount by which the effective note rate may change. A periodic interest rate cap (floor) fixes the upper (lower) limit of the actual interest rate paid by the homeowner between re-set intervals. Caps protect the borrower from rapid increases in monthly payments. Floors shield the ARM investor from sudden decreases in cash flow.

Suppose that the teaser rate was 4.75%/year, the periodic cap was 2%/adjustment, and the fully indexed rate at the first re-set moment was 7%/year. Then the effective coupon rate on this ARM would have only grown to 6.75%/year because of the periodic interest rate cap. Lifetime interest rate caps and floors govern the maximum rate adjustments that can be made to the lien's effective rate over the life of the loan. A typical maximum cap is six percentage points. Floating-rate mortgages that have reached their lifetime cap behave like a fixed-rate security with an interest rate at the variable-rate mortgage's interest rate ceiling. Not surprisingly, ARM-backed MBSs that have reached their cap trade as fixed-rate pools with comparable coupon rates do. If market interest rates fall again, then the ARM MBS will float again in price.

Some ARMs carry a *periodic payment cap*. Payment caps are typically 7.5%/year. This limitation can prevent the monthly payment from adjusting to a level corresponding to the fully indexed interest rate or even the cap-limited rate and create *negative amortization*. This means that cash flow is insufficient to pay the monthly interest charge owed on the loan. The shortfall will be added to the outstanding principal balance. Future interest computations are based on this higher loan balance, so the interest shortfall is deferred, not lost.

a. Reference Indices

The GSEs pool loans together, to package them into more liquid securities, using three broad categories of variable-rate mortgages. The types refer to the reference interest rate utilized. These are: 1. U.S. Treasury-based indices such as the 1-year *Constant Maturity U.S. Treasury* index, the 6-month Constant Maturity U.S. Treasury (*CMT*) index, and the 3-year CMT Security index, 2. various London Inter-Bank Offered Rate (*LIBOR*) indices such as 1-month, 6-month, and 1-year LIBOR, and 3. several *Cost of Funds Indices* such as the 11th District Cost of Funds Index of the Federal Home Loan Banks (*COFI*), the Federal Home Loan Bank Board Monthly COFI, the National Monthly Median COF Ratio, and the National Contract Rate.

The most common Treasury-based index is the 1-year CMT. This index is the average yield of all outstanding Treasury securities having 1 year remaining until maturity. It is calculated weekly using market quotations and is published Mondays in the *Federal Reserve Statistical Release H.15*. Because Treasury indices reflect the weighted averages of current bids and are based on weekly quotes, they closely duplicate the current interest-rate levels and direction.

LIBOR is the rate that major international banks charge each other. There are many LIBORs, one for each benchmark maturity. (A *LIBID* is the rate on the other side of the transaction; the average of the two is called *LIMEAN*. There is a PIBOR for Paris, a SIBOR for Singapore, and so forth, but no NYBOR. Why not?) This rate is often used by U.S. institutions active in overseas capital markets. International investors are attracted to this index because it allows them to eliminate *basis risk* between their asset and liability cash flows. Basis risk refers to the fact that two different floating rates, for example, 6-month CMT and 6-month LIBOR, may not move in concert.

The 11th District Cost of Funds Index (COFI) is determined by the monthly weighted average cost of savings, borrowings, and advances for member institutions of that Federal Home Loan Bank. It includes California, Arizona, and Nevada. This index is reported on the last business day of the month by the FHLBank of San Francisco. COFI reacts slowly to short-term market rate movements because of the varying maturities of the liabilities that make it up and the long lead time associated with its reporting. Because of its 2-month lagging nature, COFI ARM-backed MBSs can increase in price when market rates fall. Conversely, in a rapidly rising market-interest-rate environment, COFI ARM MBSs may trade at a discount.

Thrifts use the Cost of Fund Indices because they are closely tied to the prices that savings and loan institutions pay for monies. Banks invest in COFI-based mortgages because they closely track the yield they pay on money market accounts. COFI-based mortgages may also suffer from negative amortization (the index can be re-set monthly but the note's coupon rate is typically re-set annually).

The frequency and timing of the rate re-set determines the rate of interest paid on a variable-rate security. Floating-rate mortgages based on U.S. Treasury rates usually have annual adjustment dates. Those tied to COFI customarily fix the initial note rate for 6 months. Thereafter, the interest rate is re-set monthly or semiannually. To calculate the interest accrual rate for the forthcoming period, an investor must know the number of days in the *look-back time*. (The look-back time is the interval between the index date of record and the date when the index will be used to compute the new coupon rate.) This number, counted backward from the first day of the accrual period, fixes the effective index rate on that date. The interest accrual rate will be the new index rate plus the margin.

Infrequently one finds a variable-rate mortgage with a *carryover provision*. This means that, if the effective rate on the mortgage cannot reach the fully indexed rate because of the presence of a periodic interest rate cap, the increase may be applied to the next re-set. As an example, suppose that the current rate on an adjustable-rate mortgage is 5.5%, it has a periodic cap of 1%, and the fully indexed rate on the next re-set date would bring the rate to 7.0%. Clearly, because of the existence of the cap, the interest rate the homeowner will pay is 6.5% leaving 50 bp to be carried over. Even if at the next re-set date the fully indexed rate did not rise, then the new interest rate the homeowner will pay will be 7.5% because of the 50 bp of carryover. The possibility of carryover does not lead to negative amortization.

b. Numerical Example

As an example, consider a $225,000 ARM whose teaser rate was 5.5%/year with a maturity of 30 years. The initial monthly payment would be $1,277.53. Suppose that the periodic collar is +200 bp/–150 bp (an example of an asymmetric collar), the first rate re-set is after 1 year, the margin is 35 bp, and the index used is 7.25% per year. Then the new fully-indexed rate would be 7.25% + 0.35% = 7.60%. However, this exceeds the first periodic cap amount of 7.5% = 5.5% + 2.0%. So, the new effective interest rate would only be 7.5% per year. The remaining principal balance, after 1 year, is $221,969.05. Based on the new coupon rate, this outstanding principal amount, and 29 years, the new monthly mortgage payment would be $1,566.48, a jump of $288.95 per month (or 23%) — and so on to the next rate re-set date.

3. Valuation Considerations

The number of months remaining to the next re-set has an effect on the price of a variable-rate mortgage. If the effective rate is below the current fully indexed interest rate, and the next re-set date is a full year away, then the value of the lien will be depressed as long as market rates stay above that of the mortgage. As the re-set date approaches, the market value should rise in anticipation of the rate re-set, unless an interest rate cap will prevent the home loan from movement to the fully-indexed rate. The converse is true for an ARM security with an above-market effective note rate; it will carry a premium price. However, as the re-set date approaches, the value of this larger rate lessens and the value of the security should approach par.

Most COFI-based mortgages have negative amortization limits. The maximum loan balance increase is typically 10% of the original loan amount. If this limit is reached, then the borrower's payment is increased — notwithstanding any other payment limitations — to amortize the mortgage fully over its remaining term. Alternatively, the borrower's monthly payments are recast or adjusted every 5 years to amortize the loan fully, regardless of payment caps. Of course it is possible that, in a falling interest rate environment, an accelerated pay-down of the outstanding principal balance can occur. When this happens, the monthly payment exceeds the amount needed to amortize the loan fully. (This is a subtle form of prepayment.) Because the 11th District COFI lags behind market rates, sharply declining market rates might trigger some COFI-based borrowers to prepay their loans in order to refinance at the lower fixed rates. When a variable-rate borrower is faced with an appreciable drop in fixed-rate mortgage rates and the prospect that the floating-rate mortgage will not be re-set soon to a desirable interest rate, prepayment can be expected because it makes sense for the homeowner to exercise the option to convert the lien.

Some adjustable-rate mortgages have built-in convertibility features that allow borrowers to change their ARMs into long-term, fixed-rate loans. The exercise of this typically Bermudan option would appear as a prepayment to the investor. This feature is thought to be of little significance when the loan is close to the interest rate cap, interest rates are stable or declining, and the economics of the transaction are equivalent to a refinancing. Under such conditions, the borrower has little incentive to convert to a fixed-rate loan.

Low teaser rates may lessen the likelihood of prepayment because the borrower will probably want to hold on to the below market effective rate for as long as possible; higher margins may encourage a borrower to prepay. Approaching a rate re-set date also may increase refinancing rates, leading to faster prepayment speeds. The interest rate situation during the period of time in which the convertibility option is active may precipitate a prepayment when a borrower expects interest rates to rise and wishes to limit that risk via conversion from a variable- to a fixed-rate mortgage. Geographical distribution also is a factor in prepayments because ARMs are popular in regions of the country where mobility is high. As a result, these floating-rate mortgages tend to prepay more quickly than other, equivalent, variable-rate mortgages originated elsewhere as a result of moving frequency.

B. Adjustable-Rate Mortgage Mathematics

Suppose that you knew in advance that the annual interest rates would be $i_1, i_2,..., i_N$. The maturity of the mortgage is T years. Further suppose that the time in years for the application of the nth interest rate was denoted by t_n, where

$$T = \sum_{n=1}^{N} t_n.$$

Finally, let the payment frequency throughout the life of the instrument be m times per year. Then the monthly payment for the nth time period, MP_n, is given by

$$MP_n = UBP_0 \times F_n, n = 1,2,..., N$$

where the factor F_n is given by

$$1/F_n = \sum_{k=1}^{n} [1 - (1 + i_k/m)^{-mt_k}]/(i_k/m) \times \prod_{j=1}^{k} (1 + i_{j-1}/m)^{-mt_j}$$

C. OTHER COMMON TYPES OF MORTGAGES IN THE U.S.

1. The Graduated Payment Mortgage

The current version of the *graduated payment mortgage* was introduced by the FHA in 1976. This instrument requires an increasing monthly payment during the early years of the loan and then a constant level. By lowering the initial monthly payment and having it rise with expected increases in income, this type of mortgage made owning a home much more affordable for many people. The standard graduated payment mortgage plan is a 30-year lien with monthly payments growing by up to 7.5%/year for the first 5 years and then leveling off. For example, per $100,000 of loan amount, at an annual interest rate of 10%, the first 5 yearly monthly payments would be $667.04, $717.06, $770.84, $828.66, $890.80, and $957.62 thereafter. (For a traditional mortgage, the monthly payment would be $877.57.)

For the investor, an additional risk with this kind of mortgage is negative amortization because, in the early years of the debt, the monthly payment is insufficient to pay even the interest (in this instance $833.33 initially). The unpaid interest accrues as an addition to the principal amount. At a 10% interest rate, the outstanding principal balance reaches a maximum in the fourth year, at $105,526/$100,000 of initial principal amount. Actual amortization does not begin to occur until the tenth year.

2. Growing Equity Mortgages

A growing equity mortgage is also a fixed-rate mortgage product. The monthly payment grows over time from the base level of a traditional mortgage. The extra amount increases the homeowner's equity at a faster rate than a standard fully amortizing mortgage would. Since default rates are highly correlated with the loan-to-value ratio, this type of lien is much more secure than a graduated payment mortgage. Monthly payments normally increase at 3, 5, or 7.5% per year and a 30-year loan may be paid off in as soon as 15 years by this mechanism. There is a VA version of this product and the graduated payment mortgage.

3. Fixed-Rate, Tiered-Payment Mortgages

A fixed-rate, tiered-payment mortgage is similar to a graduated payment mortgage. The early monthly payments are well below those of a traditional mortgage with the same maturity, face amount, and interest rate. To prevent negative amortization a reserve account is established from which principal shortfalls are taken until the monthly payment has risen enough to allow for full amortization of the remaining balance. This kind of mortgage was introduced in the early 1980s (then known as a *pledged-account mortgage*). The term of a fixed-rate tiered-payment mortgage is frequently only 15 years.

4. Pledged-Asset Mortgages

A pledged-asset mortgage enables buyers to borrow up to the full amount of the sales price when there is a promise of a stable financial asset to serve as additional collateral for the loan. Thus, a pledged-asset mortgage allows a borrower to utilize savings without liquidating them. These instruments can also be used by mortgagors who have sufficient income to make the monthly payments but who have not saved the usual 20% down payment. Only a 3% down payment may be required.

5. Balloon Re-set Mortgages

Balloon re-set mortgages have an equity build-up and a refunding mechanism for the balloon payment. The monthly payment is based on a traditional mortgage amortization schedule; the reissuance of a new mortgage to cover the balloon payment (usually after 5 or 7 years) is agreed to at the beginning of the term (contingent on certain financial criteria the mortgagor must continue to meet). Even though the monthly payments are based on a 30-year amortization schedule, the initial coupon rate is based on the shorter term of the loan (assuming an upward sloping yield curve). In addition, the conditional option to refinance also allows borrowers to convert their mortgage, at its maturity, into a fixed-rate instrument.

6. Two-Step Mortgage

A two-step mortgage is a combination of two fixed-rate mortgages. The timing and amount of the (presumably upward) interest rate adjustment are set in the initial terms of the deed of trust. The two-step mortgage initially has a shorter-term pricing structure with the protection of longer-term financing. The most common forms adjust after 5 or 7 years. Pricing is frequently done based on the weekly average of 10-year U.S. Treasury Notes adjusted to a constant maturity. Interest rate increases are limited to six percentage points. Rate decreases are unlimited (given that the coupon rate is non-negative).

7. Reverse Mortgages

Reverse mortgages are designed for elderly people who own their homes outright but have no simple way of taking out some of the equity, except by selling the property. A reverse mortgage pays the homeowner a set amount for a fixed period of time and passes title back to the lender to recoup the investment when the homeowner moves or dies. HUD has a version known as the *home equity conversion mortgage* for those age 62 and older.

8. Shared-Appreciation Mortgages

Shared-appreciation mortgages are identical to traditional mortgages in terms of their payment. They allow the borrower to have a substantially below-market interest rate but assign the lender a negotiated share of the property's price appreciation upon sale (or some other agreed upon date). In an era of high housing price inflation the lender will make far more from the increase in value of the property than on a market level interest rate product.

9. Hybrid Mortgages

A hybrid mortgage is a combination of a short-term, fixed-rate mortgage and a long-term, floating-rate mortgage. It might be quoted as a 5/1, meaning that for the first 5 years the note rate is fixed and thereafter it floats and is re-set once per year. Another version might be a 3/3, meaning that for the first 3 years the interest rate was fixed and thereafter it floats and is re-set every third year. Hybrid mortgages use the standard ARM reference indices.

10. Prepayment Penalty Mortgages

A prepayment penalty in a mortgage, payable should the homeowner choose to refinance, mostly disappeared from the traditional product because neither Freddie Mac nor Fannie Mae would underwrite liens containing such provisions. Over the last few years these kinds of mortgages have made a comeback; however, now they are offered, as are adjustable-rate mortgages, at a below-market rate for the first few years (up to 5) of the life of the lien. Moreover, the prepayment penalty is solely designed to compensate the lender for the economic value of the below-market interest rate and not to inhibit the homeowner from exercising the prepayment option or to move.

11. Relocation Mortgages

Because much of the mobility of Americans is job-related and job-change driven, sometimes employers will provide housing-related benefits to the employees that they are moving or hiring. When the employer does so, for example, by subsidizing the interest rate, paying for the closing costs, or making some other substantial contribution to the new lien, this mortgage will be classified as a relocation mortgage. On account of their nature, one would expect these mortgages to prepay or refinance at much higher rates than a generic mortgage with the same amortization term.

IV. AUTOMATED UNDERWRITING

A. WHAT IS UNDERWRITING?

When one applies for a loan, the lender examines collateral, credit, and capacity. Collateral is the actual value of the land and the buildings on it in conjunction with the amount of the down payment. Credit is shorthand for the credit history of the borrower. The lender delves into what is currently owed and to whom, how long it has been owed, how regularly full and timely payments have been made, and if new debt-related activity has recently occurred. Capacity is a measure of the potential borrower's capability to make all contractually agreed to monthly payments. Capacity is evaluated using two debt-to-income ratios that involve the percentage of an applicant's income needed to cover monthly debt obligations. Borrower savings, referred to as *cash reserves*, also are used to assess capacity. While capacity is an important underwriting component, debt-to-income ratios generally are less powerful predictors of loan performance than other factors. The amount of equity and credit bureau scores are better indicators of mortgage default risk. The process of evaluating these aspects is called *underwriting*.

1. What Is Automated Underwriting?

Automated underwriting refers to the underwriting of a mortgage loan application by a computer program instead of by a human being. The automated underwriting system predicts the applicant's default risk based on his credit file and loan application information. The better automated underwriting software is able to balance a borrower's strengths in one area against risk factors in another sphere. The logic behind the decision making algorithm in these computer programs rests on the former performance of millions of mortgage loans. Econometric models of default were constructed from liens granted in the past and the payment history of the borrowers behind them. Proprietary automated underwriting technologies have been developed in the residential mortgage market by Fannie Mae, Freddie Mac, private mortgage insurers, and a number of leading mortgage originators. The scoring of government-insured mortgages and jumbo loans is also embedded in the newer versions of the GSE's systems. They evaluate more than 60% of conforming loans.

Fully automated underwriting has the same components as traditional underwriting does:

1. A collateral assessment using a statistical appraisal of the property's value.
2. A credit assessment using a credit score: most credit scoring for mortgages retrieves a summary credit score (the summary score is almost always created for the credit bureau by either Fair, Isaac Companies or by Management Decision Systems). The summary scores, along with other information, are then incorporated into a mortgage credit scoring algorithm.
3. An evaluation of the borrower's ability to carry debt based on a pair of financial ratios.

B. IMPORTANT UNDERWRITING FACTORS

1. Credit Scoring

Credit scoring is a means of evaluating the credit worthiness of loan applicants on a numerical scale. If the score exceeds a predetermined threshold, then the applicant is extended credit subject to verification of income, employment, and assets. Otherwise, the applicant is referred to a human underwriter for additional review or is denied credit. Though used for years in the credit card industry, credit scoring has only recently (post-1995) been applied to home loan applications. The huge difference in the amount to be borrowed vs. normal credit-card borrowing limits, coupled with the option theoretic approach to homeowner default, slowed the adoption of this technique. Freddie Mac did the first research that allowed it to argue that consumer credit scoring combined with other financial information can be a reliable measure of mortgage default risk.

a.   More on Credit Scoring

The three most important factors to predict the likelihood of repaying a mortgage in a timely fashion are the borrower's total equity, the *loan type*, and the credit bureau scores. Credit bureau scores can accurately summarize, in a statistical sense, the likelihood of an individual's repayment of a debt. Fair, Isaac and Co., or FICO, scores are one example of a credit bureau score. FICO scores range from about 400, denoting the highest risk, to about 900, indicating the lowest risk. In a survey of about a million home-loan records, Fair, Isaac found that one in eight borrowers with a FICO score below 600 was either severely delinquent in payments or in default. In contrast, only one in 1300 borrowers with scores above 800 had similar delinquency problems.

Borrowers possessing weak credit histories, defined as having a FICO scores under 620, have been about 20 times more likely to enter foreclosure than borrowers with FICO score above 660. For applicants with FICO scores between 620 and 660 the credit predictor is uncertain and lenders perform the same review as they would when underwriting without credit-bureau scores. Another example of a credit-bureau score is the MDS bankruptcy score for which a lower score indicates lower risk. (MDS bankruptcy scores are developed by CCN-MDS, Inc. of Atlanta, Georgia.)

The most important factor in a credit bureau score is the borrower's proven willingness and ability to repay his debts. Lower absolute scores go to those applicants with a history of chronically late payments, less than full amounts of payments, or bankruptcies. The score is based on a *credit report*, which shows debts and payment history of a potential borrower and indicates whether bills were paid on time and whether the proper amounts owed were paid. It also reveals how much debt one currently has and if there have been defaults. The more recent a delinquency, then the higher the risk.

Credit files contain information about open and closed credit accounts called *tradelines*. For each tradeline the credit file records how much of the available credit limit has been used, the consumer's history of repaying that account, and whether payment is up to date or delinquent. Credit files also document the number and nature of recent *credit inquiries*, which are requests by potential credit grantors to review a credit file. The more recent these incidents, the more negative the impact on a credit score. Historically, a high number of inquiries can indicate a higher degree of risk. Most public record and foreclosure information is retained in a credit report for 7 years (10 years for bankruptcies). The credit report also specifies the names of those authorized to obtain a copy of the credit report and indicates how often applications for credit have been made in the past 2 years. These data are kept on file electronically by three private credit bureaus: Equifax, Experian, and Trans Union.

An automated underwriting considers other important factors not related to your credit history in its evaluation of a home-loan application. These noncredit report elements include the amount of money you plan to invest or have invested in your home (i.e., the amount of your equity), your overall financial situation, your debts and income, the reason for your loan, the desired type and length of the loan, the property type, and the number of individuals applying for the loan.

2. Equity

One's financial interest in one's home is called equity; it is the difference between the fair market value of the property and the outstanding principal balance on the mortgage. A borrower who makes a large down payment or who has built up equity over time is much less likely to default on a loan than a borrower who makes a small down payment or has built up only a small amount of equity. A low loan-to-value ratio may offset other risks because the borrower no longer must be underwritten as rigorously — in effect the collateral is now backing the loan.

3. Liquid Reserves

The readily available monies after home purchase are known as liquid reserves. Some examples include checking or savings accounts, stocks, bonds, or mutual funds, the vested portion of 401(k) accounts, and funds in IRA or Keogh retirement accounts. Obviously, higher amounts of liquid reserves are more favorably viewed than lower amounts or no reserves (but not much beyond 6 months' worth).

4. Debt-to-Income Ratios

The debt-to-income ratios compare what you earn against what you owe. The back-end debt-to-income ratio is calculated by dividing your total monthly debt load by your gross monthly income. The front-end debt-to-income ratio only includes housing costs in the numerator such as the mortgage loan payment, real estate taxes, hazard insurance, and private mortgage insurance (if required by the lender). Generally, the lower the debt-to-income ratios, the better one's financial condition. A lender will verify your income by reviewing current pay stubs, bank account status, and possibly pension accounts, as well as past income tax returns or W-2 forms. It will probably contact your employer to verify your current employment status and salary. Underwriting guidelines generally recommend front-end ratios of up to 28% and back-end ratios of up to 36%.

5. Loan Purpose

The loan purpose is the reason for applying for a mortgage. It may be to purchase a home (called a purchase money mortgage) or it may be to refinance an existing mortgage. In general, buying a home represents less of a risk than refinancing an existing mortgage. Refinance transactions in which the borrower takes out little or no equity (a no-cash-out refinancing with less than $1000 additionally lent) presents less risk than those transactions in which the borrower takes out funds (a cash-out refinance).

6. Mortgage Type

Borrowers may choose among fixed, adjustable, or balloon mortgages. Analysis of historical data indicates that balloon mortgages and yearly re-set ARMs tend to be at higher risk for default than liens with longer fixed-payment periods.

7. Mortgage Term

The loan term, or amortization period, refers to the length of time it will take to pay off the mortgage; the standard is 30 years. Research has shown that loans to borrowers who choose to finance their housing over shorter terms and build up equity faster tend to default less frequently than mortgagors with longer terms.

8. Property Type

The type of home for which you have requested a mortgage is referred to as the *property type*. These might include: 1. a one unit residential property, 2. a two- to four-unit property, possibly owner-occupied, but not necessarily (The other units are presumably to be rented for investment purposes.), and 3. condominiums or co-operatives. Mortgages on one-unit residential properties have the lowest default risk, while three- and four-unit and nonowner-occupied residential properties have a much higher default risk. The number of borrowers who are contractually responsible for repayment of the mortgage loan is also a risk factor. The presence of more than one borrower on a mortgage application generally helps to reduce risk because of lower debt-to-income ratios and hence lower default rates.

9. Borrower Employment Category

A self-employed borrower is either the owner or part owner of a business. Because of the increased chance of uneven cash flows, self-employment introduces an additional element of credit risk to a mortgage application that is not present with salaried borrowers. This risk is generally considered adverse only when a self-employed borrower has other high-risk factors associated with the loan, such as a history of delinquent accounts or a low level of savings. Self-employed borrowers tend to default on their mortgages more often than salaried borrowers, all other things being equal. If self-employed, one of the ways you can offset this risk is to have a high amount of liquid reserves and a good credit profile.

PROBLEMS

1. You are offered a choice of two investments: a $45,000 face value corporate bond paying interest semiannually at 9.87% for 20 years, with the

coupons to be reinvested at 10.87%, or a $45,000 face value mortgage paying interest monthly at 9.37% for 20 years, with the coupons to be reinvested at 10.37%. Which would you choose and why? (First alternative: C = $2,220.75, terminal wealth = $432,354.50; second alternative: MP = $415.65, terminal wealth = $331,205.64)

2. If a fully amortizing, 30-year, level-payment mortgage of face amount $145,000 would have been paid off with a monthly payment of $1,114.93, what is this worth to you if you demand 12.5% per year return? What is the coupon rate? What is its Macaulay duration? ($104,466.80, 8.5%, D = 9.282 years)

3. What is the coupon rate of a 25-year, level-payment, fully amortizing mortgage of face amount $100,000 if its Macaulay duration is 5.55 years?

4. You are contemplating purchasing a 25-year, level-payment, fully amortizing, monthly payment, fixed-rate mortgage with a coupon of $8 \, ^3/_8$. Its face amount is $185,000. You are concerned about its change in duration if interest rates move ± 250 bp. Compute the market values and durations for the coupon rate and the coupon rate ± 250 basis points. (MP = $1,474.12, at i = 8.375% D = 8.481 years; at i = 5.875%, MV = $231,531.57, D = 9.593 years; and at i = 10.875%, MV = $151,800.65, D = 7.490 years)

5. Let the growth rate in the payment of a graduated payment mortgage be g, with frequency of mortgage payments m times per year. Let i be the annual interest rate and N the total number of payments. Show that the first monthly payment, MP_1, is given by

$$MP_1 = UPB_0 \times (i/m - g)/\{1 - [(1 + g)^N/(1 + i/m)]^N\}.$$

Remember that the monthly payment for the nth month is given by $MP_1 \times (1 + g)^n$. Show that the mortgage balance remaining after the nth payment is given by

$$UPB_n = UPB_0 \times (1 + g)^n \times \{1 - [(1 + g)^{N-n}/(1 + i/m)]^{N-n}\}/\{1 - [(1 + g)^N/(1 + i/m)]^N\}.$$

6. Show that the payment number M when the interest expense of a graduated payment mortgage equals the interest expense due on the mortgage is given by

$$M = N + 1 - ln[g/(i/m)]/ln[(1 + g)/(1 + i/m)]$$

7. No interest is paid in a *zero interest mortgage*; rather, each monthly payment goes completely to principal reduction. Show that the price of a P of such a lien, assuming a down payment of d percent of P, for an investor with a monthly required rate of return r is given by

$$P = P'/\{d + [(1 - d)/(N \times r)] \times [1 - (1 + r)^{-N}]\}$$

where P' is the price of the zero interest mortgage, had it been conventionally financed over N months. P will be larger than P'.

8. Show that, if mortgages were paid in advance instead of in arrears, the monthly payment formula would be given by (m = 12)

$$MP = UPB_0 \times (i/12)/\{[1 - (1 + i/12)^{-N}] \times (1 + i/12)\}$$

where the other symbols have their usual meaning.

9. Show that the total interest expense, after the nth payment, associated with a fixed-rate mortgage with N payments, annual interest rate i, and paid m times per year, is given by

$$UPB_0 \times (i/m) \times \{n - (1 + i/m)^{-N} \times \{(1 + i/m)^n - 1]/(i/m)\}/[1 - (1 + i/m)^{-N}].$$

10. Frequently one pays "points" to buy down the interest rate. A point is 1% of the original principal balance. Show that the effective annual rate of interest I is related to the coupon rate of i by

$$UPB_0 \times (i/m)/[1 - (1 + i/m)^{-N}] = (1 - p) \times UPB_0 \times (I/m)/[1 - (1 + I/m)^{-N}]$$

where p is the number of points paid.

11. Solve for the annual interest rate that will make MP equal to 1% of the UPB when the term to maturity is 30, 25, 20, and 15 years. (11.63, 11.27, 10.52, and 8.76%, respectively)

12. For a 20-year, fully amortizing, fixed-term mortgage with an interest rate of 6.78% and par value of $223,344, compute the time until half the principal is repaid, the monthly payment is 50% interest and 50% principal repayment, and the total amount, principal plus interest, paid over the life of the loan. (158 months = 13.2 years, 117 months = 9.75 years, $408,530)

5 Mortgage Securitization in the U.S.

Whole-loan mortgages are risky as an investment vehicle. They suffer from a severe lack of liquidity, credit risk, prepayment risk, potential underwriting variances, and other hazards. Finding a mechanism to enhance the attractiveness of mortgages as fixed-income possibilities would lower the cost of funds to consumers and better satisfy investors' requirements. Thus, the mortgage-backed security in its pass-through form was born. Further improvements on this one-class structure will be described in Chapter 6. Since prepayments largely determine the relative value of these securities, what is known about them is thoroughly covered.

I. WHAT IS A MORTGAGE-BACKED SECURITY?

A. BACKGROUND

1. Definitions

A mortgage-backed security is an example of an *asset-backed security* whose underlying collateral is residential mortgages. Asset-backed securities can be based on car loans, manufactured housing loans, accounts receivable, credit card debt, and so on. (Overseas, an asset-backed security is one supported by any kind of asset; only in the U.S. are mortgage-backed securities a special class. This is because of the huge fraction of the fixed-income market they occupy.)

The simplest form of mortgage-related derivative is known as a pass-through mortgage-backed security. The market for these financial instruments has grown tenfold over the last decade to $1.5+ trillion today. The backing, or collateral, of the mortgage-backed security (MBS) is the cash flows stemming from the underlying whole loans. Ultimately, the support comes from the real estate purchased by these liens. As the homeowners whose loans are in the pool make their monthly mortgage payments, these funds are distributed, in an *undivided, pro rata* fashion, to the third-party purchasers of the mortgage-backed securities.

Thus, unlike U.S. coupon-paying bonds, mortgage-related securities provide monthly income. With this form of a mortgage-backed security, the monthly interest and principal payments, scheduled and unscheduled, are passed through to the investor without any redirection of prepayment risk. For example, one who owns 1% of a 1500-pool pass-through MBS does not own 15 (= 0.01 × 1500) of these mortgages in their entirety; rather one owns 1% of all the cash flows from each of the 1500 home loans. This is what an undivided interest means.

MBS investors are unlikely to receive the same cash flow from their investment each month because of the potential for unscheduled principal payments. This is known as prepayment risk. To simplify things for the investor and to make these instruments more liquid, an effort is made to group together mortgages with similar characteristics into the pools that support MBSs. Fannie Mae MBSs and Freddie Mac Gold PCs (Participation Certificates) also have limits on the interest rates of the loans allowed in a pool, as well as other constraints, designed to make their prepayment behavior — the biggest remaining risk factor — more predictable. This type of financial instrument was first issued by Ginnie Mae in 1968.

a. Mechanics

The mortgage assets used as collateral for the security are removed from the balance sheet of the originator. The pool of mortgages is managed by a trustee with the cash flows from the liens passed on to the investor with a *payment delay*. The payment delay allows for collection of monthly payments from the homeowners, accounting of them by the firm providing the *servicing* function, remitting of funds to the secondary marketing entity, time necessary for the latter to perform its accounting of cash flows received and dispensed, and, finally, disbursement to the investors. This is typically 45 to 75 days, depending on the conduit and product type. The security usually carries some form of payment guarantee to relieve the credit risk-related concerns of the investor. Fannie Mae and Freddie Mac guarantee the investor their monthly principal and interest, for which they charge a guarantee fee. A nominal value for the guarantee fee is 25 basis points. Similarly, the servicing organization's fee is also nominally 25 basis points on the unpaid principal amount. Hence, if the consumer's mortgage interest rate was 9.75%, then the pass-through rate to the investor would be 9.25% (= 9.75% − 0.25% − 0.25%).

An entity issuing a one-class, mortgage-backed pass-through structured as a grantor trust is not treated as a taxable entity. To prevent the commingling of funds, the issuer separates the assets underlying the MBS into a separate entity, known as a *special purpose vehicle*, which is bankruptcy remote from the issuer. This means that, if the seller of the whole loans has financial difficulties, they will not carry over, or allow a claim on, the assets underlying the MBS.

b. Prepayments

A mortgage is a loan backed by collateral, namely, the land on which the house stands and the building itself, and the standard for a conforming loan has, at most, an 80% loan-to-value ratio so that the loan has an excess of collateral backing it; however, owning a whole-loan mortgage is still a relatively risky proposition. As with any fixed-income security, there is interest rate risk. In addition, there is an analog to *call risk* known as prepayment risk.

Payment of all of the outstanding mortgage debt before it is owed is called a prepayment. Although a mortgage may have a term of 40 years, most traditional mortgages are paid off well before that time (10 years or less is now used as the average life). The mortgagor is allowed to prepay the loan, in whole or in part (known as a *curtailment*), whenever he chooses to do so. Advance notice or any reason is not required, nor is a prepayment penalty demanded. Borrowers are most likely to exercise the prepayment option at a time when it is least advantageous to investors. Prepayments also include proceeds from foreclosures, condemnations, casualties, or defaults. These are of relatively minor importance compared to complete principal repayments because of moving or refinancing.

A *par security* is one that was purchased at a price equal to the face value of the instrument. For a security with an embedded option, the coupon rate has presumably been adjusted upward to reflect the increased risk. In the case of mortgages and their derivative securities, this corresponds to estimating a prepayment speed, or set of prepayment speeds, as a function of time over the life of the liens and computing an option-adjusted spread. Prepayments at the expected rate will cause no loss to the investor because they have already been factored into the price (or, equivalently, the yield).

An unanticipated decrease in interest rates will encourage homeowners to refinance their mortgages. This will cause prepayment speeds to exceed the ones projected at pricing, returning principal early in an unfavorable interest rate environment. This is known as *contraction risk* or call risk. Conversely, a sustained rise in market rates exposes the investor to *extension risk* — the peril that prepayments will slow down because it is uneconomic for the homeowners to refinance their mortgages or too expensive to trade up to more costly houses. Interest rate increases slow down the receipt of principal.

A *premium security* is one that was purchased at a price above the face value of the instrument. If interest rates then substantially decline, making refinancing attractive to mortgagors, this investor loses thrice. First he receives the principal earlier than anticipated, effectively reducing the yield because, at most, each dollar of principal will be returned at par. Second, he will have lost the interest portion of the cash flow that dominates the monthly payment for many years. Third, he faces reinvestment risk in the new, reduced interest-rate setting. Alternatively, if market rates rise, then prepayment speeds will slow, extending the life of the security and especially its interest-related cash flow component, thus allowing him to recoup the premium price paid for the certificate.

A *discount security* is one that was purchased at a price below the face value of the instrument. If interest rates then substantially decline, making refinancing attractive to homeowners, then this investor gains. He receives the principal earlier than anticipated, effectively increasing the yield (because each dollar of principal will be at least returned at par). Unfortunately, they only have the opportunity to reinvest these funds at a lower rate than was received on the discount security. Conversely, if interest rates rise, then a larger component of on-going interest-related cash flow will act to increase the total cash flow.

c.   More on Securitization

The chief legal, regulatory and accounting, and tax issues affecting the success of securitization are:

1. The main legal issue is that of a true sale of the underlying asset and the perfection of the security interest. This includes the necessity of being able to establish a bankruptcy-remote, special-purpose vehicle to separate

any losses on the secured loans from the originator of the loans. The special purpose vehicle is usually a separate corporate entity. If necessary, one also needs to have the legal right to transfer the ownership of the underlying assets in the event of bankruptcy of one of the financial intermediaries. In this way, the issuing trust's ability to continue to pay interest and principal would remain intact.

2. The major regulatory and accounting issues are the freedom of the process of securitization itself. This should include the possibility of the special-purpose vehicle obtaining credit enhancements and the ability to restructure the cash flows into more desirable patterns. These derivative securities would generally be rated by one of the credit rating agencies. A triple-A credit rating is preferred, but a double-A rating is adequate. This may be done by the special-purpose vehicle selling the securities to a trust that repackages them and actually markets them. In addition, one needs the viability of off-balance sheet treatment and nonrecourse financing for the originating institutions.

3. The most consequential tax issue is that it is important to establish the absence of double taxation or tax-neutrality with respect to other aspects of the underlying liens. The best situation is one in which only interest payments are subject to tax, with the return of the principal viewed as the redemption of the original cost. Asset-backed securities purchased at an original issue discount will be subject to capital gains taxes on the amount of the discount from par on an accrual basis.

2. Some History

Ginnie Mae issued the first MBS in 1968 (using a pool of government-insured home loans); they were pass-through securities. In 1970 Ginnie Mae followed up with the first pass-through security based on a pool of conventional mortgages. Freddie Mac issued its version, called the Participation Certificate, in 1971. Fannie Mae followed with the first sale of its mortgage-backed security, the MBS, in 1981. An agency-issued (and guaranteed) mortgage-backed security eliminates many of the risks and lack of liquidity of a whole-loan mortgage. However, it does not mitigate against prepayment risk. More complicated forms of mortgage-derivative instruments, known as REMICs (formerly known as collateralized mortgage obligations or CMOs), can do this.

The first *whole-loan pass-through security* was issued by the Bank of America in 1977. Whole-loan pass-through securities are generally backed by loans that would otherwise meet an agency's underwriting criteria except for the fact that the loan amounts exceed the conforming loan maximum level (i.e., jumbo loans). *Private-label pass-throughs* are backed by conforming loans but issued by a nonagency dealer. In 1984, the first MBSs whose underlying assets were ARMs were issued by Fannie Mae. In that same year Fannie Mae began to issue pass-through MBSs backed by multifamily mortgages.

3. Why Securitize?

Why have an asset-backed security at all? The main reason is to enhance liquidity; individual loans are usually relatively illiquid, whereas a large denomination asset-backed security is a much more saleable financial instrument. This is especially true the more standardized the collateral supporting the security is. A mixture of homogeneous instruments is easier to price than a mixture of heterogeneous ones.

For example, the GSEs bundle together mortgages of similar types — adjustable-rate, fixed-rate, government-insured or conventional, single- and multifamily properties, rental properties, variable-rate mortgages based on the same index and with a synchronization of the re-set dates, 15- and 20-year mortgages vs. 30-year instruments, comparable age since origination date (referred to as the seasoning of the loan), balloon re-set liens, and so on. The goal is to create a pool of underlying whole loans as homogeneous as possible because this will minimize the spread in prepayment speeds and their changes over time. Alternatively, the diversification of some types of risk may be the goal. Hence, a pool of underlying mortgages may be from one lender or several lenders. Similarly, the whole loans may be from one geographic area or more widely dispersed.

Fannie Mae and Freddie Mac issue MBSs with a promise of timely payment of principal and interest (a *fully modified pass-through*). Freddie Mac's older pass-throughs only guaranteed the timely payment of interest (a *modified pass-through*). Because default risk is essentially eliminated for agency securities — for a small fee — and minimized for whole-loan instruments by some form of credit enhancement, the primary risks facing investors in MBSs are interest rate and prepayment risk. The latter is somewhat mitigated by using pools of homogeneous loan types and the belief that relying on the law of large numbers will produce statistically predictable prepayment rates.

Other aspects of guaranteed mortgage-backed securities make them attractive to certain classes of investors, especially those issued by Fannie Mae, Ginnie Mae, and Freddie Mac. As with Treasury instruments, the debt of Freddie Mac and Fannie Mae and their MBSs are permitted investments for federally supervised institutions and for fiduciary, trust, and public funds held or invested under the authority of the U.S. government. Moreover, both the debt and mortgage-backed securities can be purchased in unlimited amounts by national banks, federally charted credit unions, and federal savings and loan associations. Because of their tradeability and the surety of the agency's debt and MBSs, they may be counted as liquid assets for the liquidity requirements prescribed by the Office of Thrift Supervision for federal savings and loan associations (if their maturity is within 5 years). Moreover, the debt and MBSs guaranteed by these three are eligible for collateral for Federal Reserve and Federal Home Loan Bank advances. Finally, risk-based capital regulations of the bank and thrift regulators offer preferential treatment for agency mortgage-backed securities compared with investments in commercial loans, individual mortgages, or whole-loan MBSs.

Nonagency MBSs have much wider spreads in term-to-maturity, coupon rates, and so on than do the agency versions. For instance, a whole-loan pass-through MBS might mix 15- and 30-year liens together. In addition, whole-loan MBSs typically have external (i.e., private) insurance guarantees or internal credit enhancements to soothe the fears of investors with respect to default risk.

a. Exercise

1. Compute the price difference between a Fannie Mae MBS and a Freddie
    Mac PC Gold, everything else being equal, if you know that the Fannie
    Mae payment delay is 10 days longer than that of Freddie Mac. [PC =
    $(1 + i/12)^{1/3} \times MBS$]

4. More on the Benefits of Securitization

a. To Issuers

There are several benefits to issuers from the pooling together of whole loans into pass-through securities, including: 1. lower cost of monies, 2. greater diversification of funding sources, 3. more efficient use of their capital, 4. more flexible risk management tool to accommodate further portfolio growth, and 5. enhanced financial performance. By isolating illiquid, credit-poor assets and using them as collateral for a more liquid, credit-enhanced security, a lower cost of funding may be obtained. This is the case especially if the credit rating of the asset-backed security exceeds that of the institution performing the origination and wrapping of the individual loans into the asset-backed security.

By selling relatively risky whole-loan mortgages and purchasing them back in the form of relatively riskless MBSs from an agency conduit, a bank or thrift institution can significantly reduce its capital requirements. Note that this transaction is independent of who keeps the *servicing rights*, so the potential for fee-based income has not been lost. (The capital guideline requirements imposed by the various banking and insurance regulatory authorities tend to force their management to redirect assets into those providing the highest rate of return for the lowest capital set-aside. Capital requirements can also limit the amount of portfolio growth if that increase is concentrated in assets with high risk-based capital requirements. Securitization, with credit guarantees, alleviates this type of difficulty.)

b. To Lenders

In the U.S., when a savings bank or thrift institution originates a whole-loan mortgage, it basically has four choices of what to do with it:

1. It can retain the loan in its portfolio (and therefore on the balance sheet).
    Naturally, the institution also retains interest rate, credit, and prepayment
    risks associated with the mortgage. This gives the originating bank the
    benefit of a source of interest revenue and a cash flow stream from
    servicing fees. (The servicing rights associated with a mortgage may be
    bought and sold separately.) Also, a bank holding a whole loan on its
    balance sheet is disadvantaged in that it is subject to the previously
    mentioned risks and has diminished liquidity because it has used some
    of its deposits to fund the loan. It must also meet higher risk-based capital
    regulations than with a similar dollar amount of MBSs.

2. The cleanest alternative to holding the loan in the portfolio is its sale to a secondary market conduit; this means a vending of the entire mortgage loan (rather than of a participation interest). The lender's capital is replenished so that it can continue to originate new loans and generate additional fee-related income. Cash transactions also benefit the originator because of the multiple risk reductions as the asset is no longer on its balance sheet. Moreover, the originator can apparently expand its assortment of loan types because they they will be underwritten and purchased by the GSEs. Examples might include the more esoteric adjustable-rate or hybrid mortgage types, community lending products, those oriented to very-low income borrowers, and so forth. The assets kept on the balance sheet — typically floating-rate mortgages — can be more easily matched with the bank's usual liability alternatives — short-term deposits, certificates of deposit, and so forth.

3. The whole loan could be sold to a secondary market investor for the purpose of packaging it into a pool of loans. The more liquid security would then be purchased back by the originator and the MBS retained in its portfolio via a swap-and-hold transaction. For conforming loans the security is usually issued by one of the GSEs, thus removing the credit risk from the bank and leaving an asset on the bank's balance sheet that still has interest rate and prepayment risks. This enhances the lender's portfolio quality because the originator receives a lower risk weighting on the security over holding whole loans in its portfolio (20 vs. 50%). While earning interest from the MBS, the lender also receives cash flow from the servicing fee (or its present value because the servicing rights have been sold). Furthermore, borrowing capability has been enlarged since the MBS can be used as collateral to borrow from the Federal Reserve and its member banks. Finally, the bank now has a much more liquid security that can be easily sold.

4. The institution can sell it for the purpose of packaging into a pool of loans without keeping the resulting MBS on its balance sheet in a swap-and-sell transaction. In this instance, the bank no longer has any mortgage-related asset on its balance sheet or the bank receives and quickly sells the MBS to another investor. If the lender agrees to service the loans on behalf of the investor, then it will receive the servicing fee. The originator has shifted the credit risk to the conduit and the interest rate and prepayment risks to the investor. The only remaining risk to the loan originator is that the loan be priced to generate a profit.

c. To Investors

The mechanism of an asset-backed security provides liquidity where little existed before. By mixing many different, yet similar, loans, credit risk, geographic risk, and so on can be reduced. Default risk is ameliorated because it is usual to include a credit enhancement either in the form of a third-party guarantee or in the internal structure of the arrangement. Higher returns are available because of the efficiency of pooling transactions and other intermediate activities undertaken by the conduit.

Another advantage of the MBS markets is that a very wide range of retail products exists. Fifteen-, 20-, and 30-year fixed-rate, 30-year floating-rate, various hybrid types, government-guaranteed, and so on are all available to be pooled into MBSs or REMIC classes. This means that short-, intermediate-, and long-term financially engineered mortgage-backed securities may be carved out to satisfy investor demand. Hence, investor requirements with respect to interest rate and prepayment risk can be met by the various classes of a REMIC (see the next chapter).

5. From the Originator to the Conduit

The mortgage pipeline of a mortgage lender includes all loans that are currently in process, are approved but have not yet closed, or have been closed but not yet profitably sold. *Pipeline risk* is the risk that some or all of these mortgages will not close or be sold. Fluctuations in interest rates will change the volume of loan originations as well as loan sales to third parties.

Fallout risk refers to the possibility that the consumer might not close on his approved loan application. Because many lenders sell forward the mortgages they originate to minimize their interest rate risk, this is a hazard for them. For instance, they may have promised to deliver $1 million (face value) of mortgages at 7.75% 60 days from now. If their delivery is short in amount, then the lender will have to make up the deficiency by purchasing whole loans in the secondary market or suffer an agreed-upon penalty. In either case, the lender will lose money relative to the successful closing of the approved loan applications. The opposite of fallout risk is *investor fallout* which refers to the possibility that the counterparty to the forward sale will renege. This will tend to happen in a rapidly rising interest rate environment because of the decrease in value of the loans scheduled to be delivered at a fixed price.

The interest-rate risk associated with a mortgage pipeline is known as *price risk*. This risk affects any fixed-income instrument: when interest rates go up, the market value of the security goes down and vice versa. There is the possibility that interest rates will decrease in the interim, raising the market value of the mortgage. A lender promising a conduit a particular par dollar amount at a set interest rate will lose money with this state of affairs. The usual methods for *hedging* — forwards, futures, and options — are available for fallout and price risks. (Hedging refers to the practice of balancing one risk with another. It tends to lower yield on the average by reducing the possibility of large gains as well as large losses.) One of the difficulties of dealing with pipeline risk is that the combination of fallout risk and price risk produces an asymmetric distribution of risk with respect to declining market interest rates. Forwards, futures, and options typically only provide full protection when the risks are symmetrical.

Another less common risk is referred to as *product risk*. This is a risk factor created by a lender trying to induce a particular consumer to borrow by tailoring a mortgage to suit that individual's desires. Once the lien is nonstandard, its liquidity dramatically decreases and its eligibility for delivery to an established secondary market maker is problematic.

6. Private Conduits

Private conduits also purchase mortgages for the purpose of repackaging them and then selling them to fixed-income investors. Private conduits provide a secondary market in the nonconforming and *subprime* markets. Whole-loan conduits also specialize in transforming nonconforming mortgage loans (primarily jumbo) into whole-loan securities, dealing with loans from borrowers with less than A credit ratings (i.e., alternative A, A-, and the subprime market), home equity loans, second mortgages, home improvement loans, and so forth. Demand for whole-loan and private-label MBSs, as well as the complexity of their security structures, has significantly increased over the years.

B. OPERATIONAL ISSUES

1. Servicing

The process of performing the accounting and mechanical aspects of dealing with a homeowner's loan payments and forwarding them to the investor who actually owns the loan is known as servicing. The value of a servicing portfolio for residential mortgages ranges from 1 to 2.5% of the outstanding principal balance. Lenders can utilize this cash flow to manage their earnings and balance sheets; this will include the servicing fee and float earnings on principal, interest, and escrow deposits. Expenses will include the actual cost of performing the servicing function and the charges associated with preventing and then resolving delinquencies and defaults.

Because the outlay for originating a loan usually exceeds the value of servicing it, lenders that originate a loan and keep the servicing rights must recognize an immediate accounting loss. If the lender purchases the same servicing rights from another originator, then, because the accounting practice is to capitalize the purchase price and amortize the expense, the reported earnings are positive because the net servicing income exceeds the amortization expense. Servicing rights are economically equivalent to an *interest-only, stripped mortgage-backed security* with a low coupon rate (namely, 25 bp; see Chapter 6 for a fuller explanation).

The prices for servicing have varied greatly over the last decade. They change with the level of servicing fees, local mortgage origination rates, the characteristics of the loans serviced (especially fixed- vs. floating-rate or hybrid), and the requirements of the next investor. Also, at one time the prospect of cross-selling other services to a mortgagor was thought to represent a significant potential source of servicing-related income for banks.

2. To-Be-Announced Trading

A to-be-announced trade is one in which the specific pool of mortgages to be delivered in satisfaction of the trade is not known at the time the purchase agreement is made. To-be-announced (*TBA*) trading is the preferred mode for institutional investors who frequently buy and sell large dollar amounts of MBSs. In addition, MBSs sold in the forward market normally trade in a to-be-announced fashion. For example, a banker might use a forward MBS sale to hedge his mortgage pipeline's interest rate risk. TBA trading is essential to him since it is impossible to know beforehand which of the loans being processed will close and ultimately become part of the pool backing the trade. TBA trading allows loan originators to hedge their pipeline risk without the introduction of basis risk. Remember that basis risk refers to the fact that two similar quantities (e.g., the price of gold and silver, heating oil and West Texas Crude, 6-month LIBOR and 6-month U.S. Treasury interest rates) will not be perfectly correlated in their movements.

To-be-announced trades of agency pass-throughs settle monthly on a schedule set by the *Bond Market Association*. Monthly settlement is rational because *pool factors* are released near the beginning of each month and most mortgages pay on a monthly basis. (A pool factor is a decimal fraction representing the amount of outstanding principal still left in that pool and can only be known after the previous month's scheduled and unscheduled principal payments have been made. The market value of a pool is proportional to its outstanding principal balance.) Monthly settlement on a specific date, after the pool factors are known, facilitates the ability of dealers to package the securities they want to sell in advance. The larger the inventory of pools for sale is, the smaller the bid–ask spread and the more efficient the market.

To-be-announced conforming pools are dealt with on an equal basis which dramatically increases the liquidity of trading in agency MBSs. For a TBA trade the seller and the buyer agree to the type of security (e.g., traditional mortgages, underwritten by Freddie Mac), *the weighted average coupon*, the unpaid principal balance of the pool, the price, and the settlement date, for example, a 7.5% Freddie. However, exactly which 7.5% Freddie Mac pool is not specified. The thought behind TBA trading is that any particular agency's pools are roughly equal with any other one issued by that agency (having fixed the weighted average coupon rate, product type, and allowing for seasoning). With this statistical sense of equality, all 7.5% Freddies are fungible, or interchangeable, allowing for the existence of a TBA market that, in turn, greatly adds liquidity to the entire secondary mortgage market. Investors in pass-throughs can participate in the to-be-announced market and utilize dollar rolls to fund portfolios or cover short positions. (A dollar roll is the mortgage industry's version of a repurchase agreement.)

The buyer pays when the trade is actually settled, so a seller who is late is responsible for accrued interest. If the seller is so late that settlement is beyond the *record date*, the last calendar day of the month for agency pass-through settlements, that month's proceeds from the security would be owed to the buyer too. While the buyer is waiting for the seller to deliver the pool, he can further profit by investing his funds in short-term vehicles.

Good delivery demands that, 2 days before the settlement date, the particular pool to be delivered be identified by the seller. This is known as *pool notification date* or *call-out date*. Good delivery also allows a slight variation in face value (± 0.1%; it was once 25 times higher). The Bond Market Association — the professional organization for fixed-income dealers and traders — specifies good delivery requirements for TBA pools that include the fact that each million dollars of face amount traded can be settled by delivering up to three pools. (Other rules are in effect too.) Agency pass-throughs are settled electronically by book-entry transfer. Ginnie Mae utilizes the Depository Trust Company and Participant Trust Company mechanism; Freddie Mac and Fannie Mae use *Fedwire* (an electronic data information exchange network maintained by the Federal Reserve Bank). Because of their heterogeneity, nonagency MBSs and REMICs do not trade on a to-be-announced basis. Each has a prospectus and settlement is done as outlined in that document. Standard settlement time for them is 5 business days.

a. More Details on TBA Trading

Because to-be-announced sellers have choices with respect to the makeup of collateral that can be delivered in satisfaction of the trade, one expects them to exploit them rationally. Sellers can under- or overdeliver by $\pm 0.01\%$ — and will do so depending on which way market interest rates have gone between the time the trade agreement was executed and the pool is delivered. If rates have dropped (prices increased), then the TBA seller will underfill the commitment and sell any residual loans at the higher price. Conversely, if rates have risen (prices have dropped), then the seller will overfill the commitment in order to benefit from the original higher price on the maximum amount of collateral. This is much less of an issue now that the tolerance has dropped from $10,000/$1 million dollars in 1998 to $1000/$1 million today. Finally, the dollar price paid is the product of the agreed upon price per million, the par value, and the pool factor. The accrued interest would be added to this.

In addition to taking advantage of delivery tolerances, the TBA seller has some choice over the makeup of the collateral backing the pool. This includes the range of coupon rates, maturities, average loan amounts, geographic dispersion, credit scores, and loan-to-value ratios. Each of these elements has some correlation with prepayment rates. Prepayment speeds can have a significant impact on the present value of an MBS, so sellers use their knowledge of the mortgages underlying the pool to their advantage. For example, a seller may create a pool with loan characteristics signifying higher than average prepayment rates — and a shorter than average duration — and use this pool to satisfy a TBA trade priced to an average duration. This seller might create a pool whose traits suggest lower than average prepayment speeds and choose to hold and then sell this pool as a specified pool to gain from the higher expected duration.

b. ARM TBA Trading

TBA trading occurs in generic traditional conforming pools and a TBA market exists in new production ARM pass-throughs. In general, only the most homogeneous of these agency ARM-backed MBSs trade with small bid–ask spreads in the TBA market. For similar reasons, these pools are less expensive to use to obtain financing in the dollar roll market (see below). In the past, Ginnie Mae ARM MBSs have been the favored security. As with fixed-rate MBSs, there is also *specified pool trading* with larger bid–ask price spreads than for the generic collateral.

3. Specified Pool Trading

An alternative to TBA trading is a specified pool arrangement. With this type of transaction detailed information is available to the buyer about the composition of the collateral backing the specific pool, the weighted average coupon and maturity, the geographic dispersion (or lack thereof) of the loans underlying the pool, the average outstanding loan balance, the original and current balances, the prepayment history, and the *CUSIP number*. (CUSIP is an acronym for the number, actually alphanumeric string, assigned by the Committee of Uniform Security Identification Procedure. Each security is given a unique CUSIP number.) Private-label and whole-loan issues normally include additional information, such as average credit scores, which adds to the investor's theoretical ability to price an MBS more realistically. Specified pools invariably cost more than a generic, or TBA, pool. Buyers of specified pools are usually long-term institutional investors.

4. Dollar Rolls

The mortgage securities market has a form of repurchase agreement known as a dollar roll. It is a collateralized form of short-term financing. In the repo market the securities are generally U.S. Treasury instruments; however, in this market the collateral is mortgage-backed securities. Just as the repurchase agreement market provides dealers with a liquid and flexible tool for managing temporary supply and demand imbalances in the Treasury market, the dollar roll market serves the same functions in the MBS markets. Because mortgages tend to be sold forward to manage pipeline risk, dollar rolls allow dealers a mechanism to smooth out supply and demand pressures.

The dollar roll and repo markets differ in that the former agrees to repurchase "substantially identical" securities, not the identical ones. Hence, the investor rolling over his collateral assumes *delivery* risk at the end of the roll period. In return for this right and the flexibility with respect to hedging, the dealer will offer the investor a borrowing rate from a few basis points to several percentage points below current repurchase agreement market rates. A second big difference between the repurchase agreement and dollar roll markets is that cash flows stemming from the securities go to the temporary holders. For MBSs this includes scheduled and unscheduled principal payments. Clearly, this complicates the pricing further.

There are also rules about what types of MBSs are allowed as collateral. Specifically:

1. They must be backed by similar mortgages, e.g., one- to four-family residential mortgages.
2. They must be issued by the same agency and be part of the same program.
3. They have the same original stated maturity.
4. They have identical coupon rates.
5. They must be priced to have similar market yields.
6. They must satisfy good delivery requirements, i.e., the aggregate principal amounts of the securities delivered and received back must be within 2.5% of the initial amount delivered.

These rules are specified by the Bond Market Association (*BMA*). The dollar roll market has no haircut; the investor obtains full market price. Finally, to minimize problems from fails and the accounting necessary to deal with the extra cash flows that MBSs have that Treasury instruments do not, most dollar rolls are transacted close to the monthly settlement date for these types of mortgage-backed securities. More on this and the following subjects can be found in Carlson and Tierney (1995).

a. The True Cost of Funds

Because of the difference between the repo market and the dollar roll market with respect to who gains from intermediate cash flows, when calculating the actual cost of funds obtained through a dollar roll, several vital factors should be considered. These include:

1. The price of securities sold vs. the price of the securities repurchased. (When the yield curve is upwardly sloping, the *cost of carry* is positive; hence, the repurchase price will be lower than the original purchase price. The *drop* is the difference between the initial and ending prices plus the difference between the dealer's bid–ask prices.)
2. The amount of the coupon payments.
3. The expected amount of principal payments, both prepayments and scheduled amortization.
4. The attributes of securities rolled in vs. those rolled out. (This refers to their seasoning, *burnout* level, WAC vs. current coupon rates, and so forth.)
5. The delivery tolerances. (Both parties can over- or under-deliver within 2.5% of the face amount.)

Each one of these details introduces a risk–reward opportunity for the party or the counterparty to the dollar-roll transaction. A price risk is associated with possible changes in interest rates over the term of the roll and there is prepayment risk because faster or slower prepayments than expected will reward one or the other party to the arrangement. Every characteristic defining the MBS has an associated risk because only substantially identical securities must be returned. This is compounded by the delivery tolerances.

b. The Drop

The price of an MBS declines incrementally in each successive forward delivery month. This phenomenon, known as the drop, is a consequence of the difference between short- and long-term interest rates. The more positive the tilt of the yield curve, the greater the amount of the drop. The logic is that, during the 1-, 2-, or 3-month period between the agreement to sell a whole loan and the date of settlement, a forward seller could borrow the monies to finance the purchase of the liens to fulfill the forward sale agreement. Since the funds are borrowed for a short term, the interest rate should be a short-term one. At the same time, the asset being financed, because of its longer time-to-maturity, is priced to earn a long-term yield. Therefore, assuming a positively sloping yield curve (i.e., long-term rates higher than short-term ones), earnings on the mortgages held for a few months will exceed their cost of short-term financing. Market equilibrium demands that the theoretical price drop will equal the difference between the interest earnings on the home loans and the borrowing costs to finance holding them during the commitment period.

c.   Break-Even Analysis

An assessment of the relative value of dollar rolls should include the interrelated factors of alternative financing costs (such as the 1-month repo rate), the size of the drop, and the expected prepayment rate of the pass-through. For example, the size of the drop and the expected prepayment rate determine an implied repo rate for the dollar roll transactions. If the market rate is above this level, then dollar rolls make economic sense.

Alternatively, combining a desired financing rate with an expected prepayment speed can determine the break-even level for the drop. If the offered drop is larger than the break-even level, then a dollar roll makes economic sense. However, this is still subject to considerable uncertainty from other factors, namely, that the characteristics of the pass-throughs to be returned are not known. Just as with MBSs and their pricing, dollar rolls based on current coupon MBSs have little sensitivity to prepayments, whereas those utilizing discounts or premiums are more vulnerable to prepayment rates. For instance, an increase in prepayment speed will force the implied financing rate down when using a premium security. Clearly, the opposite occurs for a discount security.

d.   Mortgage Swaps

A *mortgage swap* is an asset-backed swap between two counterparties based on the cash flows and performance of a pool of mortgages. It is economically equivalent to borrowing funds at LIBOR (plus or minus a spread) and investing in a pool of mortgages. Thus, it is a synthetic, leveraged position on the mortgages underlying the MBS.

C. STATISTICS THAT CHARACTERIZE MBSS

1.   The (Gross) Weighted Average Coupon

The most important numerical parameter used to describe an MBS is the (gross) *WAC*, or weighted-average coupon. This quantity is the unpaid principal balance weighted average of the coupon rates on the underlying whole loans. The net (average) coupon, or pass-through rate of an MBS, is lower than this by the amount of the servicing and guarantee fees. The pass-through rate is the interest rate actually earned by the investor. The WAC changes over time as prepayments, curtailments, and defaults occur. The WAC and, especially its dispersion, determine the rate of prepayments over the life of an MBS.

If T is the total number of months the pass-through will be outstanding and I_m is the pass-through rate on the mth loan, of which there are M, then the formula for the WAC is

$$\text{WAC} = \sum_{t=1}^{T} \sum_{m=1}^{M} I_m \times (\text{Total Principal})_{mt} \Big/ \sum_{s=1}^{T} (\text{Total Principal})_s$$

The quantity (Total Principal)$_{mt}$ is the total of scheduled and unscheduled principal payments from mortgage #m in month #t;

$$(\text{Total Principal})_s = \sum_{m=1}^{M} (\text{Total Principal})_{ms}$$

2. The Weighted Average Maturity

The second most important quantity of an MBS is the *WAM* (weighted average maturity) or the *WAL* (*weighted average life*). These are identical and are the time-weighted average of the principal amounts on the underlying mortgages. The WAM is measured in months. Observe that a present value is not used in its computation (nor in that for the WAC), i.e.,

$$\text{WAM} = \sum_{t=1}^{T} t \times (\text{Total Principal})_t / \sum_{s=1}^{T} (\text{Total Principal})_s$$

The WAM is normally used to indicate the remaining maturity of the mortgages comprising a pool. Theoretically, the WAM equals the pool's term minus its age. If, in fact, all the loans in a pool have the same age, then this relationship will hold true. The WAM is not the average number of months to the pool's *stated maturity date* because of the use of outstanding principal weighting in its computation. The stated maturity date is the last possible date for the receipt of cash flows from the home loans in this pool. The agencies update the WAM of each pool on a monthly basis.

One major difference between agency and nonagency pools is the homogeneity of the former with respect to original term in comparison to the latter. Hence, the WAM is a less precise concept for nonagency MBSs. A WAM of 352 months for a pool known to contain a significant proportion of 20-year liens in addition to traditional mortgages does not necessarily imply 8 months since origination. One would need to know the exact percentage of the shorter-term loans in the mixture to make a more meaningful interpretation of the WAM for prepayment purposes.

a. Exercise

1. Suppose you have a portfolio consisting of five mortgages with face unpaid balances of $123,456, $234,567, $345,678, $98,765, and $87,654 with corresponding yields of 11.11, 12.22, 13.33, 9.87, and 8.76%. Also, suppose that their remaining lifetimes are 333, 222, 111, 99, and 345 months. Compute the weighted average coupon and the weighted average maturity. (11.896%, 192.75 months)

b. The Weighted Average Remaining Maturity

The *weighted average remaining maturity* (WARM) is the weighted average remaining term computed as the number of months to the stated maturity date. On the issue date, the WAM will equal the WARM.

3. The Weighted Average Loan Age

The *WALA*, or *weighted average loan age*, is a better measure of the mean life of a mortgage-backed security than the WAM is because it tracks the lives of the individual underlying mortgages in the pool. The WALA is the best indicator of the seasoning, or aging, of the pool. The WALA is the weighted average number of months since the date of note origination of the mortgages in a pass-through. The weighting is also by principal amount and not discounted. The WALA and WAM are prepayment-, curtailment-, and default-dependent and they change over time other than 1:1 with the passage of time. An approximation to the WALA is the average original term of the pool of mortgages minus the WAM.

a. The Calculated Loan Age

The *calculated loan age* (CAGE) is an estimate of the WALA ignoring the difference between the date of mortgage origination and the *issue date*. The issue date is the date of issuance of the pool of mortgages backing the MBS, not the dates of origination of the mortgages comprising the pool. That is, it is computed as the maximum maturity date minus the remaining term. Hence, a pool backed with traditional mortgages and with a WARM of 335 months would be assumed to have an age of 25 months (= 360 − 335). Note the surmise that the pool is completely homogeneous with respect to maturity. In addition, because the WARM is not a chronological measure affected by prepayments, curtailments, and default levels, this result could be misleading.

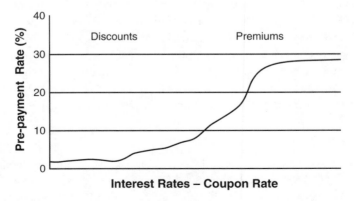

FIGURE 5.1 The prepayment ess (S) curve showing the dependence of the conditional prepayment rate on the difference between market rates and the note rate of mortgages.

4. WAC Dispersion Effects

The GSEs make considerable efforts to pool together homogeneous whole loans to underpin their MBSs. The rationale is that investors will have fewer problems in computing prepayment rates and their rates of change for similar liens than they would have if the underlying loans were more heterogeneous. The agencies can do this because of their great size and the large number of mortgages they have available to form pools. These degrees of freedom are not always present in the nonconforming markets. Hence, the potential investor in a whole-loan or private-label security should be aware of this possibility and understand how it might affect performance and valuation.

Specifically, it is the (gross) weighted-average coupon on a pool that determines that pool's prepayment characteristics rather than the yields on any particular pass-through coupon or REMIC class. As a simple example of the hidden aspects of WAC dispersion, consider two pass-through securities, A and B, with the same pass-through rate (8.5%/year) and the same gross WAC. Suppose further that A is backed by 9.0%/year loans (remember the servicing and guarantee fees) while B is backed by a 50%–50% mixture of 8.5 and 9.5% loans. Suppose interest rates first rise and then fall. As the refinancing rate drops toward 9%/year, the security labeled B will start to experience interest-rate related prepayments while the one labeled A will not. If market rates drop further, B's prepayment rate will rapidly increase while that of A will only grow slowly. Finally, if market rates stall at 8.5%/year or just below that level, then the refinancing rate of B's underlying mortgages will drop to nearly zero because those who could have refinanced will have done so, while that of A's will remain steady.

Dealers and others who actively trade in MBSs speak of the *prepayment S curve*; that is, the shape of the curve of prepayment rate vs. the spread between the contract rate and the prevailing refinancing rate. It has a shape like the letter "S" (see Figure 5.1). When the refinancing rate exceeds the coupon rate, the prepayment level is low, rising slowly as the two rates converge, and continuing to rise rapidly as the two rates diverge with the opposite sign (i.e., market rate less than coupon rate). Eventually, prepayment activity saturates and the curve levels off, hence the S-like shape. The curve bends over at its point of inflection (and not cusp).

5. WAM Dispersion Effects

The weighted average life, weighted average maturity, and weighted average remaining maturity nominally alter at the rate of a month-per-month passage of calendar time. They will shorten faster than this because of prepayments, curtailments, or defaults. An MBS priced at a discount, whose weighted average life shortens, will have a higher than anticipated yield because the principal is returned at par more quickly than expected. Conversely, the yield will decrease on the same kind of security if prepayments slow down and its weighted average life extends (i.e., decreases more slowly than one month-per-month passage of actual time). Moreover, the investor has a reduced amount of funds, relative to what was envisioned, to devote to now higher-paying fixed-income investment opportunities.

Naturally, all this is reversed if the MBS has been priced at a premium to par. What happens to the spread, or difference, between comparable duration U.S. Treasury instrument if investors foresee that discount MBSs will extend or that premium-priced pass-throughs will contract in weighted average life? The spread will narrow because the mortgage-related securities are then performing worse than predicted.

The potential heterogeneous nature in weighted average maturity of a whole-loan security can also have a forceful effect on prepayments. Because most mortgages are not *assumable* and the majority of homeowners will not quickly move once in their new house, a short WAM REMIC class will have very low initial prepayment rates. Seasoned pools, everything else being equal, will have higher refinancing or house payoff rates. The longer the WAM is, the higher the potential yield on a premium security and the lower the potential yield on a discount instrument. The reason is that, for a premium security, the WAM will shorten with the passage of time because the longer maturity loans outstanding in the underlying pool will be refinanced more quickly than the shorter maturity loans in the same pool and principal is returned at par.

6. Bond-Equivalent Yield and Mortgage-Equivalent Yield

Several derived parameters of an MBS are used to infer risk and reward; foremost is yield. Mortgages usually pay monthly while the standard (U.S.) bond pays semi-annually. Therefore, a person needs to be able to convert one yield into the other to appreciate, in a quantitative fashion, the difference that the monthly reinvestment opportunities allow. If y_m is the annual yield on a mortgage, then its annual bond-equivalent yield y_b, is given by

$$y_b = 2 \times [(1 + y_m/12)^6 - 1].$$

This computation does not fully account for the amortizing nature of a home loan.

The inverse relationship provides the *mortgage-equivalent yield (MEY)* in terms of the bond-equivalent yield (BEY);

$$y_m = 12 \times [(1 + y_b/2)^{1/6} - 1].$$

a. Numerical Examples

1. Suppose that the pass-through rate to the investor on an MBS is quoted as 7%/year. What rate must one earn on a bond for the bond's yield to be comparable, given that the monthly mortgage-backed security payments can be invested before the first semiannual bond interest payment is received? ($y_b = 7.103\%$/year)
2. If $y_b = 8.5\%$/year, show that MEY = $y_m = 8.353\%$/year.

When one writes of yield one really should be talking about the risk–reward tradeoff. The spread between a generic, current coupon, pass-through security and its comparable duration U.S. Treasury security is not constant over time. Investors are subject to fads and fashions. Some investments come into or go out of favor and the yields on them decrease or increase owing to demand and supply pressure. This is seen frequently in the U.S. Treasury market whenever some geo-political/military/economic event of concern occurs. In a flight-to-quality, fixed-income investors sell in order to purchase risk-free, U.S. Treasury Bills, Notes, or Bonds denominated in U.S. dollars.

More subtle than market mortgage rates rapidly rising or falling are the effects of the shape of the yield curve. Although we have not yet discussed it in detail, today's yield curve is not just a plot of spot rates vs. time. (Actually, it is just that but additional, hidden information is in the graph.) Precisely because quantitatively accurate interest rate prediction is impossible, many of those who deal in the mortgage markets make the assumption that today's (implied) 1-year forward rate, for example, will actually be realized 1 year from now as the then current 1-year spot rate. Moreover, almost certainly whatever interest rate model they are using to forecast interest rates or an assortment of future interest rate scenarios is based on today's yield curve and has been required to match it on the average without arbitrage opportunities. This process builds in the expectation that forward rates will be realized as spot rates in the future. Thus, the shape of the contemporary yield curve has influence in the behavior of market participants via their pricing models.

7. More on Risks and Pricing

Mortgage-backed securities are asset-backed securities whose collateral is home loans. Therefore, the issuance of new MBSs is highly dependent on the origination rate for whole loan mortgages. In turn, this rate is determined by the macroeconomic environment in the U.S., demographic and immigration trends, and the level and direction of market interest rates. With a higher level of issuance of new pass-through securities, the spread between the rate of return on these instruments and other, comparable duration, fixed-income securities tends to widen. Conversely, when the supply of new MBSs is lower, then the interest rate differential tends to lessen. These are basic supply and demand effects. One of the chief supply and demand effects influencing the interest rate spreads between MBSs and other fixed-income instruments is the activities of Fannie Mae and Freddie Mac on behalf of their own asset portfolios. The reason is simple: together they hold approximately one-third of the outstanding conforming MBSs and their mortgage investment portfolios have doubled in size in the last few years.

8. GSE Activities

Freddie Mac and Fannie Mae fund their mortgage portfolios with debt (as opposed to owner's equity). Sensibly, much of it is American-style callable to match the prepayment options in conventional whole loans (about 80 and 50%, respectively). These agencies earn most of their net income from the interest rate differential between the revenue received on their assets and their cost of funds. Therefore, they are always looking to take advantage of favorable opportunities in the fixed-income/MBS/interest rate swap markets. Because agency purchases of MBSs depend on their asset–liability interest rate spread, any widening or narrowing in these differences is likely to lead to increased or reduced purchases of MBSs as they try to maximize their profits. This increase or reduction in demand will reduce or increase supply for the rest of the market and drive prices upward or downward, resulting in narrower or wider MBS spreads to other fixed-income investment opportunities.

There is a newer, less obvious, factor at work with respect to Freddie Mac and Fannie Mae and their historical funding practices. Both of the agencies have recently tried to market their debt as substitutes for U.S. Treasury debt. This process was initiated during that brief window of time when fools predicting a 10-year glut of funds for the federal government abounded. This would have caused an absence of sufficient amounts of U.S. government debt to satisfy U.S. dollar-tropic foreign investors and resulted in a potential disintermediation of funds outside the U.S. debt markets. Who better than the GSEs to step in and fill the role that the U.S. government's outstanding debt would have played if it had been issued? Hence, the Fannie Mae Benchmark Note™ and Freddie Mac Reference Note™ programs evolved.

These modes of raising funds are explicitly designed to mimic U.S. Treasury activities with respect to a fixed calendar of issuance, the large amounts sold at auction to ensure liquidity, a high level of investor contact presale, and so forth. As the agencies combine more and more of the other debt issuance programs into these two in order to provide stability and liquidity to investors, their freedom of action to raise debt when they need it, want it, or the market is particularly receptive to it may decline. To further place this in perspective, by the end of 2001, Freddie Mac and Fannie Mae were collectively issuing more new debt than the U.S. government was.

II. PREPAYMENTS

A. EDITORIAL

Prepayment models are based on historical data and past financial circumstances, not those about to occur. A tremendous difference exists between trying to model the past and trying to predict the future with any degree of repeatable quantitative accuracy. To try to keep the models up to date, one might weigh the data by the passage of time; this will introduce statistical noise as the number of observations with significant weight becomes fewer. Model error will produce duration error, which will hurt those practicing duration-matching techniques or index performance-based investment strategies. Structural changes in the mortgage market, for example, the no-fee, no-point mortgage, automated underwriting, a large spike in the U.S. population, and so forth, will, per force, be completely missed by any extant prepayment model.

Other effects make the prediction of prepayments a dynamic enterprise, which make me shy away from trying to convince you that anybody knows how to model prepayments well. A dramatic change in the amount and quality of economic information in our daily lives has taken place over the last decade, as well as a spectacular transformation in the processing speed of consumer financial transactions. Moreover, investment knowledge available to the average person has also grown impressively.

Consider the demise of the efficacy of the Sunday newspaper's table of current mortgage rates. Today, that list is out of date before it is compiled. Gone are the days of calling all the savings banks in the (local!) Yellow Pages® to find the best interest rate and knowing that, over the day or two (or three) it took you to fulfill that chore, all the rates would still be there when you went back to the bank of your choice. Today rates come out daily. They can change hourly. You can turn your television to CNBC or the Financial News Network or some other source of up-to-date rate information. Mortgage and other interest rates are freely available over the World Wide Web from a variety of sources. Also, mortgage lending is now national; one can easily obtain a quote for a mortgage from dozens of lenders via toll-free telephone numbers. (What is amazing is how different they can be for the same loan.) The advent, and now domination, of the marketplace by automated underwriting has also been a major event.

Very few people foresaw this mixture of disparate factors in 1990, let alone their cumulative effect on the mortgage underwriting (and hence the refinancing) business. The tremendous and rapid consolidation of mortgage originators, mortgage lenders, and mortgage servicers in the 1990s, the Herculean efforts of Freddie Mac and Fannie Mae to expand homeownership, the doubling in size of their investment portfolios in the last few years, and the dramatic surge in the U.S. population point to higher origination rates and a real cheapening of refinancing. I do not know what will happen in the first decade of this century. However, you should assume that at least some of these developments will markedly change prepayment patterns yet again in unforeseeable ways in the search for market share or revenue, through the harnessing of technology, and via the utilization of the expanding communications media or financial engineering.

The discussion presented next is a broad overview of the factors determining the *post facto* principal prepayment risks for mortgage-backed securities. This is not a discussion of prepayment modeling or (what would be much better and useful) of quantitatively meaningful prepayment prediction. The reason is simple: by far the dominant factor in changing prepayment rates is the difference between the coupon rate on the extant mortgage and current interest rates for similar types of mortgages. Therefore, to predict prepayment rates accurately, one must be able, at least, to predict interest rates unerringly. That is hopeless to accomplish with any level of numerical correctness or frequency of meaningful repeatability.

Having gotten that off my chest, four major reasons behind the decision of consumers to refinance an outstanding mortgage are discussed in turn next.

B. OVERVIEW OF PREPAYMENTS

1. Definition

One way to characterize prepayments is that they are the result of: 1. normal housing turnover, 2. refinancing currently owned homes, and 3. prepayments induced by life events such as family formation or expansion, disease, unemployment, disability, divorce, retirement, or death. The most important factor affecting the change in principal prepayment speeds is the course and level of market rates since the origination of the lien. In the past, if market interest rates dropped by more than 100 to 200 basis points, then it made economic sense for the mortgagor to refinance the loan. This means that a new mortgage loan is applied for and, if the mortgagor and the property pass the underwriting standards of the issuing institution, granted. The proceeds from the new instrument are used to pay off the extant one and it and its future cash flows cease to exist.

a. Interest Rate Effects

In the "old" days (pre-1995 and the advent of automated underwriting), refinancing a mortgage was a time-consuming, expensive, and unpleasant process. Hence, the reward to endure it had to be relatively great. The present value of the interest savings needed to exceed the costs of going through the refinancing process. For those who thought in a break-even mode, at a minimum, the expenditures connected with the transaction need to be paid off by the savings from the diminished monthly payment well before any projected sale date of the property.

Today, with automated underwriting, refinancing a mortgage can be fairly quick and inexpensive (no fees, no points), but still an unpleasant experience. A 50 to 75 basis point drop in mortgage rates is enough to ignite a mini-refinancing boom. Thus, the foremost indicator of the prepayment likelihood on a mortgage-backed security is the difference between its weighted average coupon and current mortgage rates. When market interest rates are below those on people's home loans, then the prepayment option in their mortgages will be in-the-money and it may be economically rational for them to exercise their call option. Conversely, when market interest rates are above those on current mortgages, then the prepayment option in the mortgage is out-of-the-money and it is not economically rational to exercise the embedded call option (which does not mean that people will not).

2. Other Factors

Three other important factors influence altering mortgage prepayment speeds: seasoning, burnout, and *seasonality*. Seasoning refers to the aging of a mortgage from its date of origination. The events of default, moving, or economically based refinancing are relatively rare in the months following the closing of a loan. As time goes on, these start to play a larger role. Defaults on adjustable-rate mortgages can abruptly increase if interest rates are sharply rising. In general, prepayment and default rates rapidly swell in the first years after origination of the loan, increasing roughly linearly with the passage of time. (Remember that a default to an investor in an agency-issued MBS appears as a prepayment because the agency has guaranteed the timely payment of interest and principal.) The standard formula for the *conditional prepayment rate* reaches a plateau level of 6%/year on the outstanding principal balance after 2 1/2 years. Much higher, up to ten times faster, prepayment rates have been experienced during refinancing booms.

As seasoning occurs, the result is to saturate the prepayment rate after a few years. The speed at which this occurs, coupled with the interest rate environment that prevailed during this time span, can greatly diminish the future uncertainty regarding prepayments from this pool. Hence, a positively convex, or highly seasoned, pool is especially valuable and commands a premium price. The reason is that it now behaves much more like a fixed-rate, amortizing bond than a call option-embedded mortgage. Furthermore, the longer the time period since origination, the more probable that one or more favorable refinancing opportunities have occurred for those willing and able to take advantage of them. Mortgagors whose home loans remain in the pool, for whatever reasons, have not refinanced and are moderately unlikely to do so, almost independently of the course of future market interest rates.

Delinquencies and defaults tend to lessen over the time since origination because the homeowner can actually afford this mortgage. Assuming that they had a fixed-rate mortgage, a rising real income (perhaps via a promotion, a different job at a higher salary, or just income raises) has made their constant monthly payment more affordable and debt-to-income ratios are now more comfortably within the nominal ranges. This propensity to succeed at homeownership is typically aided by the general price increase that housing usually experiences. The usual elevation in housing prices drops the current loan-to-value ratio, thereby augmenting the homeowner's amount of equity in his property. If the worst should occur, selling the real estate and retaining any leftover cash is much better than defaulting would be.

A few years after the issuance of an MBS defaults and prepayments tend to stabilize, especially after the first good opportunity to refinance has come and gone. This phenomenon is known as burnout. If rates have dipped by 75 to 100 bp more than once below the coupon rate on one's mortgage and one has not refinanced, then one is increasingly unlikely to do so during future interest rate downturns. Reasons for not refinancing can range from a decrease in credit rating to a decrease in market value of the home to other personal financial problems.

Burnout can be viewed as an alteration in the composition of the mortgages underlying an MBS. As time goes on, those capable and willing to refinance do so. Those who cannot qualify for refinancing and those who are about to move will not do so based on interest rate considerations. Some homeowners may be so enamored of their original mortgage origination process that they choose not to repeat it. Finally, replacing a 5-year–old, 7.5%/year traditional mortgage with a new one at 6.5% does not, in fact, lower the total present value of the interest payments (assuming the debt is held to maturity).

Few homeowners know how or care to perform a full present value analysis, including the complications of federal income taxes, or the potential savings from various mortgage products, especially those with an array of interest buy-down opportunities by paying points. At most, one can expect a simplistic break-even analysis. Thus, a continuum of homeowners on the verge of refinancing will exist because the net present value of their embedded option is just coming into-the-money (in their view). Many will wait until the break-even analysis results look compelling, which depends on their federal tax bracket, income level, cash reserves, tolerance for debt, and so forth.

Superimposed on the background level of refinancing resulting from interest rate decreases is a noticeable seasonable pattern referred to as seasonality. The school year commences in late August or early September. Parents prefer to have their children settled in their new home and school classroom at the beginning of the school year rather than upset things in the midst of it. Therefore, home sales increase starting in the early spring and reach a peak in the late summer. This leads to a swelling of prepayments beginning in the late spring and ending in the early fall as the closings occur and settlements are completed. In the winter housing turnover reaches its minimum late in the season. This seasonal pattern is predictable in timing and magnitude — one of the few things about prepayments, beyond the underlying mobility level of the American population, that is.

a. The Effect of Curtailments

The cash flow from curtailments does affect the prepayment speed on a pool of mortgages. Curtailments tend to be quite small during the early years after origination of the loans, 1% or less, than prepayments in dollar amount. However, because of the amortizing nature of mortgages, curtailments early in the life of a pool affect the eventual amount of interest revenue to be received by an investor most. There is a different, much smaller in amplitude, periodic pattern, in curtailments too. Peaks in January and in April and May are presumably attributable to year-end salary bonuses and income tax returns, respectively, applied to the outstanding mortgage balances. Finally, there is generally an upsurge in prepayments near the end of the life of mortgages as homeowners prepay their outstanding principal balance to be freed of the tyranny of their monthly payments. This is, of course, an economically ridiculous thing to do.

Together, the effects of interest rates, seasoning, burnout, and seasonality account for the huge majority of changing prepayment behavior. Note that only one is connected to a macroeconomic variable. Mortgages may also be prepaid to the MBS investor because of default by the borrower (on insured or guaranteed mortgages).

3. Does Better Analysis Imply Better Prediction?

Today much more loan-level information is available than in the past. One can now combine these more detailed and complete data with census bureau information, commercial real estate data banks containing housing price appreciation, housing turnover rates, and so on — at least by postal zip code if not block by block within an urban zip code. Joining this information base in an intelligent manner, with correctly applied and interpreted powerful statistical analysis tools made possible by today's tremendous computing power, might make one believe that a much more thorough investigation of prepayments than has been done before can be accomplished now. Although this is all true, it does not follow that the prediction of prepayment speeds will be any better for newly issued pools of mortgages.

This is only part of the story of the new era of prepayment modeling. In addition to reams of raw data on relevant loan- and real estate-related financial information, there are also detailed regional econometric models available. These would purport to foretell the economic future of a metropolitan statistical area. Combining such a model with the real estate specific information and a more general model of interest rate prophecy, one might actually be able to convince oneself that realistic prepayment predictions at the micro-level is possible. Unless your model also predicts, by county, the significant downturn in Boeing's business, and its effect on Seattle after September 11, or the failure of Enron, and its effect on Houston in early 2002, then all this machinery is relatively useless and dangerously mis-leading for a portfolio manager. How good was your weatherman's last forecast? How good was it ten years ago?

What I would expect is, that if all this data fusion and detailed examination is carried out on pools as they season, then one could more realistically speculate about the future course of prepayments from a given pool. When successful this would make specified pool trading more of a science than an art with a stratification in prices driven by those with the capability to better successfully guess at future performance.

C. PREPAYMENT MATHEMATICS

1. The Single Monthly Mortality Rate

Single monthly mortality is used to compute the expected amount of unscheduled principal returned on a monthly basis. If the single monthly mortality is denoted by s, then the expected prepayment amount for the nth month, PP_n, is given by

$$PP_n = s \times (UPB'_{n-1} - P_n)$$

where UPB'_n is the unpaid principal balance at the end of the nth month, given that prepayments, curtailments, or defaults may have occurred in the past (i.e., $UPB'_n <$ UPB_n where the latter was defined in Equation 4.5).

a. Prepayment Speed Details

The single monthly mortality rate s measures the amount of scheduled and unscheduled principal payments during 2 consecutive months. For MBSs, the amount of principal outstanding is given by their pool factor. The pool factor for any month (PF_t for month #t) is the remaining unpaid principal balance at the end of month #t divided by the initial principal balance for this pool. It will be less than that from the previous month by the amount of scheduled and unscheduled principal repayments, curtailments, and defaults. The single monthly mortality rate (sometimes denoted by SMM) is the ratio of two successive *survival factors*. The survival factor for the t'th month, SF_t, is the ratio of the current pool factor to the amortization factor at the end of that month. The latter is computed from Equation 4.3, where i is the annual coupon rate on the mortgage and N is the total number of payments to be made, i.e.,

$$AF_t = 1 - [(1 + i/12)^t - 1]/[(1 + i/12)^N - 1].$$

The amortization factor for month t is the ratio of the current unpaid principal balance at the end of that month to the original unpaid principal balance, assuming only scheduled principal payments have been made. Therefore, the formula for SF_t is

$$SF_t = PF_t/AF_t.$$

The quantity $1 - SF_t$ equals the percentage of the initial unpaid principal balance paid at the end of month #t. Finally, the current value of the single monthly mortality rate is given by

$$s_t = 1 - SF_{t+1}/SF_t.$$

b.   Geometric Mean

Sometimes one wants an average value of the single monthly mortality rate covering many months. The correct way to compute it is via the geometric mean, i.e.,

$$(1 - s)^{n-m} = SF_n/SF_m.$$

2.   The Conditional Prepayment Rate

CPR stands for the conditional prepayment rate (not the constant prepayment rate). In contrast to the single monthly mortality rate, the CPR is an annual rate. If c is the symbol for the CPR, then the relationship between s and c is given by

$$s = 1 - (1 - c)^{1/12} \text{ and } c = 1 - (1 - s)^{12}.$$

a.   Numerical Example

The 1985 *PSA* (or *Public Securities Association*, the old name for the BMA) standard form for the time dependence of c is given, with t in months, by

$$c = 0.2 \times t\%/\text{year for } t \in [0,30] \text{ and } c = 6\%/\text{year for } t \in [30,360]. \qquad (5.1)$$

When the level of conditional prepayments equals its asymptotic value of 6%/year, the single monthly mortality rate is about one-half of 1%, s = 0.00514.

b.   Converting PSA Speeds to CPR

At saturation, 100% of PSA means a CPR of 6%/year on the outstanding principal balance. A CPR of 30%/year is five times higher than this and therefore corresponds to a 500% PSA rate. This simple proportionality holds true during the initial months as well when the PSA prepayment speed is increasing at its rate of 0.2%/month/year. Thus, 11 months into a pool's life (since origination), a CPR of 5.5% implies a multiple of the PSA rate by 2.5 times also. The mathematics underlying this is that the baseline rate at 11 months is 2.2%, a factor of 250% less than 5.5%/year.

c. The PSA Default Rate

The PSA standard default curve for the traditional mortgage, or the Standard Default Assumption (SDA) curve, is defined by the following (t is measured in months):

$$\text{Default Rate} = \begin{cases} 0.02\% \times t \,/\, \text{month for } t \in [1,30], \\ 0.60\% \,/\, \text{month for } t \in [30,60], \\ [0.60\% - 0.005\% \times (t-60)] \,/\, \text{month for } t \in [60,120], \\ 0.30\% \,/\, \text{month for } t \geq 120. \end{cases}$$

Note the low absolute values of the default rate compared to conditional prepayment rates. Thus, default effects on unscheduled principal payments are relatively minor, except in very bad economic circumstances.

D. MORE GENERALITIES ON PREPAYMENTS

1. Generalities

Jumbo loans are typically prepaid more rapidly than conforming loans are. These liens are for larger amounts so greater savings are to be garnered by refinancing. The people who have these mortgages also commonly have the cash to pay for closing costs, are financially sophisticated, and are up to date on current economic circumstances. Hence, whole-loan MBSs have a faster and different prepayment speed behavior than conforming or government liens.

There is another subtlety regarding agency prepayments and loan purpose that deserves mention. Purchase money loans, that is, borrowings made for the purpose of initially buying a property, generally prepay more slowly than loans taken out for the purpose of refinancing. Apparently, having gone through the refinancing experience results in more willingness to do so and an understanding of the potential monetary gains.

2. More on Prepayments

a. Mobility

Ours is a highly mobile society with the average family moving every 7 or 8 years. Somebody, somewhere in the U.S., is selling his current house and purchasing a new one. Such events represent prepayments for some mortgage investor. Almost all conforming (and government) mortgages now have a *due-on-sale provision*. This means that the mortgagor is required to pay off the outstanding debt fully when transferring the deed. Thus, the mobility of Americans and the resulting home sales accounts form a background, base rate, of prepayments independent of any other factor. A rate of 100 to 125% PSA seems to represent adequately the average value of mobility *per se*. (A 100% PSA level corresponds to a family moving once every 15 years or so.)

b.   The Effect of Interest Rate Differences

The response of homeowners to decreasing market interest rates is not instantaneous, so a delay must be built into prepayment models. The slowness to act allows the consumer to notice that interest rates have dropped and to make a decision about refinancing. He also must make an assessment regarding the drift of interest rates and for the underwriting and closing processes associated with refinancing to occur. The latter time is still a few weeks.

Another effect sometimes associated with changing interest rates is refinancing from a long-term instrument into a shorter-term vehicle. If interest rates drop and house prices have appreciated, then the monthly payment required of any new mortgage and the capability to qualify for a higher monthly payment will decrease because of an enhanced current loan-to-value ratio. (At least through about 75%; stratification in interest rates occurs with equity levels below this because cash-out refinancings are viewed as risky.). Thus, a traditional mortgage may be retired in favor of a 15- or 20-year substitute.

To make this concrete, consider a traditional $265,000 mortgage taken out 3 years and 10 months ago at 7.5%. Suppose that interest rates have dropped to 6.75% on 30-year loans but to 6.375% on 15-year loans. Furthermore, imagine that housing price inflation has been a robust 10%/year so that the property is now worth about $485,000 [$\cong$ ($265,000/0.8$) $\times$ 1.1^4]. As an added benefit for the current low loan-to-value ratio, the lender is offering a further $1/4$ point discount on the coupon rate. The new monthly payment on the 15-year mortgage will be about $2165 (coupon rate = 6 1/8%) compared to the old monthly payment of $1853. (The new UPB was about $254,560.)

The propensity to refinance into a shorter-term mortgage from a longer-term one is also propelled by steeper yield curves because a 15-year, fixed-rate mortgage will be priced off a shorter (i.e., lower) end of the yield curve than a traditional mortgage. Indeed, cash-out refinancings may predominate because consumers believe that they can make more on their built-up equity by investing it ways other than the real estate they live in than it will cost them to fund the source of monies. (Inventing stories to explain prepayment behavior may be fun and interesting but it will never lead to a better, quantitatively exact prepayment model.)

c.   Quarter Coupon MBSs

MBSs are mostly issued on the half percentage point. Thus, pass-through rates of 6.5%, 7%, 7.5%, and so on are the norm, while a *quarter-coupon MBS* — that is, a 6.75 or a 7.25% — is relatively rare. Although bunching current coupon issuances into half-coupon securities increases their liquidity, it can also hide the spread in the coupon rates of the loans underlying the MBS. (Remember that rates quoted to the consumer are in eighths of a point.) The operational pricing details of buying up or buying down the guarantee fees, or negotiating servicing fees, to fit neatly into these categories would take us too far afield.

3.   Government vs. Conforming MBSs

The prepayment speeds for Ginnie Mae loans are slower than those for Fannie Mae or Freddie Mac. FHA and VA mortgages were once assumable, meaning that the purchaser of a property with an FHA or VA lien on it could take over the existing mortgage if he desired to do so. However, if interest rates rise, the sale of such a home will not necessarily induce a prepayment event to the MBS holder. Also, because the maximum loan limits on FHA and VA mortgages are lower than those for Freddie Mac or Fannie Mae, the amount to be gained by refinancing is less in these cases. In addition, the income level of the Ginnie Mae-insured mortgagor population is lower than that of the Freddie Mac- or Fannie Mae-insured, so these homeowners may not be as quick to refinance because they do not have the cash resources to pay the associated costs. Finally, the default rate on FHA- and VA-approved loans is greater than that for conventional loans. However, because of the FHA and Ginnie Mae guarantees, a default results in a prepayment to the investor in one of these securities. While this acts to increase prepayment speeds, the dollar amounts are small and dwarfed by those mentioned previously. Therefore, Ginnie Mae MBSs tend to have longer Macaulay durations than do MBSs backed by conventional mortgages. Ginnie Mae MBSs are also less available than conventional ones because fewer of them are originated.

4. 15- and 30-Year MBSs

MBSs backed by traditional liens have more extension risk than do 15-year, fixed-rate MBSs. This effect is magnified for a pool consisting of relatively lower credit score mortgagors because it will be more difficult for them to refinance when the opportunity arises. The contraction risk from prepayments is less for a 30-year MBS than for a 15-year security because the 15-year mortgagor has much more to gain from the same drop in interest rates and more equity in the home to buttress the refinancing request; they may have more motive to engage in a cash-out refinancing for the same reason. The larger monthly payment on a shorter-term home loan usually means that the mortgagor is financially better off, on average, than a 30-year mortgagor and has a higher motivation to refinance should the occasion arise. Hence, the exercise of the prepayment option in 15-year home loans is more likely to be economically rational and, therefore, potentially predictable than the call option in traditional mortgages. Changing prepayments are bad from the investor's point of view, but predictable or stable prepayments are better than unpredictable ones.

Fifteen-year mortgages are preferred over 30-year liens as collateral for REMICs. Because of their shorter term, the amortization of these mortgages is much more rapid than for a traditional lien. This aspect makes it easier to devise more finely adjusted average life classes with the shorter-term, higher principal cash flow, collateral. To see how much more of the cash flow is principal, consider 15- and 30-year $300,700 mortgages with corresponding note rates of 7 and 6.75%/year. The initial two monthly payments are $2,660.92 = $1,691.44 (interest) + $969.48 (scheduled principal) and $2,000.56 = $1,754.08 + $246.48, respectively. The percentage going to principal is three times higher for the shorter-term certificate. This is also less subject to interest rate *volatility* than the interest component is. The higher the investor's certainty is that his average life expectations will be met, the more he is willing to pay. This translates into higher dealer profits. (Volatility is used in finance as a measure of uncertainty; see Chapter 7.)

The traditional instrument is the mortgage type greatly preferred by consumers because of its significantly lower monthly payment; therefore, it is in much greater supply than comparable quality 15- and 20-year-backed MBSs. The supply of 15-year loans increases when refinancing rates are very high because a big refinancing wave almost certainly means a large drop in interest rates, making the 15-year mortgage more affordable to a wider segment of the home owning population.

The slope of the yield curve has an affect on the supply of new MBSs also. When the curve is flatter, more 30-year fixed-rate MBSs will be issued because more traditional mortgages were originated. When it is steep, then the supply of these will decrease and that of ARM-backed MBSs will increase. Similarly, ARM MBSs experience a prepayment speed-up as the yield curve flattens, whereas 30-year fixed-rate MBSs may not. A more level yield curve also increases the value of the embedded call option, thereby widening MBS spreads. (The latter two are also dependent on the absolute level of interest rates.)

Because of a slowdown in prepayments resulting from a rise in interest rates, average life extension is least noticeable for discount securities. Pass-throughs closer to the point of inflection of the prepayment S curve, or bought at a premium during a bear market, will be more sensitive to interest rate changes. There are also compromises between high and low coupons as interest rates decrease (to seek call protection) and between shorter and longer term-to-maturity securities (which affects duration-based trading). (The aforementioned point of inflection is universally referred to as the cusp of the prepayment S curve.)

Finally, the exercise of the prepayment options in MBSs backed by pools of balloon re-set mortgages and hybrid mortgages is likely to be economic. Presumably the mortgagor has tried to take advantage of the asymmetric information available when he chose to take a 5-year balloon or a 7/1 hybrid over other alternatives.

a. Stratified Re-Set

The agencies make efforts to put together homogeneous pools of mortgages to use as backing for their MBSs. This is especially true for Ginnie Mae 30-year, fixed-rate MBSs. Another example is ARM-backed MBSs because of their many different features with respect to index, re-set frequency, margin, and so forth. For instance, in addition to combining variable-rate mortgages tied to the same index, they will only mix loans with the same re-set date. When the distinction needs to be made between this type and its variant, the former is referred to as a *single re-set* or *bullet pool*. Some pools are backed by floating-rate mortgages that have a set of stratified re-set dates — thus, a *stratified re-set MBS*. In the simplest version, 1/12 of the mortgages underlying the pool will have their coupon rates re-set each month (still based on the same index). This adds complexity to the valuation of the MBS and also results in a smoother response to interest rate fluctuations in its price because of the increased frequency of note rate readjustment (i.e., a lower modified duration).

III. PRICING MBSs

A. YIELD CURVE CONSIDERATIONS

1. The Main Yield Curve Effects

Consider some generic pass-through security priced at BP basis points over the Treasury curve. If the yield curve is relatively flat, for example, 125 basis points from the short- to the long-term end, then there will be relatively little difference when pricing a mortgage pass-through security if one uses the expected forward rates or a constant discount rate. Alternatively, if the yield curve has its normal upward sloping appearance (for example, at least 200 bp from the short- to the long-term end), then the effective yield spread of the cash flows early in the life of the MBS will be more than BP basis points because the short-end of the yield curve is depressed relative to the point used to price the MBS.

Since even steeply upwardly sloping yield curves rarely vary much beyond their 15-year point, the opposite effect, while occurring, is diminished in amplitude. Its leverage is further minimized by the heavy discounting and the long times to arrival that those cash flows have. Should the yield curve be *inverted*, then the long-term cash flows are mispriced but, more importantly, so are the short-term ones. The normal state of building additional yield beyond the BP basis points into the pricing will have been reversed. Such a security should be selling at a discount.

Another subtle point regarding the shape of the yield curve is the pricing convention used in the mortgage markets. We have discussed contrasting an MBS with the comparable duration U.S. Treasury instrument. This implies using one discount rate and is the simplest of comparisons to make. It would be better to compare the MBS to a portfolio of zero coupon Treasury instruments that matches the monthly cash flows stemming from the pass-through security. This mixture will, *per force*, duration-match it too. Now one can better infer the sensitivity to pricing on the shape of the yield curve.

2. More on Yield Curve Implications for MBSs

All the principal dollars will be returned at par, so a premium-priced MBS has a built-in loss potential that must be overcome by an extended life of interest cash flows. This is more likely to be the situation if the yield curve is upward tilting — the more steeply the better for the premium-priced MBS purchaser. Such a shape forecasts that mortgage origination rates will slow down, if forward rates are realized as time passes, and become spot rates because home buying will become relatively more expensive. This implies a decline in prepayment speeds and an absence of supply of new mortgage product. Any other economic factors that may have caused prepayment speeds to stabilize, if not slow down, are also better for a premium-priced MBS buyer. In addition, the level of interest rate volatility is relevant. Preferably, it is low or decreasing and thereby diminishing the probability of a large, downward, shift in interest rates.

Lower interest rate volatility decreases the value of the prepayment option embedded in extant mortgages. It also leads to a pared-down expectation that the forward rates implied by the current yield curve could be misleading by a large amount. Finally, a sharply inclined curve increases the profits available via *CMO arbitrage*, thus putting further demand pressure on the existing supply of MBSs. (CMO arbitrage refers to the pricing of REMIC securities; see Chapter 6.) Secondary factors associated with a strongly pitched yield curve are activities in the repurchase agreement and dollar roll markets (because of the cost of carry and the size of the drop). Separately, any factors that favor the supply and demand balance for premium pricing (i.e., moderate or low supply coupled with high or moderate demand) are to the good.

The dollar roll and repurchase agreement markets are affected by the form of the yield curve because those who use these markets are effectively engaging in collaterized lending with the financing cost bounded above by the short-term Treasury rate. Any yield curve shape other than the normally upward sloping one will have a negative affect on the costs of utilizing these markets and the liquidity concerns associated with them. Since the dollar roll and repurchase markets provide inexpensive financing mechanisms for holders of MBSs, activity in these markets can affect the spread between MBSs and U.S. Treasuries, especially when demand exceeds supply. When these markets strengthen, a higher level of demand for agency pass-throughs is implied; if the demand exceeds supply, then tighter MBS–Treasury spreads are the likely result. Use of leverage will increase the effect. This expense is passed on by dealers to investors who are using their MBS holdings in this fashion.

U.S. Treasury securities are more liquid collateral than mortgage pass-throughs, so it is cheaper to use them to fund via collateralized lending (e.g., a repurchase agreement) than with the latter (e.g., a dollar roll). As the collateral backing the MBS becomes less generic, the range further widens. Sometimes the absence of supply in the spot market will force a dealer to cover a short position via a dollar roll.

a. More on Interest Rate Volatility

A mortgage can be thought of as being long an uncallable, amortizing, bond and short a prepayment option. Options increase in value when volatility is magnified because investors interpret a rise in volatility to indicate a higher probability of the realization of relatively more unlikely events. This effect will be most easily seen for current coupon MBSs and those with slightly higher than current coupon rates. The reason is that these securities are sitting on or at the cusp of the prepayment S-curve. In terms of their embedded prepayment options, this means that they are at- or just slightly in-the-money. Hence, the correlation with volatility will be the highest for those MBSs considered as a function of pass-through rate (with everything else held the same). A big drop in market interest rates from their current levels, thus encouraging homeowners to refinance and leading to an increase in prepayment speeds, is assumed to be more probable when interest rate volatility is high than when it is low. (Note how one-sided this perception is: if current rates are at 11 or 12%, the uniform expectation will be that rates will decrease independent of the amplitude of the volatility. The higher the rates are, the stronger this expectation will be, even if the observed volatility is near zero. The converse is true if rates are near generational lows. This is a prime example of historical norms overriding inflexible models.)

Because an MBS holder is short a call option, one would expect MBS spreads to correlate with interest rate volatility. A decline in volatility decreases an option's value, which means that the price of an MBS increases or that its spread to U.S. Treasuries tightens. In general, higher volatility has an adverse effect on MBS spreads, with a greater negative impact on those sold at a premium as opposed to those sold at a discount. If the option is worth more, then the price of the MBS goes down, implying a higher yield. Higher volatility lowers the option-adjusted spread. Long volatility means that an increase in volatility will not antithetically affect the spread, while short volatility means that an increase in volatility will adversely affect the spread.

b. Convexity Issues

Negative convexity is not a desirable feature because of price compression and the potential for the unwelcome early return of principal. (In some of the more complicated mortgage-related securities, a real potential for losses owing to negative convexity exists.) Therefore, the spreads for the negatively convex premium MBSs are wider. MBSs are intrinsically negatively convex but seasoned MBSs need not be as interest rates vary over time. Pass-through securities that have small negative convexity, or are positively convex because of burnout, are worth more than those still strongly negatively convex. Moreover, the possibility of utilizing the negative convexity as a hedging tool should not be ignored. It is more important that the portfolio manager understand what he is buying, the cost paid for it, and the risks assumed. Investors who prefer stability to inconstant mark-to-market pricing will prefer short-duration, pass-through securities to longer-duration ones. Finally, trading off high convexity for the potential of greater total return can make callable pass-throughs desirable.

B. Other Factors

1. Seasoned MBS Characteristics

The definition of seasoning varies with issuer and market niche. Sometimes a seasoned mortgage (or pool of them) must be at least 1 year past the origination (average origination) date. Sometimes it means 2 years. For MBS pools several years past their issue date (which, itself, is typically 1 to 12 months past their mortgages' issuance dates) a short-, medium-, and long-term distinction is sometimes made. Alternative terminology would be slightly seasoned, moderately seasoned, and seasoned (or very seasoned). The time spans associated with these three groups are less than 2.5 years, 2.5 to 5 years, and beyond 10 years from issuance date.

The best information about a seasoned pool is its history of prepayments. After a few years of seasoning, prepayment prediction into the immediate future is really starting to become possible and reliable. One also needs a knowledge of the geographic distribution of the mortgages (Are they all jumbo loans in Houston just after Enron has collapsed?), the dispersion of the coupon rates, information regarding the level of underwriting that the liens have undergone (Are they all conforming to loan-to-value and debt-ratio requirements?), the credit scores of the homeowners, and so forth.

Beyond the real possibility of quantitatively accurate prepayment speed prediction as far out as a year or two ahead, seasoned pools generally have other characteristics to rely on. They tend to be of long effective duration because those who could have refinanced have already done so. They tend to be positively convex for the same reason, unlike most other mortgage-derivative securities. They may have relatively high default rates because adverse selection has kept those with a less robust financial condition or lower credit scores in the pool rather than more uniformly as at issue date. Beyond this risk, prepayments will probably be relatively slow and stable, stemming from job-related, retirement-driven, or other personal life events. Finally, their cash flow increasingly arises from principal as the loans standing behind them move further along their amortization schedules.

2. Higher Coupon MBSs

One sometimes reads of premium and discount MBSs with the adjective "coupon" helpfully added because that is what is meant. In this context, a premium coupon MBS is one with a weighted average coupon 150 basis points or more over the current coupon MBS's WAC. Similarly, a discount coupon MBS would be one whose WAC was 150 bp or more below the current coupon MBS's WAC.

A pass-through security with a WAC significantly above current rates has negative convexity. This certificate will almost certainly experience a rapid increase in prepayment speeds and, as a consequence, a cap to its price. Alternatively, should the dip in market rates be temporary, then, as they elevate from their recent low, the price of an MBS with a higher pass-through rate will not decline as rapidly as, for example, a comparable duration U.S. Treasury instrument would. Only when rates have passed the cusp of the prepayment S-curve for this instrument will it start to exhibit the standard fixed-income interest rate sensitivity of declining in value with rising rates. Secondary factors to this general behavior are the weighted average maturity of the pass-through and the actual path of interest rates in the immediate past. Both of these are indicators of the degree of burnout that the underlying pool of mortgages may have experienced.

3. ARM Evaluation Considerations

Freddie Mac and Fannie Mae own relatively few conforming adjustable-rate mortgages. The reason is simple: running a mortgage portfolio funded by short-term liabilities (i.e., depositors' funds) is much easier if one uses these funds to acquire short-term assets, namely, variable-rate mortgages. Hence, of approximately 10% of floating-rate mortgages originated during the last few years, a time of very low interest rates, most have been kept by the savings banks and thrift institutions rather than sold into the secondary market. In addition, those who desire the additional spread of a mortgage-related security over that of bonds and simultaneously require a shorter-duration asset prefer MBSs backed by ARMs.

Whenever the periodic or lifetime cap of an adjustable-rate security becomes invoked, the modified duration of the security rapidly rises from near zero to much more like that of a comparable fixed-rate vehicle. The effect is more marked if the lifetime cap or floor is operative than if it is just the periodic cap because the latter can be overridden at the next coupon re-set date. Not only the lag of the index — for instance, the relatively slowly reacting COFI vs. the more rapidly changing 6-month LIBOR or CD rate — but also the look-back time, play similar roles. A volatile interest rate environment coupled with a long payment delay can diminish the apparent responsivity of the index to market interest rate changes. Shorter look-back times generally imply smaller modified durations. The Macaulay duration of these instruments is relatively stable, the more so with the tighter the periodic cap (i.e., 1 vs. 2%). ARMs whose interest rates are re-set semiannually rather than annually will have a lower modified duration, everything else being equal.

When discussing COFI-based variable-rate mortgages the possibility of negative amortization arose because the coupon rate on these liens is frequently adjusted monthly, even though the interest rate the homeowner pays is adjusted less frequently (semiannually or annually). When coupled with a 7.5% payment cap, the possibility is increased that the gross monthly payment the homeowner will be making after the next re-set date will not cover the total interest and principal components of the mortgage. Negative amortization clearly protracts the time to receipt of principal and interest thereby lengthening the Macaulay duration of this type of mortgage. Once the contractual negative amortization limit, typically 110 to 125% of the original face value, is reached, the amortization schedule is recast with a correspondingly adjusted monthly mortgage payment that will fully amortize the outstanding principal balance over the remaining term of the loan. At this point, the security is acting much more like a fixed-rate mortgage.

From the option-theoretic approach, pricing and evaluating floating-rate MBSs is more complicated than for fixed-rate instruments. The ARM investor is long a pure floating-rate instrument, short the prepayment option, long the interest rate floors, and short the interest rate caps embedded in the lien. Hence, there are two additional financial instruments to price in order to value the ARM fully. Clearly, a consistent interest rate scenario (or set of scenarios) must be used to evaluate each component of a variable-rate security. Moreover, the use of an option-adjusted spread as only a relative value device must be especially stressed in this context (as opposed to believing that one actually earns the OAS).

The rate of origination of ARMs is dominated by the absolute level of interest rates and the steepness of the yield curve. When market interest rates are at historically low levels, the potential homeowner is very willing to trade the certainty of a 15- or 30-year fixed rate mortgage for the minor, and temporary, gain afforded by an ARM's teaser rate. The attraction of the teaser rate increases as the yield curve tends to incline more and more sharply upward. Again, the reason is simple: rates on a traditional mortgage are priced off the 10-year point of the yield curve while those for ARMs are priced off the much lower, short-term, portion of the yield curve. When a large range (say > 200 bp) from the top to the bottom of the yield curve exists coupled with the low level of a teaser rate, this combination of factors makes the variable-rate mortgage much more appealing. The risk of interest rates rising at the first re-set date is relatively far away in the homeowner's mind, especially for the 5/1 or 7/1 hybrid variations.

IV. MORE ON MBS PRICING

We review, this time in more depth, the basic valuation methods for mortgage-backed security pricing. As the reader gains a better understanding of the complexity of these instruments, he also starts to form his own opinion as to the best methodology for his purposes.

A. SIMPLE METHODS

1. The 12-Year Average Life

Not so long ago all traditional mortgages were assumed to be paid off at the end of 12 years. Thus, the pricing for these instruments was more like that for a monthly-paying, partially amortizing, bullet bond than a true long-term mortgage. Clearly, this is inadequate in today's erratic interest rate milieu but it is still approximately true. One could convincingly argue that a 10- or 8-year average life was a better estimate to today's market and forego all this option-adjusted pricing and Monte Carlo simulation. This is the basis of *cash flow yield* pricing for mortgage-backed securities. The formula for it would look like

$$PV = \sum_{n=1}^{144} CF_n / (1 + i / 12)^{(n+d/30-1)}$$

where d is the number of days delay associated with this pass-through payment delay.

In this version of the formula, all but the last cash flow have built into them the standard monthly payment for this type of mortgage at its coupon rate and an assumed, constant level of prepayments. The last cash flow includes the unpaid principal balance as of the 144th month. One can adjust the posited prepayment speed for the important characteristics of the underlying collateral (such as government-insured vs. conventional vs. whole-loan; its WAC and WAM; 15- vs. 30-year fixed-rate; geographically diverse or not; and so forth.). All the problems with more complicated prepayment models will be a difficulty for this one too, but at least this one does not overpromise what cannot be delivered. A more cogent criticism is that the modified duration and the convexity computed from the preceding model will always be positive.

2. Static Cash Flow Yield

One step up in complexity is to assume a time dependent prepayment model and compute the monthly cash flows based on it, plus the amortization schedule. Knowing the market price, one could infer the discount rate that made the discounted, speeded up cash flows equal to the price. No interest rate volatility is allowed and one would use a flat yield curve.

3. Static Spread and Zero-Volatility Spread

The next step up in reflecting reality would be to assemble a collection of zero coupon Treasury instruments whose present value of cash flows matches that expected from the mortgage (including a prepayment speed assumption). The Macaulay durations would match in this case too. The extra amount necessary to make the present value of the discounted cash flows equal the market value is known as the zero-volatility spread. It has no volatility because the computed forward rates are not allowed to vary from those implied by today's term structure of interest rates. Sometimes this is referred to as the static spread. To implement this method, one adds the value of 1/12 the annual option-adjusted spread, OAS, to the monthly forward rates r_m and computes

$$PV = \sum_{n=1}^{N} CF_n \ / \ \prod_{m=1}^{n} (1 + r_m + OAS / 12)$$

The value of the OAS that makes PV come out to be the current market price is the value of the zero-volatility, option-adjusted spread. (In Chapter 4, the spot rate version of this formula was given. Forward rates will be discussed more in Chapter 7.)

a. Why Only One OAS?

The methodology of the full option-adjusted spread technique can overcome the stability built into the zero-volatility spread method. Let us ask again, "Why is there only one OAS?" How much information do we have? We know all the characteristics of the security itself — face amount, time-to-maturity, coupon rate, payment frequency, amortizing or not, and so on. We have one additional piece of data: its market price. Because we only know one extra fact, we can, from the purely mathematical point of view, only choose one other parameter to fix.

For a European call option an obvious choice would be an option-adjusted spread in the discounting formula up to and including the call date and no option-adjusted spread thereafter (because, if the security has not been called by now, it cannot be and one no longer deserves to earn a risk premium). Alternatively for a European call option, we could have chosen the independent variable to be the probability of the call option being exercised by a certain date. I have not seen either of these suggestions developed in any depth despite their more intuitive nature. Moreover, the latter proposition could be easily extended to a Bermudan-style option with conditional probabilities.

B. Outline of the Full OAS Method

We can make the pricing process more dynamic by allowing the forward rates to depart from those implied by the current spot rate in a statistically sensible fashion. Then the preceding formula would represent the present value of this particular path of interest rates. Suppose we label the path dependence by k. Then we would write that the present value PV, on path #k, from monthly forward rates derived from the mth simulation of possible interest rate paths, $\{r_{mk}\}$, would be given by

$$PV_k = \sum_{n=1}^{N} CF_{nk} \;/\; \prod_{m=1}^{n} (1 + r_{mk} + OAS/12).$$

Note that not only the predicted forward rates are path dependent but so are the predicted cash flows, on a month-by-month basis, for this particular evolution of interest rates.

The quantity to use to compare to the actual market prices after averaging the different path-dependent values of PV_k would be

$$K = \text{total number of paths}$$

$$PV = \sum_{k=1}^{K} PV_k \,/\, K.$$

If we had a match, then the numerical value of OAS used was correct. If not, then we would adjust the numerical value of the OAS in the appropriate direction and try again until the OAS did match the price after averaging over all the interest rate paths. Clearly, to employ this algorithm fully, one needs a method of generating future interest rates. This will be discussed in Chapter 7.

How does one combine the OAS methodology with the total return framework discussed earlier? With difficulty, even ignoring the complexities introduced by attempting to generate a realistic yield curve because a reinvestment issue still exists — this time made more difficult because intermediate cash flows must be reinvested at the OAS-implied spread if the discounting yield is to be interpreted as a yield-to-maturity.

1.   More Thoughts on OAS

It seems more reasonable to tie the value of the OAS with the call probability in some fashion. Then the OAS would be time-dependent because, the longer the call is delayed, the more the investor has already gained. A particular parametric representation might be a monotonic decreasing form for the OAS (a more financially realistic scenario). For the t'th month of the security's life, we might write

$$OAS_t = OAS_0 + \Delta OAS \times t, \; t = 0,1,2,\ldots, N.$$

One of the initial values of the option-adjusted spread, $OAS_0 > 0$, or its rate of change, $\Delta OAS < 0$, was fixed (we only have one degree of freedom) and the other one determined from the price. The analytical freedom to choose is endless, limited only by our collective imaginations and what makes financial sense. Of course, easy interpretation and ultimate usefulness would be nice characteristics, too.

PROBLEM

1. Calculate WAM and the WAC for one mortgage.

6 More Complicated Mortgage Securities

The pass-through, mortgage-backed security with an agency guarantee made investing in mortgages much more acceptable to a wider investor audience. The product had virtually no default risk, was relatively liquid, and its remaining risks could be understood and therefore priced (or so investors originally thought). When the latter proved to be untrue, because of negative convexity, a demand for instruments with better-defined cash-flow horizons was created. First the CMO and then the REMIC were invented to satisfy these investors. Eventually, cash flow financial engineering and prepayment risk distribution flowered into multiple REMIC classes; the most frequently met dozen or so are discussed in this chapter. A good reference for Chapters 5 and 6 is the book by Bartlett (1994).

I. HISTORY AND DEFINITIONS

A. WHY REMICs?

1. REMIC Class Prepayment Characteristics

What do investors in mortgage-backed securities want? They want the higher yield than U.S. Treasury instruments that mortgages can provide. They do not want the credit risk nor do they want to accept too much prepayment risk. The government-sponsored enterprises and various *internal* and *external credit enhancement* mechanisms for whole-loan and private-label MBSs have effectively mitigated against the credit risk. To diminish prepayment risk required a different kind of cash-flow pattern with a more stable average life than the pass-through, mortgage-backed security. This was the primary reason that the *sequential pay class* and then the *planned amortization class* were invented.

The precipitating events were a substantial drop in market mortgage interest rates in the early 1990s. Then investors in pass-through securities rediscovered, or worse yet discovered for the first time, what negative convexity really means. Not wishing to be exposed to the uncertainty of the embedded call options in home loans, they expressed their preference for a mortgage-related instrument with more stable cash flows as interest rates varied. Thus, sequential pay and planned amortization classes were created. Investor demand increased the supply of these new financially engineered structures in the REMIC origination market and better understanding of the drifting *prepayment band* protection of a planned amortization class (or *PAC*) diffused through the financier community. At the same time, the liquidity of these classes improved in the secondary market. This was yet another reason to prefer a sequential pay or PAC class over an undivided interest in *pro rata* share of a pass-through MBS.

2. The History of REMICs

The next significant step in tailoring mortgage cash flows, beyond the pass-through MBS, to satisfy investor demands, was made in mid-1983 when Freddie Mac created and sold the first collateralized-mortgage obligation (or CMO). This instrument was backed by individual whole loan mortgages and by mortgage pass-through securities. The proximate cause of this invention was a dramatic fall in mortgage interest rates during the early part of that year and the consequent doubling of mortgage origination rates as an upshot of the refinancing wave that swept across the country. This phenomenon also abruptly brought to investors's attention the risks of negative convexity in mortgages; some losses were substantial. To continue to attract additional investors to mortgages, a more versatile device than the pass-through instrument was required.

The CMO did this and its market burgeoned but was limited by certain tax and legal constraints associated with the grantor trust used in conjunction with a CMO. To alleviate these problems, Congress passed the 1986 Tax Reform Act, which included the creation of a more efficient trust vehicle called a *real estate mortgage investment conduit* (universally known as a REMIC). In that same year, Fannie Mae introduced the first stripped mortgage-backed security (or SMBS) with *principal-only* and *interest-only* classes, although these were not the stripped mortgage-backed securities known today; initially each had a bit of the other type of cash flow. The planned amortization class (or PAC) class of a REMIC was introduced in 1987. *Floating-rate classes* of REMICs made their debut in late 1986. With these building blocks in place to satisfy a huge variety of investor demands for credit guarantee and cash flow variety, the secondary mortgage market for grouping mortgages into financially engineered structures exploded in the late 1980s.

Why do any of this? Somewhere an investor needs cash flows of this nature because his intrinsic business places him in the position of requiring nonbond-like cash flows to hedge some element of risk. By purchasing MBSs, SMBSs, or a particular class of a REMIC, he can offset a portion of that risk. A classic example is that of a servicer (whose ordinary cash flows are similar to those of an interest-only, or *IO*, strip) who buys a portion of a principal-only (*PO*) strip, thereby synthetically recreating the cash flow of a whole loan mortgage.

a. Credit Risk

At first credit enhancements for whole-loan MBSs were external, provided by private mortgage insurers or bank letters of credit. However, since the late 1980s when REMIC legislation first allowed issuance of multiclass pass-throughs, internal credit enhancements such as the *senior/subordinate* structure have been the dominant form of credit enhancement. A senior/subordinate structure involves the creation of a senior class, also known as the A class, and a subordinate piece, known as the B class. Usually the A class is rated AAA and the B class rated from perhaps AA down to NR (not rated). The B class absorbs first losses on defaulted or foreclosed home loans backing the A class. The size of the subordinate piece varies depending on the rating to be obtained on the senior piece and the credit quality of the underlying home loans. It also differs between fixed-rate mortgages (for example, a B piece of 8%) and floating- or adjustable-rate collateral (for example, a B piece of 12% for the same credit rating). The rating on the senior piece is determined by stress testing the default characteristics of the liens underlying the pool with different economic assumptions. A rating of AAA is obtained if the mortgages supporting the pool survive a stress test equivalent to the Depression of the 1930s. A rating of AA is assigned to an issue that would survive a Houston, Texas, 1980s scenario.

3. Structuring a REMIC

In general the REMIC, and the CMO before it, performed a variety of feats that large groups of investors wanted. Generic classes, or *tranches*, were created — "tranche" is from the French for "strip." (Generic is in the eye of the beholder and an *inverse floating-rate tranche* will seem exotic to some investors. However, to those active in the floating-rate markets, such a device is an important risk-management tool.) A generic security, essentially by definition, will be understood by a wider spectrum of potential investors and therefore have greater acceptance. This in turn leads to a higher level of liquidity via narrower bid–ask price spreads, perhaps a dollar roll market, or other secondary market making mechanisms.

A variety of standard REMIC tranches — sequential pay classes, *accrual or Z classes*, PACs, *targeted amortization classes (TACs), reverse TACs, support* or *companion classes,* POs and IOs, floating-rate and inverse floating-rate classes — also means that investors need only learn about a few candidate opportunities and can better appreciate the role that these new cash-flow pattern possibilities could play in their individual risk-management or yield-maximizing strategies. One of the most important things a REMIC does is to redistribute prepayment risk, as well as the rewards for taking it on, to those who want it, while simultaneously diverting prepayment risk away from those who do not want it (at a cost in their yield). The fabrication of the REMIC by the Tax Reform Act of 1986 also solved the double taxation issue of CMOs and simplified some accounting problems. (The terms CMO and REMIC are now frequently used interchangeably; however, a CMO is technically considered a sale of debt backed by mortgage assets whereas a REMIC is considered a sale of the assets.)

B. STRIPPED MORTGAGE-BACKED SECURITIES

Before describing the more complex cash flow pattern of the basic REMIC tranches, it will be helpful to better visualize what IO and PO strips really are, how they are formed, and what they accomplish.

1. IOs and POs

The individual homeowner is paying down the principal in an amortized fashion. Therefore, in pass-through MBSs, the investor receives interest and a portion of the outstanding principal with each monthly payment. A danger associated with an MBS, however, is prepayment risk. This can be approximately factored into the initial price using a hypothetical prepayment speed (or set of speeds). An MBS investor also faces a form of reinvestment risk that a bullet bond holder does not: as principal repayment occurs, even if not accelerated by prepayments, the investor must reinvest it appropriately to reach the advertised yield-to-maturity.

Suppose we strip apart a mortgage-backed security's cash flow into its mutually exclusive principal and interest components. Then we have two different financial instruments that stem from the same underlying pool of mortgages; one consists of only the cash flows from the interest payments and one consists of only the cash flows from principal payments (including any unscheduled prepayments, curtailments, or defaults). These are referred to as a interest-only stripped mortgage-backed security and as principal-only stripped mortgage-backed security.

Note that the risks of the pass-through MBS have been unequally distributed over the two derivative securities; once a homeowner refinances the mortgage, thereby prepaying the entire amount still owed, the interest payment stream completely dries up. The holder of the interest-only strip loses all subsequent cash flow while the owner of the principal-only strip receives the entire principal payment, albeit early. The sum of the prices of the two stripped instruments must closely approximate the cost of the underlying MBS for a given prepayment speed estimate; otherwise there would be an arbitrage opportunity. The principal-only strip is akin to a deep discount, amortizing bond in that accelerated prepayments increase the effective yield. Therefore, if market interest rates are falling, thereby multiplying the tendency of homeowners to refinance their mortgages or purchase more costly homes, the effective yield on a PO strip increases.

Conversely, the interest-only portion of an SMBS becomes more valuable when market interest rates are rising. This will diminish the probability of homeowners refinancing their existing mortgages or purchasing more expensive homes. This will tend to protract the time span over which the cash flows associated with the extant liens' interest payments will continue to exist, thereby effectively increasing the IO strip's yield. Put in other terms, PO SMBSs are attractive to an investor who stands to lose future cash flows from other securities in his portfolio because of falling market interest rates. The reverse set of considerations will be true for investors specializing in fixed-income instruments. For them, when market interest rates rise, the bulk of their portfolios will decrease in worth while the value of the IO SMBS will increase. (An example might be a thrift institution that maintains a portfolio of fixed-rate loans.)

Because prepayments are slow when market rates rise, the value of an IO strip will also rise because more principal on which interest can be paid will be outstanding for a longer period of time. Thus, an IO strip is a *negative duration* security. This characteristic is extremely rare in the fixed-income world and is uniquely valuable for certain hedging activities. A flattening yield curve hastens the repayment of principal as homeowners rush to lock into suddenly attractive long-term rates. Hence, an IO strip loses value in this situation. The opposite circumstance, when the yield curve grows more steep, will not enhance prepayments of principal, thereby extending the time over which interest payments will be received. This increases the value of an IO strip.

PO strip owners benefit as the repayment of principal accelerates because they receive their funds back earlier (raising the effective yield). So if the yield curve flattens, the market value of a PO will go up; the converse will occur if the yield curve grows more steep (because a more tilted yield curve will inhibit refinancing and even new home purchases). Conversely, a PO strip is necessarily a positive-duration security with, typically, a relatively large value of Macaulay duration — something else that is comparatively rare in the universe of fixed-income instruments.

a. Synthetic SMBSs

The earliest form of the stripped-MBS was known as a *synthetic-coupon* pass-through security. The term "synthetic coupon" stemmed from the fact that these were more like present-day *IOettes* (see the next section) than present day IOs: they received a fixed proportion of the principal-only cash flow from the underlying MBSs as well as a fixed (not necessarily 100%) proportion of the interest-only cash flow. Fannie Mae introduced synthetic-coupon pass-throughs in July, 1986; true IOs and POs came from that firm in January of 1987. Today IO and PO tranches of REMICs have overtaken SMBS issuance.

b. IOettes

Yet another class of IO-like instrument is known as an IOette. This is a REMIC tranche with an extremely high interest rate —hundreds of percent because an IOette is essentially an IO strip plus a bit of principal. Because a real (as opposed to *notional*), but tiny, outstanding principal balance can be used to compute an interest rate, the corresponding interest rate is very high. For example, combining one hundred parts of an 8% notional IO with one part of a PO will result in an 800% coupon IOette.

2. Valuation Considerations

When the WAC on the mortgages that form the backing for the stripped MBSs is far from the current coupon rate, their interest rate sensitivity will mimic that of a fixed-rate instrument. The reason is that, in either case, the prepayment speeds experienced by the underlying pools are already at their maximum or minimum. Similarly, one can hazard a guess that the effective convexity of PO strips based on near current coupon collateral will be positive because, if interest rates fall, the prepayment speeds of "cuspy" mortgages — mortgages whose coupon rates are near the point of inflection of the prepayment S-curve — will increase while maintaining some base level prepayment speed, even if interest rates rise. The identical scenario and reasoning applied to IO strips based on near-current coupon collateral leads one to expect negative effective convexity because the market value of an IO strip is likely to fall at a faster rate as interest rates decline and to rise at a slower rate as interest rates escalate. Finally, the sign pattern of effective convexity should be reversed for SMBSs backed by home loans with interest rates higher than those currently available.

The current coupon is likely to be near the cusp of the prepayment S-curve (almost by definition). Therefore, it will react the most when interest rates change (as opposed to higher or lower coupon securities, again, almost by definition). As interest rates decline, prepayment speeds will be greater for lower coupon rates and current coupons than for those with higher level coupon rates. After all, those MBSs with coupon rates higher than the current market ones should already be prepaying at reasonable speeds. Therefore, PO strips backed by lower-level coupon rates or current-level coupon rates will experience a greater increase in value than those backed by higher-level coupon rates.

If interest rates should rise, then IO strips whose underlying MBSs were backed by higher- and current-level coupon mortgages should perform better than those whose underlying MBSs were backed by lower-level coupon rate mortgages. The reason is that prepayments on higher- and current-level coupon pass-throughs will decrease. This will cause a loss in market price for PO strips relying on them and a gain in market price for IO strips dependent on them. For those based on lower-level coupon rate liens, prepayment speeds will not significantly slow down when market rates rise; they were already slowly prepaying because their embedded call options were out-of-the-money.

3. What Is a REMIC?

The stripped-MBS approach to redirecting the cash flows from a mortgage has been expanded via further financial engineering. In particular, REMICs are now routinely issued by the larger secondary mortgage market participants (both public and private). REMICs take the interest- and principal-only peeling apart one step further in sophistication. An MBS is a one-class financial vehicle. Its pool of underlying mortgages has been wrapped into a single instrument of large face amount. There is neither redirection nor stripping apart of the cash flows into interest- or principal-only portions. The IO and PO strips just discussed represent partitioning the original, single-class MBS into one with two classes.

By imagining the cash flows from the IO and PO to be the hot- and cold-water flows from an old-fashioned, two-faucet sink, we can create a wide variety of instruments by altering the proportion of the IO and PO flows and even changing when the IO and PO streams are allowed to be on. This is what a REMIC is: a collection of rules for mixing IO and PO cash flows over time such that the sum of the results recombines to be equal to the cash flows of the underlying pool of whole loans. By blending one fraction of the interest cash flow and a different fraction of principal cash flow, conceivably over independent time spans, one can create a multiclass MBS. Each class has a different set of prepayment and interest rate risk characteristics rooted in the fraction of the underlying interest- and principal-only cash flows comprising it and in their scheduled arrival. It also indirectly depends on the relative dollar value of this tranche relative to all the others in the REMIC.

The main advantage of a REMIC over a pass-through MBS for the ultimate investor, and the issuer who creates the security, is that, by restructuring the interest and principal cash flows into different tranches, one has created a variety of distinct cash flow streams. Different investors have different needs (usually to offset some liability) for varying coupon rates, average lives, final maturities, prepayment sensitivities, and other risk factors; REMICs offer the possibility of satisfying more investors' demands than do pass-through MBSs. The REMIC structure allows for the prepayment risk of the underlying whole-loan mortgages to be redistributed, not diminished.

Most REMICs are backed by pass-through MBSs. Backing for agency issued REMICs is agency MBSs to minimize default risk. The sum of the outstanding principal amounts of the underlying MBSs also forms the face amount of the REMIC. These MBSs have an average pass-through rate. No matter how the cash flows are divided up into the classes comprising the REMIC, the dealer creating the security must make sure that:

1. All the principal is accounted for.
2. The principal-weighted average coupons of the REMIC tranches sum to no more than that of the underlying collateral, which allows for dealer fees, profits, issuance expenses, the *residual interest class*, and so forth.
3. The sum of the interest rate and prepayment risks adds back to that of the underlying whole loans.

A critical legal detail about a REMIC is that the pool of collateral is held by a trustee in a form that is bankruptcy remote from the issuer. This protects the investor from *event risk*: the possibility that the issuer of the REMIC will have financial difficulties that are neither a reflection of the performance of the mortgagors nor a drain on the cash flows stemming from the underlying MBSs. A double-A rating company may be able to issue a triple-A rated REMIC via appropriate credit enhancements, but the rating agencies will not allow a down-graded firm to do so without external credit strengthening. Therefore, it is important in the secondary market to keep the rating of the REMIC and its tranches distinct from that of the issuer. Even more important is keeping the assets of the REMIC from being comingled with those of an issuer who might have financial difficulties.

C. THE BASIC REMIC MECHANISM

1. A Simple REMIC

In a simple REMIC structure there might be, for example, five classes. The classes are usually denoted by letters and most of them would be known as *regular interests*. One, called the *R tranche*, is known as the residual class interest. Consider the sequential pay classes A, B, C, and so forth. The A class would be a relatively short-term instrument, its tranche effective maturity date fixed by the larger amount of principal payments that holders of the A tranche receive relative to those holding the B class (of intermediate term) or the C class owners (instruments of longer term). By design, all principal payments —from any sources — stemming from all the loans underlying the supporting MBSs go first to the owners of the A tranche. Holders of the B class receive no principal payments at all until the par value of the A tranche has been fully repaid.

However, the B and C class owners receive interest on the outstanding principal balance of their tranches from the settlement date. The redirection of all scheduled and unscheduled principal payments from the entire amount of underlying REMIC collateral allows one to diminish the uncertainty of when principal will be returned to holders of tranche A compared to holders of tranche B. Another critical factor is the relative par values of the classes. A REMIC with a face amount of $100 million and an A class of $15 million will act very differently with respect to prepayment risk than the same total dollar amount of REMIC with an A class worth $85 million. Finally, the C tranche holders receive no principal payments at all until all B and A tranche holders are paid off in full. The total amount of interest rate and prepayment risk stays the same; it is just reapportioned asymmetrically within the classes of the REMIC. The sequential pay classes of a REMIC are also referred to as *plain vanilla*, *clean pay*, or *current pay* classes.

Beyond the three sequential pay classes, this example has two additional classes: the aforementioned residual or R class and the last one, the accrual or Z class. The former is a dumping ground for cash flow not required to be distributed to the other classes. Every REMIC needs an R class for legal and tax purposes. The accrual class is similar to a zero coupon bond that accrues interest. The holders of this Z tranche receive no interest payments during the early life of the REMIC; rather, the interest accrues and is added to its unpaid principal balance. Principal is paid only when the higher-priority sequential pay tranches have been fully retired. Thus, Z classes act more like a negatively amortizing mortgage than a true zero coupon bond. The maximum amount of principal addition can easily be triple the initial principal amount. Z tranches are typically the last to pay off in a REMIC structure. The interest flows owed to them went to paying down the higher-priority sequential pay classes.

Once again, you can see that the relative values of the A, B, C, and Z classes can dramatically affect the average lives and start and stop times of the intermediate classes. If $100 million of mortgages underlay the REMIC, and there are five tranches, the distribution of the par value does not need to be uniform over them. Class A could represent $32.5 million, Class B $24.5 million, and so on. A larger dollar amount devoted to the A class increases its extension risk. More par value associated with the C or Z classes decreases the A and B tranche's extension risk and vice versa. In general, the presence of the Z class reduces the average life of the sequential pay classes because the interest that would be paid to the accrual class is, instead, going to pay down the sequential classes faster than usual. As with a zero-coupon bond, Z tranches are appealing to those who do not want to deal with reinvestment risk.

One of the main advantages of creation of the sequential payment REMIC arrangement was that capital market investors with short investment horizons could be induced to place their funds in MBSs, even those backed by traditional mortgage instruments (i.e., 30-year). Simultaneously, investors with only long-term horizons benefited as they bought the C class of an A, B, C, Z, and R REMIC. This kind of specialization was only increased with the creation of planned amortization classes (PACs) and targeted amortization classes (TACs), as well as *very accurately determined maturity*-form (*VADMs*) classes. The development of these financially engineered structures and their floating-rate cousins, from fixed-rate mortgages, represented major innovations in the debt markets whose importance is sometimes overlooked when discussing the details of the derivative securities.

2. Recap

Let us review this information in a slightly different form. A plain vanilla REMIC form is one of several sequentially paying classes. Typically these are in alphabetical order, with the A tranche having the shortest maturity and the lowest yield, followed by the B tranche with a longer time to maturity and an intermediate yield relative to the WAC of the underlying MBSs backing the REMIC structure. Then comes the C tranche with a maturity date even further away and higher yield, and so forth. Each sequential pay class receives monthly interest payments from every dollar of principal still outstanding on it. All scheduled and unscheduled principal payments resulting from amortization, prepayments, curtailments, or defaults from all the mortgages forming the collateral for the REMIC flow first to the holders of the still outstanding tranche whose name is closest to the beginning of the alphabet. Thus, only when the entire amount of the principal owed to the owners of the A tranche has been paid will the B tranche holders receive any of their principal monies.

Meanwhile, the B and C tranche owners are receiving all the interest-only cash flow due to them. Once the A tranche has been retired, only B tranche holders will receive any principal. Eventually the owners of the B tranche have been fully repaid their par value, which is not necessarily the same as the par value of the A nor C tranches, and the owners of the C tranche will begin to receive their principal reimbursements (while all along having received their *pro rata* interest payments). After all the C class principal has been repaid, the possessors of the D tranche will start to collect their funds, and so on. The Z tranche accrues interest, compounded monthly at its stated interest rate, until the higher priority sequential pay classes have been retired. Then the Z tranche owners begin to collect principal and interest as it comes in (i.e., the Z tranche becomes like another sequential-pay tranche, only this conversion must wait until the real sequential-pay tranches have been paid off).

The reader should appreciate intuitively that, just as PO and IO strips of an SMBS have very different interest rate and prepayment risks, the differing tranches of a REMIC are in between them with respect to these dangers. The principal amount, average interest rate, average life, prepayment profile, and final maturities can be different for each tranche. Because their proportion of principal amount and prepayment speeds differs from those assumed at pricing, each tranche will influence all the others in complicated ways. The advantage to the investor is that, by creating varied instruments, the dealer has allowed him to match the duration of the assets and liabilities of his portfolio more closely.

a. Yield Curve Effects

Yield curve reshaping risk for REMIC tranches depends on the type of tranche. A short maturity, low dollar value, sequential pay class is relatively insensitive to yield curve reshaping because it is typically priced at par and its cash flows are concentrated early in the life of the underlying mortgages. For a longer maturity, higher dollar amount, sequential pay tranche, there is more risk from yield curve reshaping. A flattening yield curve will cause long-term forward rates to fall. This will result in short-term rates advancing and the price of a par-priced long-term sequential pay class to increase because most of its cash flows are longer-term and they will now be discounted to a lower value. If the forward rates are realized, this will have a big effect on actual prepayment rates going into the future. Therefore, a positive (negative) sensitivity to pitch alterations of the yield curve will result for long-term sequential tranches priced at a discount (premium) with respect to par.

3. The R Class

What does the owner of the R tranche receive? Mostly it is the entire package of tax advantages created by the construction of the REMIC. For this reason Wall Street dealers frequently hold onto the R tranche just in case they want to synthetically recreate the MBSs underlying the REMIC. In addition, if extra cash flows exist from the other tranches, (i.e., float income or servicing fees), these go to the holder of the R class. The sources of this cash flow are generally premium interest, coupon differential, and reinvestment income. Note that the price of an R class moves in the same direction as interest rates so the economic performance of an R tranche can easily be dominated by their tax, legal, or accounting characteristics.

Where did the R class come from? The first Freddie Mac CMO, issued in 1983, was a debt obligation backed by a particular pool of Freddie Mac pass-through securities. The underlying MBSs stayed on Freddie Mac's balance sheet as an asset, whereas the tranches of the CMO became liabilities. To complete the equilibrium of the balance sheet, there had to be an equity component, too — hence the residual class. The owner trust residual structure was created 2 years later to relieve some of the complications of the existing CMO device by allowing the sale of equity partnerships as the residual portion of the CMO. Furthermore, one could purchase *pro rata* shares of residuals, thereby minimizing on-balance sheet recognition accounting issues. Thus, the base of potential investors in R tranches dramatically widened.

When the floating-rate class was introduced in 1986 by Fannie Mae, the financial engineering possibilities for R classes further increased. Previously, residual cash flows were composed of fixed-rate coupon spread or principal from overcollateralization (a form of credit enhancement). With a floating rate class and its inverse, the interest-rate sensitivity of an R class could vary in much more appealing ways. The introduction of PAC classes enlarged this economic freedom to maneuver. The 1986 Tax Reform Law allowed the free transfer of R classes without financial statement consolidation considerations or contingent liabilities for expenses, further advancing this trend.

4. Summary

Let us look back over what the plain vanilla agency REMIC structure has accomplished. First of all, because it was issued by a GSE, with its MBSs underlying it, the timely payment of principal and interest is guaranteed. Second, the large number of mortgages pooled together can dramatically reduce the uncertainty in prepayment speed or sensitivity to local economic factors. Third, it is clear that a REMIC backed by traditional mortgages can have classes much shorter in term than either 30 years or the practical 8- to 10-year life of the typical 30-year lien. The A tranche is a short-term instrument, the B tranche is an intermediate term instrument, the C tranche is a longer-term instrument, and the Z tranche is a long-term security that is not retired until every mortgage in the underlying pool has been fully paid off. Many different types of investors, with varying needs for cash flows over very different periods of time, could now have their needs much better met.

a. Callable MBSs and REMICs

A new development in the mortgage-backed security market is that of a *callable pass-through* security. Freddie Mac introduced this in June of 1995. The basic pass-through is a one-class security with each owner receiving an undivided interest and a *pro rata* share of the monthly cash flows. A callable pass-through is a two-class instrument in which the callable class receives all of the principal and interest from the underlying collateral and the call class receives none. (The owners of the callable class can be multiple as with the noncallable version.) The owner of the call class has the right to exercise his call option on the underlying pass-through, at a specified price plus accrued interest, from the callable class holders. Typically, there is a no-call or lockout period and a Bermudan call structure.

Investors in the callable class are still effectively long an amortizing bond and short a call option but the call option has one more component. One would expect that the owner of the call class will exercise his option in an economically reasonable fashion, whereas the individual homeowners whose mortgages are backing the pass-through may not. Therefore, the holders of the callable class will face reduced performance relative to a noncallable pass-through supported with comparable home loans. Consequently, the yield on a callable pass-through would be expected to be higher than that on a noncallable one (by about 20 to 50 bp).

A *callable REMIC* is one in which the REMIC is divided into two parts: the ordinary REMIC holders and the holder of a call option on the REMIC. The owners of the REMIC's other classes receive their cash flows according to the priority schedule outlined in the REMIC's prospectus. When the REMIC is called, all the outstanding tranches will be redeemed at par (with the option holder retaining all the outstanding collateral). Customarily there is a short lock-out or no-call period. The two main determinants of the probability of the call option being exercised are interest rate volatility and yield curve slope reshaping.

Higher volatility supposedly makes options more valuable because the belief is that the higher the volatility is, the more probable that the option will come into-the-money. Thus, if interest rate volatility is high, the holder of the call option will continue to wait until market interest rates have further moved his way, extending call protection to the holders of the callable REMIC. This is the standard logic of a call option holder who can, at most, lose the value of his call premium while, theoretically, being able to gain quite a bit. A steepening of the yield curve will enhance the call holder's interest in calling the REMIC to take advantage of the CMO arbitrage built into it upon issuance (see the next subsection).

Even a small decline in interest rates would encourage the exercise of the call because the call holder could finance the collapsed REMIC at lower short-term interest rates while receiving the higher, long-term rates owed to the longer-lived REMIC tranches. Moreover, if the yield curve steepens, then forward rates are increasing and thus diminishing prepayment speeds and extending the life of the REMIC tranches. This improves the prospect of receiving interest cash flow, the dominant component of the first decade's payment stream, and of increasing yield.

A *re-REMIC* is a newly issued REMIC partially backed by REMIC tranches already outstanding from earlier deals, instead of based upon newly manufactured mortgage-backed securities. I have seen REMIC structures with 50 to 60 different classes upheld four levels deep with other REMIC and re-REMIC tranches. Computing the interactions among all these parts, with varying prepayment speeds and changing interest rates, to determine the worth of what you are buying is effectively unattainable.

5. CMO Arbitrage

Suppose that you are considering constructing a plain vanilla REMIC. The yield curve is in its normal configuration of upward sloping. You, the dealer, will make money off the CMO arbitrage. The method that you will use is to price the A tranche, because it has the shortest anticipated life, off the short end of the yield curve. Thus, it will carry a relatively low interest rate with respect to the weighted average coupon of the underlying MBSs serving as collateral for the REMIC. As the next shortest, the B class will be priced a bit further along the yield curve and carry a slighter higher interest rate, and so on down to the Z class. You try to structure the REMIC such that the sum of [(the interest rate per tranche) × (the tranche face amount)] does not add up to (the pass-through rate on the underlying MBS) × (the total principal amount). As a dealer you want the former to sum to less than the latter so that you can take the difference as profits. The more steeply the yield curve is upwardly sloping, the easier this is to accomplish and the more you stand to make via this mechanism. Therefore, REMIC issuance usually increases as the yield curve steepens because of the CMO arbitrage effect and the ability to differentiate more clearly among the sequential and PAC tranches of a REMIC by coupon rate. The larger demand for product further increases the price, decreasing the spread to Treasuries.

Consider what happens when the yield curve is flat or inverted. Now there is very little or no CMO arbitrage to be had. Furthermore, investors will not want to purchase longer duration securities when faced with a flat or inverted yield curve. They expect long-term interest rates to rise rather than to fall further and this makes longer-maturity instruments currently unattractive. One consequence of this is a decrease in demand for traditional MBSs in the secondary market to serve as collateral for new REMIC deals. Hence, their prices drop owing to supply and demand considerations.

D. WHOLE-LOAN REMICs

The huge majority of whole-loan MBSs and REMICs are backed by jumbo mortgages. Savings and loan institutions, commercial banks, investment banking firms, and other secondary market mortgage conduits issue whole-loan MBSs. The collateral in a whole-loan MBS or REMIC is likely to be more heterogeneous with respect to many characteristics of the liens than those for a comparable agency-issued MBS.

The dispersion of coupon rates will be larger, as will the amount of seasoning. Loan balances will range from just above the conforming loan limit of the agencies to several times that amount. Whole-loan MBSs will contain liens amortizing over 30 years, plus 15- and 20- year amortization schedule loans. Geographic dispersion is likely to be less than in agency-issued securities that attempt to diversify on this basis (e.g., a Fannie Mae Major). The reason is that high house prices tend to be concentrated in California and the Northeast; therefore, such securities are much more subject to default risk because of this geographic concentration. For example, loans originated in Silicon Valley during the late 1990s are more likely to simultaneously go into default now that the dot com bubble has burst.

The A piece of a whole-loan REMIC is usually further divided up into classes by average life, for example, sequential pay classes, PACs, TACs, and so forth. The B piece, on the other hand, is frequently separated by credit risk. It may consist of several tranches representing first loss, second loss, and so on through last loss positions. These are referred to as *mezzanine tranches*.

1. The Servicer's Role

The role of the trustee and of the (master) servicer is more important for whole-loan MBSs than for agency-issued securities. For instance, when the homeowner is delinquent in making the monthly payment, will the servicer pay the investor? It depends on what type of *servicer advances* have been outlined in the REMIC's prospectus. Three varieties of advances are common:

1. The strongest is *mandatory advancing*, which means that, if the servicer fails to advance payments owed by delinquent homeowners, the servicer is in default.
2. Next in protection for the investor is *limited advancing* in which, if the servicer can demonstrate a high probability of recovery of delinquent amounts should the property go into foreclosure, then the timely advancing of missed payments is not required. Alternatively, a specified fraction of the amounts unpaid and overdue may be dictated to be forwarded.
3. Finally there is what is known as *optional financing*, which implies just what you think it does.

Another key role of the firm providing the servicing function concerns the issue of *compensating interest*. If a lien is refinanced mid-month, then the homeowner will not pay interest for the remainder of the month because the outstanding balance is now zero. However, the investor is expecting interest to be paid through the end of the month as is the norm with agency-issued securities. The apparent deficit of interest payment is known as compensating interest and may or may not be paid in full by the (master) servicer. It is clearly to the investor's benefit for compensating interest to be fully paid. The source of the compensating interest is usually the *excess servicing spread*. (There is also a compensating interest issue with respect to curtailments. Typically the servicer will not forward a part of a month's interest on any curtailments made by the homeowner.)

a.   A Cleanup Call

Most whole-loan REMICs have what is known as a *cleanup call* provision. For example, once the outstanding principal balance drops below 10% of its original amount, the servicer or residual class holders may decide to call in the outstanding amount. The main reason to do this is to benefit from not performing the allocation of cash flows and accounting tasks associated with such a small remaining dollar amount. Long-paying sequential classes, POs, and Z classes may have sudden drops in average life should the cleanup call be exercised. Freddie Mac uses a 1% cleanup call; Fannie Mae does not use one (but has one in its MBSs).

II. OTHER COMMON REMIC CLASSES

A. PLANNED AMORTIZATION CLASSES

While plain vanilla REMIC structures and stripped mortgage-backed securities can satisfy the demands of many investors, prepayment uncertainty still exists at a level beyond what some market participants want to bear. This led to the construction of two other REMIC tranches: PACs and TACs. A planned amortization class (PAC) is a tranche of REMIC with a much more precisely defined temporal cash flow structure than a sequential pay class. This is achieved by using two multiples of a standard prepayment speed curve to provide an upper bound on the maximum potential cash-flow rate and a lower bound on the minimum potential cash-flow speed. The narrower the width in the speed collar of the PAC's prepayment, the easier it is to compute the expected life of the tranche and the higher the probability of its realization.

This two-sided prepayment protection is arranged as follows: a typical PAC will have upper and lower prepayment speed bounds associated with it, for example, an 80 to 250% PSA PAC. This means that prepayments are designed to flow to this PAC at no less than 80% of the standard PSA speed given in Equation 5.1 and no faster than 250% of that rate. Since an investor knows the expected minimum and maximum prepayment rates, he can determine the maximum and minimum times to recoup his par value. The interest rate on a PAC will be lower than that on a sequential pay class because of the trade-off between risk and return.

1.   PAC Bands and Effective Collars

A PAC tranche normally has a companion class to absorb excess prepayments when they speed up above the ceiling of the prepayment speed collar and to provide cash flow when prepayments slow down too much to meet the floor of the initial PAC prepayment speed collar. One can carve out a series of PAC tranches with ever narrowing prepayment speed collars. First created in 1989, such classes are differentiated by referring to them as PAC I (the widest prepayment speed band), PAC II (the next widest), and so on down to the narrowest prepayment speed collar. The PAC I tranche can act as a companion class to the PAC II tranche, which in turn can act as a companion class to the PAC III tranche, and so forth.

A high level of prepayments will eventually drain down the prop provided by the companion class; therefore, the ceiling of the PAC collar can be broken in this circumstance. Rising interest rates leading to a significant slowdown in prepayment speeds are less likely to affect the floor of the collar similarly. The reason is not that the companion classes are so structured with sufficient capacity to provide cash flow in any circumstance; rather, the lower limit of the PAC band is generally chosen to be at the historical level of slow prepayments so that it will not be stressed. One does need to be concerned about the division of principal between the PAC class and its support class. Once a PAC collar's upper bound is breached by faster than expected prepayments, the ultimate shortening of the life of the tranche hinges on this ratio and the ability of the support class to absorb future prepayments. Once the support class is fully paid off, the PAC behaves like a sequential pay class. It is also said to be *busted*. If one is purchasing a PAC tranche within a multilevel PAC structure, such complications are even more difficult to work through and anticipate.

PAC band drift refers to the phenomenon that the actual PAC band changes from its initial values over time as prepayments wax and wane. This can occur even if prepayment speeds remain within the original PAC bands, something difficult to fully grasp. Consider what happens to the effective PAC bands if the prepayment speed of the underlying collateral is very high throughout the early years of the PAC, but still below the ceiling on the initial PAC prepayment speed collar. Because prepayments have been faster than expected at pricing, more of the support class will have been used up than was anticipated. As this is occurring, the effective upper bound of the collar will decrease.

Conversely, if prepayments are slower than expected at pricing, but still within the original PAC collar, then less of the support class will have been retired than was forecasted. As this is happening, the effective upper bound of the collar will increase. The key point is that all of this faster and slower talk is relative to the prepayment speeds used when the PAC class and its support class were apportioned their par amounts and the initial prepayment speed band determined at pricing. The *effective collar* for a PAC class is the combination of prepayment speeds that can occur in the future and still ensure that the PAC will not be "busted." Since prepayments, curtailments, and defaults occur, or do not occur, every month, the effective collar changes every month too.

a.   Special Cases

PAC II classes can exhibit complicated behavior with respect to prepayments because of alternatives in the principal cash-flow characteristics between it and the level I PAC. One variation is known as the *level-payment schedule*. This means that the amount of principal comprising the PAC II pay down schedule is the difference between the principal payments between the lower bound of the PAC I collar and the lower bound of the PAC II collar. This would be the case because the total amount of principal available, especially for shorter-life PACs, is dictated by the lower bound of the PAC band. Only if prepayments are faster than expected when the deal was constructed will cash flow be available to the subordinated classes.

Sometimes a PAC class is issued with a *lock-out structure*, meaning that no principal is paid to this class for the first few years after the issuance of the REMIC. (It still receives interest.) By incorporating this kind of feature, greater prepayment protection is afforded to all the other classes of the REMIC. Since the level I PAC cannot collect any principal, the second tier PAC is in danger of being rapidly paid down if prepayment speeds increase.

The last common variation is known as a *barbell payment schedule*, meaning that the principal cash flow is scheduled to come early in the life of the REMIC tranches and then later with relatively little to arrive in between. Structures with 5 to 10 years between the bulk of the cash flows have been tailored. Another alternative is to change the principal pay down rules of the standard REMIC so that excess principal is paid to the longer-dated PAC classes within a REMIC, rather than the shorter-dated ones, after the companion classes have been exhausted. This is known as a *reverse PAC*.

2. PAC Class Value Considerations

PAC classes designed to be short-term in life rarely have their prepayment speed bands "busted" because, even if significant changes occur in market interest rates over the lifetime of a 3- to 5-year PAC, the companion classes are still extant with a high enough principal balance to supply principal or absorb it. Remember too that the principal cash flows from a traditional mortgage are back-loaded in the sense that it takes a long time to reach the 50% principal to 50% interest level. This also accounts for the comparative certainty of expected cash flow from a short-average-life PAC class. Relatively speaking, buying a PAC makes one long in volatility while buying its companion class would make one short in volatility. The PAC's cash flows are much more protected from large interest rate alterations than the companion class's.

Because of the shorter maturity of the underlying collateral, both sequential pay and PAC tranches carved out of 15-year liens tend to be more stable than those whose support is the longer-maturity liens. The shorter maturity of the loans is amplified by the tendency for the mortgagors who hold loans of this type to prepay faster than those with longer-term instruments. Fifteen-year loans also have much more scheduled principal in the early monthly cash flows than do traditional ones. This makes it easier to structure a greater dollar value of PAC classes relative to their support classes. The trend is to make these classes appear more like fully amortizing bonds.

Super PACs are a less popular creation along these lines. These PAC classes have principal allocated to support classes twice that normally seen in a REMIC structure. Thus a super PAC can have a wider prepayment collar and a higher degree of certainty of remaining within it.

B. Support Classes

Except to mention the existence of support or companion classes, not much space has been devoted to describing them. Clearly, they represent the inverse of whatever they are propping up. By analyzing the class that they are sustaining, one can infer, at least in the simpler REMIC structures when the relationship is one-to-one, what the risks and rewards of a companion class will be. Just as clearly, the more stable the supported class is, the less likely that one is able to gauge cash flows for the support class. Consequently, they are sold at a considerable discount or have a high coupon rate.

Support tranches are sometimes divided up by expected average life. The risks of the shorter-term securities are mostly connected with extension risk, while those of the longer-term instruments are mostly associated with call risk. A short-term security can hardly shorten anymore and a long-term security can hardly lengthen anymore.

C. Targeted Amortization Classes

A REMIC tranche known as a targeted amortization class (TAC) is for an investor only interested in one-sided protection, specifically against extension risk. For this class, the one-sided prepayment protection is assured by quoting a maximum prepayment speed at which they may be received by the TAC owner. He earns a higher yield than if he had purchased a PAC because he is still accepting contraction risk while obtaining the kind of prepayment risk protection desired. If prepayments overshoot the prepayment speed when assumed for pricing the tranche, then the excess will be paid to its support class. This degree of safety is not as high as that of a PAC because, for a PAC class, any excess prepayments are first paid to its support classes and then to any TACs in the REMIC. Finally, if principal prepayments fall below the speed assumed when the deal was priced, then the TAC will extend.

1. Reverse TACs

A reverse TAC has call risk rather than call protection. A reverse TAC is a targeted amortization class with only downside prepayment speed protection. Thus, while a TAC is shielded against extension risk, a reverse TAC is sheltered against contraction risk.

2. More on IOs and POs

One can have *PAC POs* and *PAC IOs, TAC POs* and *TAC IOs, super POs* (which are highly leveraged), and so on. A PAC PO, instead of containing just a PO strip, has the PAC prepayment speed bands working in its favor. Hence, it will be much less sensitive to interest rate fluctuations than a straightforward PO strip will be. Similarly, a level II PAC PO is better protected than a level I PAC PO. Analyzing a particular tranche of a REMIC really depends on where it lies in the distribution rules for cash flow among all the other classes comprising the REMIC, on the evolution of interest rates and its effect on changing prepayment speeds (not to mention what underlies the REMIC, especially if it is a re-REMIC). Writing in generalities or showing one numerical specific example (tied to a particular interest rate set of circumstances and prepayment model) is of extremely limited predictive value.

D. FLOATING-RATE AND INVERSE FLOATING-RATE CLASSES

A floating-rate class of a REMIC is one whose coupon rates float with some index, for example, 6-month LIBOR. Since the collateral that lies beneath the REMIC is typically an MBS composed of fixed-rate whole loans, an inverse floating-rate class must be fashioned too. In the case of the inverse floating-rate, the coupon rate on the tranche moves in the direction opposite to market rates. The floating-rate class acts like the companion to the inverse floating-rate class and vice versa. The principal amounts and interest rates of the two tranches are adjusted such that the sum of their principal amounts equals some fraction of the total unpaid balance of the underlying whole loan mortgages; weighted by the principal amounts, the average coupon of the floater and the inverse floater is equal to the WAC of the REMIC.

One way to understand floating-rate tranches and their inverses is to start with a more basic class, for example, some sequential pay class or a PAC. We divide the principal amount and cash flows from this class into the floating-rate class plus the inverse floating-rate class. This is normally done with some leverage $L > 1$, so

$$\text{Some PAC of a REMIC} = \text{Floater} + \text{Inverse},$$

becomes, in terms of their prices,

$$(1 + L) \times P_{PAC} = P_{inv} + L \times P_{fl}.$$

As a specific numerical example, suppose that the desired leverage was 3:1, the PAC had a par amount of $200 million, and we wanted an inverse class worth $50 million. Then, since $L = 3$, the floating-rate class would have a par amount of $150 million. The price of the PAC tranche and that of the floating-rate tranche are market-based prices. The price of the inverse floater has been created based on them plus the required degree of leverage. The interest rate of the inverse is not relevant to its price. If we turn the formula around to read

$$P_{inv} = (1 + L) \times P_{PAC} - L \times P_{fl},$$

then we can see that one who purchases an inverse floating-rate tranche has effectively leveraged the PAC tranche and sold short, or financed it, by using L units of the floating-rate tranche. The PAC that was partitioned by this method has been priced off a particular point of the yield curve, so yield curve reshaping centered on this point can have large effects on P_{inv}.

The interest rates associated with the floating-rate and inverse-floating rate classes can be divided up in even more complicated ways. One proviso is that there always be a cap on the interest to be paid because you, the dealer, do not want to have an open-ended liability. Such tranches typically have floors too. First, consider dividing up a sequential pay tranche, with an 8% interest rate and $50 million of principal, into two different sequential pay classes with different interest rates. One way to do so would be to have $30 million at 10% plus $20 million at 5%. Note that the sum of the principal amounts equals that of the partitioned sequential pay class and the weighted average coupon equals the rate on the underlying sequential pay class (i.e., with the millions understood, $50 = $30 + $20 and $50 \times 0.08 =$ $30 \times 0.10 + 20×0.05).

The interest rate formula of a leveraged floating-rate tranche looks like

$$L \times (6\text{-month LIBOR}) - \text{Spread}.$$

There are usually two critical levels for the floating rate: the one that makes the inverse floater hit its cap and the one that makes the floater hit its floor. The interest rate on the inverse floater is of the form

$$\text{Maximum} - L \times (6\text{-month LIBOR}).$$

The maximum amount is the cap for the inverse floater; the floor is typically zero. Sometimes, floaters with $L > 1$ are known as *super floaters* or *leveraged floaters*. Those with $L < 1$ are referred to as a *de-leveraged floating rate* class. Every now and then, excess interest spread relative to the WAC of the divided up class will be stripped off to create an inverse IO. Pilpel (1995) treats this subject well.

a.   Numerical Example

Consider a floating-rate class whose interest rate is given by $3 \times (6\text{-month LIBOR})$ $- 16.5$ with a cap of 12% and a floor of 6%. Let the interest rate of the inverse floating-rate be $47.5 - 5 \times (6\text{-month LIBOR})$ with a cap of 10% and a floor of 0%. If 6-month LIBOR is less than 7.5%, the floater reaches its floor of 6% while the inverse realizes its cap of 10.75%. If 6-month LIBOR should attain 9.5%, then the floater reaches its cap of 12%. Simultaneously the inverse floater hits its floor of 0%.

1.   Duration and Yield Curve Considerations

Because the duration of the underlying PAC or sequential pay tranches in these examples must be conserved even upon division, the inverse floating-rate tranche can have a very large duration. With a factor of three leverage, and the PAC having a Macaulay duration D of 7 years, then $D_{inv} = 28 = 7 \times (1 + 3)$. The existence of the leverage with respect to the PAC shows how the prepayment sensitivity of that tranche can dramatically change the duration of the inverse floating-rate tranche. For inverse IOettes and inverse IOs in which the leverage might be 10:1 or higher, larger durations are also the norm. One way to understand how very high modified durations may be obtained is to remember that the modified duration of a floating-rate class is very near zero because its interest rate is always adjusting, so its price is always near par.

As mentioned previously, in addition to conserving duration in this subdivision process, the gross yield must be conserved. Thus, high effective yields of the derivative classes can be generated through leverage, depending on how one wants to manipulate the formulas so that some desired goal is reached for the characteristics of one or the other pieces of the broken up sequential pay class or PAC. Thus, yields on inverse-floating rate tranches can be 10 to 20%; those on IOs and IOettes can be hundreds of percent because of the small amount of real principal to be repaid.

To summarize, inverse floating-rate tranches are a leveraged derivative of a more basic (and stable) tranche — such as a sequential pay class, PAC, or TAC — and the floating-rate tranche. The yield of the inverse floating-rate tranche can move independently of its price; therefore, yields are not very informative of the value of such a class. The modified duration of an inverse floating-rate tranche can substantially understate its effective duration (that is, including the optionality component introduced by the prepayment options in the underlying MBSs). Finally, inverse floating-rate cash flows can be replicated by purchasing one unit of a fixed-rate tranche, entering into L swaps to receive the fixed-rate tranche coupon in exchange for paying (for example) 6-month LIBOR, and buying L interest rate caps. Therefore, the swap market has a direct effect on floating-rate tranche prices and on the prices for inverse floaters. Similarly, the swap and interest cap markets may be used to convert inverse IOs and IOettes into instruments whose cash flows resemble those of a fixed-rate instrument.

a. Example

Consider another example of creating a floater and an inverse-floater from a fixed-rate security. Suppose that you have $270 million of 8.25% mortgages in an MBS. You split the $270 million into two packages, one with a face value of two-thirds of this amount (i.e., $180 million) and one with a face value of one-third, or $90 million. The latter will trade at the Federal Home Loan Bank 11th District Cost of Funds Index (or COFI) plus 85 basis points. In addition, a cap of 13.5% is attached to this floater. The larger amount, representing the face value of the inverse-floater, has a coupon rate set equal to 11.95% – COFI/2 with a floor of 5.2%. The weighted average coupon is always 8.25%, whether or not the cap or the floor is in effect. To verify this, observe that $270 × 8.25 = $180 × (11.95 – COFI/2) + $90 × (COFI + 0.85) and that at COFI = 13.5, 11.95 – COFI/2 = 5.2.

2. Yield Curve Risk

Floating-rate and inverse floating-rate tranches are especially subject to yield curve risk (a change of shape of the yield curve particularly with regard to a dramatic increase or decrease in its the slope). Normally the inclination of the yield curve is taken to mean its average rate of change between the 2- and 10-year pricing points. Accepting this definition, one can compute the change in value of an interest sensitive security by imagining a ± 20% change in yield curve slope. One would do this by allowing for the change of shape, computing the new forward rates that this revised form of the yield curve implies, and then recalculating the present value of the contingent cash flows based on the new forward rates. The difference between the two prices is a sensitivity measure with respect to yield curve tilt alterations. Note that the absolute level of interest rates is not the paramount factor in this discussion.

For an inverse IO floating-rate class, a decline in interest rates is good, as is an amplification in the tilt of the yield curve. It is easy to understand the first part of the statement — decreasing interest rates will result in the yield of an inverse floater moving the other way. For the latter part, an increase in the slant of the yield curve will be interpreted as higher forward rates which, if realized, will decrease the incentive to refinance, thereby extending the life of the tranche carved up to form the floater and its inverse. However, the floating-rate tranche will prepay faster now; therefore, the inverse floater will extend.

E. OTHER CLASSES

1. VADMs

A very accurately determined maturity (VADM) tranche of a REMIC is a special type of accrual or Z class. The interest accruing to the Z class is not diverted to a sequential-pay class; instead, it is utilized to pay down the VADM. Thus, the VADM has relatively little extension risk because interest that can be used to pay it is always accruing to the Z class. A VADM is subject to contraction risk in the event that prepayments are extremely rapid. A VADM is similar to a reverse TAC and VADM tranches respond similarly to PACs with respect to their prepayment speed and yield curve risks.

2. Jump Zs and Sticky Jump Zs

A *jump-Z* tranche will move ahead in payment priority over the other tranches in a REMIC if a certain event, such as prepayment speeds exceed a particular level or interest rates cross the bounds of a collar, occurs. Normally the jump-Z tranche maintains this priority only as long as the trigger event is ongoing. *Sticky jump-Zs* maintain their higher priority to cash flows even if the trigger is no longer satisfied. Clearly, a sticky jump-Z will have a dramatic change in duration if the triggering event occurs.

One can take a PAC and slice off part of its cash flows to construct a Z tranche. This *PAC Z* will have the stability of the PAC to provide for a more constant average life and, consequently, less exposure to reinvestment risk. Support Z tranches for a PAC or TAC are another variation. Their cash flows are relatively unpredictable, with little or no call protection; hence, they are priced at a steep discount from par.

3. Notional IOs

Suppose that a considerable dispersion in coupon rates exists among the whole loan mortgages used to form the pool to construct an MBS. If this MBS is then used as collateral for a REMIC, excess interest may not be paid out to any of the REMIC's tranches. These cash flows once went to the R, or residual, class. Now one is likely to find, instead, an additional tranche of the REMIC whose cash flows are based solely on this excess coupon income: a *notional interest-only* or *nominal IO* class. This is not quite the same as the standard stripped MBS IO class. The notional principal is inferred based on computed the cash flow. If the total par value of the REMIC handled in this fashion is par and the amount of excess interest not apportioned to other tranches is ΔWAC, then the notional principal associated with the nominal IO is given by par $\times \Delta$WAC/WAC, where WAC is the weighted average coupon on the MBSs underlying the REMIC.

4. WAC IOs

Another feature is sometimes found in a whole-loan REMIC that is not normally found in an agency issuance — a *WAC IO*. A normal IO strip is created by peeling apart the interest-only part of the monthly cash flows from the principal-only part. In the usual situation the interest rate quoted on the IO is similar to the weighted-average coupon of the underlying pool of mortgages, but may be less. In some cases a sufficient number of mortgages may be in a pool with coupon rates higher than the quoted pass-through rate (known as the *remittance rate* in this circumstance) to provide cash flow to yet another tranche. If so, and this is done, then we would have created a WAC IO. Similarly, if the principal cash flows from all the liens with coupon rates in excess of the remittance rate are packaged together, these can form a *WAC PO*. It is the heterogeneity of the collateral with respect to an agency MBS that allows this to occur.

III. CREDIT ENHANCEMENTS

In mortgage investments a credit enhancement is a means of providing investors with greater certainty with respect to lack of loss from defaults, thereby increasing pricing efficiency and liquidity. A credit enhancement can be external or internal. For a whole-loan MBS or REMIC tranche, a triple-A credit rating from the usual bond rating agencies is desired. To accomplish this, with the exception of the nonrecourse sale of uninsured whole loans, almost all nonagency mortgage invest-ments include some type of credit enhancement. The economic motivations for credit enhancements are that: 1. from the perspective of the mortgage-backed security's issuer, its cost is exceeded by the increase in value of the investment (i.e., the revenue exceeds the expense), 2. for the third-party guarantors or insurers of the home loans, the revenue received in return for the assumption of credit risk, and 3. to the investors, the implied increased level of certainty with respect to the timely return of all the cash flows owed to them.

Especially in the fixed-income markets, investors (individual and company) are accustomed to using credit-related ratings to determine the yields that they will demand, or offer to pay, on a given type of security. In addition, regulatory require-ments or their own internal investment policies may prohibit institutional investors from purchasing assets below minimum rating levels (i.e., investment grade now by definition). When not forbidden, the higher risk-based capital requirements of lower-rated assets may make them uneconomic to own. The usual bond rating agencies specify the minimum levels of credit enhancement necessary to achieve a specified evaluation by employing historically based, statistical, econometric models that subject the underlying collateral to an economic stress. This would include a large variation in interest rates, high levels of unemployment, a decrease in housing prices, etc. The level of credit enhancement needed to endure the strains implies the appropriate rating. The more severe the economic scenario survived by the collateral (actually by the mortgagors) is, the higher the rating. Normally, an AAA or AA rating is desired for the senior tranche of a whole-loan security.

External credit enhancements are usually in the form of third-party guarantees that protect the first loss position of the senior tranche (up to a specified level, such as 10%). External credit enhancements most commonly come in the form of a corporate guarantee, a letter of credit, pool insurance, or bond insurance. Today a senior/subordinate structure is by far the most widespread form of internal credit enhancement for nonagency-eligible loans. Under this arrangement, the issuer, or a nonrisk adverse investor, assumes the bulk of the credit risk by taking a subordinate position in the issued security. A subordinate position holder might assume 100% of the credit losses up to a predetermined percentage of the pool's par value.

A. External Forms of Credit Enhancements

1. Pool Insurance

Primary mortgage insurance covers each loan, without regard to the aggregate amount of previously paid claims. Primary mortgage insurance can be borrower-, lender-, or investor-paid. Supplemental mortgage insurance is an additional layer of protection (usually a *pool policy*) that pays the actual loss remaining after the insured collects from the primary mortgage insurer. The insurance pool may also include loans without primary mortgage insurance. Frequently purchased from a *monoline* insurance company, pool insurance indemnifies each loan at the outset. Whether a claim will be paid when a default occurs depends on whether the aggregate amount of previously paid claims has equaled a *stop loss* or a *benefit cap* amount. Traditional pool insurance insures each loan for the full extent of the loss after a sale of the property and receipt of any primary mortgage insurance benefits, subject to the benefit cap of the pool. *Modified pool insurance* coverage is provided by a policy that has a pool-level stop loss and also a stop loss level on each loan. A *fill-up pool* is a policy to which loans can be added over a designated time period.

A pool insurance policy covers losses from defaults and foreclosures on the underlying mortgages up to the amount required to obtain the desired AA or AAA rating. Policies are normally written for a fixed dollar amount of coverage that remains in force throughout the life of the pool. The insurance company providing the pool policy must have a rating equal to or higher than the desired rating on the pass-through. There is also the quandary of event risk, meaning that, if the insurer is down-graded by the rating agency, then so will be the security that they insure (even if no negative occurrences have been associated with it). This transpired repeatedly in the 1980s when commercial banks that had guaranteed whole-loan MBSs had monetary difficulties because of their exposure to large amounts of defaulting Latin American debt.

Since default rates on home loans typically rise, peak, and then lessen, some pool policies are written with a decreasing coverage amount as the collateral seasons (somewhat analogous to decreasing term life insurance, sometimes suggested for a mortgagor). The rating agency must approve this and might do so because the loss record of this pool is less than the average rate. Finally, losses occurring because of bankruptcy on the part of the mortgagor are usually not covered because bankruptcy court judges, and many state bankruptcy laws, tend to favor homeowners. Pool policies were a commonly used form of credit enhancement on whole-loan MBSs issued in the 1980s and early 1990s. Then the mortgage insurance companies stopped issuing pool policies or priced them at very expensive levels to recoup their losses on earlier policies. For jumbo collateral with an A credit rating, the senior/subordinate structure is much more economical.

2. Bond Insurance

Bond insurance is currently the preferred means of credit enhancement for subprime and 125% LTV issues. (This means that the homeowner can take out a mortgage whose face amount exceeds that of the property's current evaluation by 25%.) Bond insurers are similar to pool insurers in that they cover losses on foreclosure but differ in that they guarantee the entire senior class rather than just a percentage of the losses. Because they guarantee the entire senior class, the rating on the pass-through is equal to the bond insurer's corporate debt rating. It is customary for bond insurance to play a secondary role (that is, as a supplement to another form of credit enhancement).

3. Other Forms

Other forms of external credit enhancement include letters of credit or a corporate guarantee; these are also subject to event risk. The bank issuing a letter of credit must be rated at least as high as the related bond issue. Risk-based capital regulations have made the issuance of letters of credit unattractive for banks. Also, only a few mortgage originators are able to obtain letters of credit on an unsecured basis; therefore, their capital is tied up too. Thus, letters of credit are not commonly used today as mortgage credit enhancements.

B. INTERNAL CREDIT ENHANCEMENTS

1. Senior/Subordinated Structures

For nonagency securities, the most prevalent form of credit enhancement is the senior/subordinate structure. When using this configuration, the bonds are divided into classes by credit risk, known as the A piece and the B piece. (These are not the A and B sequential pay tranches of a REMIC.) The intent is for the A piece to be rated AAA or AA, while the B piece may range from nonrated to AA. With principal amounts of 6 to 8% (10 to 12%) for fixed-rate (floating-rate) mortgages devoted to the B portion, the senior or A slice can typically receive a triple-A rating.

Both the A and B pieces are usually further divided up, but in different ways. The A portion is separated by average life and prepayment protection (as in a sequential-pay REMIC structure, though it might include PACs) while the B member is separated into other tranches by credit risk exposure. These classes are sometimes referred to as mezzanine tranches. Within the B piece, different priority positions are established that determine the order in which losses from foreclosures are absorbed, such as first loss piece, second loss piece, third loss, and so forth.

Assume that an issuer takes a 1% first loss position and sells a 2% second loss position on a $200 million issue. Let the losses on foreclosures average 25% of the principal amount. If the issue experiences a 7% foreclosure rate, then the total losses would be $3.5 million (7% × 25% × $200 million). The first loss position would absorb its full 1% × $200,000,000 = $2,000,000 in losses. Then the second loss position would absorb the remaining $1,500,000. Assuming no additional losses, the second loss position would eventually recover $2.5 million of its original $4 million position. Meanwhile, the A piece would be fully protected.

2. Reserve Funds

Two other methods used to ensure that sufficient cash flow is available from the subordinate pieces to cover losses are *reserve funds* and a *shifting interest structure* (which, confusingly, has nothing to do with the interest payments owed on the loans). Reserve funds come in two forms: *cash reserve funds* and excess servicing spread generated. Cash reserve funds are deposits of monies spawned by the issuance process. They derive from the underwriting profits of the deal and are used to compensate the first loss holders in the event of default or foreclosure. If insufficient cash is deposited to attain the desired credit rating for the senior tranche, then another form of credit enhancement, e.g., a letter of credit, might be used in combination. Excess servicing spread accounts are created because of a difference between the gross weighted average coupon and the net weighted average coupon (exclusive of servicing fees). The amount in such an account will gradually increase over time and can be used to pay off the first loss holder in the event of default or foreclosure. This is exactly analogous to a guarantee fee charged by an agency (i.e., it is essentially a low coupon IO strip).

3. Shifting Interest Structure

A shifting interest structure is a financial device used to divert cash flows from the higher-risk B piece to the lower-risk A piece. It requires that prepayments and curtailments be disproportionately transferred from the subordinate class to the senior class, for example, during the first 5 to 10 years of the life of the security. Moreover, this deviation from *pro rata* receipt of prepayments might decrease over time — for example, 100% of prepayments to the A piece for the first 5 years, 70% for the next year, 60% for the next year, 40% for the 8th year, only 20% for the 9th year, and none thereafter. As a result, the senior class is paid down more quickly, causing the B class outstanding principal balance to grow relative to that of A's. By accelerating the rate at which the owners of the A tranche receive their monies, less of its principal is at risk for a shorter period of time. Hence, the A piece holder is protected against losses later in the life of the underlying mortgages. Furthermore, because all prepayments and curtailments go to the senior tranche, its average life can be considerably shortened if a refinancing boom takes place.

a. Overcollateralization

Overcollateralization refers to the situation in which the outstanding unpaid principal balance of the collateral is greater than the issue amount. The extra cash flow received on a monthly basis is reserved to cover potential cash flow shortfalls in later months. Upon the stated maturity of the deal, any remaining excess funds would be distributed to the residual holder.

7 Interest Rate-Related Topics

What do we need to know about the term structure of interest rates and the yield curve? Aside from the definitions, it would be wonderful if we understood what drove them from day to day or even month to month. Then we could attempt to predict interest rates or perhaps just interest rate trends. With this information we could price assets and liabilities and forecast cash flows and mark-to-market values. These curves also provide hidden information regarding interest rates for future times for agreements that we enter into today. These forward rates are an important component in arbitrage-free pricing. They are also utilized in interest rate modeling and interest rate cap, floor, and swap pricing, all of which will be treated. Finally, several small sections on what can reasonably be accomplished and how are presented.

I. THE TERM STRUCTURE OF INTEREST RATES AND THE YIELD CURVE

A. DEFINITIONS

"The term structure of interest rates" is the curve that shows the time dependence of interest rates on U.S. Treasury instruments **without** coupon payments, i.e., on zero coupon bonds (or their equivalents). "The" yield curve is the graph that illustrates the time dependence of interest rates on U.S. Treasury instruments **with** coupon payments. Both are usually exhibited by plotting interest rate against time to maturity from 3 months to 30 years. One can define other types of yield curves and term structures — for instance, the yield curve for corporate AAA bonds, that for AA bonds in the manufacturing sector of the economy, and so on. The only requirement to make these diagrams meaningful is that comparably risky debt products that are traded in a reasonably liquid fashion be all along the time axis. When one speaks of "the" yield curve or "the" term structure of interest rates, then the U.S. Treasury curve — that is, risk-free rates — is always understood.

The yield curve has existed only since the mid-1970s, following the repeal of Regulation Q, rapid inflation as a result of not raising taxes to pay for the Vietnam War, taking the U.S. off the gold standard in 1972 and thus allowing the dollar to float, the first Arab oil embargo following the 1973 Yom Kippur war, selling of 30-year Treasury bonds in volume starting in 1977, and the resulting volatility launched into heretofore relatively stable borrowing and lending markets.

1. The Differences among Them

When the term structure of interest rates is upward sloping, then the term structure always lies above the yield curve. The reason is that a coupon-paying bond returns some monies to an investor earlier than if he had purchased a zero coupon bond. The quicker return of funds results in a lower discount rate for the fastest returning monies and a higher discount rate for the more slowly returning payments. Similarly, with an upward sloping yield curve, the forward rate curve lies above the zero coupon rate curve. When the yield curve is downward sloping, this order is reversed, with the yield curve lying above the term structure that serves as an upper bound to the forward rate curve.

2. Appearance

The normal (most common) shape for the yield curve or the term structure of interest rates is upward sloping from the short-term rate to the long-term rate. Upward sloping can mean a long to short difference of 300 basis points or only 100 basis points. See Figure 7.1. The former would be referred to as a steeply upward sloping curve, the latter as a shallow or nearly flat upward sloping curve. "Short-term" once referred to 3 months but, with the introduction of the 1-month T-Bill, it now means 1 month. "Long-term" once referred to 30 years but, with the termination of the sales of those bonds, it effectively now means 10 years (and refers to the 10-year U.S. Treasury Note). Obviously, old 30-year T-Bonds are still outstanding.

A flat yield curve would be one constant in time. Historically these are extremely rare in practice. An inverted yield curve is one that has short-term rates higher than long-term rates. A *humped yield curve* is one that rises from low short-term rates, reaches a maximum at some intermediate term, and then falls. In the past decades these two types were mostly seen coming into or going out of a recession. In the last few years, however, many of the abnormal yield curve profiles have appeared much more frequently because of supply and demand effects.

3. "Explanations" for the Curves

There are no good explanations for the shapes of these curves. The liquidity premium hypothesis, anticipated inflation hypothesis, and supply and demand considerations are believable stories (some of the time) but not of any predictive, quantitative use. Among others, the expectations explanation anticipates that investors believe that the forward rates embedded in the yield curve will be realized as spot rates. Since the yield curve is normally upward sloping, this immediately has the embarrassment of predicting ever increasing interest rates. One modification of this is to confine the fulfillment of one's expectations to only short-term forward rates. Another is to introduce statistical noise into the exposition and essentially argue that the best predictor of tomorrow's spot rate is today's. This is an historically true fact and belies the use of a binomial lattice model interest rate computation (see below).

The market segmentation explanation argues that different investors have different time preferences and liquidity concerns. Hence, it will take an exceptional opportunity to make a short-term investor purchase long-term securities and vice

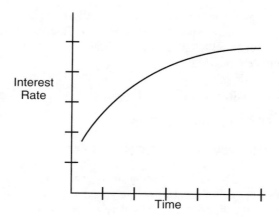

FIGURE 7.1 A heuristic version of the standard upward sloping yield curve. Many more complex shapes have been the norm in the last few years. The spread between the long-term and short-term ends has also varied from about 100 bp to several hundred basis points.

versa. Thus, in general, there will be independent and nonmixing forces (investment amounts) driving short-, intermediate-, and long-term rates. This is sometimes referred to as the preferred habitat explanation. (Cute names with no real information content are just cute names.)

a. The Liquidity Premium Hypothesis

This hypothesis asserts that the normal, upward-sloping shape of the yield curve can be understood because investors prefer to keep their fixed-income assets in a relatively liquid state. To induce them to rent out their money for ever increasing periods of time requires an ever increasing premium to be paid. Hence, longer-term interest rates must be higher than medium-term rates, which, in turn, must be higher than shorter-term ones to compensate financiers for lost investment opportunities and a higher default risk. The interest rate for some time span t, i(t), must include the underlying interest rate R(t) plus the liquidity premium at that time, L(t);

$$i(t) = R(t) + L(t) \text{ and if } T > t, \text{ then } L(t) > L(T).$$

The liquidity premium is assumed to be a monotonically decreasing function of time ($\partial L/\partial t < 0$). This accounts for the asymptotic approach to the longest term rate of the normally upward-sloping yield curve. The amplitude of the time dependence of the liquidity premium, that is, its large rise in between short- and medium-terms and not between medium- and long-terms, is unexplained.

b. Supply and Demand

The abnormally severe consequences in the fixed-income markets of the Russian government default of August, 1998 was a classic case of supply and demand factors determining the shape of the yield curve. The invisible results of the Argentinian government default in the fall of 2001 was a more reasoned instance of what should happen when some tangential economic/political/military event occurs — nothing.

Nonetheless, supply and demand factors are much more likely to produce unusual yield curve shapes than the standard explanations. Because human beings are controlling the markets, and their money is at stake, no meaningful prediction of direction or amplitude is possible.

B. TYPES OF INTEREST RATES

1. Spot Rates (Discrete Compounding)

The basic set of interest rates defining a term structure of interest rates (or the yield curve) are spot rates. These are the interest rates quoted today for borrowing or lending for one, two,..., N periods, starting today. The interest rate for one-period lending or borrowing, beginning now, or the one-year spot rate, is denoted by s_1; similarly s_2 will be the symbol for the interest rate for two-period lending or borrowing commencing today, and so on, and s_N for the rate for N-period lending or borrowing beginning today. (Note the continuing and explicit neglect of transaction costs; the borrowing rate is taken to be equal to the lending rate. This unrealistic assumption makes it simpler to formulate no-arbitrage arguments.)

Spot rates are used to compute more reasonable present values than the assumption of a flat, or never-changing, yield curve. The present value (PV) for a single, one-time cash flow of a future value amount FV, occurring N periods out, in terms of s_N, is given by

$$PV = FV/(1 + s_N)^N, N = 1,2,... \tag{7.1}$$

The inverse relationship is given by

$$s_N = (FV/PV - 1)^{1/N}, N = 1,2,...$$

a. Exercise

1. Let the Nth spot rate be $s_N = 0.0987$ per year, the future value be FV = \$5,696.11, and N = 10 years. Compute the present value PV. (PV = \$2,222.22)

The present value of a bullet bond with a nonflat yield curve is the sum of each coupon payment C discounted back to the present by its own spot rate plus the redemption amount similarly treated. Let $\{s_n\}$ be the set of spot rates, one for each payment period, n = 1,2,..., N. Let F be the face amount of the bond, in dollars. In addition, let N be the total number of payment periods and let PV signify the present value in dollars of the N coupon payments and the repayment of the principal F, discounted at $\{s_n\}$. Then, by extension of Equation 7.1,

$$PV = C/(1+s_1)^1 + C/(1+s_2)^2 + \cdots + (C+F)/(1+s_N)^N$$
$$= \sum_{n=1}^{N} C/(1+s_n)^n + F/(1+s_N)^N.$$

b. Numerical Example

Let the annual spot rates be $\{s_n\} = \{0.0555, 0.0666, 0.0777, 0.0888\}$, the coupon $C = \$123.45$, and the face value $F = \$15,000$. Then, since $N = 4$, the formula for the present value is

$$PV = C/(1+s_1)^1 + C/(1+s_2)^2 + C/(1+s_3)^3 + (C+F)/(1+s_4)^4$$
$$= \$123.45/(1 + 0.0555)^1 + \$123.45/(1 + 0.0666)^2 + \$123.45/(1 + 0.0777)^3$$
$$+ (\$123.45 + \$15,000.00)/(1 + 0.0888)^4 = \$11,085.24.$$

The present value formula for any series of cash flows, $\{CF_n\}$, each discounted by its own spot rate s_n, $n = 1,2,\ldots, N$, can also be written by adding up the separate present values from Equation 7.1:

$$PV = CF_1/(1+s_1)^1 + CF_2/(1+s_2)^2 + \cdots + CF_N/(1+s_N)^N$$
$$= \sum_{n=1}^{N} CF_n/(1+s_n)^n. \tag{7.2}$$

c. Mortgages

For a traditional mortgage, the present value, PV, with a nonflat yield curve and no principal prepayments, if MP is the monthly payment amount in dollars, looks like

$$PV = MP/(1+s_1)^1 + MP/(1+s_2)^2 + \cdots + MP/(1+s_{360})^{360}$$
$$= \sum_{n=1}^{360} MP/(1+s_n)^n.$$

d. Spot Rates (Multiperiod Payments)

With m payment periods per year, an amount of PV dollars, after N years, would be worth FV dollars, where

$$FV = PV \times (1 + s_N/m)^{mN}.$$

e. Spot Rates (Continuous Compounding)

If the interest is compounding continuously, then the relationship between the present value of a \$1, zero coupon bond at time t, maturing at a later time $T \geq t$ [for example, $PV(t,T)$] is related to the continuously compounded spot rate at time t for maturity $T- t$ later, $s(t,T)$ by

$$PV(t,T) = \$1.00 \times \exp[-s(t,T) \times (T - t)]. \tag{7.3}$$

Solving for the spot rate in terms of the price results in $(T \neq t)$

$$s(t,T) = -ln[PV(t,T)]/(T - t). \tag{7.4}$$

The formula is written in this form so that both the numerator and denominator are positive (remember that $s > 0$ and $PV < \$1$, so its logarithm is negative).

2. Forward Rates (Discrete)

Forward rates are one set of interest rates implicitly defined by a term structure. The forward rate $f(t,T)$ is the interest rate quoted today, that is, at time 0, for borrowing money starting at time t $(t \geq 0)$ and lasting for a period of $T - t$ (≥ 0) years into the future. Note the three moments of time associated with a forward rate: 1. now, the time of the pricing (time 0 in this example), 2. the instant that borrowing or lending commences with this forward rate (time t), and 3. the instant that borrowing or lending terminates with this forward rate (time $T \geq t \geq 0$).

Continue to use discrete time periods, for example, a year, and to denote the 1-year spot rate as s_1, the 2-year spot rate as s_2, and so forth. Instead of writing $f(1,2)$ for discrete forward rates, utilize subscript notation, $_2f_5$, to indicate the forward interest rate for borrowing or lending money commencing 2 years from now (the leading subscript of two) for 3 years (deduced from the difference between the trailing subscript of five and the leading subscript of two: $5 - 2 = 3$) and agreed to now. In general, $_nf_m$, where $0 \leq n < m$ will denote a forward rate commencing n years (or whatever basic time interval is used) from now and terminating $m - n$ years after that. If $m = n$, then $_nf_m$ vanishes. Note that $_0f_N$ is identical to the N-period spot rate s_N.

To deduce the forward rate $_1f_2$ from s_1 and s_2, observe that the interest cost of borrowing or lending \$1 for 2 years, starting now at time 0, can be equivalently expressed, assuming the absence of an arbitrage opportunity, as

$$\$1.00 \times (1 + s_1) \times (1 + {}_1f_2) \text{ or as } \$1.00 \times (1 + s_2)^2. \tag{7.5}$$

In the first expression the assumption is that \$1 was borrowed for 1 year at the 1-year spot rate starting now at time zero. It was also known, at time zero, that the loan could be rolled over for another year, in 1 year, at today's quoted 1-year forward rate. In the second expression the assumption is that \$1 was borrowed for 2 years at the current 2-year spot rate. Absent an arbitrage opportunity, these two interest expenses must be equal. It is not possible to overemphasize the fact that all the internal mathematics about spot, forward, and short rates are really statements about the borrowing or lending costs of money over multiple time periods in various ways. That is why the \$1 factor in front of these expressions has been stressed.

The pricing rule can be expanded to 3- and 4-year intraperiod rates by writing all the equivalent ways for borrowing for a 3- or 4-year term and equating the resulting costs. For 3 years the results are

$$\$1.00 \times (1 + s_3)^3 \equiv \$1.00 \times (1 + {}_0f_3)^3 = \$1.00 \times (1 + s_1) \times (1 + {}_1f_2) \times (1 + {}_2f_3)$$
$$= \$1.00 \times (1 + s_1) \times (1 + {}_1f_3)^2 = \$1.00 \times (1 + s_2)^2 \times (1 + {}_2f_3). \qquad (7.6)$$

All the possible four-period formulas are

$$\$1.00 \times (1 + {}_0f_4)^4 \equiv \$1.00 \times (1 + s_4)^4 = \$1.00 \times (1 + {}_0f_3)^3 \times (1 + {}_3f_4)$$
$$= \$1.00 \times (1 + {}_0f_1) \times (1 + {}_1f_2) \times (1 + {}_2f_3) \times (1 + {}_3f_4)$$
$$= \$1.00 \times (1 + {}_0f_1) \times (1 + {}_1f_4)^3 = \$1.00 \times (1 + {}_0f_1) \times (1 + {}_1f_2) \times (1 + {}_2f_4)^2$$
$$= \$1.00 \times (1 + {}_0f_1) \times (1 + {}_1f_3)^2 \times (1 + {}_3f_4) = \$1.00 \times (1 + {}_0f_2)^2 \times (1 + {}_2f_4)^4$$
$$= \$1.00 \times (1 + {}_0f_2)^2 \times (1 + {}_2f_3) \times (1 + {}_3f_4).$$

There are $N(N + 1)/2$ intraperiod rates in an N element of the term structure but only N of them are independent. One fundamental set is the spot rates $\{{}_0f_n\} = \{s_n\}$. Another is the set of *short rates*. The most general expression involving two spot rates and the implied forward rate between them is given in the next exercise.

a. Exercises

1. Show that, or explain why, $(1 + {}_mf_n)^{n-m} = (1 + s_n)^n/(1 + s_m)^m$.
2. If the rate for 3-year money today is 11.55% $(= {}_0f_3)$ and the rate for 2-year money today is 10.99% $(= {}_0f_2)$, then what is the rate for 1-year money 2 years from today $(= {}_2f_3)$? $[(1 + {}_0f_3)^3/(1 + {}_0f_2)^2 = 1 + {}_2f_3; 12.678\%]$
3. Given the numbers from the preceding exercise, if the current rate for 1-year money is 9.87% $(= {}_0f_1)$, then what is the rate for 1-year money 1 year from now $(= {}_1f_1)$? $[(1 + {}_0f_2)^2 = (1 + {}_0f_1) \times (1 + {}_1f_2); 12.121\%$ and note that $(1.0987 \times 1.1212 \times 1.1268)^{1/3} = 1.1155]$
4. Suppose that ${}_0f_4 = 14.319\%$, ${}_1f_4 = 13.229\%$, ${}_2f_4 = 12.145\%$, and ${}_1f_3 = 14.315\%$. Determine the underlying 4-year term structure of interest rates. (17.652%, 15.429%, 13.212%, and 11.088%)
5. Show that if the yield curve is flat at some level i, then all the forward rates equal i too.

3. Short Rates (Discrete)

Short rates are the forward interest rates for a single time period. The short rate S_n is identical to ${}_nf_{n+1}$. The relationship between the spot rate s_N and the short rates S_0, $S_1,\ldots, S_{N-1}$, is given by

$$(1 + s_N)^N = (1 + S_0) \times (1 + S_1) \times \bullet\bullet\bullet \times (1 + S_{N-1}) = \prod_{n=1}^{N} (1 + S_{n-1}).$$

The relationship between the forward rate ${}_nf_m$ and the short rates S_n, $S_{n+1},\ldots, S_{m-1}$ is given by

$$(1 + {}_nf_m)^{m-n} = (1 + S_n) \times (1 + S_{n+1}) \times \bullet\bullet\bullet \times (1 + S_{m-1}) = \prod_{k=n+1}^{m} (1 + S_{k-1}).$$

a. Short Rates and Expectations

Observe that, under the hypothesis that forward rates will be realized as future spot rates, the short rates do not change with time except to roll down the yield curve. If today's short rates are $S_0, S_1..., S_N$, then next year they will be $S_1, S_2,..., S_{N-1}$ and the year after that they will be $S_2, S_3,..., S_{N-2}$, and so on. This is one reason why short rates are the preferred independent variables in interest rate models.

4. Spot Rates (Continuously Compounded and Continuous)

The continuous spot rate, s(t), is usually defined in terms of the continuous forward rate. If f(t,T) is the continuously compounded forward rate, at time zero (i.e., now), and with $T > t \geq 0$, then the continuously compounded spot rate s(t) = f(t,T). More properly one should take the limit as $T \to t$ to produce the instantaneous, continuously compounded, spot rate at time t, s(t)

$$s(t) = \lim_{T \to t} f(t,T).$$

a. Spot Rates (Simple and Continuous)

In analogy with Equation 7.3, one can define a continuously compounded simple spot interest rate S in terms of the price, or present value, of a zero coupon, $1 bond, PV(t,T);

$$PV(t,T) = 1/[1 + S \times (T - t)] \text{ or } S = [1/PV(t,T) - 1]/(T - t).$$

5. Forward Rates (Continuous)

The continuously compounded forward rate $f(\tau,t,T)$ is given by the ratio of the present values of two one-dollar zero coupon bonds from time tau τ to T and one from time τ to t ($T \geq t \geq \tau \geq 0$);

$$PV(\tau,T)/PV(\tau,t) = \exp[-f(\tau,t,T) \times (T - t)]. \tag{7.7a}$$

The inverse relationship is given by

$$f(\tau,t,T) = -\{ln[PV(\tau,T)] - ln[PV(\tau,t)]\}/(T - t). \tag{7.7b}$$

Writing it in this form, when we take the limit and let $T \to t$, the result will be

$$f(\tau,t) = -\partial ln[PV(\tau,t)]/\partial t. \tag{7.7c}$$

a. Going Backward

From the definition of the continuously compounded forward rate as a partial derivative, we can go backwards and solve for the present value $PV(\tau,t)$ as a function of $f(\tau,t)$. The result is

$$\int_{\tau}^{t} d\ln\,[PV(\tau,t')] = -\int_{\tau}^{t} f(\tau,t')\,dt' = \ln[PV(\tau,t)] - \ln[PV(\tau,\tau)].$$

The last expression is the value of a \$1 zero coupon bond at maturity, or \$1. Since the logarithm of unity is zero, this formula reduces to

$$\ln[PV(\tau,t)] = -\int_{\tau}^{t} f(\tau,t')\,dt', \text{ or } PV(\tau,t) = \$1.00 \times \exp\left[-\int_{\tau}^{t} f(\tau,t')\,dt'\right]. \qquad (7.8)$$

This is an important alternative to the Equation 7.3 pricing formula for a zero coupon bond.

b. More Details

For the case of continuous compounding, forward rates are merely arithmetic averages ($n \geq m$ implying $t_n \geq t_m$)

$$\exp(s_n \times t_n) = \exp(s_m \times t_m) \times \exp[{}_m f_n \times (t_n - t_m)]$$

so that

$${}_m f_n = (s_n \times t_n - s_m \times t_m)/(t_n - t_m).$$

Moreover, if the spot rate curve is flat, $s(t) = s_0$, then all the forward rates are equal to s_0 as well.

c. Forward Rates (Continuous Simple Interest)

$$f(t,T_1,T_2) = [1 - PV(t,T_2)/PV(t,T_1)]/(T_2 - T_1) \text{ where } T_2 \geq T_1 \geq t \geq 0.$$

C. CONSTRUCTING THE TERM STRUCTURE

The Wall Street Journal publishes every business day. Almost every day that it is printed it contains a plot of the yield curve for the previous day. (For a few days after September 11, 2001 there was no plot.) Where does this curve come from? Why does it have the smoothness that it does? Let us address these issues in turn.

1. Statistical Issues

There is much ado about little in discussions of fitting observations of zero coupon or coupon-paying bond prices to a term structure or a yield curve. They tend to center around

- The liquidity, or lack of liquidity, of a particular maturity date
- The relative importance of the *TED* spread (the difference between the U.S. Treasury spot rates and those on Eurodollar deposits)
- The comparative prominence of the LIBOR yield curve vs. the Treasury yield curve with respect to liquidity and the number of benchmark rates, especially long-term ones
- The fungability of cash and the role that the interest rate swap markets play as alternative investments —and therefore pricing
- Whether or not an arbitrage-free result is of paramount importance (as opposed to actually matching the real data, which often reflect nontrivial supply and demand factors)
- The role of the futures and options markets in inferring interest rate volatility
- The esthetically desired appearance of the plot, and so forth

The uses to which this particular fit will be put also play a significant role in determining how and what to use to fit what to and why. I have neither read nor heard a thoughtful, informed discussion of the appropriateness or, more significantly, the lack of appropriateness, of the actual numerical techniques utilized to perform the statistical smoothing and adjustment processes to financial data. Least squares, spline-fitting algorithms, exponential smoothing, and so forth have their uses, but not necessarily here.

The next two subsections show how to perform the computations in an ideal world without these practical considerations (that is, after choice of the raw pricing data base, its initial smoothing by statistical means, the weights assigned by the number of dollars invested (?), and the formation of the benchmark prices along the term structure or yield curve).

2. Using Zero Coupon Instruments

Suppose that one has the following prices (in 32nds) for three comparable 1-, 2-, and 3-year-to-maturity, zero-coupon bonds. "Comparable" means the same credit rating, liquidity, and so forth.

$$\text{Year 1: Price} = 94{:}7 = PV_1;$$

$$\text{Year 2: Price} = 87{:}5 = PV_2;$$

$$\text{Year 3: Price} = 79{:}13 = PV_3.$$

If the face value of each bond is F = \$100, then we can infer the 1-, 2-, and 3-year zero-coupon spot rates s_1, s_2, and s_3, by "boot-strapping"; for it must be true that the following equations all simultaneously hold:

$$PV_1 = F/(1 + s_1), PV_2 = F/(1 + s_2)^2, \text{ and } PV_3 = F/(1 + s_3)^3.$$

Straightforward computation reveals that (refer to Equation 7.1) s_1 = 6.136%/year, s_2 = 7.115%/year, and s_3 = 7.990%/year.

3. Using Coupon-Paying Instruments

Constructing the term structure from comparable coupon-paying bonds is performed in a similar manner; simply remember the coupon payments. You again have three bonds priced with cash flows as shown in the following table. Each bond has a face value of \$100:

Bond	Year 1	Year 2	Year 3	Price
#1	\$5.55	\$0	\$0	100–01
#2	\$6.66	\$6.66	\$0	99–15
#3	\$7.77	\$7.77	\$7.77	99–07

Then we can infer the 1-, 2-, and 3-year spot rates s_1, s_2, and s_3 as follows; it must be that the following equations simultaneously hold, lest there be an arbitrage opportunity:

$$PV_1 = (F + C_1)/(1 + s_1), PV_2 = C_2/(1 + s_1) + (C_2 + F)/(1 + s_2)^2,$$

and

$$PV_3 = C_3/(1 + s_1) + C_3/(1 + s_2)^2 + (C_3 + F)/(1 + s_3)^3.$$

Start with Equation 7.2 and PV_1 = (\$100.00 + \$5.55)/(1 + $_0f_1$) = \$100.03125 and deduce for the 1-year spot rate the value of s_1 = $_0f_1$ = 5.517%. Next use this, plus the formula PV_2 = \$6.66/(1 + $_0f_1$) + (\$100.00 + \$6.66)/(1 + $_0f_2$)^2 = \$99.46875, to infer that the 2-year spot rate must be given by s_2 = $_0f_2$ = 7.002%. Finally, combining these two results with the last equation, PV_3 = \$7.77/(1 + $_0f_1$) + \$7.77/(1 + $_0f_2$)^2 + (\$100.00 + \$7.77)/(1 + $_0f_3$)^3 = \$99.21875, it follows that the 3-year spot rate is given by s_3 = $_0f_3$ = 8.204%. The formula connecting the forward rates for two periods was provided in Equation 7.5. Using these formulas and the values we have so far results in $_1f_2$ = 8.508%. The formulas connecting forward rates for three periods were given in Equation 7.6. The remaining intraperiod forward rates are $_2f_3$ = 10.649% and $_1f_3$ = 9.573%.

a. Exercise

1. Suppose that one has the following prices and annual coupon payments for three comparable bonds, each having 1, 2, and 3 years to maturity: $C_1 = \$5.55$, $PV_1 = 98:7$; $C_2 = \$6.66$, $PV_2 = 100:5$; and $C_3 = \$7.77$, $PV_3 = 102:13$. Let the face value F of each of them be $100. Compute the spot rates. ($s_1 = 7.464\%$/year, $s_2 = 6.545\%$/year, and $s_3 = 6.035\%$/year)

II. INTEREST RATE SWAPS, CAPS, AND FLOORS

The notional amount of interest rate swaps outstanding was in excess of $14 trillion by mid-2001. This exceeded the total amount of U.S. government debt, the entire fixed-income market, and almost everything else now that the Euro has diminished foreign exchange market complexity. What is an interest rate swap? Why participate in an interest rate swap? What are the kinds of interest rate swaps? What about interest rate caps and floors — how, and why, do you price them?

A. INTEREST RATE SWAPS

1. Basic Definitions

A *plain vanilla*, or *generic*, or *fixed-for-floating, interest rate swap* is one in which two parties agree to trade, or swap, their interest payments on an outstanding amount of debt. This occurs on the *trade date*. Interest rate swaps do not need to be on a real debt. Two parties could agree to swap their interest payments — in arrears — on a made up, or *notional principal,* amount. The interest would accrue from the *effective date* of the swap. To be even more efficient, we would not actually swap the interest payments on the next *settlement date* but would only agree to exchange the net difference between the two payments as they become due over the course of time. When the swap ceases to exist, it has reached its *maturity date*. Even if real debts are outstanding, by engaging in an interest rate swap, we only agree to exchange the interest payments — the obligations for the principal repayment are never bartered. Thus, relatively little is at risk in an interest rate swap, especially when compared to an over-the-counter option, foreign exchange forward, or the like.

The cash flow associated with an interest rate swap can be viewed as the difference between the cash flows from two equal face amount coupon paying bonds — one making payments based on a floating-rate and the other making payments based on a fixed-rate. Hence, the swap can be valued by discounting the differences between the two expected payment streams with an appropriate forward rate curve. In all instances, the economic value of an interest rate swap is zero at the commencement of the agreement; otherwise, one of the counterparties would be giving away money for nothing. This can be arranged by using a spread between the two rates, making a payment for the present value of the difference, or a combination of both, or via some other mechanism.

a.   Basis Swaps and Other Varieties

An interest rate swap between two floating interest rates, for example, 6-month LIBOR and the U.S. 6-month CMT rate, are referred to as *basis swaps*. In these types of swaps the floating or fixed nature of the interest rate is the same on both sides of the swap; the difference between two rates of the same nature is exchanged.

2.   Why Participate in One?

Why engage in an interest rate swap? There might be several reasons for executing an interest rate swap. Suppose that you had a liability with a fixed-interest rate associated with it but you believed that market rates were going to increase over time. Then, if you could induce someone to carry out a fixed- for floating-rate interest rate swap, and your guess regarding the direction of short-term rates turned out to be true, you would win. What you and the counterparty had agreed to exchange, or swap, was the value of the interest payments on the equal amounts of debt outstanding, at each coupon date going forward. Because you owe a fixed-rate but would be receiving the increasing floating-rate, the difference would be in your favor. This type of interest rate swap, in which a fixed-interest rate is exchanged for a floating-interest rate (or vice versa, if you are on the other side of the swap) is known as a generic interest rate swap or a plain vanilla interest rate swap. Note that the debt obligations are not exchanged, just the interest payments on them. Swaps can have maturities out to 15 years.

Conversely, if you owed a floating rate on a liability and believed that short-term rates were going to decrease, then if you could induce someone to engage in a floating- for fixed-rate interest rate swap you would gain (if your belief proved correct). This time, the counterparty would pay you the previously agreed-upon, and now higher, fixed rate, while the amount you owed would be decreasing.

Another reason for engaging in an interest rate swap is given by the comparative advantage argument. This is much the same as the comparative advantage argument made in the international trade area of economics (and with roughly the same relevance). For some natural business reason you would prefer to obtain floating-rate debt. Similarly, some other firm would prefer a fixed-rate liability on its balance sheet. However, it costs you too much to borrow in the short-term funds market and it costs them too much to borrow in the long-term bond market. So, it is possible for both parties to engage in the interest rate swap, to borrow funds in the sectors of the market where they each have the comparative advantage, and then agree to swap their interest payments. In this way both will end up paying less than if they had not engaged in the interest rate swap.

3.   Swap Dealers

Two firms trying to find each other in the financial markets, intent on engaging in a specific type of interest rate swap, is very inefficient. Therefore, a few large commercial firms manage interest rate swap desks. All the market participants know this and the company treasurer merely approaches the dealer on the swap desk with the type, or side, of the swap in which he wants to enter. The dealer quotes a price and takes on the swap and the risk of not finding a counterparty to take the opposite side of the swap quickly enough. Since the number of such dealers is very limited, the odds are high that the dealer will be able to find a counterparty (or counterparties, if the notional amount is appreciable or the swap is long-term) before having to place his own capital at risk.

Note that the swap dealer in this situation is playing much the same role as a bookmaker in Las Vegas does on sporting events. The bookmaker does not care who wins or loses the next game that Team A plays. What the bookmaker (swap dealer) desperately cares about is that he not lose any money acting as the intermediary for those who do have a definite opinion of the likely victor (direction of interest rates). The bookmaker controls the amount of money bet on either side via the point spread (bid–ask spread).

Even if Team A sentiment is high, once the point spread that Team A must overcome becomes large enough, the less fervent Team A supporters will start to bet on the opposition —Team B — because they do not believe that Team A can win by $10^{1}/_{2}$ or $20^{1}/_{2}$ points. (The half-point is to prevent ties.) Some point spread exists that will turn the flood of Team A money into a stream of Team B betting. When the equilibrium point-spread is found, equal amounts of cash are being bet on both sides and the bookmaker's (swap dealer's) capital is no longer at risk. The bookie takes a fee, or haircut, from both sides, the losers pay off the winners, and the bookmaker stays in business for the next game.

B. Why an Interest Rate Swap Really Works

In all the finance textbooks that I have read, the economic consequences of an interest rate swap are worked out with hypothetical fixed- and floating-rate numbers already in place. I have never seen the source of these quantities nor the underlying mathematics that really shows how an interest rate swap must benefit both parties as long as one simple condition is fulfilled. Hence, I will go over the basic algebra behind this so you can comprehend swaps more thoroughly. While demonstrating the full mathematics of an interest rate swap, I will make the unrealistic assumption that there is, in fact, no intermediary. After the detailed analysis is presented, along with a concrete numerical example, you are invited to repeat the problem analytically, with an intermediary in place who takes unequal fees from the two parties, and then show that the basic result is still true.

1. The Mathematics

Think of two imaginary firms, GCR, Inc. and BCR, Inc. (for the **G**ood **C**redit **R**isk and **B**ad **C**redit **R**isk corporations, respectively). GCR, Inc. is a well-known international firm with a very strong financial position and is always able to obtain a favorable interest rate for floating- or fixed-rate borrowing. BCR, Inc. is a small, domestic firm and has a mediocre balance sheet. It must always pay more for loans than GCR, Inc. does, especially in the fixed-interest rate market. (Actually, it would more likely be the other way around, but for the purposes of exposition the swap is constructed in this fashion. See immediately below.) Thus, in the fixed- and floating-rate debt sectors the GCR Corporation has an absolute advantage over the BCR

Corporation: a lower interest rate will be demanded of GCR in either of the debt sectors. The fact that the GCR, Inc. rates are lower than those required from the BCR Corporation in the fixed- as well as in the adjustable-rate markets does not mean that the **differences** between the two pairs of interest rates are the same. The key to an interest rate swap being profitable for both parties is that the spread between the two pairs of rates is not equal.

To perform our analysis of the problem let us define some symbols:

$$i_G = \text{GCR's floating interest rate,}$$
$$i_B = \text{BCR's floating interest rate,}$$
$$I_G = \text{GCR's fixed interest rate, and}$$
$$I_B = \text{BCR's fixed interest rate.}$$

We need two more symbols —the differences between the two pairs of similar types of interest rates:

$$\Delta I = I_G - I_B < 0 \text{ and } \Delta i = i_G - i_B < 0.$$

Both ΔI and Δi are negative because of GCR's absolute advantage in both interest rate markets. GCR, Inc. can always borrow for less than BCR, Inc. can. I assumed that the **spread** between the two same-type interest rates will be larger in the fixed-rate market than in the variable-rate market; $|\Delta I| > |\Delta i|$. (The absolute value bars are used to denote the magnitudes; remember that these two quantities are intrinsically negative because of GCR's absolute advantage in both markets.) This is the key to the swap to be presented.

I have not set the problem up to guarantee the result. Only three possibilities exist: 1. $|\Delta I| > |\Delta i|$, corresponding to the swap described, 2. $|\Delta I| < |\Delta i|$, corresponding to the reverse swap (the more realistic case), or 3. $|\Delta I| = |\Delta i|$, corresponding to the case in which no beneficial swap can be executed. Hence, if the problem had been posed the other way around, the entire discussion would have been reversed, but the conclusion regarding the profitability of the swap to both counterparties would be unchanged.

GCR, Inc. has a comparative advantage in the fixed-rate market. This means that $|\Delta I| > |\Delta i|$ or the absolute value of the difference between the two companies' rates in the fixed-rate market is bigger than the absolute value of the difference between their rates in the floating-rate market. Apparently, GCR Inc. should always borrow in the fixed-rate market to obtain the best deal. However, each firm can borrow in the market in which it has the comparative advantage and swap its interest payment liabilities (not those of the principal); both will save money.

How can this be arranged? GCR, Inc. accepts from BCR, Inc. fixed-rate interest payments at the rate $(I_G + E)$ per dollar of principal balance where $E > 0$. The GCR, Inc. treasurer wants E to be non-negative so that he is getting at least as much from BCR, Inc. as it will cost his firm to pay for its (unwanted) fixed-rate debt. GCR can do this because of its superior financial might. In compensation, GCR, Inc. will pay BCR, Inc. floating-rate interest payments in the amount of $(i_G - e)$ per dollar of principal amount where e > 0 too. This constraint on e ensures that GCR, Inc. is paying less than what it would have had to pay if it gone directly to the floating-rate debt market in the beginning. The net amount that GCR, Inc. owes per dollar of principal amount borrowed is (debt obligation plus swap cash flows):

$$-I_G + (I_G + E) - (i_G - e) = -i_G + E + e.$$

The two e values have been defined so that GCR, Inc. benefits on both legs of the interest rate swap; however, these are not the key constraints. (I set it to appear as one-sided as possible to demonstrate that these considerations are, in the end, immaterial.) To induce the GCR treasurer to engage in the swap at all, he demands that the net cost of the entire transaction be less than it otherwise would have been if GCR, Inc. had gone straight to the floating-rate market to obtain its funding. This latter amount is $-i_G$ per dollar of principal amount borrowed, so the relevant condition is that

$$-i_G + E + e > -i_G \quad \text{or that} \quad E + e > 0.$$

In contrast, BCR Corporation's treasurer borrowed in the floating-rate market at i_B per dollar of principal amount. BCR, Inc. is receiving a variable interest payment in the amount of $(i_G - e)$ per dollar of principal amount from GCR, Inc., while simultaneously paying GCR a fixed-interest payment in the amount of $(I_G + E)$ per dollar of principal borrowed. The BCR, Inc. treasurer would, of course, like the former at least to equal i_B and the latter not to exceed I_B, but this is not his main concern. For the sum of the floating-rate borrowing plus the interest rate swap to make economic sense to him, the net cost must be less than that which BCR, Inc. would have had to pay if it had gone straight to fixed-rate market. Thus, the BCR Corporation treasurer demands that net outflow be no more than $-I_B$ per dollar of principal value, or

$$-i_B + (i_G - e) - (I_G + E) > -I_B.$$

This can be rewritten as

$$(I_B - i_B) - (I_G - i_G) - (E + e) > 0,$$

or as

$$-\Delta I + \Delta i > E + e \ (> 0 \text{ from above}).$$

We already know that the sum of the e values must be positive for the arrangement to be beneficial to the GCR Corporation. Hence, we can conclude that, for the swap to work for both parties, the following inequality must be satisfied:

$$-\Delta I > -\Delta i.$$

This is exactly where we started. Therefore, it is not the construction of the swap payments in terms of the two e's *per se* that makes this bargain work to mutual benefit; rather it is the fact that the sum of the e's is non-negative and that GCR, Inc. and BCR, Inc. are each borrowing in debt markets in which they have the comparative advantage. Finally, observe that the interest differential, per dollar of principal, that can be gained from the swap is precisely $-\Delta I + \Delta i$. This is the amount, per dollar of principal, that the two firms can share, reducing both their costs of borrowing.

a. Numerical Example

Now attach some concrete numbers to the symbols (all per-year):

$$i_G = \text{GCR's floating rate} = \text{LIBOR} + 50 \text{ bp},$$
$$i_B = \text{BCR's floating rate} = \text{LIBOR} + 100 \text{ bp},$$
$$I_G = \text{GCR's fixed rate} = 9\%,$$
$$I_B = \text{BCR's fixed rate} = 10.5\%.$$

Assume that the two firms agree to split equally the 100 bp that $-\Delta I$ (= 150 bp) $+ \Delta i$ (= -50 bp) represents, or $E + e = 100$ bp. Then GCR winds up paying a floating-rate equal to just LIBOR (rather than the LIBOR + 50 bp that it could have obtained on its own). BCR Inc. ends up paying a fixed rate of 10% (rather than the 10.5% that it could have obtained on its own). Everybody wins! Finally, note that the 100 bp does not need to be split evenly and that both firms will still benefit (albeit one more than the other).

b. Exercise

Now put a swap dealer in the middle of the swap transaction. The dealer takes a fee from each swap counterparty for performing the service (i.e., book-keeping, bringing the two companies together, taking on some of the risks, and so forth). Let the fee charged to the GCR (BCR) Corporation per dollar of notional principal balance be denoted by f_G (f_B). There is no need to assume that these are the same. Re-perform the swap analysis and show that the key inequality is now

$$-\Delta I + \Delta i > (E + e) - (f_G + f_B) > 0.$$

Also, explain why the amount that can be gained from the swap by the corporate participants is only $-\Delta I + \Delta i - (f_G + f_B)$ because of fees paid to the swap dealer.

C. MORE ON INTEREST RATE SWAPS, CAPS, AND FLOORS

Forward rate agreements may be considered the building blocks of interest-rate swaps. An interest rate swap allows the counterparties to settle on a set of pairs of interest rates for a series of interest valuations, on a specified principal amount, at a precise set of future payment dates. A forward rate agreement allows the same for a single interest rate on a single cash flow at one payment date in the future.

1. Forward Rate Agreements

A forward rate agreement is a contract in which the buyer and seller lock in an interest rate for a prespecified period of time beginning at a particular date in the future. A notional principal amount is also specified to complete the interest payment computation. For instance, a buyer and seller may consent to fix in place a 6-month interest rate at 6.5% starting 6 months from now. The reference rate used to evaluate the contract, perhaps 6-month LIBOR, is determined by the counterparties in 6 months' time. If this rate is higher than the specified level of the forward rate agreement, the seller of the forward rate agreement (FRA) pays the buyer the present value of the interest rate differential applied to the notional amount. If this rate is lower than the FRA rate set on the original trade date, then the buyer of the FRA pays the seller the present value of the spread.

a. Mechanics

On the trade date the two counterparties agree to the forward rate agreement. On the *fixing date* the reference rate is determined and the contract is settled a few days later on the settlement date. The difference between the fixing date and the maturity date depends on the type of reference rate. For instance, if the maturity is 6 months after the fixing, the rate fixed might be 6-month LIBOR (or 6-month U.S. Treasury). Forward rate agreements are cash settled; when the actual level of the reference rate is observed on the fixing date, the contract is completed without any borrowing or lending occurring on that date. The ready money settlement reflects the difference between the forward rate at the time of the pact and the reference rate at the fixing date. The full formula is:

> Value of FRA = Present Value [Settlement rate × (number of interest payment days/day count convention for the settlement rate) × Notional amount] − Present Value [Contract rate × (number of interest payment days/day count convention for the contract rate) × Notional amount].

In practice this is equivalent to

> [(Settlement rate − Contract rate) × (number of interest payment days/day count convention for the settlement rate) × Notional amount]/[1 + Settlement Rate × (number of interest payment days/day count convention for the settlement rate)].

For example, if the forward rate had a $150 million notional principal amount, the 6-month LIBOR forward rate agreement was placed at 7.35%, and the spot rate at settlement was 7.10%, then the value of the FRA would be

$$[(0.071 − 0.0735) × 90/360 × \$150,000,000]/[1 + 0.071 × (90/360)]$$

or −$92,115. The negative sign point outs that the buyer of the FRA must pay the seller this amount because the settlement rate was below the contract rate.

2. The Mechanics of a Fixed- for Floating-Interest Rate Swap

One way to try to understand an interest rate swap is that it is the exchange of the coupon payments from a floating-rate bond with those from a fixed-rate bond of equal principal amount. We can imagine combining all the coupon payments and ignoring the principal amounts. (Remember that there is no exchange of principal in an interest rate swap and the amount of the principal is merely notional.) Unless the set of floating-rates over the term of the swap averages out to be equal to the fixed-rate, one counterparty will win and the other one will lose. (Note that we are ignoring present value considerations for the moment.) In any case, the net difference between the fixed- and floating-rate coupons each period is actually paid to the other party to the swap.

a. Swap Quotation Terms

Standard fixed- for floating-rate swaps are quoted in terms of the fixed rate, so a swap payer is the *fixed-rate payer* and the *floating-rate receiver*, while a swap receiver is the *fixed-rate receiver* and the *floating-rate payer*. The terms of a swap are:

1. The notional amount used to compute the interest payments must be specified.
2. The fixed interest rate needs to be designated.
3. The frequency of interest payments must be determined.
4. The day count convention associated with the fixed-rate is required.
5. The term or maturity of the swap is crucial.
6. The re-set dates for the term of the swap for the floating-rate index determine the basis for computing the new interest rate payments.
7. The reference index used to determine the floating-rate is key.
8. The day count convention associated with the floating interest rate is obligatory.
9. The beginning date of the swap needs to be known. (This can be now or some time in the future; these are referred to as spot or forward, respectively.)
10. The payment exchange dates are requisite.

One can induce complications by using different currencies to determine the interest rates and having more convoluted versions of the principal, for example amortizing or accrediting.

3. Pricing Considerations for an Interest Rate Swap

An interest rate swap has no net economic value when entered into. The market fixed-rate is the at-the-money swap rate, or the rate that would cause the interest-rate swap to have a value of zero on the swap start date. This assumes that, if the forward rates implied by the current yield curve were realized, neither counterparty would profit from the swap transaction because the cash outflow would equal the cash inflow for both counterparties on a net present value basis. However, it will be an extraordinary instance when the forward rates implied by the current yield curve are actually realized as spot rates. Hence, the theoretical value of the swap after the start date is almost never zero, making it possible for one of the counterparties to profit at each payment date.

a. Counterparty Risk

In addition to interest rate exposure risk, both counterparties face the credit risk of the opposing participant. However, the characteristics of interest rate swaps make them much less risky from a default viewpoint than other types of swaps or over-the-counter forward agreements. The main reason is that no principal is at stake — only the net difference between the interest expense of both sides is at risk. Naturally, one would not enter into an interest rate swap without the *proviso* that, if the counterparty should default, no financial obligation is left to carry forward.

b. Other Types of Interest Rate Swaps

A few common, nongeneric swaps are in use today most notably *LIBOR-in-arrears* and *spread-lock interest rate swaps*. A LIBOR-in-arrears swap agreement is a fixed-for floating-rate swap, with the floating-rate set as the LIBOR value determined at the end of the interest accrual period instead of at the beginning. A spread-lock interest-rate swap is a derivative whose payments are tied to the level of TED spread (the spread between the yield on a U.S. government bill, note or bond and a Eurodollar rate of equal maturity). Spread-lock interest-rate swaps can be for one time period or extend over multiple time periods. A multiperiod version would be called a *rolling spread-lock interest rate swap*. Sometimes interest rate swaps are executed using two different currencies' interest rates.

c. "Swaptions"

A *swaption* is a nonexchange traded option contract that provides the right, but not the obligation, to enter into a specified interest rate swap at a future date. When the option expires, it may be settled in cash (the counterparties exchange the monetary value of the option based on the forward rates that day) or settled by actually entering into the swap agreement. A swaption has the same types of terms as any other option with regard to an expiration date, the exercise style, the option premium, and the detailed terms of its contract (i.e., the underlying swap). The most common version of a swaption is a forward starting fixed- for floating-rate interest swap.

4.   Interest Rate Caps and Floors

An interest rate cap is used to limit the maximum exposure to a variable rate of interest on one's liability side, that is, a cap would be used for protection against mounting interest rates when one has a payment stream determined by floating rates. In return for the cap premium, the cap seller will reimburse the cap purchaser for interest costs resulting from the reference floating rate rising above the cap level (also known as the *strike rate*). Interest rate caps are commonly used by funding managers to limit their interest expense exposure to variable-rate funding instruments such as short-term bank debt, commercial paper, and floating-rate notes.

Conversely, an interest rate floor shields interest revenue against exposure to falling interest rates. An interest rate floor puts a limit on how low a variable rate of interest can fall before compensation will be received from the counterparty. Interest-rate floors are used by asset managers to protect the yield of their portfolio holdings from declining below a minimum level.

a. Parameters

A user of an interest rate cap will specify, beyond the notional principal amount, the cap strike level, the reference index rate, the term, and the *tenor*. In turn, the provider of the cap will calculate the premium for the protection required. The cap strike is the maximum level of interest rate to which the cap buyer is exposed. If rates go above the cap strike point, then the seller of the cap will compensate the cap buyer for the difference between the market rate and the cap strike rate. The reference index rate is the rate that will be used to determine the payments of the cap. The term of the cap is the time period over which the cap is in effect. The tenor, or re-set period, of the interest rate cap determines how frequently the reference index rate is settled on and potential payments fixed.

The factors that specify an interest rate floor are identical to those of an interest rate cap. The difference in the two instruments is the way in which the strike value is used. The strike value of an interest rate floor determines the level to which the reference index rate can fall before the floor begins to recompense the buyer of the floor for the spread. By providing the buyer payments equal to the difference between the floor strike and the market rate, the seller of the floor effectively limits the buyer's exposure to falling yields to the level of the floor strike.

III. INTEREST RATE MODELING

First I will go over the basic mathematical ideas necessary to understand how today's interest rate models are formulated and put to use. Then I will provide an editorial on the major flaw of these models and that of their most common mode of numerical implementation. I will also suggest some improvements on what is currently done if this is the way you want to proceed. Fully appreciating the information requires knowing a minimum amount regarding several sophisticated statistical and numerical (not financial nor economic) ideas. This level of experience, knowledge, and practice exceeds that of an MBA- or the typical Ph.D.-level economist. In the next chapter I suggest how to more profitably manage an interest-rate sensitive portfolio that does not rely on these techniques.

Finally, this book is more about mortgages *per se* than it is about all the background wisdom and learning necessary to appreciate my comments. Therefore, some of the next several pages will seem disjointed until my editorial comments.

A. Basic Probability Ideas

1. The Normal Distribution

The normal (or Gaussian or bell-shaped) distribution, or frequency function, is given by the form ($\wp$ stands for the probability of)

$$\wp\{w \in [w - dw/2, w + dw/2]\} = \exp[-(w - \mu)^2/(2\sigma^2)]\ dw/(2\pi\sigma^2)^{1/2}.$$

This expression indicates the probability that the random variable w will be in the small range $w - dw/2 \leq w \leq w + dw/2$. The normalization constraint is given by (the probability of something happening must be one)

$$1 = \int_{-\infty}^{\infty} \exp[-(w - \mu)^2/(2\sigma^2)] \, dw/(2\pi\sigma^2)^{1/2} = \int_{-\infty}^{\infty} \wp(w) \, dw.$$

The mean or average value mu, μ, is given by

$$\mu \equiv \int_{-\infty}^{\infty} w \times \exp[-(w - \mu)^2/(2\sigma^2)] \, dw/(2\pi\sigma^2)^{1/2} = \int_{-\infty}^{\infty} w \times \wp(w) \, dw.$$

The variance, or the square of the standard deviation, about the mean is computed from

$$\sigma^2 \equiv \int_{-\infty}^{\infty} (w - \mu)^2 \times \exp[-(w - \mu)^2/(2\sigma^2)] \, dw/(2\pi\sigma^2)^{1/2} = \int_{-\infty}^{\infty} (w - \mu)^2 \times \wp(w) \, dw.$$

In these three cases, the expressions given on the far right-hand side are true for any meaningful probability distribution (though not all meaningful distributions have finite second moments).

The Gaussian distribution is beloved by statisticians because of the central limit theorem and its relative ease of use to obtain closed form results. The central limit theorem essentially states that the sum of any number of random variables will have a Gaussian distribution. Therefore, if something is repeated over and over (flipping a coin, selling a stock, buying a T-Bill), then the characteristics of the resulting distribution will tend to normality. The full theorem is an even stronger result than this and really powerful. The Gaussian distribution also frequently allows for closed form analytical results — the favorite of anybody who does applied mathematics. They are pretty, neat, easy to use, and can make you feel that you really have mastery over the underlying (nonstatistic) subject because the **mathematical** result came out so nicely.

2. The Log-Normal Distribution

One big disadvantage of the normal distribution in financial applications is that it is two-sided: it allows for positive and negative prices, interest rates, and so on. It also does not represent the actual outcome of financial events especially well. The simplest arithmetic cure for these difficulties is to use the ratio of two successive measurements of the relevant financial variable as the random quantity. If we took the logarithm of the ratio of two successive measures, then we would solve both these thorny problems and provide a better fit real stock price, interest rate, and so forth historical data. Thus the log-normal distribution is important in finance. It is related to the normal distribution as follows: if u is a normally distributed random variable, then the variable v = exp(u) has a log-normal distribution. The log-normal distribution is given by

$$\wp\{v \in [v - dv/2, v + dv/2]\} = \exp\{-[ln(v) - \mu]^2/(2\sigma^2)\}\ dv/[v \times (2\pi\sigma^2)^{1/2}].$$

The mean and variance (about the mean) of u are given by μ and σ^2. The mean value of v is given by $\exp(\mu + \sigma^2/2)$. Its variance, or the square of the standard deviation about its mean, is given by $\exp(2\mu + \sigma^2) \times [\exp(\sigma^2) - 1]$.

3. The Volatility Parameters

Volatility in finance is defined as the standard deviation from the mean of some price, interest rate, or other monetarily variable quantity (unless we have already transformed to the logarithm, in which case it refers to the standard deviation of that quantity about its average). It is meant to provide a risk-related measure. Larger volatility means that more extreme values may be reached and this potential arguably increases the value of options. Historical (post-1973) interest rate volatility is in the 10 to 20% range. Short-term interest rates are usually more volatile than long-term rates. Volatility usually increases with the magnitude of the interest rate and generally increases in a downward moving market relative to that in an upward moving market.

The main (and financially considerable) defect of volatility as a risk-indicate measure is that it is a **two-sided** appraisal. Actual financial risks are almost always **one-sided**. For instance, if you were a buy and hold par bond investor, then the "risk" of interest rates dropping and staying low is not something that you would worry about. If that occurred, you would own a portfolio with a built-in capital gain and paying higher than market rates. Similarly, if you were purchasing the common stock of the XYZ Corp. for its expected increase and saw that increase occur, the stock split 3:1, and rise further yet, you would not be disappointed. Short-sellers have the diametrically opposed point of view, but that perspective is still one-sided.

a. Historical or Empirical Volatility

Historical or empirical volatility is a measure of volatility based on actual experience of the market's inconstancy. It is the only accurate way to understand the market's past pricing of volatility. One must choose a time span over which to compute it; some of the financial considerations in doing so include whether to: 1. assume long-term macroeconomic stability and obtain (formally) higher precision estimates by averaging over many business cycles, 2. cover only the most recent economic cycle (the far past is no longer believed to be relevant) and to try to be more financially up-to-date, or 3. try to catch the time evolution of any recent trends. One also must define a reasonable sampling frequency based on the availability of data for liquid trading: daily, weekly, or monthly, it depends on the actual behavior of the economic variable in question.

Separate issues exist between mathematical and economic precision. For the latter, one wants a long-time series of trades executed in an efficient market with depth and liquidity. One also wants stability in the underlying market. Hence, quoting stock index returns, for example, before the advent of program trading is a questionable practice. Similarly, before the coming of a huge increase in trading volume and the number of trades of 10,000 blocks of shares, things were different. On the purely mathematical side, the standard deviation of the sample mean, based on a random sample of size N, owing to sampling error, is equal to σ^2/N where σ^2 is the variance of the underlying distribution.

Thus, one could argue that, as the number of observations increases, so does the precision of the sample estimate. This is a statement about convergence in probability (i.e., mathematics), not about finance or about economic stability or real fiscal and monetary policy history. (There is a corresponding mathematical result for the sample deviation too.) However, do not expect more precise or more accurate (and those words do not mean the same thing) estimates for the means or standard deviations of economic variables because the number of observations increases if the underlying financial process driving the price series in the data base is secularly time-dependent. One needs to balance the accuracy of the underlying economic model very carefully with the accessibility of truly useful data. Only someone well-versed on both sides of this issue should be allowed to pursue it for profit.

For interest rate statistical computations, the standard procedure is to assume $N + 1$ observations of an interest rate I_n at the end of nth time interval, $n = 0,1,\ldots,$ N (daily, weekly, monthly, and so forth.). Define L_n as the logarithm of the ratio of two successive measured interest rate values, $L_n \equiv ln(I_n/I_{n-1})$ (i.e., the anticipation of a log-normal process). For the variance of the process, use the symbol σ_L^2 (the standard deviation of L about its mean). Then the standard formulas for computing historical volatility of an interest rate I are

$$(\text{volatility estimate})^2 = \sigma_L^2 = \sum_{n=1}^{N} (L_n - <L>)^2/(N-1),$$

when $<L>$ stands for the average value of L,

$$<L> = \sum_{n=1}^{N} L_n/N = \sum_{n=1}^{N} ln(I_n/I_{n-1})/N.$$

If these observations were not performed daily, then, to compute the annualized volatility, we must renormalize by the number of trading days in a year (i.e., the number of observations per year)

Annual Volatility = (Number of Trading Days/Year)$^{1/2}$ × Daily Volatility.

Alternatively, if weekly estimates were utilized, then the formula would be modified to

Annual Volatility = (Number of Trading Weeks/Year)$^{1/2}$ × Weekly Volatility.

b. Expected Volatility

More important than historical or empirical volatility is the expected volatility. This is the value that the volatility will assume in the future, specifically over the time period when the financial instrument under study is to be priced and will have cash flows. It is the expected interest rate volatility that should determine the option-adjusted spread in MBS pricing. The difficulty is that the expected volatility is neither observable nor predictable from the present.

c. Implied Volatility

Another related concept is that of implied volatility. It is defined as the value of the volatility which reproduces the observed market price, based on some model for the value of the embedded option. Unfortunately, it is explicitly model dependent and, even if predicted correctly, does not imply that the model to price the option was correct.

B. STATISTICAL PROPERTIES OF FINANCIAL SECURITIES

Some stochastic process, that is, a mechanism generated in a probabilistic fashion without any financial content, is used to generate future changes in interest rate in most of today's models. A simple one, known as a random walk, complemented with the Gaussian distribution is common because this frequency function is very well understood and tends to generate analytical (i.e., closed form) mathematics. It also has the central limit theorem behind it. Somewhere I read that mathematicians believe in the central limit theorem because the physicists have experimentally demonstrated it to be true (which is empirically false, by the way), while the physicists believe in the central limit theorem because the mathematicians have proved that it is true with logical rigor (which is true, but irrelevant to real data).

Much, much better would be to use the historical range of variations in interest rates ever since interest rate volatility become a real issue in the U.S. markets — for example, post-1973. One could still take random samples from this information data base. Its financial importance is that this particular set of records represents the only economic reality with which we have any familiarity and experience. Coding an analytically convenient formula, for example, the Poisson distribution, whose mathematical properties are simple to deal with and build models from is what statisticians do, not people genuinely interested in trying to learn from real-world geopolitical/military/fiscal/monetary experience and to use it to govern their future investment behavior in that realm.

1. The Definition of a Random Walk

The variable z is going to represent my left–right displacement along the sidewalk in front of my house, from my front door. So $z(t)$ measures my net displacement from the origin at time $t \geq 0$. My position is sampled at times t_n, $n = 1,2,\ldots, N$, and is denoted by $z(t = t_n) = z_n$. It is my front door, so I define $z(0) = 0 = z_0$. Suppose that we infer, from the observations of $z(t)$, that a good model for $\{z_n\}$ appears to be given by (with Δt some short, constant span of time)

$$z(t = t_{n+1}) = z_{n+1} = z_n + \varepsilon_n \sqrt{\Delta t}, \; n = 1, 2,\ldots \text{ with } t_{n+1} = t_n + \Delta t.$$

The random variable epsilon, ε, is assumed to be distributed in a Gaussian fashion. Its average value is zero and its variance equal to unity. Therefore, I have an equal probability of taking steps to the right or to the left and they all average out to the same size. Furthermore, different values of ε are assumed to be uncorrelated (that is, the jerkiness of by-chance movements is independent of past motion's history; I am not allowed to become tired or energized, for instance). If this did accurately model my haphazard walking pattern with a time step of a few seconds, then I would be said to be following a random walk or a discrete time Wiener process.

Consider the difference between and z_n and z_m for $n > m$:

$$z(t_n) - z(t_m) = \sum_{l=m}^{n-1} \varepsilon_l \sqrt{\Delta t}.$$

Δt is a constant and the epsilon values have been assumed to be independently distributed with a zero mean. Therefore, after taking an expectation with respect to the underlying Gaussian probability distribution, the mean displacement terms out to be

$$\langle z(t_n) - z(t_m) \rangle = 0. \tag{7.9}$$

Thus, on average, I will have no net displacement from my front door. However, the variances of the differences do not vanish. In fact, it is just a few steps to algebraically show that

$$\mathrm{var}[\,|z(t_n) - z(t_m)|\,] = t_n - t_m.$$

The proof rests on the independence of the epsilon values and the fact that they are uncorrelated with unit variances, to wit:

$$\mathrm{var}[\,|z(t_n) - z(t_m)|\,] = \left\langle \left[\sum_{l=m}^{n-1} \varepsilon_l \sqrt{\Delta t} \right]^2 \right\rangle = \left\langle \sum_{l=m}^{n-1} \varepsilon_l^2 \Delta t \right\rangle = (n - m)\Delta t = t_n - t_m.$$

The square root of Δt is used in the defining process so that the variance would be proportional to Δt instead of its square (and more easily adaptable to the statistical interest rate modeling to come; we need not be concerned with some other technical reasons here).

2. The Definition of a Continuous Time Wiener Process

We can obtain a continuous time Wiener process by taking the limit of the discrete random walk process as $\Delta t \to 0$. It is still true that $\varepsilon(t)$ is a standardized normal random variable uncorrelated on any time scale. This continuous time process is represented by writing

$$dz = \varepsilon(t)\sqrt{dt}.$$

(For historical reasons, this is also known as a Brownian random walk.) For any value of $t < T$ the quantity $z(T) - z(t)$ is still a normally distributed random variable with zero mean and variance $T - t$.

a. A Generalized Wiener Process

The generalization of the simple Wiener process is given by

$$dx(t) = a\ dt + b\ dz. \qquad (7.10)$$

where a and b are constants. This stochastic (and no longer ordinary because of the probabilistic origins of dz) differential equation for the time evolution of the quantity x may be integrated to

$$x(t) = x(0) + at + bz(t).$$

In the context of the sidewalk excursion, I now have some mean drift velocity, given by a, plus a random component whose amplitude is determined by b. Think of the difference in motion between a well-hit golf ball (minimal buoyancy and wind effects, not going to fly high enough for minor changes in gravity; e.g., a small value of b) and that of a balloon (a large value of b).

b. Geometrical Brownian Motion

A geometrical Brownian motion process is one whose stochastic differential equation is given by a change of variable to the natural logarithm, i.e.,

$$d\mathit{ln}[x(t)] = A\ dt + B\ dz \qquad (7.11)$$

instead of Equation 7.10. When A and B are constants, this stochastic differential equation can be integrated as well, with the result

$$\mathit{ln}[x(t)] = \mathit{ln}[x(0)] + At + Bz(t).$$

Using angular brackets to denote an average, the mean value of $\mathit{ln}[x(t)]$ is given by $<\mathit{ln}[x(0)]> + At$. This mimics x(t) increasing as if it were based on the principal amount, x(0), growing at a continuously compounded interest rate of A but subject to fluctuations in rates of magnitude given by the absolute value of B.

3. An Ito Process

The next step up in complexity is an Ito process; A and B are now allowed to be functions of x and t. The Ito process used in standard interest rate modeling is given, where z(t) is a Wiener process and with S(t) the short rate, by

$$dln[S(t)] = dS(t)/S(t) = (\mu - \frac{1}{2}\sigma^2) \, dt + \sigma \, dz. \tag{7.12}$$

The underlying stochastic process for the short rate has a mean equal to μ and standard deviation σ. The time dependence of S(t) is governed by a geometric Brownian motion process

$$dS(t) = \mu S(t) \, dt + \sigma S(t) \, dz. \tag{7.13}$$

(Yes, you did miss something in going from the stochastic differential equation for S to that for its logarithm and vice versa. See Hull's 1997 text.)

With the temporal evolution of the random variable S(t) governed by Equations 7.12 and 7.13, the first two moments of S are given by, respectively,

$$E\{ln[S(t)/S(0)]\} = (\mu - \sigma^2/2)t, \quad E[S(t)/S(0)] = \exp(\mu t), \tag{7.14}$$

$$var\{ln[S(t)/S(0)]\} = \sigma^2 t, \text{ and } var[S(t)/S(0)] = \exp(\mu t) \exp(\sigma^2 t - 1).$$

a. Numerical Integration of the Model

To go from the continuous formula Equation 7.13 to its finite version, for a small time step Δt, write

$$S(t_{n+1}) - S(t_n) = \mu S(t_n) \, \Delta t + \sigma S(t_n)\varepsilon(t_n) \, \sqrt{\Delta t}.$$

This implies that the evolution of the short rate S is given by

$$S(t_{n+1}) = [1 + \mu\Delta t + \mu\varepsilon(t_n)\sqrt{\Delta t}] \, S(t_n), \, n = 0,1,2,\ldots$$

Because the parameters of the model and S(0) are known, the time evolution of S(t) can now be generated by a set of epsilon values, $\{\varepsilon_n\}$. The multiplicative coefficient above is normally distributed; however, S was assumed to be log-normally distributed. For the sake of consistency with the log-normal distribution, it is better to write the discrete time evolution equation in terms of the logarithm from Equation 7.12,

$$ln[S(t_{n+1})] - ln[S(t_n)] = (\mu - \sigma^2/2) \, \Delta t + \sigma\varepsilon(t_n) \, \sqrt{\Delta t}, \, n = 0,1,2,\ldots$$

Now,

$$S(t_{n+1}) = S(t_n) \times \exp[(\mu - \sigma^2/2)\Delta t + \sigma\varepsilon(t_n)\sqrt{\Delta t}],$$

going forward in time and the random coefficient is log-normally distributed.

At this point, we have about two-thirds of the mathematical machinery necessary to perform the more popular versions of simple interest rate modeling. The next step involves tying together the pricing formulas for a zero coupon bond from the probabilistic and deterministic points of view. Here is a place where the spot, short, and forward rates will all meet.

C. The Relationship among Interest Rates and Statistics

1. The Spot-Rate Version

Let us begin by reviewing the no-arbitrage argument for a zero coupon bond with a \$1 face amount. Let $PV(t,T)$ be the present value now (at time t) for this security, which matures at time $T > t$. First, suppose that $PV(t,T)$ exceeded what we think its present value is, namely, $\exp[-r \times (T - t)]$, where r is the constant continuously discounted interest rate. [If we were to allow for changing interest rates, then r would need to be a function of time, for example, r(t). We will include this complexity later on.] Then, one can sell the bond short during the time period [t, T] and invest $\exp[-r \times (T - t)]$ of the proceeds in risk-free lending. At time T, when the bond matures, the short position in it is worth \$1 while the risk-free lending will return \$1. Hence, at time T, the net cash flow will be zero. However, at the earlier time t, the investor had excess monies because we assumed that $PV(t,T)$ was greater than $\exp[-r \times (T - t)]$. These could have been invested at the risk-free rate and returned more funds at time T. Clearly, this unbalanced situation cannot be maintained for any length of time.

Another possibility is that $PV(t,T)$ is less than $\exp[-r \times (T - t)]$. Then, at time t one would borrow $\exp[-r \times (T - t)]$ dollars and purchase a \$1 zero coupon bond at a price of $PV(t,T)$. When the maturity date arrives, the net cash flows will again sum to zero. The \$1 received from the bond can be used to pay off the loan. However, at the earlier time t, there was again net excess of cash because this time we assumed that $\exp[-r \times (T - t)]$ exceeded the cost of the \$1 zero coupon bond or $PV(t,T)$. These funds, too, could have been invested over the maturity of the zero coupon bond at the risk-free rate to produce more funds. The only condition that would eliminate such arbitrage opportunities is if the standard bond pricing equation holds and, as we know,

$$PV(t,T) = \exp[-r \times (T - t)]. \tag{7.15}$$

This is a simplified version of Equation 7.3. From this perspective, this relationship is not really a definition; rather it is a consequence imposed on bond prices by the no-arbitrage requirement.

2. The Forward-Rate Version

Now let us reperform the no-arbitrage argument in terms of the forward rate. Let the continuously compounded forward rate be $f(\tau, t, T)$, $T \geq t \geq \tau \geq 0$. The relationship in Equation 7.7a was between two different bonds, namely,

$$PV(\tau,T)/PV(\tau,t) = \exp[-f(\tau,t,T) \times (T - t)]. \tag{7.7a}$$

We should, in principle, be able to extract all the necessary information concerning the forward rate $f(\tau,t,T)$ from $PV(\tau,T)$ and $PV(\tau,t)$. This is not just a statement about inverting the preceding formula. The point is that, between the two prices $PV(\tau,T)$ and $PV(\tau,t)$, for two different \$1 face amount zero coupon bonds of separate maturity, we have pricing information extending from time τ to time t and, independently, from time τ to time T. These two intervals completely cover the range from t to T — the time period over which the forward rate is the interest rate.

Repeating the formulas from earlier in this chapter, the inverse relationship is given by

$$f(\tau,t,T) = - \{ln[PV(\tau,T)] - ln[PV(\tau,t)]\}/(T - t). \qquad (7.7b)$$

Taking the limit and letting $T \to t$, the result will be the instantaneous forward rate

$$f(\tau,t) = -\partial ln[PV(\tau,t)]/\partial t. \qquad (7.7c)$$

From this partial differential equation, it was possible to go backward and derive

$$PV(\tau,t) = \$1.00 \times \exp\left[- \int_{\tau}^{t} f(\tau,t')\, dt'\right]. \qquad (7.8)$$

At this point, we could repeat the no-arbitrage argument utilizing this form of the pricing equation (with similar results, but now expressed in terms of the forward rates). Once more, we could view the last formula as a consequence of a no-arbitrage argument instead of as a definition of a forward rate.

3.   The Random Interest-Rate Version

When the instantaneous spot rate $r(t)$ becomes stochastic, then the pricing formula will need to change because we no longer know in advance, nor can we argue ahead of time from a no-arbitrage perspective, how randomly generated interest rates will behave. We can make progress, but only in small (technically infinitesimal) steps. We also must place restrictions on the underlying probability mechanism generating the interest rates so that no unrealistic financial opportunities occur. Because most interest rates are built up from the risk-free rate with a differential for credit risk, liquidity risk, and so forth, the essential variable to model is the risk-free rate.

Suppose that R_f represents the risk-free rate earned during the infinitesimal interval $[t, t + dt]$. R_f is known at time t, although its future value will rise and fall according to the random process described earlier, for example, that we have used to alter it over the passage of time. Now we are considering a \$1, zero coupon U.S. Treasury Bond maturing at time T with present value of $PV(t,T)$. What value of this bond do we expect as a function of the risk-free rate $R_f(t)$? (Note that time dependence is not because of secular changes in the risk-free rate; rather, it is a consequence of the randomness introduced into its forecast.) We need to have some sort of expectation that we formally write as

$$PV(t,T) = \$1.00 \times E\{\exp[-R_f(t) \times (T - t)]\}. \qquad (7.16)$$

This expectation is with respect to the underlying stochastic process chosen to generate the changes in $R_f(t)$. What must be special about this probabilistic mechanism? It must be a **risk-neutral** measure because we are pricing off the risk-free rate now. So the term $E\{\exp[-R_f(t) \times (T - t)]\}$ can be reinterpreted as the average value of a random discount factor applied to the a par value zero coupon bond of $1.

This is as far as a book about mortgages can go without delving much further into probability theory, describing Markov and Martingale processes, and further wrapping up our simple financial problem of trying to price a $1 zero coupon bond in more statistical theory (but only if we can carry it out analytically else it is not convenient to use that frequency function). However, something has been accomplished if one wants to develop statistically based interest rate models. We have succeeded in connecting three relationships, Equations 7.8, 7.15, and 7.16, with the price of a zero coupon bond.

The first two formulas can be regarded as definitions, or forced upon us by a no-arbitrage argument. The last relationship was the result of computing the anticipated value of varying financial quantity under a risk-neutral measure that would turn out to be equal to the current arbitrage-free price of the instrument. Put another way, the first two relationships, based on the no-arbitrage condition, can be viewed as definitional pricing equations. We can view the last one in that fashion, in that, given a proper model for the risk-free rate of return, it can be used to obtain the correct market price for the bond also. The latter pair form the basis of the two broad approaches to pricing interest rate-sensitive securities. What is now referred to as the classical approach uses the second relation, whereas the Heath, Jarrow, and Morton (1990) approach uses the third.

4.   What Is Done in Practice

Pricing interest rate-sensitive securities can now proceed in two different ways, depending on which of the two arbitrage relations is used as a starting point. One method is to commence with a set of bond prices that can reasonably be argued to be arbitrage-free. Then the spot rate relation, e.g., Equation 7.15, can be used to go backwards and infer a model for the short rate. Because the relations involving these interest rates hold under no-arbitrage conditions, the model obtained will also be said to be risk-adjusted. That is, it will be valid under the risk-neutral measure used in Equation 7.16 (which has not really been fully described). Beyond the ever-lengthening string of statistical assumptions, the drift of the spot rates will be computed and we can calibrate to the observed volatility. Finally, one can then exploit the arbitrage-free characteristic of this spot-rate model to price interest rate sensitive instruments other than zero coupon bonds.

The other algorithm uses the second arbitrage condition, Equation 7.8, and obtains arbitrage-free evolution of the forward rates $f(\tau,t)$. (In practice, one picks a basic interval of time, for example, 3 or 6 months, and a total time span, say 5 years; this determines the number of forward rates actually modeled — 20 or 10, respectively, for these examples.) It involves no drift modeling of the spot rates because they no longer appear, but the volatilities along the forward rate curve need to be calibrated from data available on the short rate process. In different terms, the second methodology to pricing interest rate-sensitive securities is an attempt to extract the fundamental no-arbitrage relations among the forward rates from the observed zero coupon bond prices and then summarize them within an arbitrage-free, spot-rate model.

5. Summary

If PV(t,T) is the price of a zero coupon bond at time $t > 0$ that pays \$1 at time T, then it is given by Equations 7.5, 7.8, or 7.16. Thus, the spot rate can be determined from the expected value of the price of a \$1, zero coupon bond. That is, the term structure of interest rates, at any time, can be obtained from those values and the risk-neutral process, and its parameters, initiating the changes in the risk-free rate of return.

In the standard nomenclature with the short rate as the fundamental independent variable, a one-factor model for the short rate S(t) is one in which the stochastic process underlying the evolution of S(t) has one source of uncertainty. In a risk-neutral world, these are of the form of an Ito process seen in Equation 7.12. In the one-factor model, μ is the symbol for some mean level drift and σ stands for a standard deviation about the mean. The initial condition is S at $t = 0$, S(0); this differential equation specifies the stochastic evolution of S from S(0). The one factor in these models is the Wiener process dz. Multifactor models are built with multiple (independent) Wiener processes. For example, if one were trying to model the short- and long-term interest rates, one would need two independent Wiener processes: one to alter the short-term rate and another to change the long-term rate. With one-factor models changes in the short rate are instantaneously propagated throughout the entire term structure of interest rates.

D. Binomial Lattices

We briefly examined the possibility of numerically integrating the stochastic differential equation proposed as a model for interest rate evolution when we turned differential equations into difference equations. Those procedures would produce a short interest rate, or a continuously discounted spot rate, evolving in time under assumptions built into the model (e.g., the statistical basis, the meager financial content beyond a no-arbitrage constraint, and so on). The straightforward numerical integration procedure will not easily allow us to determine the outcome from call and put options embedded in fixed-income instruments.

An alternative methodology that allows us to perform both types of computation in a unified manner is based on the concept of considering short-time changes in rates superimposed upon a lattice; see Figure 7.2. The vertex of the lattice represents time zero (now). As we move through the lattice, to the right, in uniform time steps

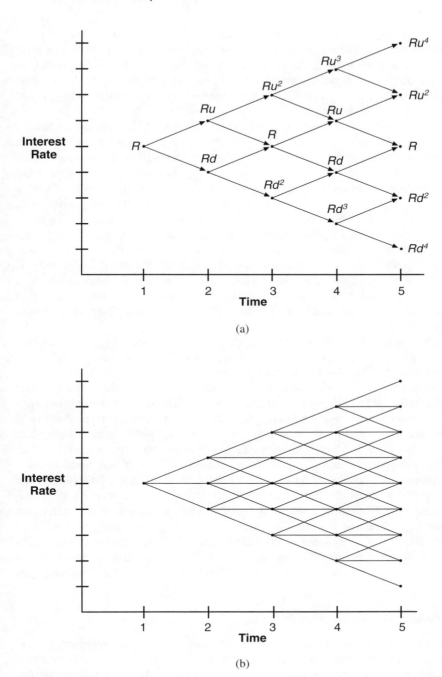

FIGURE 7.2 (a) A binomial lattice illustrating how to compute the change in the interest rate R after successive up (u) and down (d) moves through time. (b) A trinomial lattice showing the same type of interest rate changes over time. Note how many states are available in this lattice that do not appear in the binomial version and that these are the most probable.

(usually for computation simplicity), we compute new values for the interest rates. At each node, we interrogate the optionality components of any contingent cash flows to see if they are in- or out-of-money. If they are in-the-money, then we adjust the conditional cash flows accordingly and move on to the next node, at the same time step, in the lattice. Eventually, we examine all the nodes at one time step and then advance the entire procedure in time.

To use a lattice one must define the basic unit of time. It might be an hour, a day, or a week; this is a detail. However, the basic conceit of the model, as a computational tool, is that the economic variable modeled has *only* two possibilities at the next time step. This is usually implemented via a multiplicative change (to make things log-normal eventually). If, for instance, the short rate S increases, it goes up to $uS(0)$, $u > 1$; if S decreases, it goes down to $dS(0)$, $0 < d < 1$. From $S(0)$, one time step in the future, the numerical value of the short rate will be $S(1) = uS(0)$ or $S(1) = dS(0)$, depending on whether S increased or decreased, respectively. There are no other possibilities at any time step in the entire lattice. Finally, what makes this a binomial lattice, rather than a binomial tree, is that the product of u and d is restricted to be one. This means that the lattice closes because, for instance, $u^2d^2S(0) = S(0)$ and $u^3d^3S(0) = S(0)$, and so forth. Had this not been true, the lattice would not recombine and we would have a more flexible tree model (but still severely deficient in only being binomial).

Knowing how much the short rate might potentially increase or decrease reveals nothing about the relative probability of one of these occurrences, which is an independent variable. Hence, the last parameter needed is the probability that S increased, for example, $1 \geq p \geq 0$. With only two possibilities, the probability that S decreased must be given by $1 - p$. (For my very much preferred trinomial numerical implementation, there would be two independent probabilities: p, the probability of an upward move, and q, the probability of a downward move, with $1 \geq p, q \geq 0$, and $1 \geq 1 - p - q \geq 0$ the probability of a stationary value.) The probability of an increase or decrease could change with each step taken through the binomial lattice, but one usually assumes, again only for the sake of computational simplicity, that p is a constant across the lattice. (Computational simplicity is always easier to deal with but should never be used as an excuse when it comprises the underlying financial, physical, or engineering process so much as to distort the outcome.) Building up this progression over many time steps results in a discrete time estimate to the continuous process. Theoretically, if we make the time step short enough and include many of them, the approximation will be sufficiently accurate, numerically, for our purposes.

1. Parameter Specification

How are the parameters u, d, and p to be specified? Within the boundedness constraints mentioned above, they can be specified any way we want. A common assumption is to utilize the logarithm of the change in the short rate as the key variable. Indeed, this was implicitly done by specifying a multiplicative change in value rather than an additive one. Standard choices for u, d, and p in terms of the expected value of the logarithm and of its variance, given in Equation 7.14, are

$$u = \exp(\sigma\sqrt{\Delta t}), \; d = 1/u = \exp(-\sigma\sqrt{\Delta t}), \; \text{and} \; p = \frac{1}{2} + (\mu/2\sigma)\sqrt{\Delta t} \quad (7.17)$$

where Δt is the small interval of time between sets of nodes on the lattice.

2. Trinomial Lattices

What do trinomial lattices have to do with any of this? The most popular numerical method of implementing a random walk and simultaneously computing the cash flows from option-embedded instruments, such as callable bonds or mortgages, appears to be the binomial lattice tactic. This is also true for option pricing *per se*, although, in the latter case, there is a technical problem with constructing equivalent value portfolios composed of three elements instead of two. Of course, the **bi**nomial model only allows for two possible changes in the level of the relevant financial quantity, e.g., an interest rate, a stock price, a put option premium. The fundamental premise of the binomial technique is that whatever is considered can go up or go down. There are no other choices. This is financially unrealistic because the most probable outcome for almost all economically determined variables is no significant change at the next time step.

Whether S represents a short interest rate, the price of a share of common stock, the premium for a put option on pork bellies, or almost any other economically determined variable, its empirically best predictor at the next time step is its value at the last time step. In particular, unless significantly new information is available across a time step, an interest rate or price has no reason to change. (Consult a finance text, such as Copeland and Weston, 1992, on the various efficient market hypotheses formulations.) So the best predictor, most of the time, for S(1) is S(0), whatever financial variable S represents. Thus, the binomial aspect is a critical, and probably fatal, limitation of the binomial lattice methodology for computing interest rate, common stock price, or any fiscally related evolution.

My intuitive numerical concern, honed by decades of experience, is that not allowing this basic, and apparently empirically essential, possibility when pricing via a binomial lattice intrinsically biases the results beyond any other advantages of the scheme. If this concern is truly warranted, then a deep, inherent structural flaw exists in the interest rate modeling process that shorter time intervals, bigger computers, or better pre-payment models will never deal with nor solve. Does the physicist give up the essential physics because a simplified numerical method will not accommodate it? At least a trinomial model, with the triplet of possibilities for S(1) = {dS(0), S(0), uS(0)}, appears to be crucial to obtaining **financially** meaningful results (assuming that the rest of the statistical folderol associated with interest rate modeling is worth anything).

There are more technical issues concerning the actual operations of financial markets and the underlying mathematics of a tree vs. a lattice. We believe that most financial markets in the U.S. satisfy the weak form of the efficiency hypothesis. This is equivalent to stating that the underlying statistical process is Markovian. Trees can represent Markov processes; lattices cannot because they are explicitly path dependent. Moreover, after n steps, a lattice can only reach n + 1 different values for the short rate between $u^nS(0)$ and $d^nS(0)$, while a trinomial lattice has twice as many possibilities between the same pair of limits (2n with this counting convention). Therefore, the pricing resolution of a trinomial lattice is always twice that of a binomial lattice over the same time span. This advantage can never be overcome by a supercomputer.

3. More on the Binomial Lattice

Consider applying the expectation operator to the binomial lattice from time 0, when the short rate is S(0), to time 1 (in effect Δt later), when the short rate will be S(1). Because we are using a log-normal distribution for the short rate, we want the expectation of the logarithm of S(1) to be accurately given by the lattice after moving one step forward in time. The probability of an upward (downward) move is p (1 − p), the resulting value of the short rate is uS(0) [dS(0)], so the expectation is given by (the correlation coefficient is zero by definition)

$$E\{ln[S(1)]\} = p \times ln[uS(0)] + (1 - p) \times ln[dS(0)].$$

One can take S(0) = 1 without loss of generality; it represents an overall scale factor in a multiplicative model. This is done from now on. The variance of $ln[S(1)]$ about its mean value is given by

$$\begin{aligned}
\text{var}\{ln[S(1)]\} &= p \times ln^2(u) + (1 - p) \times ln^2(d) - [p \times ln(u) + (1 - p) \times ln(d)]^2 \\
&= p \times (1 - p) \times [ln(u) - ln(d)]^2.
\end{aligned}$$

Thus, the appropriate choices to match the parameters of the lattice with those of the underlying probability distribution (see Equation 7.14) are

$$(\mu - \sigma^2/2)\,\Delta t = p \times ln(u) + (1 - p) \times ln(d),$$

and

$$\sigma^2\,\Delta t = p \times (1 - p) \times [ln(u) - ln(d)]^2.$$

The relationship between u and d is still not fixed and ud = 1 is the simplest. Doing so, and imagining Δt to be small, reproduces Equation 7.17 for u, d, and p.

4. The CIR Model

As a specific example of one of the many stochastic differential equations proposed for generating the temporal evolution of the short rate, the Cox, Ingersoll, and Ross (1985) model is presented here. It incorporates mean reversion and a more realistic function than most for the volatility of interest rates. Mean reversion dampens the tendency to allow negative interest rates or unrealistically large values for them. Specifically, their stochastic differential equation takes the form

$$dS(t) = \lambda(\mu - S)\, dt + \sigma\sqrt{S}\, dt.$$

The mean value is specified by μ and the speed at which the mean is approached is given by lambda, $\lambda > 0$. Observe that the mean reversion term must be of the form shown, that is, $\mu - S$ rather than $S - \mu$, to have the correct behavior. If S gets too large, specifically larger than μ, then $\mu - S$ will be negative, making the next alteration in S negative and driving $S(t)$ downward and vice versa. This is what mean reversion connotes. The speed with which the reversion to the mean occurs is driven by λ. The larger it is, the more rapidly a departure from the mean value μ will be corrected. Unfortunately, real short rates do not appear to exhibit mean reversion, but long-term rates tend to. The variation in the short-rate depends on the magnitude of the short-rate in conformance with actual values.

One can solve this model in closed form and thereby explicitly demonstrate that it is capable of representing a wide variety of historically observed yield curve shapes. This has nothing to do with actual ability to predict real future yield curve shapes, given a numerical set of values for λ, μ, σ, and $S(0)$.

5. Principal Component Analysis

Interest rate data, in the form of the yield curve, are naturally interpreted as a plot of spot rates over time. Usually one utilizes a set of benchmark dates corresponding to the maturities of U.S. Treasury instruments because they are traded in a liquid fashion. Suppose that there is a set of N of them. This set of parameters to model the full yield curve does not mean that the evolution of the yield curve is best described in terms of a model that attempts to predict these particular N spot rates (or some denser set of 2N of them, and so forth). More subtle combinations of the full suite of spot rates may have more explanatory statistical power.

The purpose of principal component analysis is to try to reveal such unobvious combinations if they exist. An analogy might be trying to model a circle in rectangular coordinates. A circle with center translated to the position (a,b) would have an equation given by $(x - a)^2 + (y - b)^2 = R^2$, where R is the radius of the circle. To analyze this formula requires the solution of a quadratic equation, possibly a parametric representation to simplify it, and so forth. If, instead, we translated the rectangular coordinates by $-a$ and $-b$ respectively (that is, back to the origin), and then transformed the description from rectangular to polar coordinates, what would we find? Just $r = R$, which would be simple and much easier to understand. This is the kind of simplicity that principal component analysis might reveal.

When principal component analysis has been applied to the analysis of the yield curve (or the term structure of interest rates), three quantities show up with the most explanatory power. One is the absolute level of interest rates or the mean height of the yield curve. Another is a measure of the slope of the curve from the short-term end to the medium-term — for example, a slope measure based on the 2-year and the 10-year points. These two factors together have the statistical power to explain about 85 to 90% of yield curve reshapings.

The third element is related to the curvature. Together, according to Knez, Litterman, and Scheinkman (1994), the three of them explain almost all the variation observed in the yield curve over time. (Considering their mathematical significance, this should not be surprising.) After much more numerical experimentation, over longer time spans than the above-cited work covers, one would want to be able to develop an interest rate model that concentrated on these three quantities, used them as the independent variables, incorporated their financial dynamics, and had minimal statistical content. Unfortunately, this cannot be easily accomplished.

E. EDITORIAL

Have you seen any finance in the last few pages? Any economics? There are at least a dozen interest rate "models" in the literature that purport to contain the "dynamics" of the change in the term structure of interest rates. None of them have been seriously back-tested and none of them have any demonstrable predictive quantitative value going forward. In fact, they have the tiniest bit of financial content plus a huge dose of analytically convenient statistical theory that generates more applied mathematics.

Contrast this with the situation in a real science. How many models of gravity are there? One: Einstein's theory of general relativity. It has been back-tested over centuries of increasingly precisely measured data within and without the solar system (indeed to the ends of the observable universe); it has been tested in multiple, independent ways. It predicts entirely new phenomena that have been verified to the best of our measurement capabilities and it has neither arbitrary probability nor statistical content. (For those few of you who know quantum theory and will counter that it has statistical content, you are wrong; it has not one iota of statistical content. In one of its mathematical expressions, it can be easily formulated with a probabilistic interpretation. These are not nearly the same things.)

At one time McDonalds® was advertising its hamburgers (a **meat** product) in a jingle, sometimes sung backwards, that lauded its special sauce, its lettuce, its cheese, its pickles, its onions, and its sesame seed buns. In January, 1984, Wendy's® countered with the Clio® award-winning commercial in which Clara Peller, asked the critical question: "Where's the beef!?!?"

F. A FINAL REVIEW OF THE OAS METHOD

We now have all the pieces in place to more fully appreciate how option-adjusted spread computations are performed for mortgage pass-through securities. At the least complicated level, we would use monthly mortgage-adjusted (for credit risk, lack of liquidity, reinvestment risk, but not interest rate volatility) spot rates $\{s_n\}$ and write

$$\text{Market Value} = \sum_{n=1}^{N} CF_n/(1 + s_n)^n.$$

The cash flow at the nth month would be given by the sum of the monthly payment, MP, plus any unscheduled prepayments, curtailments, or defaults

$$CF_n = MP + (Prepayments + extras)_n.$$

This probably will not work well because the market price will not be reproduced if we discount by spot rates not allowed to fluctuate, even though we have interest-rate dependent cash flows. Uncertainty in the realized spot rates will translate into uncertainty regarding prepayments so that the true cash flows will be impossible to predict. This will lead to the investor demanding a higher rate of return than really deserved for investing in this type of security because he is risk averse. So, we add in an option-adjusted spread that will be positive. A better formula would be, with m = 12 for a monthly payment,

$$\text{Market Value} = \sum_{n=1}^{N} CF_n/(1 + s_n + OAS/m)^n$$

The option-adjusted spread, or OAS, is the premium in the interest rate, expressed as a decimal on an annual basis, required to compensate the investor for the embedded options and their uncertain valuation. The option-adjusted spread is the additional reward, over the on-the-run U.S. Treasury instruments that form the basis of the yield curve, demanded for credit, liquidity, reinvestment, and option risks. (More properly, a suite of on-the-run zero coupon U.S. Treasury debt vehicles would be used to match expected cash flows and therefore automatically match the Macaulay duration too.)

When added to the Treasury rate and used as a discount rate, the OAS makes the present value of the cash flows equal to the market price, thereby compensating the investor for the additional element of risks. We understand why there is only one OAS; only one extra piece of information (i.e., the market price) can be used to modify the option-free, fixed-income pricing formula.

We can have a static OAS, a fixed spread over and above the entire current Treasury spot curve. This would also be referred to as the zero volatility OAS. The reason is because only one scenario for future interest rates has been allowed: that observed to be embedded in the current spot rate curve. We can alter the current yield curve in some statistically and financially well-defined ways and compute an average of prices over many possible future evolutions of the current yield curve. Holding the set of future interest rate paths constant, one value of the OAS will match the market price. One financial constraint is that the average departures from the current spot rate curve are zero in an arbitrage-free fashion. In other words, the suite of scenarios produced with our interest rate models will conform to the current forward rate curve. (We might even do the same for the volatility structure of the curve if we were using an interest rate generation model that had a time-dependent volatility component.) The purely statistical properties can essentially be chosen at will, subject to these restrictions.

1. More Details

Let us use the following notation:

M = the total number of interest rate paths to be used in the Monte Carlo simulation,

CF_n^m = the monthly cash flow at period #n on interest rate path #m. It is important to realize that nth the cash flow on interest rate path #m is explicitly path dependent because of the embedded call options and

s_n^m = the mth monthly interest rate path value for the Treasury instrument's spot rate at payment time #n.

Then, the mth estimate of the present value of the contingent cash flows PV_m, as a function of the currently guessed value of the annual option-adjusted spread, oas, would be given by

$$PV_m = \sum_{n=1}^{N} CF_n^m / (1 + s_n^m + oas/12)^n.$$

(We must guess because we cannot invert this formula as was the case for the yield-to-maturity computation.) The computed market value, MV(oas), is given by averaging over the individual values obtained via the Monte Carlo interest rate simulation;

$$MV(oas) = (1/M) \times \sum_{m=1}^{M} PV_m.$$

Either MV(oas) reproduces the observed market value or it does not. If it does, then the true option-adjusted spread (i.e., the OAS) is equal to oas. If it does not, then we alter the value of oas and repeat the computation until the observed market value is successfully matched. To reiterate, the OAS method is one in which

• A large number of hypothetical Treasury interest rate futures are simulated.
• A (constant) trial value for the actual option-adjusted spread is added across the entire purported yield curve.
• The cash flows for this discount rate are computed explicitly, including the monieness of the call option.
• Their present values are calculated and then a price.

When, after the generation of sundry interest rate scenarios, the average of the computed price equals the actual (or observed) market price, then we have inferred the true value of the option-adjusted spread and we label it the OAS.

a. Technical Details

Should we be averaging the final prices to infer the OAS or should we be averaging the cash flows at each node of the interest rate model first? This is reminiscent of computing a portfolio duration; portfolio OAS is similarly complicated. How the mean is computed will affect the result; one could first average the cash flows from all the simulated interest rate paths and then compute the OAS as the spread that equates the present value of the aggregated cash flow means to the market price. One could also define the OAS as the spread that equates the mean of the individual prices for each hypothetical interest rate path to the market price. Usually, the OAS is defined as the spread that equates the average simulated price to the observed price — the method that the preceding formulas encapsulate.

The better procedure is to compute the portfolio weighted average OAS as was done with duration vs. a portfolio-wide internal rate of return. However, correlation is a much more important issue here. Suppose that two assets in the portfolio would separately be computed to have OAS of BP basis points. Then, if the two are highly correlated, the OAS of the portfolio will also be near BP basis points. However, within the set of simulated scenarios, when one is performing well so is the other and vice versa. Therefore, the dispersion for the portfolio's OAS will be wider than that for either individual asset (and by the square root of two or about 140%). Conversely, if the two assets are negatively correlated in performance, then there will be a cancellation effect and the actual portfolio will appear to have a smaller dispersion than either asset alone while having the same value of BP basis points for the OAS. Obtaining the full distribution of OASs is a much better alternative if one knows how to read and interpret it.

2. Pros and Cons

Advantages of the option-adjusted spread methodology over merely discounting cash flows are that: 1. it allows for interest rate volatility, 2. it permits cash flows dependent on interest rates, 3. it can be computed for both assets and liabilities, and 4. using it, one can meaningfully compare the OASs of different instruments because all were priced as a spread to the same on-the-run Treasuries over the same maturity via the same interest rate model and set of future scenarios.

Some disadvantages of the option-adjusted spread methodology include the facts that: 1. it is based on the current yield curve, implying that forward rates will be realized as future spot rates, 2. the values produced are highly dependent on the interest rate and the prepayment models, and 3. one must have a systematic method for preventing values outside the realm of financially realistic quantities — a full log-normal probability distribution allows for unrealistically high and low interest rate possibilities. Other problems include the fact that the true OAS should approach zero as the maturity date approaches, just as the price of a fixed-income security approaches its par price as the maturity date nears. Another difficulty with the use of an OAS in the standard present value implies that reinvestment of the intermediate cash flows until the maturity date is at that higher rate of return too.

The procedure does not capture interest rate path-independent events such as a REMIC tranche down-grading. (More properly phrased, the option-adjusted spread methodology does not capture events that cannot be explicitly expressed in terms of interest rate changes.) Another obstacle to realistic pricing for mortgage-backed security analysis is the use of a deterministic formula for prepayments. It is better to use a probabilistic prepayment model, but this imposes a significant computational burden because one would need a double stochastic averaging process.

On the purely statistical side of the interest rate generation process, adding a constant offset to a randomly generated interest rate sequence alters the statistical properties of that distribution. An alternative procedure that overcomes some of these difficulties is the following:

$$\text{Market Value} = (1\,/\,M) \times \sum_{m=1}^{M} \sum_{n=1}^{N} CF_n^m\,/\,(1 + p \times s_n^m)^n,$$

where the multiplicative factor of p plays the role of the OAS.

8 Portfolio Management

This chapter discusses portfolio management and its theoretical underpinnings in the mean-variance mode. The former requires as much art as technical understanding, knowledge, and judgment as a facility with present value formulas or forward rate computation. The latter rests on a very weak statistical foundation usually only appreciated by experts, who have dealt with reams of real data, whether scientific or economic, and come to understand that the world is not random. The mathematics of the basis for linear correlation will be thoroughly explored so that you can be aware of the very strong assumptions made to adopt an inappropriate statistical model for financial risk. The chapter concludes with a suggestion on how to do better at portfolio management.

I. INTRODUCTION

What are you trying to do? Make a reasonable amount of money in the short-term? Manage to a particular benchmark index over the long-term? Provide stability of nominal cash flow for liability matching purposes? Are you attempting to preserve purchasing power as well? Are you performing asset and liability management with a goal to preserving capital first and providing a stable income stream second? Is your main goal the rapid growth of the value of assets under management so that excellent short-term performance can be used as a marketing tool? Do you expect new infusions of cash to invest (and on what time scales) or is this a *de novo* setup? More generally, is this a buy-and-hold operation or is a certain amount of trading required/expected/allowed? How does the potential for price or yield volatility interact with your stated performance objectives? Do tax, accounting, or regulatory limitations override maximizing the net present value of your cash flows? You must answer these questions in concert with your clients and customers. No book can do this for you.

In general, you need to assemble a consistent investment policy with three key elements: 1. an *asset allocation strategy*, 2. a set of operating instructions for buying and selling securities known as *market timing*, and 3. a methodology for *security selection* within chosen asset classes. It is best to place significant thought into the development of these three critical elements, understand and make your client comprehend why you have made particular choices, and then to stand by your selections. You must hope that your client will honor his contract with you, follow through with performance measurements on the agreed-upon time scale with the agreed-to measurement barometer, and understand your fee structure.

Market fads come and go. This week Argentina defaults, next week/month/quarter it might be another country that does not really matter in the U.S. fixed-income and mortgage markets. Even if there is another "dot com bubble" (or another tulip bulb bubble!), the value of a Freddie Mac PC Gold will not be fundamentally affected, although its market price might dramatically change for a few weeks. You also should have a deep and thorough knowledge of financial history. The following names and issues should trigger an informed alarm bell in your mind:

The Franklin National Bank collapse
The Conrail/Penn Central default
Barings Bank and derivative trading
The Latin American debt crisis of the mid-1980s
The Hunt brothers trying to corner the silver market in 1979–1980
The savings and loan failures because of failure to employ duration-matching
    techniques, greed, fraud, and lack of Congressional action
The Bank of Commerce International (BCCI) and lack of oversight
Milken and junk bonds
The 1991 Gulf War
Foreign currency traders' attack on the European monetary system in the fall
    of 1992
The Saloman Brothers U.S. Treasury bond market share imbroglio
Any Mexican peso collapse
Orange County, California, and leveraged derivative trading in late 1994
Sumitomo and copper futures
The collapse of Daewoo, the second largest chaebol in South Korea, in
    mid-1999
Enron in 2001, WorldCom in 2002, …

The point is that, by now, you should expect something untoward to occur once every 6 to 12 months. It may not be in your market niche but may still have consequences that overflow into your preferred investment segment. The general administration of your fiduciary responsibilities should already have a plan, well-developed before the next problem arises, on how to deal with it when it comes. One danger of not being so prepared is that market breaks tend to panic investors in the same direction. This

- Complicates the liquidation of securities via thin trading with wide bid–ask spreads.
- Pushes the prices of sought-after instruments far beyond their fundamental values.
- Damagingly reveals inappropriate or underappreciated leverage.
- Rapidly depletes margin accounts.
- Highlights the misallocation of funds away from the basic strategy of the investment portfolio.
- Makes lines of credit or other quick cash-raising schemes very expensive.

Note that the irregularly periodic, and roughly annual, occurrence of troublesome economic, political, or military events makes any reliance on analytically convenient probability functions exceedingly risky. Almost all of them have high contact at infinity —meaning that they asymptotically approach zero probability levels rapidly (read the absence of many standard-deviation departures from the norm events). Relying on models built on such formulas can be expensive; the failure of prepayment models for mortgages before the large 1992 interest rate drop exposed the meaning of negative convexity, portfolio insurance and the 1987 stock market crash, Long-Term Capital Management's convergence strategy, and so on. Life is much more interesting than the set of Pearson distributions is.

Finally, life and markets change over time in permanent ways. The swiftly enlarging pool of international investors, their goals, the changing nature of global investment vehicles, and the speed of information flow and trading make immutable alterations in the behavior of market participants over the course of years (sometimes even sooner). Model building and historical wisdom must be continuously updated, in the presence of considerable and confusing background noise, to integrate the new realities.

A. ASSET ALLOCATION

An asset allocation strategy refers to defining the set of all possible asset classes that one might invest in and rating them according to some logical scheme; it could be explicitly by risk level. If so, then one assumes that the client expects a risk–reward trade-off in the yield. It could be within a specific class, such as mortgage-related derivative instruments, and you must choose between nonagency pass-through MBSs or REMIC tranches. Beyond the generic agency vs. special nature of any other collateral underlying an MBS — with respect to the volume of product and the nature and amelioration of its embedded credit risk — are hazards associated with the price of the security with respect to par and its negative convexity.

Moreover, once a model portfolio has been chosen you should expect to rebalance it over time as different portions of it grow or shrink in value. From the perspective of stable portfolio management the frequency of this would presumably be low, unless you deliberately chose to manage the portfolio with a technique such as *value-at-risk* (VaR). The management strategy that determines your frequency of trading and the rules that define how and when, or if, you buy and sell should be clearly promulgated. However, sudden market breaks might engender a greater volume of trading activity, for example,

Common stocks in October, 1987
The liquidity crisis of February, 1994
The collapse of the Japanese real estate and stock markets in the early 1990s
The foreign-currency shambles in East Asia in late 1997
Fixed-income securities in August, 1998, because of the Russian default (and only $40 billion, mostly to the Germans!?!)
Technology stocks during 2000

Using an index-matching strategy usually requires only passive tactics. However, if the necessity were to outperform the specified index, for example, by 50 bp in yield, an active portfolio management strategy would be called for as the portfolio manager dynamically searched for relative value within the other constraints he needed to observe. One constraint might be a duration-matching restriction for the purposes of portfolio immunization. Convexity-matching may also be an important consideration. Here the function of specified trading in seasoned MBS pools could play a large role.

Rather than to try to match an index one-for-one, a subset of it might be employed. Time studies of correlation could indicate that holding a small group of key securities has a high coefficient of linear correlation with the gross performance of the index. If these crucial instruments were also the more liquid ones, then trading and other transaction costs would be minimized as one sought to keep the degree of responsiveness high. The main dangers are that the inappropriate time period for performing the correlation would have been chosen coupled with a lack of decreased time weighting for older events. Markets change and evolve, sometimes with frightening speed.

1.   Model Fixed-Income Portfolios

A suggestion for a conservative, U.S. fixed-income portfolio might have the following composition:

1. U.S. Treasury instruments: 20%
2. Agency debt (meaning principally Freddie Mac and Fannie Mae): 15%
3. Mortgage-backed securities: 35% (of which the majority would be pass-throughs as opposed to REMIC tranches)
4. About 25% AAA and AA corporate bonds
5. The remaining 5% split between *commercial MBSs* and other types of asset-backed securities, for example, 3 and 2%, all with a AAA rating

(Why have such a small weighting in any type of asset class? To make a huge amount of money if it becomes a home run? To limit your losses because you do not really understand the security or how it evolves over time?)

If you were attempting to increase yield, then you would trade ownership of Treasury instruments for callable agency debt or a heavier weighting of A and BBB quality corporate debt. Independent of yield *per se*, the main reason to stay resolutely invested in U.S. Treasury instruments is their unique liquidity, the existence of many exchange-traded futures and options based on them, and the ability to manipulate a blend of investments synthetically with respect to duration and convexity. The tight correlations with the interest rate swap markets and the TED spread, plus the ability to perform similar kinds of artificial creation with liquid instruments traded on them, should not be ignored either.

a.   Price Discovery

There is a physical place called the New York Stock Exchange. Around the corner you can find the American Stock Exchange. There is a common, albeit electronic, "place" known as the NASDAQ market. Nothing comparable exists for the universe of fixed-income instruments. It is essentially an over-the-counter marketplace. The absence of a centralized trading platform makes price discovery difficult, time consuming, and expensive. Transaction costs or wide bid–ask spreads can easily prevail beyond those required for traders to make a reasonable profit. (Remember the 1/8 to 1/4 point systematic difference scandal on the most heavily traded NAS-DAQ stocks a few years ago?) In addition, the fixed-income market has a huge range of securities that are different from but similar to U.S. government debt instruments. These range from junk bonds, agency and nonagency pass-through MBSs, REMICs, and other types of asset-backed securities to foreign debt, and so on. A share of common stock in the XYZ Corp. is the same as any other share. This is not true of their bullet bonds, even if they have the same issue amount, time-to-maturity, sinking fund provisions, and so forth. A different CUSIP number means a different security.

b. Hedging

Hedging, in the financial context, means to protect against one risk by investing in a second venture. The simplest example is the wheat farmer and the baker. The farmer wants to grow his crops and receive enough at harvest time as recompense for his supplies and labor. The baker wants the wheat at a known price so that he can make bread. In April, they agree to delivery of the wheat in September at a price fixed in April, thereby off-setting each of their respective risks.

The Chicago Board of Trade introduced a mortgage-backed futures and options contract in June of 1989, but it has not been successful — for reasons that neither they nor I understand. Moreover, most of those who purchase a REMIC tranche want that particular set of cash flow characteristics, so using exchange-traded options or futures for them would not work. Over-the-counter derivatives are available for hedging pass-throughs and the forward markets exist for TBA trading. However, given its huge size, comparatively little organized future or option trading takes place on mortgages.

For mortgage-backed securities, Macaulay duration increases with rising interest rates and decreases with falling interest rates. This is a direct effect of the prepayment option going out of- or coming into-the-money. As rates decline the phenomenon of price compression occurs — the same absolute drop in interest rates brings ever-smaller increases in price. If one is managing a mortgage portfolio with a specified duration range, then it may mean rebalancing the mixture when rates drop. The simplest method of doing so is to purchase options on U.S. Treasury securities (just as the simplest method of hedging interest rate risk in general for mortgage-related securities is to purchase options on comparable duration U.S. Treasury instruments). One can add convexity relatively simply to a mortgage portfolio. One purchases call options because the downside risk is the cost of the option premium and there is little limit to the upside gain or one purchases put options (for the opposite set of reasons).

Subtracting convexity from a mortgage portfolio can also be executed in two relatively simple fashions, namely, writing call or put options depending on one's views with respect to the market. Here, too, the risks and rewards are basically one-sided. Someone trying to hedge dynamically — that is, to adjust the duration of his mortgage portfolio continuously as interest rates move up and down — is required to purchase futures to lengthen duration after prices have risen (rates have fallen). He must do the opposite when rates have risen, namely, sell futures after prices have fallen. Naturally, the more one hedges away the negative convexity risk in his mortgages, the less of the option-adjusted spread (literally interpreted) one can expect to earn.

B. MARKET TIMING

The operating instructions for the portfolio that you are running should also include a set of rules regarding market timing. Will you consistently attempt to buy low and sell high (doomed to fail over the long term)? Will you buy heavily whatever asset class is momentarily extremely depressed in price with no real fundamental weakness — perhaps temporarily overriding your basic asset allocation strategy? Buying during downturns, to reap the reward of the upturn, also implies that you have the funds to do this. These monies have been lying idle (or essentially idle in some short-term, low interest rate investment) or must be quickly and, possibly expensively, borrowed. In the former case the frequency of good buying opportunities coupled with the amplitude of any gains (and your ability to garner them) must outweigh the long-term losses resulting from a continuously large cash holding at a low rate of return. In the latter instance it is obvious that borrowing costs must be exceeded by profits. A not-so-visible expense was maintenance of the ability to borrow a large amount of funds on short notice. Perhaps you will follow a much more conservative strategy, such as building a *laddered fixed-income portfolio*?

You might have a disciplined trading system designed to forecast market moves or predicated on your ability to discover hidden values. Alternatively, you project perceived risk and act, in a contrarian fashion, on that. These possibilities could be referred to as timing-based approaches too. The major differences among them, if carefully thought through and consistently executed, and attempting to buy low and sell high, are considerable. Finally, note that doing nothing, for instance not rebalancing a portfolio, is a form of market-timing too. In reality, you are choosing not sell this (perhaps accepting a loss now) to purchase that (to garner a gain in the future), thereby failing to remain true to your strategic vision.

1. Duration and Portfolios

There are two simple types of fixed-income portfolios designed to deal with duration. The *barbell strategy* involves purchasing short- and long-term instruments; intermediate-term securities are avoided. The durations of the portfolio, both Macaulay and modified, are altered by changing the allocation mix. This method demands an active management strategy because the short-term assets are always maturing and their funds must be reinvested. This requires a decision about the relative proportion of new short- and long-term assets to be purchased with these monies. Second, with the passage of time, a long-term instrument evolves into an intermediate-term certificate. To keep to the barbell policy, these must be sold and the proceeds reinvested in short- and long-term fractions whose relative amounts need deliberation. In both instances, transaction costs must be paid. Finally, though interest rate volatility is concentrated in the short-term end of the market, the price volatility of fixed-income instruments is concentrated in the long-term versions of these investments.

Thus, an equal dollar amount at the two extremes does not translate into equal price sensitivities (if this is a goal of the client).

A laddered portfolio is one in which fixed-income instruments of all maturities, out to some maximum tenor, are purchased in equal dollar amounts. As the shorter-term instruments mature, their proceeds are used to buy new maximum life certificates; the bulk of the portfolio automatically ages forward 1 year per year of time. This type of structure requires minimum management effort and consumes little in transaction costs. (This assumes that the security classes have been fixed and that bond swapping to try to pick up extra yield is not routinely done.) Hundreds of billions of dollars are invested in bond funds in this format, especially in U.S. government debt. Since there has been no 20-year Treasury Bond for a long time, you can see one reason why the sudden demise of the 30-year U.S. Treasury Bond produced such anguish among bond fund managers.

a. Other Possibilities

The simplest method of matching a liability requirement over time is to purchase zero coupon bonds that will provide the compulsory cash flows. This requires no active management, is inherently interest-rate risk-free and can be simple to execute using U.S. Treasury instruments via *STRIPS*. (The Treasury STRIPS program was introduced in January, 1985. STRIPS is the acronym for separate trading of registered interest and principal of securities.) This method is known as *defeasance*. Liability payback management is mostly practiced by insurance and pension funds which primarily face interest rate risk. Beyond this, they also face repayment and reinvestment risk. As an example, an annuitant may or may not exercise various options in the insurance product delaying or accelerating funds owed to him.

The next step up in complication is known as running a *dedicated* portfolio. The intent is to optimize the difference between future cash inflows and outflows at a minimum cost. Because the implementation of this technique is interest rate sensitive, rebalancing or reinvestment issues frequently cause departures from the desired result. The immunization of a fixed-income portfolio, as discussed in Chapter 3, was the next step in portfolio management sophistication. Really long-term duration instruments are relatively rare, so matching 15-year or longer-term liabilities is effectively impossible. The active supervision of a duration-matched assortment of assets, with rebalancing as demanded by convexity considerations, is the preferred mode of operation.

The Yale University endowment fund pioneered *absolute return* investing about 15 years ago. Their aim was to produce equity-like returns from fixed-income investments by concentrating on discovering undervalued investments, accepting the buy-and-hold risks associated with illiquid securities, and capitalizing on exogenous events to their advantage. This required a high level of portfolio management, extensive research, and a generally short time horizon for this portion of their asset allocation. Yale's success is well known. However, this technique is difficult to succeed at over the long term because of secular changes in the market, asymmetric information, and turnover among portfolio management staff that depart with the historical corporate memory of the inevitable unprofitable mistakes.

b. Value-at-Risk

Value-at-risk is an example of one type quantitatively based portfolio management strategy. Its main feature is the putative estimation of the maximum amount of loss, at some stated level of probability, which you can expect over a particular time horizon. This apparently meaningful numerical estimate is provided, given the composition of the portfolio, its (linear) correlation matrix, and your model of how the relevant markets are going to perform in the future. (VaR's main weaknesses are the necessity of all these assumptions, how up-to-date they are, and how complete the knowledge base behind them is.) You might have a goal of limiting daily risk to $1,000,000 of the value of assets under management with a probability of 1% or less or limiting daily risk to $1,234,567.89 of the value of assets under management with a probability of 0.98765% or less. If you do not believe that the second VaR estimation was a reasonable proposition, then why did you believe the first one? You believed it because it used round numbers. If a VaR model can do the first computation with believability, it can do the second one too; you must have equally deep faith in both results.

2. Callable Bonds

Embedded options in bonds make the accurate pricing of these instruments difficult. Usually, these will be call options with a lock-out period. A European-style call option, to be exercised by a rational debtor, can be straightforwardly valued once you have the value for market interest rates at the expiration of the no-call time interval. Moving from there to a Bermudan- or American-style option renders even an approximate assessment problematical. You must accurately estimate an entire suite of future yield curves until the maturity date of the bond. It is impractical to guess a value for more complicated options. A thorough study of a consistent callable debt issuer, such as Fannie Mae or Freddie Mac, would provide insight into the true yields of their instruments. As an example of what might be revealed, historical *post facto* analysis of credit risk has shown that investors routinely overdemand compensation in the form of higher yields, usually by hundreds of a percent.

C. SECURITY SELECTION

Security selection refers to the methods and procedures used to analyze competing potential investments. In the mortgage markets are a variety of different interest rate and prepayment risk products:

Pass-through MBSs
Stripped MBSs (i.e., IOs and POs)
Various REMIC tranches such as sequential pay classes, level I PACs, level
    II PACs, TACs, and reverse TACs
Companion classes to these tranches
Accrual classes
Floating-rate and inverse floating-rate classes
WAC POs, VADMs, etc.

There is additional diversity among seasoned and newly originated MBSs, those with underlying collateral that conforms or does not, and so on. Searching for mispricing opportunities, especially among the more illiquid whole-loan and private-label securities, is most likely to be profitable and add relatively little actual default risk because most of these investments will have various credit enhancements.

A static security selection decree some times will cause you to lose out on undervalued prospects within your asset class. (This is a minor concern to those with a short-time horizon.) Remaining true to a strategic vision is very good, but tactical flexibility is highly desirable. Knowing that this chance is the one to be taken differentiates the good from the mediocre portfolio manager and keeps the art in investment science (misnomer though that that phrase is).

1. Model Mortgage Portfolios

A conservative, mortgage portfolio might have the following blend: 1. about 20% of government-guaranteed pass-throughs spread around the current coupon, 2. a mixture of 30- and 15-year agency pass-throughs divided up 55% and 15%, spread within 100 bp of the current coupon, and 3. ten percent of balloon re-set mortgages MBSs and AAA commercial MBSs. Observe the absence of any private-label securities or even sequential-pay or PAC REMIC tranches (even if backed by agency collateral). Given this, it is not surprising not to see whole-loan certificates. One can take on significantly more risk, but not necessarily gain a great deal in yield, by devoting a higher percentage of assets to the riskier REMIC tranches (e.g., IO strips, floating-rate and inverse-floating rate classes, support classes, and so on).

2. Yield

What is the best yield available in the MBS market today? What do you mean by the best? Is it the highest stated yield? Is it the MBS with the highest static spread to the 10-year U.S. Treasury Note? Are we considering only agency-issued securities or are whole-loan MBSs under consideration too? Do you have a specific time frame in mind? How important is being duration-matched vs. the potential for extra yield? Are there convexity bounds within which to stay? Is interest rate volatility anticipated to increase or decrease? Is the shape of the yield curve likely to change and, if so, which pass-through securities will benefit and which will be harmed? Are supply and demand factors driving the rich or cheap assessment of MBSs that dominate other factors? Does one MBS, or a group of them, have sufficient seasoning that their future prepayment speeds are likely to be predictable? Will the different risk-based capital guidelines for the various securities significantly affect return on equity? Are there accounting regulations to obey? Are the rewards commensurate with the risks?

These are just some of the questions that a portfolio manager should ask himself when selecting assets to purchase. If the universe of MBSs is widened to include REMICs — even sequential pay classes and PACs — then the difficulty of answering this question exponentially increases. So does the risk. The reward for being right usually does not, however.

a. Leverage

Financial leverage can appear in a portfolio in unexpected and unwelcome ways. Many derivative instruments have a high degree of leverage built into them. Some fee-generating schemes, such as lending collateral in the repurchase agreement or dollar roll markets, are less extreme examples of being leveraged. Using devices that provide leverage and understanding the nature of the relevant hedge ratios is one thing. Using securities that provide leverage and not appreciating their inter-action with the rest of the holdings or their potential to magnify bad outcomes possibly places the portfolio manager in an embarrassing situation, beyond devi-ating from their basic asset and security allocation strategies, to risking the bonus, if not the job.

3. On Diversification

The mantra in modern portfolio management is diversification based on the mean-variance framework made popular by Markowitz. Also, assets can be allocated with respect to an efficient frontier in order to maximize returns for an assumed level of risk. However, the information base is invariably biased and incomplete and the statistical assumptions made in constructing these models are usually overly sim-plistic, if not incorrect. In addition, I appreciate how mathematically and financially thin that the arguments behind this dictum are; it rests on feeble statistical grounds because the actual trading markets where stocks, bonds, and other investment prices are set are not anywhere near random. I am referring especially to the standard assumption of two-sided risk aversion. (Random means something much weaker than normally distributed or in conformance with the central limit theorem; hence, one might hope for randomness, if not normality.)

Therefore, because of this compromise, the results obtained regarding diversi-fication and risk diminishment rest heavily on the concepts of linear correlation and variance minimization. Because a particular statistical theory is already built, taking over the edifice of standard, two-sided statistics and analytical probability theory and applying them to finance (rarely governed by rational human beings!) is a poor excuse for not really thinking about the relevant problems.

There are other difficulties with the mean-variance framework, even if you accept all its caveats. It (theoretically) forces you to purchase the security with the highest level of return for a given level of risk without considering price *per se* because the methodology implicitly assumes an efficient market — at least in the weak sense of the phrase. Moreover, no natural, internally consistent, rebalancing philosophy with a close relationship to the actual world of considerations exists with regard to a lack of liquidity or transaction costs. While it can be adapted to overcome some of these shortcomings, a fully developed theory of investments would, from the beginning, coherently and consistently address them in the beginning, instead of misappropriating a simple statistical superstructure. Finally, the technique is difficult to make realistically dynamic, basing risk estimates and correlation matrix values on some (necessarily externally and arbitrarily specified) set of time scales.

a. Financial Risk

Nobody wants to put all his eggs in one basket because it is too risky. If you drop the basket, you might break all the eggs. Your basket might be stolen, leaving you bereft of eggs. The same concept applies to investments; rarely does an individual investor or investment manager own only one security or one type of investment. One hopes that by diversifying the portfolio over many uncorrelated investments the overall risk of the combination will be less than the worst risk of any one, the average risk of the whole or some other meaningful measure of risk. The quantitatively interesting problem is how to assess the risk of a portfolio made up of $N > 1$ securities. No one knows because no one really knows how to define risk in the financial context quintessentially. Financial risk can be easily defined in a mode that allows standard mathematical techniques to be used to assess it, but that is not the same thing as having specified it in an economically sensible manner.

The risk to you, the investor or portfolio manager, in a specific project might be quite different. The project may pay off handsomely, garnering you a big return, it may be only middling successful, earning a return comparable to what you could have obtained, for example, in AA corporate bonds, or it may be an abysmal failure, barely allowing you to recoup 50¢ on the dollar. Here the risk is associated with the fact that you do not know the outcome and that there is such a wide range of potential results. A project with three prospective results of 12.5% profit, 12.0% profit, or 11.5% profit would not be said to be risky. This is not because a 12% return is a particularly high (or even a satisfactory) rate of return; it is because the variation among the possible outcomes is tightly limited. People much prefer certainty to uncertainty and investors and investment managers (who are usually people but increasingly are computer programs) are generally risk averse.

In truth, you only care about the risk of loss; that is, financial risk is only one-sided. While an investment with potential outcomes of +10, +20, and +35% can be said to be risky because of the wide range of possible end results, very few investors would be disappointed with any one of them. Conversely, an investment with the three highly probable conclusions of +1, 0, and –2% does not have much variation but it also does not have much return. Nonetheless, because of the narrow spread of possible end results, this investment would be said to not be risky (as well as not be particularly profitable). Mathematically, it is very difficult to deal with a one-sided probability distribution. Therefore, the first steps in the analysis of portfolio risk, by Harry Markowitz in the early 1950s, were based on two-sided distributions taken from standard, extant mathematical techniques. Developing a mathematically tractable, one-sided, (or mostly one-sided) technique for evaluating risk would greatly benefit the investment community.

Before delving into the mathematics of portfolio risk, which actually involves nothing more than the concept of linear correlation, note that not all risks can be minimized via the diversification of a portfolio. In finance, the phrase *unsystematic risk* is used to denote that portion of the risk associated with investments that can be diversified away by constructing an appropriate mixture of assets. (Other names for the same quantity are unique risk, residual risk, specific risk, and diversifiable risk. This proliferation of terms really helps the student focus on the key idea.) Therefore, you should not expect to be rewarded for accepting risk of this type and the financial markets should not price securities such that you can make excess rewards by allowing for this type of risk. (Excess is circularly defined as those above the mean for this level of nondiversifiable risk.)

An example of unsystematic risk that can be eliminated by diversification is to own only the production side of some commodity (a gold mine, an oil well, a wheat field, and so forth). If wholesale prices were to drop, then you would lose money. However, if you also owned the retail side of the same commodity (a jewelry company, a gas station, a bakery, and so forth), then that type of firm would benefit from a drop in cost of its raw materials. Hence, by owning a portfolio containing a mixture of both types of business, you would be (partially) shielded from a drop in the pertinent commodity prices. That is, you would have lowered your overall risk via the mechanism of diversification.

In contrast, systematic risk refers to something that affects the entire market. For example, when the Dow Jones Industrial index rises, so does the price of your stock.

II. THE MATHEMATICS OF PORTFOLIO RISK

A mortgage portfolio is subject primarily to interest rate risk and, via that, prepayment risk, although some default risk on the part of the mortgagors is present too. Asset diversification outside of mortgages is not usually a consideration for a buy and hold mortgage investment firm because mortgages are the only asset class that they own in large amounts. Moreover, such a business typically specializes in fixed- or adjustable-rate mortgages and the latter have minimal price-related interest rate risk.

However, the prepayment characteristics of 15-year fixed-rate liens are different from those of 30-year mortgages. In addition, differences in risk exist among government-insured mortgages, conforming conventional mortgages, and jumbo mortgages. Therefore, a more general understanding of portfolio diversification and risk management is a worthwhile side issue to discuss. In this section I consider a two-asset investment portfolio in detail and fully develop the mathematically relevant issues. I enjoy working out analytically tractable problems; it is really neat that all you have heard about portfolio diversification, hedging, and so on just falls out of the formulas. That is an aesthetic statement from a mathematician, not a practical statement from an investment advisor worth his pay.

A. A TWO-ASSET PORTFOLIO

1. Overview

Having gone through the mathematics, it turns out that a two-asset portfolio has all the statistical and financial complications that might arise with a much larger collection of securities. Hence, by providing a thorough discourse of this (apparently limited), topic we can cover all that is embodied in more complex scenarios. When it is convenient, we use results from calculus to facilitate the discussion. Of course, if your calculus is rusty or you never learned it, then you will not make much pedagogical progress. However, the key presentation aspects of the discussion can be developed only using high-school algebra, which is included too.

A rational way to proceed might be to compute the average rate of return based on a probability distribution that describes the conceivable outcomes for the security under consideration. From what does this probability distribution arise? It might be from an arbitrary function analytically convenient to use; the log-normal distribution is very heavily overused for this purpose. It could be from a probability distribution that has some reasonable theoretical underpinnings to warrant its use (as the normal distribution does from the central limit theorem — an amazingly powerful, sometimes practical and utilitarian, result). It also might be from a mathematical function that has been fit to empirical data for this security (by far the best choice, assuming that the underlying price dynamics are either static or slowly changing with time).

What can you compute with this distribution, beyond an expected value? You can compute the second moment and try to understand what it is telling us about the relative probability of different outcomes. The most common usage of the second moment is to inform us of the amount of spread the various end results have about their mean value. (The average value is also known as the first moment of the distribution.) This standard deviation would be computed from the same probability distribution utilized in the construction of the mean value mentioned earlier. This measure, known as the variance (its square root is known as the standard deviation) plays the part of the main risk-measuring variable in finance.

In the financial context, risk is interpreted as the relative uncertainty of an outcome. The larger the possible range of results about the mean —good or bad — is, the more apprehension is associated with that investment. In particular the level of risk is defined to be equal to the standard deviation of a financial instrument's return about its mean value. One then speaks of the *risk-adjusted return*, which is equal to the expected rate of return divided by the standard deviation about the mean.

The main purpose of this section is to understand, in general, how to compute the variance of a portfolio consisting of an arbitrary number of assets. When you attempt to perform the relevant computation for a two-element portfolio, then you immediately encounter an intricacy. The difficulty is the potential for interaction between the rates of return of the two assets. In the mortgage markets an obvious interaction is between the coupon rate on a traditional mortgage and the interest rate on a 10-year U.S. Treasury Note. The mathematical issue is the nature of this association. Do the two rates of return under consideration move together, at least partially, or are they partially independent? If they do move together, is it in the same or opposite direction, with some degree of confidence?

The statistical theory available for off-the-shelf usage is well developed if and only if the two quantities are linearly correlated. Just as no accessible general theory of one-sided risk exists, there is no general theory of non-linear correlation. Without this enormously strong and, therefore, highly simplifying assumption, most of the current formalism of portfolio risk management would not exist.

The real issue for someone trying to manage a portfolio in a risk-averse fashion is not the ease of the mathematical computation, which increased computing power has made moot, but what happens in the genuine world of financial markets over time. It is easy enough to gauge whether or not two time series (i.e., sets of prices for two stocks, bonds, interest rates, commodities, financial derivatives, and so on) are linearly correlated or not and, if so, to what extent. The standard statistics books contain numerical details of computing the linear correlation coefficient (defined in Equation 8.6). If the correlation is other than linear, you are operating in nearly virgin statistical territory and are essentially on your own. Assuming the price history of two assets is linearly correlated in order to utilize the existing mathematical superstructure is, at best, naïve.

Accepting the importance of linear correlation, the next most critical problem is the time period over which to perform the calculation. Do we go back to the stock market crash of October, 1987, or earlier? (Back to that of 1929, when the Federal Reserve first had a real influence?) Do we return to the most recent Mexican peso crisis or the one before that? Do we revisit the Russian default of 1998? Pick your date and look back in time. Independent of how far in the past we go to utilize the available price data, do we use equal weights? Would it not be preferable to decrease the weight of the older values relative to the newer ones to better track the ever-changing markets and broad economic environment? (Yes, in general.) What kind of diminution of influence is preferable? (It depends on how fast you want to react to every little political, economic, military, and social change.) Are there any good theoretical guides on how to do so? (No.)

You can begin to see the nature of the complexity of an issue that has no right answers. Does the amount of dollars already invested in one asset determine its weight? People have reasons for preferring T-Bills to T-Bonds. Financial judgment, extensive statistical experience (which means more than dumping data files into a canned computer program), and a real appreciation for the nature of the underlying economics and mathematics are required here.

Return to the restriction to linear correlation. This is extraordinarily important because the statistical theory is well developed only in this instance. For assets whose rates of return are nonlinearly correlated, no simple measure is analogous to the linear correlation coefficient; we tend to use it to quantify the extent of the link between two rates of return. Indeed, all of portfolio diversification theory really is contained in one formula for the variance of two linearly related quantities. (See Equation 8.5 below.) In finance, the variance is used as the principal measure of risk; from this follow two of the standard dictums in investment theory: 1. diversification is the way to minimize risk and 2. if you want to earn a higher than expected rate of return, you must accept a higher level of risk.

If the price history of two quantities were positively correlated, whether linear or not, then we know that they move together. If one goes up (down), then so does the other one. If they were in fact positively *linearly* correlated, then they would move up and down together in a proportional fashion. If they were positively, but not linearly, correlated, then they would move up and down together in a more complicated way (e.g., perhaps with a quadratic relationship such as $Price_1 = Price_2^2$). If the price history of two quantities were negatively correlated, whether linear or not, then we know that they move in opposite directions. If one goes up (down), then the other one goes down (up). If they were, in fact, negatively linearly correlated, then they would move down and up in a proportional fashion. If they were negatively, but not

linearly, correlated, then they would move down and up together in a more complicated way (e.g., perhaps a cubic relationship such as $Price_1 = -Price_2{}^3 + Price_2/3$).

The financial importance of negative correlation is that it can reduce the level of
risk whereas positive correlation can only increase the level of risk. In the mortgage-
related context, think of the combination of an interest-only strip and a principal-
only strip, the sum of a targeted amortization class and a reverse TAC, the fusion of
a floating-rate tranche of a REMIC and the inverse floating-rate tranche of the same
REMIC, and so forth as examples of securities whose correlation is negative.

B. THE EXPECTED RATE OF RETURN OF A PORTFOLIO OF ASSETS

1. The Expected Rate of Return for One Asset

Before proceeding any further, we should first discuss exactly how to calculate
the average rate of return for an individual security. To do so requires that we
have a complete set of possible future values. In the real world these estimates
and their relative probability of coming to fruition are your responsibility. In any
case, suppose that some investment has five possible annual rates of return:
$R_1 = -15\%$, $R_2 = 5\%$, $R_3 = 15\%$, $R_4 = 35\%$, and $R_5 = 75\%$. Further imagine that the
probability of realization associated with each one is the set of values $p_1 = 0.15$,
$p_2 = 0.25$, $p_3 = 0.35$, $p_4 = 0.15$, and $p_5 = 0.10$, respectively. Then the expected annual
rate of return, commonly denoted by $E(R)$, is given by forming the product of each
potential rate of return by its probability of occurrence and then summing over all
possible circumstances (assuming that the *per force* non-negative probabilities are
properly normalized, meaning that they sum to unity). In this instance, the result of
the computation is

$$E(R) = 0.15 \times (-0.15) + 0.25 \times 0.05 + 0.35 \times 0.15 + 0.15 \times 0.35 + 0.10 \times 0.75 = 17\%.$$

In terms of the summation convention discussed earlier in the text, the average rate
of return can be compactly written as

$$E(R) = \sum_{n=1}^{N} p_n R_n = (p_1 R_1 + p_2 R_2 + \cdots + p_N R_N). \tag{8.1}$$

For clarity in this section, "a times b" will mostly be written as "ab" instead of
as "a × b." There are two other common ways to indicate an average. One is to
surround the quantity whose mean value is constructed by angular brackets as in
<R>. The other is to place a superior bar over the quantity. $E(R)$ is the notation that
will be used because it is easy to read and to typeset.

2. The Result for a Two-Asset Portfolio

Now let us see how to compute the expected return from a portfolio of two securities,
labeled A and B. Assume that we are fully invested. This does not mean that one
of A or B is not cash; rather it means that there can be no second cash account.

Denote the percentage dollar amount invested in security A (B), or its weight in the portfolio, by w_A (w_B). The relationship $w_A + w_B = 1$ (i.e., 100%) follows because all of our funds are invested. For the moment also maintain the constraint of no short-selling. Hence, $0 \leq w_A \leq 1$ or $w_A \in [0,1]$, meaning that both security weights are non-negative.

Now let R_A (R_B) indicate the instantaneous annual rate of return on security A (B). The portfolio's annual rate of return, R_P, will be given by the weighted average of the two components or

$$R_P = w_A R_A + w_B R_B.$$

Alternatively, because of the conservation of our funds, the instantaneous rate of return of the portfolio could have been written in terms of one independent variable, for example, w_A, without loss of generality, i.e.,

$$R_P = w_A R_A + (1 - w_A) R_B. \tag{8.2}$$

The instantaneous rates of return on the two securities A and B will fluctuate with the economic circumstances of the market. We use our knowledge of past history and the current economic state to construct our own estimates for the future average behavior of R_A and R_B from Equation 8.1. The average rate of return for the portfolio, with the average understood to be taken with respect to the hypothetical probability distribution that defines the possible outcomes for each component of the blend, $E(R_P)$, is given by the expression

$$E(R_P) = w_A E(R_A) + w_B E(R_B).$$

The hypothetical probability distribution referred to previously is a joint distribution, for it tells us the probability that A will have rate of return r_A while B simultaneously has rate of return r_B (for some pair of values r_A and r_B). Because $w_A + w_B = 1$, an equivalent formula is

$$E(R_P) = w_A E(R_A) + (1 - w_A) E(R_B). \tag{8.3}$$

To be concrete, assume that the expected annual rate of return on asset A is $E(R_A) = 0.05$ (or 5%) and on asset B is $E(R_B) = 0.15$. For a 50% to 50% mixture of investments in the two securities, the expected annual rate of return on the portfolio would come, from Equation 8.3, to $E(R_P) = 0.10$ or 10%,

$$E(R_P) = w_A E(R_A) + w_B E(R_B) = 0.5 \times 0.05 + 0.5 \times 0.15 = 0.10.$$

If, instead, we were 75% invested in security B, i.e., $w_B = 0.75$, then $E(R_P)$ would have the value 12.5%:

$$E(R_P) = w_A E(R_A) + w_B E(R_B) = 0.25 \times 0.05 + 0.75 \times 0.15 = 0.125.$$

Investing more heavily in the security with the higher expected rate of return moves the expected rate of return from the portfolio in that direction; this can be seen from Equation 8.2.

a.   Digression

Consider the rate of change of E_P with respect to w_A, $\partial E(R_P)/\partial w_A$. It is given, from Equation 8.3, by

$$\partial E(R_P)/\partial w_A = E(R_A) - E(R_B).$$

Several important points can be made. First, because the expected rates of return $E(R_A)$ and $E(R_B)$ are constants (once their underlying joint probability distribution is specified), a graph of $E(R_P)$ vs. w_A would be a straight line because the slope of the $E(R_P)$ – w_A relationship is a constant. Second, the slope of this line will be positive (negative) if asset A has a larger (smaller) anticipated rate of return than asset B. The steepness of the line, or the potential for gain, depends on the difference between the two rates of return. If their anticipated rates of return were equal, then the slope of the portfolio's mean rate of return with respect to the percentage invested in asset A would be zero; the line would be flat. This is because, statistically, no difference exists between the two securities, so altering the allocation to prefer one over the other would not gain more (lose less).

3.   The Variance of an Asset

Having learned how to calculate the expected rate of return on an individual security in Equation 8.1, as well as how to compute the average rate of return for a two-element portfolio of securities in Equation 8.3, it is time to move on to the next step — evaluating variances and standard deviations. The reason for interest in variances is that these quantities serve as proxies for risk in the financial milieu. First, review the method for computing the variance of an individual asset. The variance with respect to the mean value of the rate of return is given by:

$$\sigma_R^2 \equiv \sum_{n=1}^{N} p_n[R_n - E(R)]^2 = \sum_{n=1}^{N} p_n R_n^2 - E^2(R). \tag{8.4}$$

The lower case Greek letter sigma, σ, is universally used to denote this quantity.

It is possible to compute the second moment, or the variance, with respect to any arbitrary point, not just the average value. In other words, we did not need to first subtract the mean value of the rate of return from each possible rate of return in this summation. If we had not done so, that quantity would contain different information than the one computed.

The detailed result of the application of this formula to the same set of hypothetical rates of return and probabilities presented above yields

$$\sigma_R^2 = 0.15 \times (-0.15 - 0.17)^2 + 0.25 \times (0.05 - 0.17)^2$$
$$+ \ 0.35 \times (0.15 - 0.17)^2 + 0.15 \times (0.35 - 0.17)^2$$
$$+ \ 0.10 \times (0.75 - 0.17)^2 = 0.0576 = (0.24)^2,$$

or the standard deviation (about the mean) is 24%.

The potential complication for a mixture is the correlation, or dependence, of the rate of return of one asset on another. (In the mortgage markets, A might represent the 2-year U. S. Treasury Note rate and B might represent an adjustable-rate mortgage teaser rate.) Denote the standard deviation of the rates of return of the assets A (B), about their individual expected values, by $\sigma_A(\sigma_B)$. Then, by definition,

$$\sigma_A^2 \equiv E\{[R_A - E(R_A)]^2\}, \text{ and } \sigma_B^2 \equiv E\{[R_B - E(R_B)]^2\}.$$

Also note that $\sigma_A^2 \equiv E(R_A^2) - E^2(R_A)$. The standard deviation of the rate of return on the portfolio as a whole, σ_P, about its mean value $E(R_P)$, is defined similarly,

$$\sigma_P^2 \equiv E\{[R_P - E(R_P)]^2\} = E\{(w_A R_A + w_B R_B) - [w_A E(R_A) + w_B E(R_B)]\}^2$$
$$= E\{w_A^2[R_A - E(R_A)]^2 + w_B^2[R_B - E(R_B)]^2$$
$$+ \ 2w_A w_B[R_A - E(R_A)][R_B - E(R_B)]\}.$$

After replacing quantities already defined and using $w_A = 1 - w_B$ again, we have

$$\sigma_P^2 = w_A^2 \sigma_A^2 + (1 - w_A)^2 \sigma_B^2 + 2w_A(1 - w_A)\rho_{AB}\sigma_A \sigma_B \qquad (8.5)$$

In the last term on the middle of Equation 8.5 a short-hand notation has been introduced to represent the simultaneously averaging of the expected value of the product of the two rates of return R_A and R_B. The variance of the portfolio, σ_P^2, is not a linear combination of its component variances; an additional cross term stems from the linear correlation coefficient between the rates of return of A and B. The linear correlation coefficient between A and B, ρ_{AB}, is defined as

$$\rho_{AB} \equiv E\{[R_A - E(R_A)] \times [R_B - E(R_B)]\}/(\sigma_A \sigma_B). \qquad (8.6)$$

The numerator is known as the covariance of A and B and is normally denoted by σ_{AB}. It is always true that $\rho_{AB} \in [-1,+1]$ as well as that it is dimensionless. Another form for ρ_{AB} is

$$\rho_{AB} = [E(R_A R_B) - E(R_A)E(R_B)]/(\sigma_A \sigma_B) = \sigma_{AB}/(\sigma_A \sigma_B).$$

If the returns on the two assets A and B were independent, this would mean that $E(R_AR_B)$ factors, i.e., $E(R_AR_B) = E(R_A)E(R_B)$. In this special circumstance, the correlation coefficient (and the covariance) between the rates of return on the pair vanish. *The converse statement is not necessarily true. The absence of linear correlation does not imply the absence of correlation.*

Again use the values $E(R_A) = 0.05$ and $E(R_B) = 0.15$. For $w_A = 0.5$, $E(R_P) = 0.10$, while for $w_A = 0.25$, $E(R_P) = 0.125$. Suppose that the two variances were $\sigma_A = 0.1$ and $\sigma_B = 0.25$. (Note that the asset with the higher rate of return has deliberately been made the riskier of the pair. Doing anything else would violate one of the canons of finance: namely, that the risk-averse investor is willing to accept more risk only if he also has the chance to earn a higher reward.) If, in addition, their correlation coefficient were equal to +3/8, implying a weak relationship and that they move together (the plus sign), then, from Equation 8.5, the variance of the portfolio would be equal to $0.022813 = (0.1510)^2$ and $0.039297 = (0.1982)^2$ in the two instances (i.e., $w_A = 0.5$ and $w_A = 0.25$). By investing more than 50% in the riskier asset (which is B because its standard deviation is larger), we have increased the expected rate of return from the portfolio above its mean value of 10 to 12.5% with the concomitant increase of risk of nearly one-third ($= 0.1982/0.1510 - 1$).

Suppose that the correlation coefficient had been instead –3/8, implying one asset's rate of return increases as the other's decreases, and vice versa. Then the results for the portfolio variances — with the same proportions of investment as previously — would be equal to $0.013438 = (0.1159)^2$ and $0.032266 = (0.1796)^2$, respectively. The portfolio variance has decreased for both weight assignments. The ratio of risk vs. the percentage of funds invested in asset A is different now that the correlation coefficient has changed sign because this has ameliorated part of the risk induced by the more than 50% allocation to asset B. As we shall see, a much more negative correlation coefficient can dramatically reduce the overall risk level of the mixture. From this comes the concept of hedging.

4. The Minimum Variance Portfolio

If we are going to use the variance of a combination of securities as the measure of their risk, then it behooves us to find that particular mixture that has the least risk — thus, our curiosity in what is known as the minimum variance portfolio. We can find this special blend, which minimizes σ_P^2 with respect to w_A, by computing the partial derivative of σ_P^2 with respect to w_A and next finding the value of w_A that makes the result vanish. (A purely algebraic demonstration is provided in the next subsection.) The result is

$$\partial\sigma_P^2/\partial w_A = 2w_A\sigma_A^2 - 2(1 - w_A)\sigma_B^2 + 2[(1 - w_A) - w_A]\rho_{AB}\sigma_A\sigma_B.$$

This expression will be null when w_A is given by the quantity denoted by W_A; its measure is given by

$$W_A \equiv \sigma_B(\sigma_B - \rho_{AB}\sigma_A)/(\sigma_A^2 + \sigma_B^2 - 2\rho_{AB}\sigma_A\sigma_B). \tag{8.7}$$

The test for a minimum is that the second derivative be positive when $w_A = W_A$. In this particular circumstance, the second derivative is independent of the value of w_A because it is always equal to

$$\partial^2\sigma_P^2/\partial w_A^2 = 2(\sigma_A^2 + \sigma_B^2 - 2\rho_{AB}\sigma_A\sigma_B)$$

$$= 2[\sigma_A^2 + \sigma_B^2 - 2\sigma_A\sigma_B + 2(1 - \rho_{AB})\sigma_A\sigma_B]$$

$$= 2[(\sigma_A - \sigma_B)^2 + 2(1 - \rho_{AB})\sigma_A\sigma_B]$$

after completing the square in the intermediate step. This quantity is always non-negative. Hence, the solution $w_A = W_A$ represents an absolute minimum. (A corresponding value of $w_B = W_B$ is given by $1 - W_A$.)

What if the second derivative were zero? It must be that $\sigma_A = \sigma_B$ and $\rho_{AB} = 1$ unless we assume that both assets are risk-less (so that $\sigma_A = \sigma_B = 0$ by the definition of a risk-free security). If $\sigma_A = \sigma_B$ and $\rho_{AB} = 1$, then the corresponding value of W_A is zero. All the investment should be in asset B. However, this is of no real import because the equality of the two variances would mean that they are statistically identical with respect to their riskiness (i.e., they have same the standard deviation). Moreover, at the moment, they are assumed to be perfectly linearly correlated too. In this circumstance, you should expect that no way exists to change the portfolio variance by altering your relative percentage contribution.

If we keep the two assets equally risky but delete the requirement that they be perfectly linearly correlated, then the value of W_A becomes one-half independent of the value of ρ_{AB}. This makes sense for the same reason that we discussed earlier. Lastly, note that the second term in the second derivative can vanish if one of the assets is risk-free. Adding a risk-free asset into the portfolio is discussed in detail later. Finally, from Equation 8.7, we see that if the asset labeled B was in fact risk-free, then the minimum variance portfolio has no funds allocated to the risky asset, asset A (i.e., $W_A = 0$).

The value of the variance of the portfolio at its minimum is given by

$$\sigma_P^2|_{min} = \sigma_A^2\sigma_B^2(1 - \rho_{AB}^2)/(\sigma_A^2 + \sigma_B^2 - 2\rho_{AB}\sigma_A\sigma_B).$$

Keeping to same set of numerical values, from the formula for W_A, Equation 8.7, $W_A = 0.988$ and $E(R_P) = 0.051$ with $\sigma_P = 0.100$. For the negative correlation coefficient of $-3/8$ the results are $W_A = 0.788$, $E(R_P) = 0.071$, and $\sigma_P = 0.006$. The negative correlation has decreased the amount to be invested in A, raised the expected rate of return, and simultaneously diminished the overall level of risk.

a.   An Algebraic Demonstration

Instead of thinking of $\sigma_P^2|_{min}$ and W_A as the quantities just defined and computed, think of them as designated (with perfect hindsight!) as

$$W_A \equiv \sigma_B(\sigma_B - \rho_{AB}\sigma_A)/(\sigma_A^2 + \sigma_B^2 - 2\rho_{AB}\sigma_A\sigma_B)$$

and

$$\sigma_P^2|_{min} \equiv \sigma_A^2\sigma_B^2(1 - \rho_{AB}^2)/(\sigma_A^2 + \sigma_B^2 - 2\rho_{AB}\sigma_A\sigma_B).$$

Return to the general expression for the portfolio variance in Equation 8.5 and discover that it can be rewritten:

$$\sigma_P^2 = (\sigma_A^2 + \sigma_B^2 - 2\rho_{AB}\sigma_A\sigma_B)(w_A - W_A)^2 + \sigma_P^2|_{min}.$$

Since each term above is positive definite, a minimum value for σ_P^2 will be obtained if we can arrange the weight-dependent term, which is the only place the variable w_A appears, to vanish, i.e., if and only if $w_A = W_A$. [Remember that $\sigma_A^2 + \sigma_B^2 - 2\rho_{AB}\sigma_A\sigma_B$ is the same as $(\sigma_A - \sigma_B)^2 + 2(1 - \rho_{AB})\sigma_A\sigma_B$.]

b. Special Circumstances

From the expression for $\sigma_P^2|_{min}$, we can see three special values for ρ_{AB} and two for σ_A and σ_B that should be considered. One is zero for ρ_{AB}, which signifies no linear correlation between the two assets. The other two special values occur when $|\rho_{AB}|$ is equal to unity. If the correlation coefficient vanishes, then W_A will be given by $\sigma_B^2/(\sigma_A^2 + \sigma_B^2)$ with W_B given by the symmetrically related quantity $\sigma_A^2/(\sigma_A^2 + \sigma_B^2)$. The weights are now inversely proportional to the risks presented by the other asset. The minimum value of the portfolio variance, $\sigma_P^2|_{min}$, is a symmetrical function of the squares of the variances equal to $\sigma_A^2\sigma_B^2/(\sigma_A^2 + \sigma_B^2) = 1/(1/\sigma_A^2 + 1/\sigma_B^2)$ in this situation. This quantity is related to the harmonic mean of the two variances. Lastly, observe that, if $\sigma_A = \sigma_B = \sigma$ and the correlation coefficient is still zero, then the portfolio variance is just $\sigma^2/2$. Hence, the risk can be reduced by half at most.

If $|\rho_{AB}| = 1$, then, with probability equal to one, it implies that the rate of return from asset A is a linear function of the rate of return from asset B. If ρ_{AB} is equal to +1 (−1), then the two assets move perfectly together (oppositely) in a proportional fashion. Conversely, if the rates of return on the two securities A and B were, in fact, wholly linearly related, then $|\rho_{AB}|$ would be equal to unity.

Consider first the case of equal variances $\sigma_A = \sigma_B > 0$ and further assume perfect positive linear correlation between them or that ρ_{AB} is equal to one. Now we find that the expression for σ_P^2 in Equation 8.5 reduces to

$$\sigma_P^2 = \sigma_A^2[w_A^2 + (1 - w_A)^2 + 2w_A(1 - w_A)] = \sigma_A^2[w_A + (1 - w_A)]^2 = \sigma_A^2!$$

What does this mean? If we assume that the two securities are equally risky and perfectly positively linearly correlated, then no difference exists between them, statistically speaking. Therefore, creating a portfolio out of them cannot result in any real risk reduction and the variance of the mixture is identical to the (equal) variance of either one of them.

c. Exercise

1. Show that, if $\rho_{AB} = 0$ and $\sigma_A = \sigma_B = \sigma$, $\sigma_P^2/\sigma^2 = 2(w_A - \frac{1}{2})^2 + \frac{1}{2}$.

If we keep the two assets equally risky, but relax the requirement that they be perfectly correlated, then what can we anticipate for the volatility of the mixture? Building on what we just learned, we would again expect no risk reduction by choosing to invest in one rather than the other. This implies that the value of w_A, which minimizes the portfolio variance, will just be $W_A = 1/2$. A straightforward computation from Equation 8.7 verifies this. Now the variance of the entire portfolio is given by

$$\sigma_P^2 = \sigma_A^2(1 + \rho_{AB})/2.$$

Recognize that it appears as if we can entirely eliminate risk if we have total, negative, linear correlation (i.e., $\rho_{AB} = -1$). This situation represents what is known as a *perfect hedge*.

Let us pursue this point further. Suppose that ρ_{AB} was equal to -1. Then, from the preceding analysis of the minimum portfolio variance, the value of w_A will be equal to $\sigma_B/(\sigma_A + \sigma_B)$ and that of W_B will be equal to $\sigma_A/(\sigma_A + \sigma_B)$. Since there is perfect negative linear correlation between assets A and B, the total variance of the portfolio can be computed to be

$$\sigma_P^2(\rho_{AB} = -1) = w_A^2\sigma_A^2 + (1 - w_A)^2\,\sigma_B^2 - 2w_A(1 - w_A)\sigma_A\sigma_B$$

$$= (\sigma_A w_A - \sigma_B w_B)^2 = [\sigma_A w_A - \sigma_B(1 - w_A)]^2.$$

Now substitute the aforementioned values of w_A and w_B (i.e., $W_A{:}W_B = \sigma_B{:}\sigma_A$) and obtain zero for the total variance (= riskiness) of the portfolio. Thus, the portfolio has no financial risk stemming from the two assets. The portfolio can still have risk because both securities are common stocks and the Dow Jones average is dropping precipitously. As measured by the standard deviation, the existence of complete negative linear correlation has led to a perfect hedge. Clearly, with merely negative linear correlation $(0 > \rho_{AB} > -1)$, one can accomplish almost the same thing by weighing the asset allocation in an appropriate fashion.

As we just saw, the general portfolio variance, when $\rho_{AB} = -1$, is a perfect square. What does this mean? First examine the case $\rho_{AB} = +1$ more closely. For $\rho_{AB} = +1$,

$$\sigma_P^2(\rho_{AB} = +1) = w_A^2\sigma_A^2 + (1 - w_A)^2\sigma_B^2 + 2w_A(1 - w_A)\sigma_A\sigma_B$$

$$= (\sigma_A w_A + \sigma_B w_B)^2 = [\sigma_A w_A + \sigma_B(1 - w_A)]^2.$$

As long as we stay within the conventional bounds, namely σ_A, $\sigma_B > 0$ and $w_A \in [0,1]$, then the expression squared just above is non-negative. Thus, we have the linear relationship between σ_P and w_A

$$\sigma_P = \sigma_A w_A + \sigma_B(1 - w_A).$$

Remember that the expected level of return is also a linear function of the weight allocated to asset A; see Equation 8.3. Thus, in this special case, we have a one-parameter system of two equations. Eliminating w_A to deduce the direct relationship between $E(R_P)$ and σ_P yields

$$E(R_P) = \sigma_P[E(R_A) - E(R_B)]/(\sigma_A - \sigma_B) + [\sigma_A E(R_B) - \sigma_B E(R_A)]/(\sigma_A - \sigma_B).$$

Instead of a curvilinear relationship implicitly given by Equations 8.3 and 8.5 for the boundary of accessible $E(R_P)$–σ_P space, when the linear correlation is equal to one, it is a straight line whose slope is given by

$$\partial E(R_P)/\partial \sigma_P = [E(R_A) - E(R_B)]/(\sigma_A - \sigma_B) > 0.$$

This is positive because, if $E(R_A) > E(R_B)$ then $\sigma_A > \sigma_B$ and vice versa (i.e., the conventional view that higher risk brings higher rewards).

The most interesting value of w_A, still when $\rho_{AB} = +1$, is given by

$$\omega_A = \sigma_B/(\sigma_B - \sigma_A).$$

At this percentage of investment in asset A, the entire portfolio variance vanishes. If we assume that $\sigma_B > \sigma_A$ ($\sigma_B < \sigma_A$), then this value of w_A is positive (negative). That is, it lies inside (outside) the normal bounds of $w_A \in [0,1]$ and is (is not) normally a reachable state. To accomplish this requires short-selling, which is the interpretation we would give to a value of w_A less than zero. Hence, we borrow one asset to use to purchase the other.

If we return to the case $\rho_{AB} = -1$ to examine the other boundary in $E(R_P)$–σ_P space, we will find that it is linear too,

$$\sigma_P^2 = w_A^2 \sigma_A^2 + (1 - w_A)^2 \sigma_B^2 - 2w_A(1 - w_A)\sigma_A \sigma_B$$
$$= (\sigma_A w_A - \sigma_B w_B)^2 = [\sigma_A w_A - \sigma_B(1 - w_A)]^2.$$

From here the analysis is trickier because, in order to take the square root, we must assume that we know the sign of the radical. Once again the net result is to define one of the boundaries in $E(R_P)$ –σ_P as a straight line in this special case. See Copeland and Weston (1992) for more details.

5. A Risk-Free Asset

The discussion changes significantly if a risk-free security is introduced into the mixture, for example, replacing asset B. It earns the risk-free rate of return R_f (by definition). The portfolio's expected rate of return becomes $E(R_P) = w_A E(R_A) + (1 - w_A)E(R_f)$ now, but the expectation of the last term is always equal to R_f. Also, the variance of the rate of return of the risk-free asset is zero by definition. Thus, the variance of the portfolio is now given simply by

$$\sigma_P^2 = (w_A \sigma_A)^2.$$

Keeping to the conventional view that $w_A \in [0,1]$, we can express the volatility of the portfolio as

$$\sigma_P = + w_A \sigma_A > 0.$$

An alternative way of thinking about this is that w_A is serving as a parameter relating $E(R_P)$ to σ_P. The relationship between the expected rate of return on the portfolio and its volatility may now be expressed as

$$E(R_P) = (\sigma_P/\sigma_A)E(R_A) + [1 - (\sigma_P/\sigma_A)]R_f = R_f + (\sigma_P/\sigma_A)[E(R_A) - R_f].$$

Can we go to the point where σ_P exceeds σ_A? Yes, but that would mean that w_A exceeds 1 and to do so would imply that we were *leveraged* with respect to asset A. The anticipated rate of return from the entire portfolio would now exceed that envisioned from asset A alone. This would be the reward for having accepted ever higher levels of risk.

What happens if we go in the other direction, that is, below the limit of 0% for w_A? Now

$$\sigma_P = -w_A \sigma_A > 0.$$

The relationship between $E(R_P)$ and σ_P is still a linear one, but the slope is now negative;

$$E(R_P) = -(\sigma_P/\sigma_A)E(R_A) + [1 + (\sigma_P/\sigma_A)]R_f = R_f - (\sigma_P/\sigma_A)[E(R_A) - R_f].$$

In other words, we would be short-selling asset A and overinvesting the proceeds in the risk-free asset, consequently reducing risk and return.

C. MULTIPLE-ASSET PORTFOLIOS

Consider a multiple-asset portfolio and revert to using numerals instead of letters to separately signify each security with rates of return $\{R_n\}$ and normalized dollar proportions $\{w_n\}$, $n = 1,2,\ldots, N$. Using the summation notation, the portfolio return is given by $R_P = \Sigma w_n R_n$, where the summation commences at unity and ends at N. The expected rate of return formula is similarly given by $E(R_P) = \Sigma w_n E(R_n)$. For the portfolio variance, the explicit formula includes the variance of each security in the mixture plus its covariance with all the others. This can be written in compact form as

$$\sigma_P^2 = \sum_{n=1}^{N} w_n^2 \sigma_n^2 + \sum_{m=1}^{N} \sum_{\substack{n=1 \text{ and } m \neq n}}^{N} \rho_{nm} w_n w_m \sigma_n \sigma_m. \tag{8.8}$$

Using the variance abbreviation, var, this can be shown to be the same as

$$\sigma_P^2 = \sum_{n=m+1}^{N} \sum_{m=1}^{N-1} \text{var}(R_n + R_m) - (N-2) \times \sum_{n=1}^{N} \text{var}(R_n).$$

This provides an easy way to compute σ_P^2 as securities are added to the blend and allows us to infer the following key result of theoretical portfolio diversification.

1. Only the Covariance Really Matters

It turns out that only the covariance really matters. To see how this happens, suppose, for simplicity, that all the weights $\{w_n\}$ are equal. Then each one must be equal to $1/N$ if they are properly normalized. Let us bound the two terms appearing in Equation 8.8. Suppose that the largest that any security standard deviation can be is S. In other words, $0 \leq \sigma_n \leq S \ \forall \ n \in [1,n]$. Then, for the first term we have the result for the upper bound

$$\sum_{n=1}^{N} w_n^2 \sigma_n^2 \leq \sum_{n=1}^{N} (1/N)^2 S^2 = N(1/N)^2 S^2 = S^2 / N.$$

Therefore, as N becomes infinitely large (i.e., as $N \rightarrow \infty$), this term approaches zero as long as S is finite. In other words, for diverse portfolios with a large number of assets, the dominant contribution to the portfolio variance must arise from the covariance terms.

How large are the covariance terms? First, notice that $N(N-1)/2$ covariance terms are in the double sum for σ_P^2. Let the average value of any single covariance be denoted by s;

$$\sum_{n=1}^{N} \sum_{\substack{m=1 \text{ and } n \neq m}}^{N} \rho_{nm} \sigma_n \sigma_m \equiv [N(N-1)/2]s.$$

With this definition, we can rewrite the mean covariance contribution to the portfolio variance as

$$(1/N)^2 [N(N-1)/2]s = (1 - 2/N)s \rightarrow s \text{ as } N \rightarrow \infty.$$

The covariance terms remain finite even in the case of an arbitrarily large number of securities comprising the portfolio. Therefore, as the number of separate investments increases, the variance of a diverse portfolio tends to approach the value of the average covariance among them. Theoretically, this implies that a 15- or 20-security portfolio, with little linear correlation among the choices, is sufficient to protect someone against risk.

D. PORTFOLIO CONSTRUCTION FORMULAS

The above mathematical formalism tells us how to formulate a minimum risk portfolio. To this we might add the fact that we want the minimum cost portfolio of assets whose cash flows at least meets those of our liabilities over time. We could put these two together and develop a formal expression for asset choice among the allowed alternatives given their mean rates of return and their covariance matrix. We could do this in a present value sense, a duration-matching way, or so on. Each particular requirement would have its analytical expression and the resulting minimization, or maximization, problem would be solved by a linear or quadratic programming technique. This part of the process really adds nothing new. Everything else has already been (implicitly) determined once the set of assets, their expected rates of return, and the above mean-variance formalism adopted.

III. A NEW STRATEGY FOR OPTIMIZING FIXED-INCOME PORTFOLIO VALUE

(The method described in this section is protected by a pending U.S. patent application.)

An old cliché says, "If you can't beat 'em, join 'em." That is the essence of the technique expounded in the next few pages (with some extra degrees of sophistication). This section contains a novel method for more profitably managing a portfolio of interest rate-dependent financial assets and liabilities utilizing derivatives. The aim is to increase net wealth by earning income or fees from derivatives and by protecting against potential capital losses — paper or otherwise.

Instead of defensively constructing the portfolio to assure a desired net interest margin and protecting against interest rate risk by duration-matching (i.e., immunization), you can construct the optimum yield curve for your particular asset and liability combination. As long as they depend on interest rates and their time rates of change, the embedded optionality components will be fully incorporated. Once this unique yield curve has been specified, then it may be compared to the current market yield curve, an historical average curve, the forward rate curve, and so forth; alterations of your assets or liabilities, via derivative instruments, can be made to bring the portfolio's optimal yield curve more closely into alignment with the specified empirical one. By following this procedure and accepting a certain amount of additional risk, further wealth may be garnered. This method can be extended to managing a foreign exchange swap book, physical commodity deliveries over time, and so forth. The requirements are an efficient market, a forward pricing structure, and a liquid options market. As a first example, consider why this technique cannot be accomplished in the equity markets.

A. THE EQUITY MARKETS

You own 100 shares of stock in the XYZ Corporation. Your investment strategy is to continue to own these shares without suffering any sizeable capital loss, potential or realized, because of changes in their price. You are not opposed to finding some mechanism of receiving additional compensation from your long position, perhaps by lending the shares to be sold short. You would earn a fee for furnishing your shares to the short-seller. Alternatively, if you believed that their price might significantly dip in the near term, you might want to purchase a protective put. Generally the time to expiration would be fairly quick, a few months, though if LEAPS (Long-term Equity AnticiPation Securities) are available on XYZ Corporation stock, you can extend the exercise date to a few years. If you are correct regarding future prices for XYZ Corporation shares, then your losses will be minimized because you will exercise the put option. You also maintain your desired long position in the stock. If you are incorrect regarding future prices for XYZ Corporation shares, then the put option will expire worthless while you preserve your long position.

Another, significantly riskier, method to try to make an extra profit from your holdings would be to write a covered call on these shares. You would do this if you did not expect share prices to improve significantly. Writing a covered call on your XYZ Corporation stock means that you sell a call option on these shares with an exercise price higher than the current market price and higher than you expect the price to rise during the lifetime of the option. If you are correct regarding future prices for XYZ Corporation shares, then you maintain your long position in the underlying stock and your net wealth increases from the option premium. If you are incorrect, then the call option will be exercised. As a consequence you will suffer a significant loss, though still a much smaller one than if you had written a naked call, because you actually already own the underlying equities to deliver. If, instead, you held specific views regarding the price volatility of XYZ Corporation stock, you might engage in a butterfly spread, a straddle, and so forth.

Even more complex option-based strategies are available, but they are all essentially static in concept. Calendar spreads, interest rate strips, Asian options, lookback options, and, especially, delta or dynamic hedging explicitly recognize this. These schemes represent instantaneous measures; there is no way to forecast a common share's price accurately. That was one reason for the development of dynamic hedging. Indeed, the standard rationale for rebalancing a portfolio of stocks and options via delta hedging is precisely that the stock price changes with the passage of time in an unpredictable fashion. This results in a newly written option share price different from those outstanding and the need to make an adjustment to remain delta neutral. Let us see how and why it is different in the fixed-income markets.

B. THE DEBT MARKETS

In the fixed-income markets, the situation is dramatically different for two reasons:

1. There is a well-known, precise relationship between the present value of an option-free, fixed-income, security and anticipated interest rates.
2. There is a market-clearing consensus expectation for what future interest rates will be in the form of an arbitrage-free yield curve, forward rate curve, or its equivalent.

The combination of these two facts means that a consensus valuation going forward in time can be placed on any option-free, fixed-income, instrument. Aside from (time-dependent and not easily predictable) spreads between debt securities of different quality and liquidity, one yield curve, say that for U.S. Treasury instruments, suffices to price the entire, option-free, fixed income market for today and tomorrow. Surely some procedure must exist that can be used to try and maximize wealth, by taking on some additional risk — analogous to covered calls, protective puts, portfolio insurance, and dynamic hedging for common stocks — for fixed income investments but that will explicitly take into account the no-arbitrage forward rates embedded in the yield curve.

C. The Underlying Problem

Consider the management of many endowment, pension, and bond funds, as well as the problems faced by the supervisors of life insurance companies, savings banks, and mortgage investment portfolios. Organizations of this type have definitive liabilities (e.g., projected payment streams) stretching relatively far into the future or are running a highly leveraged business. They are in one of these two postures because: 1. they owe a consistent cash flow stream to their clientele, usually at some desired (or promised) rate of return on an initial plus recurring investments, or 2. they borrow the huge majority of the monies available for investment purposes — as opposed to using owner's equity — on which they are expected to make a reasonable rate of return. These portfolio managers take the capital provided to them, or borrowed for them, and use the cash to purchase income producing assets. The key to providing their service successfully, their business profitability, and their commercial longevity is that the time averaged cash flow from their investments meets, and preferably exceeds, the time averaged cash flow demanded by their customers.

These financial managers and portfolio directors have an income cash flow stream that is highly interest rate dependent and an expense cash flow stream very sensitive to the market level of interest rates. If they can maintain a positive spread between the interest revenue and expenses, then their customers' needs will be met and their ongoing commercial future assured. A new accounting and public relations complication facing these types of enterprises is that changes in generally accepted accounting procedures (GAAP) have arrived, specifically the Financial Accountant Standards Board's Statement of Financial Accounting Standards #133. Enforcement of this standard requires marking-to-market the value of assets and liabilities and more fully justifying hedge accounting.

These valuations are interest rate-sensitive, too, representing the discounted value of forecasted cash flows. Therefore, as the balance sheet is restated on a quarterly basis, variations in owner's equity will occur as market interest rates go up and down. Owner's equity now becomes merely the difference between the mark-to-market value of the assets and liabilities; it no longer can be viewed as a stable element of their risk-based capital. The proposed strategy can also be used to help shield owner's equity from large, market-driven fluctuations and unwanted attention by misinformed financial communications media.

D. CURRENT PRACTICE

Portfolio managers typically adopt a standard, increasingly protective, stance by following a series of well-known steps. First they make sure that the balance sheet actually balances in the accountant's sense (i.e., the assets equal the sum of liabilities plus the owner's equity). Next they try to immunize their asset and liability portfolios by matching the (Macaulay) duration of the cash flows from the two sides of the balance sheet as closely as possible. Modified duration, to effect price equality, must be considered too. An even more sophisticated measure requires matching the convexities of the asset and liability portfolios.

The purpose of these procedures is to try to control the differences between the asset and liability sides of the balance sheet, the differences between their time rates of change (the duration-matching constraint of portfolio immunization), the dollar difference between the two sides of the balance sheet (the modified duration restriction), and the difference between the rate of change of their rates of change (for convexity-matching). The operational controls invoked to support these precautions help to ensure sufficient cash flow from the revenue generating side of the balance sheet to at least support, if not exceed, the expenses incurred by the liability side of the balance sheet. Other (purely defensive) tactics can be tried and prediction methodologies used to make an effort to ascertain potential status given certain interest rate scenarios (e.g., VaR). However, they provide no particular clue on how to maximize profits or net wealth by taking on slightly more risk. This is the aim of the innovative format of doing business explained next.

Finally, given the intrinsic type of financial activity of endowment funds, pension funds, money market funds, life insurance companies, savings banks, mortgage investment portfolios, and so on, there is usually one side of the balance sheet that they cannot do too much about. Participating in and succeeding at the line of business at which they are proficient demands that either the asset or the liability side of their balance sheets have a particular kind of structure. This implies not only restrictions on the nature of the financial securities utilized but also on their maturity pattern and the kind of embedded option characteristics contained. To a considerable extent, these elements are all predetermined (or at least highly constrained) by the nature of the core business enterprise or the client's wishes. So, given this set of constraints, how can you pro-actively do better for your clients and yourself?

1. The Ideal

If you could project the future path of market interest rates, then you could also predict the changes in revenue and expense cash flow streams as well as the alterations in the mark-to-market values of assets and liabilities. This would enable the management team to limit the fluctuations in owner's equity. Moreover, you would be able to adjust — ahead of time — the constitution of asset or liability mixtures in an effort to gain from the forecasted movements in the yield curve. You might actually alter the composition of your assets or liabilities but, alternatively, you could certainly synthetically do so through the use of the appropriate derivative instruments. Unfortunately, this is an ivory-towered approach.

a. The Basics of the New Idea

The methodology described next is a generalization of the types of option strategies mentioned earlier, to be operated in conjunction with a preexisting style of managing a financial portfolio that is geared to maximizing the net present value of the securities held by accepting some added risk. Specifically, it provides a mathematically deterministic way to alter a given composite of interest rate-sensitive assets and liabilities, possibly via derivative securities, so that their maturity and option structures more closely conform to the most profitable yield curve given the constraints of your portfolio's basic commercial purpose. By following the concrete recommendations of this procedure, you can increase the spread between your interest revenue and expense, thereby swelling your net wealth and profits.

How, exactly, can this be done? The ordinary method is to approach this problem from the front end and try to predict the course of interest rates, and so forth. To do this accurately is unfeasible. What you can do, instead, is to solve the inverse problem. That is, given your current mixture of assets and liabilities, and their individual and collective dependencies on interest rates (including any embedded option features), you can compute the unique yield curve that makes the present value of the difference between your revenue and expense cash flows an extremum. Knowing this special yield curve, and comparing it to some long-term, historical average yield curve, the current yield curve, or the yield curve most likely to be realized over the next year or so, you can see in advance how to modify your asset or liability portfolios to more closely reach the possible extremum for the present value of your revenue and expense cash flows. Moreover, you could do this without negatively affecting your desire for a small duration gap, should this be a business pressure.

To reiterate, this goal will be successfully accomplished by computing the one yield curve which will optimize the difference between the present values of the cash flows from the existing blend of assets and liabilities. The determination of this optimal yield curve is executed via the calculus of variations. Knowing this singular yield curve, which is a function of the current maturity and option structure of the securities already held by a firm, its management can then see how to alter their assets and liabilities, to increase net interest income without violating the principles on which the portfolio was constructed (that is, its business purpose, duration requirements, client desirements, and so on).

The main advantage of this innovative method of doing business is that, by turning the problem inside out, the preferred path of (future) interest rates will be known. Hence, you need only compute the optional elements of your asset and liability portfolios given one interest rate scenario. While this is still not a deterministic, quantitatively exact procedure, it is much easier and much more reliable than trying to predict the future of the yield curve from the beginning and then inferring the functioning of any call or put options. Finally, the embedded option elements of the securities held or owed must be modeled, no matter how their management is attempted, so this criticism is not particular to this method of doing business.

2. The Essential Mathematics

The general formula for the continuously discounted present value of some time-dependent cash flow CF(t), out to a horizon T > 0 from now, when the flat yield curve is specified by R, has the form

$$PV = \int_0^T CF(t) \, \exp(-Rt) \, dt.$$

Now allow for a more realistic case in which the continuously paid interest rate R is time dependent, for example, R(t), and cash flows are contingent on the value of R. Extend the functional dependence of the cash flow on the interest rate by writing it as CF[R(t),t]. This allows for the possibility of callable or puttable bonds, prepayment options in mortgages, and so on. The formula for the present value PV formally remains the same, i.e.,

$$PV = \int_0^T CF[R(t),t] \, \exp[-R(t)t] \, dt.$$

If we generalize yet again to allow the cash flows to depend not only on the level of the interest rate R(t) but also on its rate of change, R' = dR(t)/dt (even closer to the real case of some of the more complex embedded options), then we would enlarge the functional dependence of the cash flow CF but still express the present value of the discounted cash flows by a similar looking, Laplace-transform type, integral,

$$PV = \int_0^T CF[R(t),R'(t),t] \, \exp[-R(t)t] \, dt. \tag{8.9}$$

A fund's net present value is the difference between the discounted cash flows of its assets, A dollars per year, and its liabilities, L dollars per year, i.e.,

$$CF(R,R',t) \equiv A(R,R',t) - L(R,R',t). \tag{8.10}$$

Ideally, you would want to maximize the net present value PV in Equation 8.9, given the structure of $A(R,R',t)$ and $L(R,R',t)$ determined by your underlying business, subject to a particular interest rate path $R(t)$. Without knowing in advance what form $R(t)$ will take, this is not a solvable problem. We already have the rules, implicit in Equation 8.10, that specify how the cash flows change with interest rates and their rates of change. Positing an interest rate curve completes the mathematical specification of the problem and you can move on to computing the net present value PV from $C[R(t),R'(t),t]$ and $R(t)$. Not knowing the actual path that interest will take in the future, that is, $R(t)$, renders this effort fruitless.

3. So What is New?

Suppose, instead, *that we turn the problem inside out,* and ask, for a given functional dependence of your revenue and expense cash flows on the course of interest rates $R(t)$, and their rate of change $R'(t) = dR(t)/dt$, what particular interest rate path maximizes the net present value PV. If we can solve this problem, then knowing how that maximizing interest rate curve differs from the actual yield curve that you expect to be realized (on whatever basis), you might be able to tailor the cash flows — in actuality or synthetically via derivative instruments — from the assets $A[R(t),R'(t),t]$ or the liabilities $L[R(t),R'(t),t]$ to try to maximize your net present value. That is, without really taking an aggressive posture with respect to the immediate future of interest rates or materially affecting your actual liability and asset structure, you can still position fund allocation (= normal business portfolio + derivatives) to produce more wealth (or at least conserve it).

The mathematical method of looking for the extrema of the net present value, expressed as an integral of the form given in Equation 8.9, is known as the calculus of variations. To discover the differential equation that $R(t)$ must satisfy to effect an extrema for PV heuristically, you can imagine a variation in the interest rate path away from some base interest rate path $R(t)$, where $\delta R(t)$ represents a small departure, via

$$R(t) \rightarrow R(t) + \delta R(t).$$

Keeping the starting and ending times of our portfolio's horizon fixed (i.e., 0 and T), we then consider the resulting change in the net present value, $PV \rightarrow PV + \delta(PV)$ caused by the alteration $R(t) \rightarrow R(t) + \delta R(t)$ in the future path of interest rates. We only consider variations $\delta R(t)$ such that the magnitude of the change, $|\delta R(t)|$, is small. To emphasize this, we will rewrite the variation of the future path of interest rates by writing it as $\varepsilon r(t)$ where epsilon is positive and small in magnitude and $r(t)$ is some continuous function of the time t, which vanishes at $t = 0$ and at $t = T$.

In Equation 8.9, the cash flow is a function of the interest rate and its time rate of change. The exponential term depends on $R(t)$ too. With the kind of variation in $R(t)$ being considered, and similarly for $R'(t) \rightarrow R'(t) + \delta r'(t)$, the leading terms in the Taylor series for the changes in $CF[R(t),R'(t),t]e^{-R(t)t}$, as a function of epsilon, are given by

$$\delta\{CF[R(t),R'(t),t] \exp[-R(t)t]\} \cong CF[R(t) + \varepsilon r(t),R'(t) + \varepsilon r'(t),t] \exp\{-[R(t)$$
$$+ \varepsilon r(t)]\} - CF[R(t),R'(t),t] \exp[-R(t)t]$$
$$\cong \varepsilon r(t)\partial\{CF[R(t),R'(t),t]\exp[-R(t)t]\}/\partial R + \varepsilon r'(t)\partial\{CF[R(t),R'(t),t]$$
$$\exp[-R(t)t]\}/\partial R' + \text{terms of order } \varepsilon^2 ...$$

The resulting variation in the present value, $\delta(PV)$, becomes approximately equal to

$$\delta(PV) \cong \varepsilon \int_0^T \{r(t)\partial[CF(R,R',t)e^{-R(t)t}]/\partial R - r'[\partial CF(R,R',t)e^{-R(t)t}/\partial R']\} \, dt.$$

Integrate the second term in the above by parts and realize that the integrated term must vanish, because we originally assumed that $r(0) = r(T) = 0$, to derive

$$\delta(PV) = \varepsilon \int_0^T \{\partial[CF(R,R',t)e^{-R(t)t}]/\partial R - d[\partial CF(R,R',t)e^{-R(t)t}/\partial R']/dt\} \, r(t) \, dt.$$

For this first-order change in the present value PV to represent an extremum, it must be null. We know that $r(t)$ is any continuous function that vanishes at the limits of integration and that $\varepsilon > 0$. In these circumstances, by the fundamental lemma of the calculus of variations, the condition for $\delta(PV)$ to vanish requires that the quantity in curly brackets is always zero. Hence, Euler's differential equation for the determination of $R(t)$ is given by

$$\partial[CF(R,R',t)e^{-R(t)t}]/\partial R - d[\partial CF(R,R',t)e^{-R(t)t}/\partial R']dt = 0. \qquad (8.11)$$

You can (numerically) solve this partial differential equation for the interest rate path that makes the net present value of your particular portfolio an extremum. Then you can compare the computed yield curve with the expected yield curve and modify your holdings appropriately or buy and sell interest rate-related derivative products to accomplish the desired changes.

a. A Special Case

To examine what this method produces in a particular instance, suppose that CF in fact is independent of R and its first derivative. Then Euler's equation, Equation 8.11, will reduce to

$$t \, CF(t) \exp[-R(t)t] = 0.$$

The integrated form of this, over the life of the portfolio, is clearly the customary duration-matching constraint. You might object that this is a considerable amount of mathematical overhead to deduce a well-known result, but the point of the demonstration is to show the potential reasonableness of the full method. In addition, it brings up the larger question of how to deal with a duration-matching strategy explicitly.

4. Incorporating Macaulay Duration

When dealing with financially complicated portfolios of assets and liabilities, the simple goal of maximizing the net present value, as a proxy for customer or share-holder wealth, is not necessarily optimum because liability and asset cash flows can extend over a decade or so. Hence, a standard interest rate risk management tool is to ensure that the average discounted cash flows from the two components of the balance sheet match over time also. Therefore, they would concentrate on keeping the duration gap — the difference between the (Macaulay) duration of the assets (D_A) and the duration of the liabilities (D_L) — close to zero. We also know that, when the yield curve is relatively flat, we can enforce the constraint of matching modified duration. The key part of the computation of the duration is its numerator. In the notation that we have been using, this would be expressed as

$$D \propto \int_0^T t \, CF[R(t),R'(t),t] \, \exp[-R(t)t] \, dt. \qquad (8.12)$$

In keeping with these interest rate risk management goals, instead of finding the extreme value of the net present value while varying $R(t)$, you might, instead, want to minimize $|D|$ alone. This would lead to a differential equation of the same form as above but based on the duration D. (The presence of the absolute value would greatly complicate the purely mathematical aspects of the problem.) A better alternative, and one much closer to real business practice, would be to find the extreme value of the net present value of the portfolio subject to the constraint that the duration of the entire portfolio vanish (or be minimal). In this case, a Lagrange multiplier technique would be used (the lower case Greek letter lambda, λ, is normally used to symbolize this) and we would consider looking for an extreme value of

$$PV + \lambda|D|,$$

or better, of

$$PV + \lambda D^2$$

with D given in Equation 8.12. It is straightforward to extend the original extremum problem to include duration. Further generalizations, for example, to demand positive convexity, can also be handled, but much less easily.

PROBLEM

1. Suppose you manage a duration-matched portfolio of assets and liabilities that are also in balance. Let the annual cash flows at time t be denoted by CF(t). Interest rates may change from their current annual value r, to r + R. The net present value of the portfolio, NPV, is equal to 0 when R is zero because it is in balance and its first derivative vanishes when R is equal to 0 too (because it is immunized against interest rate changes). Finally take the liability to be a $1 amount owed at time t = T > 0. Next, use d(t,r) to designate the t year discount factor at an annual interest rate of r; $d(t,r) = (1 + r)^{-t}$. Then the fact that the net present value of the portfolio is zero can be expressed by

$$NPV(R = 0) = \sum_{t=1}^{T} CF(t) \times d(t,r) - d(T,r).$$

Remember that the liability is $1 and this amount just acts as a scale factor. The duration-matching constraint takes the form

$$dNPV(R = 0)/dr \times (1 + r) = \sum_{t=1}^{T} t \times CF(t) \times d(t,r) - T \times d(T,r).$$

The problem is to show that, for any constants A and B, the following is true;

$$d^2NPV(R = 0)/dr^2 \times (1 + r)^2$$

$$= \sum_{t=1}^{T} (t^2 + At + B) \times CF(t) \times d(t,r) - (T^2 + AT + B) \times d(T,r).$$

2. Next prove that A and B can be selected such that the quadratic form $t^2 + At + B$ has a minimum value at time T as well as a value of unity there. (You have two constants to use to enforce two restrictions.) Show that this implies that $d^2NPV(R = 0)/dr^2$ is positive or that the convexity is positive.

9   Other Topics

Two major mortgage markets have not yet been covered: the American commercial mortgage market and non-U.S. markets. Commercial mortgages are very different from residential ones in their underwriting standards, default characteristics, prepayment possibilities, and variety. Only the briefest introduction to this hundreds of billions of dollar market is given here. (It deserves its own book.) This chapter is mainly restricted to defining the key terms and concepts. Outside the U.S. Germany has the most developed mortgage-backed securities market. With the advent of the euro and concomitant minimization of foreign currency risks, and Europeans copying many of the features found in the American MBS markets, this is the most likely place to sojourn outside the U.S. Because information about foreign markets is very scattered and not always in English, the second section of this chapter is intended as a succinct guide through the plethora of foreign mortgage market products.

I. COMMERCIAL MORTGAGE-BACKED SECURITIES

A. Background

As with residential (one- to four-family) mortgages, the process of pooling similar assets together to form an asset-backed security is common for multifamily and business properties. The assets are commercial mortgages and the securities derived from them are known as commercial mortgage-backed securities. Issuances have dramatically grown in dollar amounts and frequency over the last decade. Mortgage-backed securities are now a critical source of liquidity for the residential housing market; commercial mortgage-backed securities fulfill a similar role for the commercial mortgage industry.

Historically, the primary sources for commercial real estate funding included life insurance companies, pension funds, commercial banks, savings institutions, and tax shelter syndicates. By the late 1980s capital for commercial real estate mortgage investments had become scarce. The reasons for this include plummeting real estate values, the savings and loan industry collapse, a U.S. recession, and new laws affecting the treatment of investments in real estate. Consequently, the number of investors willing to buy commercial mortgage-backed securities (*CMBSs*) was very limited, as was the availability of CMBSs.

In the early stages of the CMBS market, commercial real estate owners and developers represented the majority of the issuers; however, the market has evolved. Now, lenders such as commercial banks and investment banks join borrowers in the packaging of commercial mortgages into a greater number of larger face amount, further standardized, and liquid securities. The emergence of conduits — entities formed for the sole purpose of originating commercial loans to be repackaged into a CMBS — are another growing sector of the CMBS market. The nature of the underlying collateral has also shifted; pools increasingly comprise small loans and multiple borrowers instead of multiple properties from a single borrower.

Prior to the early 1980s a market for trading commercial mortgages existed but was limited and the loans were typically not sold in security form. Instead, financial institutions would trade these loans among themselves, either as whole loans or as commercial mortgage participations. The first pooled commercial mortgage security was issued in 1984 — a $205-million CMO issued by Penn Mutual Life Insurance Company. In 1985 the estimated issuance of pooled commercial mortgage securities totaled almost $3 billion. Issuance slowed thereafter and totaled approximately $11 billion by 1992. Compared with the single-family market in 2002, where roughly 50% of outstanding mortgages are securitized, the proportion of securitized commercial mortgages was initially quite small. It was not until the real estate recession of the early 1990s that CMBS issuance increased.

The Financial Institutions Reform, Recovery and Enforcement Act (FIRREA) of 1989 was the catalyst for the CMBS market. The legislation chartered the Resolution Trust Corporation (RTC) and consigned to it responsibility for the many thrifts, formerly insured by the Federal Saving and Loan Insurance Corporation (FSLIC), that had been placed in receivership. FIRREA also included new regulations making it more onerous for savings institutions to hold certain amounts of commercial real estate loans. Under FIRREA commercial real estate loans held by commercial banks and thrifts had a 100% risk-weighting classification.

By 1992 the new capital standards also required savings institutions to maintain total regulatory capital equal to 7.2% of their total risk-weighted assets and at least 8% thereafter. In addition, the 1989 act imposed categorical asset restrictions on savings institutions, limiting secured nonresidential real property loans to 400% of regulatory capital. Those new requirements were difficult for many thrifts to satisfy, so they were forced to liquidate commercial mortgages or, at a minimum, to curtail originating them.

Early issuance of commercial mortgage-backed securities was driven by weak real estate markets, rising loan losses, and the RTC's need for an efficient loan exit strategy. Over the years the source of commercial mortgage-backed security collateral used to back issuance moved from the RTC's distressed loans to commercial mortgages specifically originated and pooled for securitization purposes. By 1997–1998, outstanding issuance was sufficient to justify third-party reporting services and dealer secondary trading efforts. These have increased liquidity and better enabled relative value comparisons with other fixed-income debt products.

1. More on the RTC

The Resolution Trust Corporation was created in 1991 to consolidate and sell off the foreclosed assets of the bankrupt savings and loan institutions. This included approximately $100 billion worth of commercial real estate. The RTC began to play a role similar to that of the FHA and Fannie Mae in the 1930s, especially with regard to developing homogenized paperwork and underwriting standards. The traditional lack of liquidity in the commercial whole-loan markets, and the special nature of the properties, led the RTC to apply the model of creating pools of similar commercial loans and selling off undivided interests of *pro rata* shares in them. Although the CMBS was not new, the size and frequency of the RTC's offerings in this form were able to make investors feel more comfortable with commercial MBSs as an investment vehicle. Moreover, the RTC worked to expand the base of investors. The changes in risk-based capital rules, as well as these other factors, combined to increase CMBS issuance from $8 billion in 1991 to $61 billion in 2000.

CMBSs can be an appealing investment because of their relatively higher yields, the lack of substantial prepayment risk, and opportunities for diversification. (Most commercial mortgages have prepayment restrictions with severe economic penalties; therefore, they have limited prepayment risks.) In addition, the introduction of stricter risk-based capital charges for insurance companies assisted the growth of the CMBS market. These 1993 regulations were similar to those forced onto banks by the Basle Accords. In particular, the new guidelines required insurance companies to hold larger capital reserves for whole-loan commercial mortgages than for commercial mortgages repackaged into CMBSs. As a consequence the insurance companies increased their ownership of CMBSs.

The borrower on larger mortgages (more than $1 million) is usually structured as a special-purpose entity. This insulates the property's cash flow from the parent company. The special purpose entity is usually restricted via covenants to owning and operating only the property and prevented from incurring further liabilities. Often, on larger loans, the special purpose entity will have a special legal opinion declaring it to be separate from its parent's operating activities. This is referred to as being bankruptcy remote; it is an effort to prevent involving the loan in any future bankruptcy proceeding that might evolve from a troubled parent company.

Commercial mortgages usually require the borrower to fund an escrow account with one month's payment of debt service as well as ongoing reserves for real estate taxes and property insurance. The borrower is also required to provide annual financial statements and tenant rent rolls to enable the servicer to monitor property performance.

To analyze final balloon repayment risk, investors and rating agencies focus on the property's loan-to-value ratio and expected balloon mortgage balance at maturity. The current loan-to-value ratio is a dynamic quantity and is used in conjunction with the *debt service coverage ratio* (DSCR) to determine how highly a property is leveraged. Multifamily properties typically fall in the 75% range, while hotels and offices may be as low as 50 to 55%. As with the debt service coverage ratio, the range of loan-to-value ratios within the pool must be considered. The number of high LTV loans, defined as over 75%, should be limited to under 15% of the par value of the loans within the pool.

Geographic diversity in asset-backed pools is desirable since it can lessen some of the risks of regional and economic business cycles. Geographical dispersion limiting the concentration to 40% or lower in any single state is generally considered good. A diversification of the types of property within a CMBS is also desirable.

a. Prepayment Terms

Commercial mortgage loans have a number of provisions that limit or penalize borrowers who prepay their loans. This prepayment protection (or call protection) is a primary reason that investors purchase CMBSs. The most common types of prepayment protection include a lock-out period, a significant prepayment penalty, or a *yield maintenance agreement*. The advantage of a lock-out period is that it restricts the borrower's ability to prepay the loan for a certain number of years after loan origination. Hence, the resulting cash flows are simple to model and it provides complete protection against prepayment. Lock-outs typically only cover the first few years of a loan and are usually combined with at least one other method of prepayment protection.

To prepay the mortgage for refinancing purposes the borrower must pay a *prepayment penalty*, computed as a percentage of the prepayment amount. The penalty level generally declines over time. A commonly used prepayment penalty schedule is 5% of prepayment in year one, 4% in year two, 3% in year three, and so on down to 1% in the fifth year.

Yield maintenance premiums are designed to compensate the lender in the event that the borrower prepays. A yield maintenance agreement provides for a prepayment charge that allows investors to attain the same effective yield as if the borrower made all scheduled mortgage payments until maturity. CMBSs with a yield maintenance agreement make investors indifferent to prepayments and make refinancing uneconomical to the borrowers. A declining fee proportional to the remaining balance is usually utilized; for example, a 5–4–3–2–1 schedule means that the penalty is equal to 5% of the outstanding loan balance in the first year of the penalty period, 4% during the second year, and so forth. Defeasance is when the borrower pledges U.S. Treasury securities whose cash flows equal or exceed that of the mortgage to the mortgage holder. Restrictions on prepayments usually end about 3 to 6 months before the balloon date; this time interval is referred to as the *free* or *open period*. The objective is to allow the borrower time to refinance the loan and thus make the balloon payment.

2. CMBS Format

Because of the significantly larger dollar amounts associated with commercial property and the different economics of their loan payback patterns, the structure underlying the mechanics of the securitization and servicing processes for CMBSs is more complicated than that for residential MBSs. As a result one can expect to have an originator/seller, a trustee, an investment bank, an underwriter, a rating agency, a *master servicer*, a *special servicer*, a *subservicer*, and investors in a CMBS deal. The duties of the orginator, underwriter, conduit, trustee, and rating agency are now familiar. Any subservicing agreements are negotiated between the master servicer and the subservicer. Usually, ultimate accountability rests with the master servicer.

An important aspect of any housing loan is that the borrowers fulfill their obligations, convenants, and other responsibilities required under the mortgage contract. Such liens are known as *performing loans*, whereas a *nonperforming loan* is one in which some of these conditions have not been satisfied. The trustee must notify the investor of the appropriate status of each loan in the pool and acts as a supervisor for the master and special servicers, ensuring that they act in accordance with the terms of the *pooling and servicing agreement* summarized in the prospectus. This agreement details the servicer's obligations to the other parties. If the agreement is violated, then the trustee has the right to assume the servicing function or to appoint a new servicer. This agreement is intended to make each component of converting mortgage cash flow from the mortgagor to the investor very mechanical.

The major responsibilities of the servicers include preparing reports for the trustee, collecting and keeping records relating to monthly payments, monitoring the condition of the underlying properties, maintaining property escrow accounts (for taxes and insurance purposes), and transferring collected funds to the trustee for payment to the investor. Mortgage debt service payments for CMBSs are collected and aggregated by the master servicer. Payments are remitted once a month to the trustee, who in turn makes them to the certificate holders. If a loan defaults, then the certificate holders are insulated from possible short-term cash flow shortfall by the master servicer. This firm is obligated to make principal and interest advances to the trustee and pay property taxes and insurance payments to the extent that such advances are recoverable from the underlying mortgage obligation.

The special servicer may be a separate entity from the master servicer and is responsible for loan collections on defaulted loans. This organization has an obligation to work out the loan with the objective of maximizing the net present value of the proceeds realized from the loan. A special servicer is one expert in default and asset administration. They are usually engaged within 60 days of the moment when a loan goes into default. The special servicer is responsible for delinquency collection efforts, any modifications to the loan terms such as forbearance or workout agreements, the inspection of the property, foreclosure proceedings, bankruptcy processing, and the final liquidation of the real estate (if necessary). The special servicer usually has extensive commercial real estate expertise enabling it to evaluate whether to foreclose and liquidate the loan or to restructure the loan to enable it to be returned to the master servicer.

3. Types of Commercial Property

There are about 45,000 shopping centers in the U.S. *Retail buildings* are classified as low-, mid- or high-rise. They are also categorized by their location with respect to the city center or suburban or commercial building district. *Industrial properties* are grouped as owner-occupant (single- or multitenant), light industrial (high-technology or research and development), or bulk warehouse. Industrial properties include warehouses and special use technological facilities. Since industrial space is usually designed simply, it tends to earn lower rents. Location, product type, construction details, zoning laws, amenities, and market perception also drive industrial rental revenues. Commercial mortgages, particularly industrial and warehouse properties, may be subject to more environmental risk than single-family properties.

A multifamily property is defined as a building with five or more residential units. They are usually classified as high- or low-rise, or garden apartments. The majority have 150 to 200 units and standardized loan underwriting characteristics.

Multifamily rents are measured on a rent per unit basis, i.e., $875/1-bedroom unit. They may also be measured in monthly amount per square foot. Multifamily loans that have been securitized are generally considered more desirable because their short-term leases allow revenues to rise with expenses and inflation. They are believed to be more susceptible to economic downturns and lower occupancy rates; their higher loan-to-value ratios make them riskier. As part of their mission, Ginnie Mae, Fannie Mae, and Freddie Mac issue forms of CMBSs. Ginnie Mae also issues securities on loans backed by nursing home projects and heath care facilities.

The fundamental source of value for multifamily properties is the excess of rents collected over the expenses. This margin is called *net operating income*; it does not include noncash expenses such as depreciation. Accordingly, a property's value arises from the level and dependability of this margin in the future. The capitalization rate is the rate at which net operating income is discounted to determine the value of a property. It is one method utilized to estimate property value. Generally, higher capitalization rates indicate higher expected returns and higher perceived risk.

A *commercial office building* would similarly be classified as low-, mid- or high-rise. In addition, it too would be characterized with respect to its location relative to the city center, namely, suburban or commercial. More heterogeneous, they typically have nonstandardized loan underwriting. Since these buildings are rented, the lease–tenant analysis is critical for ascertaining whether sufficient rental income will be forthcoming to cover the mortgage payments. The annual rental rate per square foot is the common standard used to evaluate a commercial building's worth, e.g., $28 per square foot. Rental rates are based on the leaseable space (that is, net rental area); office properties have longer-term leases than most other property types. While this can offer a steady cash flow during the lease's term, upon lease expiration, make-ready expenses (e.g., repairs, improvements, repainting, redivision of internal spaces, and so on) and advertising costs incurred in attracting new tenants can be quite high.

Suburban office type refers to property located outside the city proper. Suburban offices are generally located along major traffic routes; suburban office buildings are often constructed in office parks erected by one developer. Downtown office buildings are generally high-rise and are located in or near a city center — the central business district.

The rating agencies analyze the ability of a property's income to support its mortgage and the amount of the balloon payment owed at maturity. The rating agencies also look at the expiration dates for major leases in the property relative to the maturity date of the mortgage to assist in determining vacancy potential and the releasing risk exposure on the balloon date. If many leases expire near the loan maturity date, then the loan will usually be structured to accrue a sufficient releasing reserve to mitigate against the risk of nonrepayment of the outstanding principal balance. To the extent that the rating agencies perceive lease rollover risk, they will increase their probability of default assessment and sometimes decrease their specific estimated loan recovery, leading to higher subordination levels.

Finally, the viability of income-producing property depends on its tenants and ability to attract replacement tenants. The loss of a major tenant can cause insolvency. Most recent commercial mortgage defaults have been caused by lease expirations or leases taken out by an essentially bankrupt entity. Rating agency models favor multitenanted buildings and, in addition, will look to the credit worthiness of the individual tenants. The anchor tenant in a shopping center is always critical. Single-tenant buildings are usually penalized with higher subordination levels to ensure a sufficient loss recovery if the tenant should vacate and cause a default.

Listed from least risky to most volatile, property types are multifamily, mobile home, anchored retail, industrial, office, unanchored retail, full-service hotel, self-storage, nursing home or health care, and limited-service hotels. The agencies may also penalize the more volatile property types with a higher probability of default in addition to the tougher valuation parameters to reflect their less stable cash flows.

The cash flow stability of a new property can differ significantly from that of a property in operation for a number of years. Newly developed properties may have many of their leases expire in the same year, leaving significant lease rollover risk. This may occur if the tenants find that they signed leases that charge unjustifiable rents for the untested property. A property that has operated for a number of years usually has stabilized tenant rental levels and a set of diversified tenancy lease expirations. Therefore, the rating agencies usually require 3 years of financial statements to review the property's cash flow stability and adjust their underwritten cash flow based on the property's operating history. Any newly built property with no operating statement is penalized; properties that have no statements because they were recently purchased are penalized to a lesser extent.

a.   Credit Enhancements

Just as with whole-loan residential MBSs, subordination, or credit enhancement, reallocates the default risk of a CMBS. Examples of credit enhancements include:

1. Accrual classes are junior tranches, structured as zero coupon bonds, that increase in value over time in lieu of receiving interest payments.
2. Advance payment agreements are timely payment guarantees made by the issuer. These may be limited to a specified number of payments after default.
3. Cross-default and cross-collateralization provisions mean that all the properties in a pool serve as collateral for individual loans so that, if one mortgage defaults, then the lender may accelerate prepayments on all mortgages that are a part of the agreement. (Cross-collateralization cannot occur among the assets of different borrowers.)
4. Hyper-amortization is when there is accelerated pay down on senior classes by allocating all principal payments to these classes. This is analogous to a shifting interest structure.
5. In issuer guarantees, the issuer of the CMBS agrees to absorb losses subject to certain conditions and might guarantee the timely payment of principal or interest.
6. Letters of credit or surety bonds are agreements that may guarantee interest and principal payments provided by a bank or insurance company; they may also be used in addition to issuer or third-party guarantees.

7. Overcollateralization occurs when the sum of mortgage balances in the pool exceeds the nominal value issued.
8. Reserve accounts set aside a portion of sale proceeds to absorb losses on the pool for some period of time.
9. In seller representations and warranties, the seller certifies certain credit-sensitive information about the underlying collateral and agrees to some remedy that might include paying monetary damages or substituting collateral.

4. Key CMBS Financial Ratios

The two most important indicators of the quality of the collateral backing a CMBS are its debt service coverage ratio and the its loan-to-value ratio. The debt service coverage ratio (DSCR) equals the net operating income divided by the mortgage payment. It characterizes how much cash flow a property generates vs. that required to make the loan payments. For example, if the net operating income from an apartment building is $135,000 and the debt service is $100,000, then the debt service coverage ratio is 1.35. The DSCR is the primary indicator of the credit quality of a commercial property (as defined by default and loss risk). A DSCR of less than unity means that insufficient cash flow is being generated by the property to cover required debt payments. As the DSCR rises, the default risk declines.

Lenders use the debt service coverage ratio as a broad classification to judge the credit quality of potential investments. For example, a lender may require apartment enterprises to have a minimum debt coverage ratio of 1.25 and may require shopping centers to have a minimum value of 1.10. In CMBS transactions, acceptable levels vary depending on property types, loan type, rating level, and the nature and depth of any credit enhancements. The complete range of DSCRs in the pool must be considered when evaluating a CMBS, not just the weighted average. (Remember that a similar warning applied to residential MBS parameters such as WAC and WAM.)

The mortgages on commercial properties tend to have shorter stated maturities than their residential counterparts. The typical commercial mortgage is a balloon loan, with a 30-year amortization schedule and a balloon payment due after 10 years. However, many commercial mortgages are either nonamortizing or partially amortizing and thus mature with a significant outstanding principal balance or balloon payment owed at maturity.

5. CMBS Pool Types

There are four common transaction types:

1. A *regular conduit*, which is a pool containing more than 50 loans, usually with no one loan representing more than 10% of the total balance.
2. A *fusion*, meaning that the pool contains fewer than 50 loans with one loan representing more than 10% of the pool.

3. A *large loan* in which a pool contains less than 30 loans with several loans each more than 10% of the total pool balance.

4. A *single asset/single issuer* pool collateralized by a single asset or a pool of assets owned by the same entity.

The rating agencies can usually give an investment-grade rating to a low-leverage loan on a stand-alone basis. Some floating-rate conduit pools are collateralized by a variety of loans with mortgages paying based on a floating-rate index.

II. NON-AMERICAN MORTGAGE MARKETS

A. Overview

By now you have seen that the most common American mortgage is the 30-year, fixed-rate, fully amortizing, monthly-paying, level-payment instrument. This is the most common lien for several reasons:

1. It has a long history in the U.S. as the standard product.
2. With the embedded prepayment optionality, it is much better for most borrowers than any other type of lien.
3. At year-end 2001 interest rates were at a generational low so that the one advantage of an adjustable-rate mortgage barely existed.

In the rest of the world things are very different. Therefore, this section provides a very brief summary of the world's other major mortgage markets, sometimes concentrating on their history and sometimes on the variety of their products. Much of this information is difficult to summarize concisely or to find in one place. Consider this an abbreviated overview of a very diverse subject.

One of the largest, best-developed non-American mortgage markets is that of Germany. Their legal structure, naming convention, risk management techniques, financing methods, and other aspects of their mortgage market have been copied by several European countries. As the Germans have shown with their *Jumbo Pfandbrief*, the search of European domestic mortgage markets for funds has begun to reach deeply into the international capital markets. In Western Europe, with the advent of the euro — and its implications for a minimization of foreign currency risk, a more homogeneous legal structure (one day), and a relatively large, wealthy, home-owning population — opportunities for American investors in jumbo-type securities will only increase. Hence, there is a considerable amount of material on the German market and its offshoots in nearby countries. The Canadian, English, and Australian markets have the same origins as the U.S. market and therefore share some similarities.

B. OTHER NORTH AMERICAN MARKETS

1. The Tradition of English Law

The origins of Canadian and U.S. mortgage lending practices and law can be traced back to English feudal times. During that period the relative power of the lords and royalty diminished and private ownership of *fee simple* interests in land became common. To expedite investments in land, loans secured by the right of ownership became common. (One could own the land and all the benefits from it outright, separately own the productive capacity of the surface of the land for agricultural, forestry, or grazing purposes, have detached subsurface rights to coal and other minerals, and so forth.) Initially the seller supplied credit to the purchaser, a system similar to today's Canadian vendor mortgage or mortgage take back.

A major difference between the modern and medieval era was that the seller not only kept the legal title but also retained the right to occupy and use the property (i.e., physical possession). The feudal buyer obtained control of the legal title and the real estate only after the full amount of the purchase price and all interest owed had been paid. This system offered the medieval seller a very high measure of security against default; by today's standards, the feudal lender was in a much better position than the borrower was. In fact, the borrower was generally not even entitled to the income stemming from the property before acquiring title to it. Furthermore, should the mortgagor fall in arrears with respect to the payment of the lien, then the right to take possession of the property could be forfeited (as well as all payments made to that date —just as today). Gradually, as property ownership and mortgaging became more widespread, the separation between possession of the legal title and possession of the physical property became more distinct. Eventually this evolved into our system of full title (i.e., the actual deed) to the real estate passing on its sale.

This evolutionary change came about principally because the British Courts of Equity recognized that a property purchaser who had been granted a mortgage had the right to the profits from the grounds. Thus, there was no longer any advantage to the seller to retain material control of the land and the buildings on it. However, sellers still held the legal title as a means of default protection. Eventually, the borrower was acknowledged as the legal owner of the property and the seller merely held the right to obtain repossession of the property if the mortgagor was unable to repay the borrowed monies.

2. The Canadian Mortgage Market

Jumping forward a few centuries to the first three decades of the 20th century, Canadian mortgage financing was characterized by long-term loans in which only interest was paid periodically (generally monthly) throughout the life of the loan (as was the case in the U.S.). Partial payments of principal seldom occurred; rather, the entire principal amount was repaid (or refinanced) upon maturity. Repayment was not amortized and generally followed one of two methods: periodic payment of accrued interest (quarterly, semiannually, or annually), with the principal owed and payable on maturity or the periodic payment of accrued interest plus fixed amounts of principal, with the outstanding balance owed at maturity.

This 5-year balloon mortgage form, coupled with periods of stable interest rates, low inflation, and steady property values, resulted in interest-only loans being regarded as a satisfactory investment (and borrowing) vehicle. During these decades prevailing interest rates were 6.0 to 6.5%/year and most loans were made at about 50% of the market value. Institutional lenders could not advance funds in excess of 60% of value. Also, in Canada rather than having an escrow account, borrowers typically made their own property tax payments, producing receipts as proof of payment to their lenders.

The economic collapse during the Depression greatly altered lenders' and borrowers' perceptions of the quality of these liens. Many lenders found themselves with the full amount of principal outstanding on a large number of loans whose property was worth considerably less than the borrower's indebtedness. Moreover, the mortgagors had lost their source of income and were forced to live off savings rather than try to retire a home loan. The market response to this situation was a shift to repayment plans in which the periodic payment of interest and principal occurred during the term of the financial arrangement (i.e., a fully amortizing instrument). The most common form of these repayment plans was similar in structure to the traditional mortgage in the U.S.

Another major Canadian innovation during the middle of the 20th century was the use of mortgage default insurance. This developed from the Canadian federal government's attempts to stimulate demand for and supply of housing during the post-World War II period. Direct federal intervention in housing is precluded by the Canadian Constitution (formerly the British North America Act), so the federal government utilized indirect measures to implement its housing policies. It attempted to motivate financial institutions to increase the supply of funds for mortgage lending by reducing the risk of loss in the event of default. The most successful method (and the one still in use) took the form of government insurance against default on mortgage loans granted under the terms of the National Housing Act; the borrowers paid the insurance fees. The insurance program played a major role in attracting new lenders to the mortgage market, particularly the chartered banks.

However, by the end of the 1960s fundamental changes had occurred in the Canadian economy. The most visible of these was the onset of rapid inflation inherited from the U.S. This also was a period of rising consumer demand. The increase in consumer buying intensified competition for the supply of capital between investment and consumption. As a consequence interest rates rose significantly and long-term lenders found themselves with the risk of duration mismatching. Mortgagors were protected from holding long-term debt at higher rates by rights granted by the Canada Interest Act; however, mortgage lenders had no comparable protection from being locked into long-term loans at rates below the current market interest rate.

The 30% increase in conventional mortgage interest rates in the 3-year period commencing in January, 1972, was followed by a 75% increase between September, 1979, and September, 1981. Naturally, these rapid market interest rises concerned holders of fixed-rate, long-term debt instruments. From the lender's perspective, it was desirable to modify the mortgage agreement to give the lenders increased protection against the risk of unexpected interest rate fluctuations.

The *partially amortized mortgage*, which offers such a shield, emerged. This scheme involves periodic payments based on a long period of time for amortization purposes. However, the loan matures on a short-term basis. At maturity, the full amount of the outstanding balance must be repaid or refinanced at the rate prevailing when the term expires. In other words, this is equivalent to the U.S. market's modern re-set balloon mortgage. Rates on these shorter-term liens (1, 2, 3, or 5 years) were generally less than rates on the longer-term mortgages because the yield curve is normally upward sloping. The partially amortized mortgage, in effect, permits the periodic readjustment of mortgage rates, allowing lenders to better match the rates offered on their liabilities (deposits) and their assets (mortgages). As in the U.S., with the adjust-able-rate mortgage, the transference of interest rate risk from the professional banker to the unsuspecting consumer does little for the latter. The main source of Canadian housing funds is lenders' sales of fixed-rated guaranteed investment certificates or other interest-bearing securities whose terms match those of the mortgages that they permit. One reason for this is that the standard Canadian mortgage is a 1- to 5-year, re-set balloon, 25-year amortizing, level-payment, monthly paying mortgage.

Between August, 1978, and September, 1981, Canadian interest rates increased from 10.3 to 21.5%. Rapidly swelling monthly loan payments (particularly during the 1982 recession) attracted significant attention to risks of the partially amortized mortgage to the borrower. Although such a sharing of risk makes good economic sense from the lender's point of view, the risk of homeowners having to refinance at much higher market rates — the consequence of partially amortized mortgages and rising rates of interest — prompted the federal government to introduce an interest rate insurance program in 1984. Under this program, by paying an initial insurance fee, borrowers could buy protection against making payments based on an interest rate more than a specified number of percentage points greater than the rate in the original mortgage. In effect, the mortgagor purchased an interest rate cap.

The Canadians have also devised their own solution to the tilt problem, that is, as a borrower's income increases over time, the debt-service ratio will likely decline over time. Because the borrower's housing purchasing power is usually constrained to a level based on income at the time the loan is initiated, if gross debt-service ratios could be adjusted to reflect expected increases in borrowers' income, then families would be able to obtain a larger mortgage or purchase a house sooner than would otherwise occur. In response to this common circumstance, a number of mortgage repayment schemes were developed under government auspices that make provision for increasing, rather than constant, monthly payments. These are similar to graduated payment mortgages in the U.S.

In 1986 the Canada Mortgage and Housing Corporation (CMHC) launched a new program by creating a financial instrument called the National Housing Act Mortgage-Backed Security. As in the U.S., these publicly traded MBSs (explicitly modeled after the Ginnie Mae security) were designed to help provide a steady flow of mortgage funds into housing. Only National Housing Act (NHA)-insured mort-gages are allowed to be pooled to construct an MBS and these mortgages are all guaranteed by the CMHC. These MBSs offer a double guarantee: the NHA insurance on the underlying mortgage and the government guarantee of timely payment on the MBS certificate.

A recent mortgage-related security is the Canada mortgage bond. The Canada Housing Trust recently completed the first issue of Canada mortgage bonds with a $2.2 billion issue featuring a 5.527% coupon rate. This inaugural issue is the largest syndicated bond ever issued in a single tranche in Canada. The 5-year bond matures on June 15, 2006, with interest payments made semiannually. Canada mortgage bonds carry the full faith and credit of the government of Canada, and the timely payment of interest and principal to investors is guaranteed through the CMHC. To provide investors with a bond-like investment, the Canada Housing Trust transforms monthly NHA MBS cash flows through swaps into nonprepayable, nonamortizing bond cash flows that are bullet bonds.

a.   Canadian Mortgage Mathematics

The financial aspects of a Canadian mortgage differ slightly from those in the U.S. Instead of converting a mortgage yield to a bond-equivalent yield, Canadians start with a bond yield and convert it to a mortgage-equivalent yield. A numerical example will make this clear: suppose you are considering a 10%, 25-year, fully amortizing, fixed-rate, level-paying, monthly paying loan. Based on U.S.-type calculation, your monthly payment amount would be $908.70/$100K borrowed. In Canada, it would be $894.49 per $100K of principal. You first turn the 5% (= 10%/2) semiannual bond-equivalent yield into a mortgage-equivalent yield $[1 + BEY/2 = (1 + MEY/12)^6]$ of 9.7978%/year, in this case, and then use that quantity in the standard mortgage formulas. To verify that you understand this computation, show that, for an 8%/year interest rate, the Canadian monthly mortgage payment would be $763.21 (with an MEY of 7.8698%/year) per $100K borrowed.

3.   The Mexican Mortgage Market

Mexico is very different from the U.S. and Canada in that it has a special type of financial institution to provide mortgage financing opportunities for low-income borrowers. SOFOL (*Sociedad Financiera de Objeto Limitado* or Limited Scope Financial Society) is a relatively new creation. These institutions can lend funds but cannot accept deposits. Since 1994 they have rapidly increased their market share to 50%, primarily by lending to families with monthly incomes below $400. This swift market penetration is a consequence of the huge gap between the household formation rate of about 1 million per year and the construction of new housing units at about a third of that level. (The remainder occurs in the informal housing construction segment of the market where people build their own homes from scratch.)

The basic reason for this circumstance is that Mexico, like many South American countries, has a highly bifurcated economic and demographic structure. There are the rich (1 to 2% of the population) and a modest middle class (3 to 5%). The remainder are poor (about 25%) or poorer (the bulk). The banks satisfactorily serve the upper few percentage points of the population with traditional mortgage products. The SOFOLs serve the next segment downward in income and wealth. Government agencies, such as the housing pension funds INFONAVIT — for private sector workers — and FOVISSTE — for federal workers — serve the poor. These agencies collect monies through mandatory payroll deductions of 5% and then make housing loans to their members. (Some second-rank banks also function as lenders for these people. An example is *FOVI,* a housing trust fund of the Mexican central bank established in 1963. FOVI stands for *Fondo de Operación y Financiamiento Bancarioa a la Vivienda.*) These three funds generally lend to families whose income level exceeds twice the minimum wage.

Mexican mortgage interest rates were in the low- to mid-teens in the late 1990s. However, the standard mortgage instrument, the *price level adjusted mortgage* or PLAM, has a principal balance linked to inflation so that the interest rate is a **real** rate of interest, not a nominal one. This system is partly a consequence of the periodic peso devaluations experienced (every 6 years in synchrony with the Mexican presidential election cycle). The Mexican central bank computes an artificial unit of account based on the Mexican consumer price index. This quantity, known as a unit of investment (UDI for *Unidades de Inversion*) serves as the conversion factor between nominal and real prices. This was not an easy instrument to manage the interest rate risk because no inflation-linked funding sources were available. When the optimistic assumption that real rates of return would decrease turned out to be false because of the 1994–1995 peso devaluation of 140%, the banks lost.

A different instrument, known as a *double-indexed mortgage,* or DIM, has become popular. It was introduced by FOVI in 1984. For this security the payments are indexed to inflation — specifically the Mexican minimum wage level — and the loan is amortized using short-term market interest rates (thus, the dual nature). This type of lien was a much easier loan for the banks to handle. Bankers and newly formed banks rushed to issue this mortgage without appreciating its more subtle features. Borrowers began to default as interest rates rose from 8%/year in 1992 to 11.5% just 2 years later. One of the causes was that a DIM is not a fixed-term instrument; if the interest rate used for interest charge accrual increases or the wage level decreases, then the maturity of the DIM will increase (and vice versa). While this feature minimizes borrowers having to accept a large increase in monthly payment (by extending the term), it also increases the time to full ownership and decreases the rate of equity buildup.

One of the consequences of the 1994 peso devaluation was that real interest rates rose and real wages fell. Regardless of the type of mortgage that homeowners had, many were unable to meet their monthly payments or negative amortization occurred. Delinquency rates rose to 40%. FOVI invented a new product to prevent this from happening in the future. It is basically a fixed-rate double-indexed mortgage plus an insurance fund (known as the *SWAP*). The amount of the insurance fund is sufficient to prevent negative amortization. The cost of the insurance premium, the SWAP fee, is bundled into the borrower's monthly payment as primary mortgage insurance coverage as frequently done in the U.S. This instrument appears to an investor as a price-level adjusted mortgage because the proceeds from the insurance fund hide any payment shortfalls, while simultaneously appearing to a homeowner as having their payments adjusted based on wage levels. Finally, from the perspective of the FOVI, the instrument behaves like a PLAM with reduced credit risk because the insurance fund protects the borrower against severe payment shocks.

The current legal structure in Mexico will not support a mortgage-backed securities market.

B. The Major European Mortgage Markets

1. The German Mortgage Market

One of the most common means of mortgage financing in Germany (and Austria) is the *Pfandbrief* — an intermediate-term, fixed-rate, noncallable, annual paying bond with first claim on the property underlying the mortgages that it funds. The standard maturities are 3, 5, and 10 years. Pfandbriefe require a much lower loan-to-value ratio than in the American market: a maximum of 60%. Actually, two types of Pfandbriefe exist: *public Pfandbrief* to finance public-sector lending and *mortgage Pfandbrief* to finance residential housing (two-thirds) and commercial property construction (one-third). (There are ship-related Pfandbrief, too, based on the Ship Mortgage Act of 1943.) Despite the well-known aspects of the German mortgage market and the fact that it serves as a model for much of Europe, homeownership rates in Germany are a relatively low level of 40%.

Public Pfandbrief, also known as *Kommunalobligationen*, are loans made to the German federal government, the 12 state governments (or Länder via the Landesbanken or Central Savings Banks), local authorities, public-sector agencies, and corresponding institutions in other European Union countries. A 1998 amendment expanded this to include the purchase of public debt securitized in the form of bonds. Mortgage Pfandbrief are restricted to mortgage loans, that is, real estate-secured loans for housing construction, housing purchase, housing renovation, housing refinancing, and commercial properties. The latter are mostly office and administration buildings. Public Pfandbrief are for public sector activities.

German mortgage banks are specialist banks and do not engage in the full suite of banking activities. Their scope is limited by the Mortgage Bank Act of 1900 to granting loans on domestic real estate and issuing mortgage bonds on the basis of the mortgages thus acquired. They are also permitted to grant loans to domestic corporations and institutions governed by public law and issue bonds on the basis of those claims. Moreover, they are now allowed to lend in Switzerland, to the other member states of the European Union, or to the member states of the European Economic Area. Investors in the U.K., the Netherlands, Spain, and France are the German mortgage banks' top borrowers, with commercial lending predominating (90% of the total). The size of the market now exceeds one trillion euros; about 80% is in the form of public-sector lending.

In more detail, the legally stipulated core competency of a German mortgage bank comprises public sector and mortgage lending. (Two banking institutions are grandfathered under the Mortgage Bank Act. The 23 other banks issuing Pfandbrief are pure mortgage banks; the Pfandbrief issuance of the Landesbanken are governed by the Public Pfandbrief Act of 1927. There are 18 public-sector Pfandbrief issuers.) Because the issuance of Pfandbrief takes place under the supervision of the Federal Banking Supervisory Authority, an extra degree of security exists over and above that provided by the German Banking Supervisory Authority. The latter approves the very conservative property valuations a mortgage bank uses and regularly inspects the *coverage* a bank has for its mortgage bonds. Thus, the lien is granted based more on the value of the collateral than on the credit worthiness of the borrower.

The cover is the total pool of assets a mortgage bank has to back its mortgage and public Pfandbriefe. This means that an individual mortgage is not allocated to a specific Pfandbrief: all the mortgages in their entirety serve as cover for the mortgage Pfandbriefe as a whole (and normally the mortgage and public pools are kept separate and not comingled). In particular, mortgage Pfandbriefe may only be issued for mortgages on properties that yield a permanent return. (Mortgages on new buildings that are not yet completed have no earnings capacity and, therefore, construction loans are not allowed.)

Another provision of the Mortgage Bank Act explicitly states that income from the bonds be invested in assets that, throughout the life of the bonds, sufficiently cover the resultant liabilities. That is, the capital and interest claims under the Pfandbriefe must be supported by interest and principal repayments from the mortgages and public sector loans granted. This limits the funds that the mortgage banks raise by issuing mortgage and public Pfandbriefe to mortgage and public sector loans and for no other purposes. German law requires that, in addition to liens and Pfandbriefe balancing in nominal amount, the asset and liability management ensures a maturity, if not a duration, match. The purpose of this is to minimize liquidity problems and interest rate risk.

a.   History

The German mortgage banking system was started in an effort to repair the ravages of the Seven Years War (1756–1763). Friedrich II of Prussia issued an edict in August of 1767, the cabinets-ordre, which formed the basis for the Pfandbrief. On its basis, the Silesian Landschaft, an association of estates belonging to the aristocracy, churches, and monasteries, was set up in 1770. The estates were named in the pfandbrief, or pledge letter, as security in the event of default. The funds were originally used to finance agriculture because paper money had lost its value in the war. Second-generation Pfandbrief were issued following the creation of the *Crédit Foncier de France* in 1852.

Now Pfandbrief issuers changed from public law corporations to private real estate credit institutions whose legal form was that of joint stock companies. Moreover, instead of issuing the mortgages *per se* as securities, they issued bonds. The major difference between these mortgage bonds and ordinary bank bonds was (and still is) that the holder of a Pfandbrief had a preferential right in the event of bankruptcy with respect to the bank's entire mortgage loan portfolio. Also, as agriculture was diminishing in importance in mid-19th century Germany, the monies raised by these instruments went instead to fund the development of growing towns and cities.

The modern German mortgage bank was established in 1862 and now about two dozen of them are governed by the Mortgage Bank Act of 1900. After the unification of Germany in 1870, the bulk of Pfandbrief issuance went to urban housing construction. Limited commercial lending, primarily to Prussian factories or others in which a continuous return was highly probable, were granted. With the start of the first World War, the public need for funds shifted to armaments and the success of the mortgage banks came to a rapid end. Recovery did not come until after World War II. The regeneration of the German economy, the eventual reestablishment of consumer savings, and the rapid growth in population supported and increased the demand for housing. Cross-border lending was permitted starting in 1963, when the German Mortgage Banking Act was amended to allow lending within the European Economic Community. This capability was further expanded in 1974 to the European Union.

b. Status Today

Pfandbriefe comprise the largest segment of the German bond market, even larger than German government bonds (*bunds*). Pfandbriefe are very safe because of the stringent underwriting requirements of German mortgage banks (for instance, their 60% loan-to-value ratio), an extremely conservative view of the forward-looking market value of the property, and a rigorous appraisal system. Consequently, they usually receive a triple-A rating from Moody's. In fact, mortgage Pfandbriefe must be backed by first mortgages of at least nominal value. Public Pfandbriefe must be backed by public-sector loans yielding at least the interest owed on the bonds.

By law mortgage banks have the right to suspend the right of prepayment (on fixed-rate loans) for a maximum of 10 years after disbursement, so there is effectively no prepayment risk for an investor in German residential mortgages during this lock-out period. A mortgage bank may allow prepayment but then will almost certainly charge an economically determined prepayment penalty. Finally, a mortgage bank may issue what Americans would call a second mortgage; however, these loans are not eligible to be the collateral backing a Pfandbrief. Moreover, the total value of the junior loans may not exceed 20% of the bank's mortgage loan portfolio.

Interest rate volatility in the early 1970s threatened to disrupt the strict rules under which German mortgage banks had been operating. Long-term, fixed-rate loans fell out of favor in the capital markets. As a consequence, the type of mortgage product offered to potential homeowners significantly widened to include adjustable-rate mortgages, balloon mortgages, and hybrid mortgages.

c. Jumbo Pfandbriefe

A significant development in the German mortgage bond market was the creation of a standardized jumbo Pfandbrief product. (Here jumbo refers to the total size of the issue, not that the underlying home loans are particularly large in par value.) This instrument was created specifically to increase international investor excitement and demand in the German mortgage market. The capital market's requirements for transparency, standardization, liquidity, common issuing techniques, and product design had to be satisfied. A jumbo Pfandbriefe has a minimum size of euro 500 million or DM 1 billion. (In contrast, most Pfandbrief issues have face values from DM 10 million to DM 1 billion, with DM 300 million a typical par amount.)

Jumbo Pfandbriefe are issued by a syndicate of at least three banks promising to make a market in the issue. The practical consequence is the existence of continuous bid–ask spreads on jumbo Pfandbrief. The minimum trading size is DM

25 million (or euro 15 million). The large face amount size of an issuance, homogenization of documentation, standardized issuing procedures, meeting of international standards (accomplished in stages through March of 1997, a few years after the first issue in May, 1995), and continuing presence of market makers dramatically increases the liquidity of the jumbo Pfandbriefe over the traditional Pfandbriefe. Today jumbo Pfandbriefe comprise over one-third of the German pfandbriefe market (the sixth biggest debt market in the world). Approximately 25% are placed with non-German investors and there is an active Jumbo Pfandbriefe repurchase agreement market. Prior to the innovative introduction of the jumbo Pfandbrief, Pfandbrief were viewed as heterogeneous, illiquid, and local.

Finally, to meet investor demand, Pfandbriefe are now structured with many of the characteristics of REMIC tranches seen in the U.S. market. Most common are floating-rate tranches tied to LIBOR or FIBOR (Frankfurt InterBank Offered Rate), inverse floating-rate classes (called reverse floaters in Germany), zero coupon issues, floating-rate tranches with caps and floors, callable classes, step-up callables, tranches indexed to a constant maturity index, EURIBOR-linked bonds, step-up floaters, foreign currency tranches, and so forth. Pfandbrief are usually issued in bearer form (about 75%) though those bought to hold to maturity are issued in registered form (*Namen Pfandbrief*). The latter are favored by accounting regulations and normally held, at book value, on the balance sheets of insurance companies. Other than the insurance companies (20 to 25% ownership), the next largest two holders of Pfandbrief are banks (25%) and foreign investors (20% and rapidly growing). Private households and investment funds each own comparable, smaller, shares (about 15%).

2. The British Mortgage Market

At the beginning of the 1990s, the British standard floating mortgage note rate was at 15.4%/year. In contrast, in the 1950s, the rate was 5%/year and only six rate changes over that decade occurred. By the 1960s, the mean floating rate had increased to 6.75%, rising further to 10.1% in the 1970s. By the 1980s the average had further climbed to 12.5%. In November, 1984 the Building Societies Association stopped setting the official mortgage rate; the era of a free market in British mortgage rates began in 1986. Unlike the U.S., the adjustable-rate mortgage is the predominant form there. Since the housing boom of the 1980s, the mortgage market is much more complex with a far wider choice of loans. At present, over 1000 mortgage types are available in the U.K. Main mortgage categories are listed next and a brief introduction is given to each form. This subsection is written using British English, instead of American English, to give the reader some of the flavor of the U.K. marketplace.

Approximately 68% of British households own their home; a proportion very similar to that in the U.S. In Britain one generally borrows up to three times the amount of the first income of a family plus half of the second income, or two-and-a-half times the joint income. Most lenders are prepared to offer up to 95% of the property's value but, as in the U.S., they will charge less interest with a bigger deposit. In fact, the 100% loan is routinely available. In general a deposit of between 3 to 10% of the asking price of the property is expected from the borrower. Borrowing more than 75% of the property's assessed valuation requires the mortgagor to pay for insurance to protect against default. As in our country, solicitor's fees, valuation, arrangement, and mortgage indemnity costs rapidly mount up at settlement time.

The basic mortgage choices are a variable-rate loan, a fixed-rate loan (usually at a higher interest rate than the variable-rate), or a discount-rate loan. The latter offers a discount on the variable rate. Many fixed-rate loans and virtually all discounted offers have prepayment penalties or other constraints. This means that the homeowner effectively gives up the right to refinance because of the high redemption penalty. These punitive costs may be as high as 6 months' repayments if the borrower wants to make a significant curtailment of the outstanding principal balance or to refinance.

A *repayment mortgage* is one in which the monthly installments (or payments) contain two elements: one to repay interest and the other to repay some of the capital borrowed (their phrase for the unpaid principal balance). This is identical to the fully amortizing instrument in the U.S. Usually mortgages are for 25 years, although shorter ones are available. This instrument is portable — that is, it goes with the borrower and not to the combination of the borrower plus the property — which means that each time the homeowner moves and remortgages (British for refinancing) the homeowner is extending the period to repay the original mortgage. The lender may require life insurance for the outstanding mortgage balance.

A *fixed-rate mortgage* is one with an interest rate set for a period of time. The rate then reverts to the lender's basic mortgage rate, commonly known as the *standard variable rate*. (As the name indicates, this is an adjustable interest rate.) These mortgages sometimes have early cancellation penalties that can lock one into staying with the lender for a time after the introductory fixed-rate period expires. Some fixed-rate mortgage products specify that borrowers will be offered a further constant rate once the initial period has expired.

A *variable rate mortgage* offers the potential homeowner a mortgage at the lender's basic mortgage interest rate, *the standard variable rate*. This fluctuates with interest rate changes made by the Bank of England. Usually there are no penalties for cancellation, for transferring to another mortgage product, or to another lender (known as redemption penalty and lock-in periods; a redemption penalty is the British phrase for a prepayment penalty).

A *tracker rate mortgage* is a variable rate mortgage with interest that rises and falls in line with a specific benchmark, usually the Bank of England base rate. The tracker rate would be expressed as a certain percentage rate above the benchmark. There are two standard repayment methods for tracker rate mortgages. (One is the repayment mortgage discussed above and the other variety is considered next.) Lenders argue that they have responsibilities toward their savers as well as to borrowers. Therefore, lenders offering standard variable rate loans do not always pass on decreases in the base rate. To overcome this, the tracker mortgage always follows the Bank of England's base rate up and down. The difference, or spread, between the tracker's rates and the base rate will remain constant for the lifetime of the mortgage. A second benefit of the tracker mortgage is that the difference between its variable rate and the base rate is normally smaller than the margin on an ordinary variable rate mortgage. On the latter, the average margin is around 1.5%; on a tracker it can be as little as 75 bp.

An *interest only mortgage* means that the monthly installments will cover only the interest on the loan as with the U.S. old-style balloon mortgages. Of course, one still needs to repay the capital. The interest only mortgage keeps the monthly installments low and gives the homeowner the flexibility to invest in a range of savings plans, some of which can have tax advantages (e.g., individual savings accounts — a sort of British IRA —or pensions). Another problem is that, even if the freed-up cash flow is used for investments or savings plans, there is no guarantee that the savings will accumulate enough funds to cover the unpaid principal balance when it becomes due.

Standard investment or savings plans are offered as options to repay the capital on an interest only mortgage. With an *investment linked repayment* plan the monthly installments cover interest and contributions to an investment or savings plan such as an endowment. The latter combines deposited funds with life insurance cover (the British phrase for the decreasing term mortgage insurance sometimes advocated in the U.S.), an individual savings account, or a personal pension plan. The aim of the design will be to increase the funds sufficiently to repay the mortgage at the end of the period and possibly provide a surplus. This is an opportunity to invest in tax-efficient savings plans and to benefit from a rising stock market. Sometimes, the plans include life cover such as with *endowment mortgages*.

A *cash back rate mortgage* offers money back when the mortgage is finalized. (This is not the same as cash-out refinancing in the U.S.) The amount of cash back is often a percentage of the loan. This option can be attractive to first time buyers who need extra funds for home improvements or furniture. Rates are usually set at the lender's standard variable rate for a fixed term. Additional cash back can add to the term or to the cost of the mortgage. Cancellation penalties are charged to alter the mortgage within its initial years (to offset the lender's losses from providing the extra funds at closing).

A *capped rate mortgage* offers an interest rate with a maximum rate for a set period of time. During the capped period the interest installments will not rise beyond the capped amount, even if interest rates increase sharply. Although one is protected from increases in interest rates, one also will not benefit from any decreases in market rates. Interest rate collar variants of this mortgage are available too.

An endowment mortgage is also an interest-only mortgage. With this, and *pension mortgages,* the capital is not repaid until the end of the mortgage period. The monthly repayments are interest-only. In addition to the interest, one also takes out a life assurance policy —an endowment. This payment is split in part between a life insurance policy and an amount used to purchase investments (i.e., stock market mutual funds known as unit trusts). At the end of the mortgage period the accumulated monies are used to repay the amount of capital borrowed.

If one has a personal pension scheme, then a pension mortgage may be an appropriate option. This is similar to an endowment mortgage, in that interest only is paid off during the mortgage period. The difference is that the lump sum generated by the pension scheme is used to repay the capital. Rather than paying premiums on an endowment policy the mortgagor makes contributions to the pension scheme sufficient to ensure the repayment of the capital element and a retirement. The borrower will also need a separate life insurance policy to cover the capital sum, if the borrower should die before retiring.

A *flexible rate mortgage* offers the adaptability to change monthly payments with a variable- or fixed-rate mortgage. This provides the elasticity to manage mortgage payments to suit cash flow needs as circumstances change. Flexible mortgages are also known as choices, daily interest, or current account mortgages. Though only recently offered in Britain, they are well-established in Australia where they originated. Flexible mortgages suit certain groups better than others; they are particularly attractive to self-employed people or those who work on fixed-term contracts. Flexible mortgages allow one to repay capital early, to take back some monies paid in, or to postpone payments. Some are run as substitutes for current and savings accounts, so all one's funds are working to minimize interest on the mortgage. There are no standard repayment methods; each lender specifies the extent of the freedom on its flexible mortgage. The interest rate may be variable or fixed.

With the most adaptable flexible mortgages, freed from constant monthly repayments, borrowers can repay all or part of the loan without penalty at any time, saving on interest simultaneously. Because interest is calculated on a daily rest system, all capital repayments have an immediate effect on the debt owed. Some flexible mortgages even allow customers to borrow back overpaid sums (i.e., curtailments) or to take payment holidays. Interest rates on these mortgages are typically a little higher than the standard variable rate. Fixed and discounted interest rates are not usually an option with this product.

A *low start capital repayment* option, usually only available to first-time homebuyers, is essentially one in which, for a given period of a few years, interest-only is repaid. Then a gradually increasing capital element is repaid. It is usual for the lender to take out a life insurance policy to cover the repayment of the capital in case the borrower dies before the loan is repaid. This would probably be a term policy, co-terminating with the final repayment of capital on the loan.

A *discount rate mortgage* offers an interest rate set at an amount (discounted) below the lender's standard variable rate. Normal terms are between 1 and 5 years. This gives the homeowner the opportunity to pay less than the standard rates while payments fall with interest rates. However, the longer the period of discount is, the smaller the amount of the discount. These mortgages sometimes have early cancellation penalties. The initial rate, paid by borrowers for the duration of the discounted rate period, is a direct reduction from the standard variable rate, and rises and falls with the lender's base rate. Some discount mortgages specify a further discounted rate once the first has expired. Other products will revert to the lender's standard variable once the first discount period has expired.

A *current account mortgage* is a very flexible mortgage product linked to a current account (a checking account in U.S. parlance). These mortgages take the benefits of the flexible mortgage and combine what the borrower earns and what he owes. Periodic salary payments into a combined mortgage and current account are made each month. The unpaid principal balance is instantly reduced and therefore the interest charge is abated too. Borrowers can also incorporate their savings accounts into these accounts to reduce the amount owed.

Integrated banking refers to a range of accounts, all with the same institution, working together to maximize savings or to minimize borrowings. The interest rates for these accounts are then pooled together and the money in the savings and current accounts is offset against the money borrowed, for example, for a credit card, a personal loan, or a mortgage. The main difference between current account mortgages and integrated banking is that the former represents a single account combining all the facilities of a mortgage and current account whereas the latter comprises separate accounts with one institution and the money saved is offset against the money borrowed.

The British have a term known as *remortgaging*, which is when the mortgage is moved to a different lender without actually moving the home. In other words, it is comparable to refinancing in the U.S. The British remortgage for many of the same reasons: to release the built-up equity in their property, to cover home improvement costs, to consolidate existing debts, or to obtain a better mortgage rate. Redemption penalties (fees paid for repaying the mortgage early) might make remortgaging not worth while. Borrowers currently on fixed, capped, or discounted mortgages may encounter such penalties.

Some mortgage deals also come with overhangs. That is, the borrower is tied to the lender's standard variable rate for a period of time after the fixed, capped, or discount incentive rate expires. This allows the lender to recoup the cost of providing the inducement. Just as in the U.S., the fees and costs incurred for remortgaging are similar to those for buying a property, although no stamp duty is paid (i.e., local sales taxes). Likely costs and fees are lenders' booking and arrangement fees and a valuation (i.e., appraisal) fee. In Britain a lender may be willing to accept the original purchase valuation report (typically expiring in 6 months in the U.S.). Other costs will be those for solicitors and conveyancing, and the usual players in obtaining a home loan. The British also have a MIG fee (mortgage indemnity guarantee) analogous to U.S. private mortgage insurance. It may be payable if the loan-to-value ratio is a high.

A *buying-to-let mortgage* offers a potential landlord a mortgage to buy a property not intended to be his residence but to be rented out to tenants. To accommodate this providers will expect an estimate of the annual rental income, which should be a significant percentage of the loan amount, e.g., 10%, evidence that a professional letting or managing agent will be appointed, proof of income to supplement the rental income, a significant deposit for the property, e.g., 30%, and that reasonable demand exists for rental property in that area. Buy-to-let mortgages tend to be around half a percentage point more than the standard variable rate, but discounted, fixed, and capped rate variations are available. Elastic terms are also offered with some schemes, allowing borrowers to overpay and take payment holidays when necessary.

The British have a fully developed mortgage-backed securities market. The National Home Loan plc, an independent mortgage loan company, issued the first one in 1987 with a face amount of 50 million pounds. The market grew to over £10 billion by the end of 1996. The British use the special purpose vehicle model and have no government support for their MBSs. Most British MBSs are rated AAA by Standard and Poor's or Moody's Investor Service. The credit enhancements for these securities usually take the form of pool insurance and the senior/subordinate structure discussed earlier. Pool insurance generally covers the default risk on 7 to 13% of the outstanding principal balance. Eventually, structured MBSs, much like our REMICs, appeared in the British market.

3. The Irish Mortgage Market

Ireland has an extremely high homeownership rate: 80%. The Irish mortgage market has expanded since the mid-1990s with 46,500 new houses built in 1999 and just under 50,000 more constructed in 2000. Mortgage approvals exceeded £9 billion on over 80,000 houses in 2000 for new and second-hand properties (Irish for used or previously owned). This was up 17% over 1999. Mortgages actually drawn down exceeded £7.5 billion, also up 17% from 1999. Prices for new houses increased 14% in 2000 (19% in 1999) and second-hand homes went up 17% (21% in 1999). The average new house (at year-end 2000) cost £180,000 in Ireland, with Dublin the most expensive area of the country. The average second-hand house cost £199,000 in Ireland, with Dublin again the most expensive at £256,000.

Loan limits in Ireland are strictly a function of gross income. The conservative rule of thumb is two and one-half times the main gross income plus the second income. The more liberal lenders will allow three times the main gross income plus one and one-quarter times the second. Lenders insist that a valuation be carried out for about £100. Private mortgage insurance in Ireland is referred to as an indemnity bond; it is an insurance policy that has a one-off payment made by the applicant. The policy is designed to protect the lender in the event of a shortfall in the proceeds following a forced sale. The indemnity bond is only applicable on loans over 75% of valuation or purchase price.

A life assurance is a life insurance policy taken out at the start of the mortgage. The policy normally covers the lives of all parties to the mortgage. In the event of one person dying before the mortgage is repaid, the policy is designed to clear the outstanding amount of the mortgage. All lenders will also insist on a building's insurance policy (i.e., hazard insurance) in place prior to issuing the cheque (check) at closing. It is a requirement of the Bank of Ireland that a building's insurance policy be in place. As in the U.S., mortgage interest is tax deductible.

As an example of the sensitivity of the Irish (and other EU countries) to the European Central Bank, floating rates in Ireland now depend on the level of the euro. Having joined the euro region in January, 1999, Irish variable mortgage interest rates are now driven by the European Central Bank's repurchase agreement rate. A modification of this rate will prompt a change in variable mortgage rates. Normally, banks and building societies have a corresponding movement of variable deposit rates and variable mortgage rates. Their fixed-rate mortgage rates respond to yield movements in the Irish government bonds (also called gilts). The Bank of Ireland has launched a European Central Bank tracker mortgage that will never exceed the European Central Bank's interest rate by more than 135 basis points. It also guarantees that any European Central Bank rate changes will be passed on to customers within 5 working days.

There are two basic types of Irish mortgages: *annuity* and *endowment*. An annuity mortgage is one in which the repayments cover the interest element of the mortgage and the capital balance (i.e., the amount originally borrowed). The amount of the mortgage's outstanding principal balance progressively reduces and by the end of the term the mortgage and the interest are completely paid off. The normal length of time over which a lien will be repaid is 20 years, but it can range from 10 to 30 years — a fully amortizing lien, in other words. With an *endowment mortgage*, the monthly repayment only repays the interest on the lien. To repay the capital balance, one needs to take out an additional endowment policy with an assurance company and pay a monthly premium.

There are three common interest rate options in Ireland: fixed-rate, variable-rate, and *split-rate*. A fixed rate means that the rate of interest is fixed for 1, 2, 3, 5, 10, or 20 years. The same amount is repaid every month for the agreed-upon time period. In the case of a fixed-rate loan, the borrower will be liable to pay a compensatory sum, that is, a prepayment penalty, for refinancing. This is a form of yield maintenance and it is calculated as

$$\text{Amount} \times (r - r') \times T/36500.$$

"Amount" means the average balance of the amount repaid early or converted from the date of repayment or conversion to the end of the fixed-rate term, allowing for scheduled payments. In the case of an endowment loan, this will equal the full amount of the early repayment or conversion. The quantity denoted by r is the cost of funds for the bank loaning the funds for the fixed-rate period as incorporated in the existing interest rate applying to the loan. Similarly, r' is the interest rate on the available funds to the bank for monies placed in the money market on the date of early repayment or conversion for the remainder of the relevant fixed-rate period. Finally, T denotes the number of days from the date of early repayment or conversion to the end of the relevant fixed-rate period. (Imagine selling this product to the American consumer.)

With a variable-rate loan, the rate can go up or down depending on market interest rates. A split-rate loan allows the security of a fixed rate and the money-saving potential of a variable rate. For example, you could set 50% of your mortgage principal balance at a fixed rate and 50% at a variable rate. Other proportions are available at the discretion of the borrower.

In addition to the above, there are many special programs. One is known as *deferred start* and is only for first-time home buyers. With this instrument the mortgagor need not pay for the first 1, 2, or 3 months of the life of the lien. Then monthly repayments are readjusted so that the mortgage will be fully paid off in the originally contracted time period. The *low start* product is also for first-time home buyers. With this option you can make repayments at a reduced rate for a 3-year period (15% in year 1, 10% in year 2, and 5% in year 3). When this time interval is over, the repayment level is increased so that the mortgage is fully paid off in the original term.

Most foreign mortgages have much more adaptable forms than those found in the U.S. One example in Ireland is a *flexible month mortgage*. For this instrument, repayments are made over 10 or 11 months each year instead of every month. One repays the same amount over the mortgage term but has 1 or 2 months each year when no payments are due. Even more fascinating is a *mortgage break* loan. With this device there are no mortgage repayments for 3 consecutive months. When the break is over repayments are readjusted so that the mortgage will be fully paid off in the original time period.

The Irish have several other specialized options. One is a *lump sum payment* option (known as curtailment in the U.S.). For example, an annual bonus can be applied to the outstanding mortgage balance by making a lump sum payment. A fee would be charged for a lump sum payment on a fixed-rate mortgage. Instead of a graduated payment mortgage, the Irish have an *index linking increase* capability. In this instance, the borrower's repayments are annually altered, for example, by 1, 2, or 3%. Even though this option was chosen, one can go back to the original mortgage repayment schedule at any time. Another possibility is the *fixed overpay increase* in which the repayments are increased by a set amount; this can be reduced back to the amount of the original mortgage repayment level at any time.

Further flexibility is indicated by the *level pay* option for those with a variable-rate lien; the repayments are set at a fixed amount for 1 year. At the end of the year the repayment levels are readjusted so that the mortgage is paid off in the originally agreed-upon time period. A last variation is the *equity release equity* feature (i.e., a second mortgage). One can use this equity to borrow money at a much lower rate than would be the case with an ordinary personal loan.

4. The Austrian Mortgage Market

Austria shares the Pfandbrief concept with Germany. Its mortgage banking laws — the main one was passed in 1939 — largely correspond with those of Germany. Austria has a higher homeownership rate, though — about 50%. The smaller size of Austria means that its mortgage bond market is also relatively modest. Only ten banks, eight of them state-owned regional mortgage banks (called *Landes-Hypothek-enbanken)* and two of the private universal banks, issue Pfandbrief. One big difference between the German and Austrian mortgage banking laws is that in Austria holders of Pfandbrief have no recourse to special assets. Instead, they have a priority claim in the event of bankruptcy. In 1998 Austria passed a law allowing its banks to use loans and mortgages originated from other European Union countries (and Switzerland) as collateral for Pfandbrief. This, plus the existence of the euro, may rapidly enlarge Austria's tiny mortgage market via subsidiaries of German banks looking to expand throughout Europe.

5. The French Mortgage Market

The term "mortgage" derives from the Middle English term "mortgage," which, in turn, came from the old French "mort" and the German "gage" meaning to pledge upon death. That is, in case a mortgagor did not retire the claim on his property at the time of his death, the mortgagee was allowed to take back the title. This usage dates back to the late 14th century. The French mortgage bond market dates back to February 28, 1852, when establishment of the first banking institutions to fulfill the mortgage origination function was authorized.

Mortgage banks such as the Crédit Foncier de France (created at the end of 1852 from the merger of three local property credit companies) could grant long-term loans secured by property with annual repayment of principal. The original loan-to-value ratio was capped at 50% and only first liens were allowed. To fund these loans mortgage banks were authorized to issue interest-bearing bonds with a certain special legal status with respect to the recoverability of claims against those in default. An 1860 modification permitted lending funds to local authorities (departments and municipalities in France) and then to hospitals and other public institutions. France, too, has special mortgage bond instruments for ships and aircraft.

Today the French have a home ownership rate of about 55% and a mortgage instrument known as an *obligation foncière*. These are distributed by a variety of bank-related entities that issue them through subsidiaries known as *Sociétés de Crédit Foncier*. (In France, mortgage banks can also engage in all the traditional banking activities.) They were normally funded by medium- and long-term mortgage bonds. In 1969 however, the laws were changed to allow more flexibility to generate external financing as long as repayment was still guaranteed by the mortgage loans supported by these funds. As in Germany and Luxembourg, there is bankruptcy remoteness, meaning that the bankruptcy of the parent company or the Sociétés de Crédit Foncier does not affect the credit worthiness of the mortgage, the obligation foncière.

Obligation foncière (usually denoted as OF) are issued with a 60% loan-to-value ratio, though, as in Germany, lending on real estate can go higher with alternative securities (up to 90% for French residents). The 1999 revision of the French mortgage banking laws makes their OF market very similar to Germany's Pfandbrief with the specialist nature of the Sociétés de Crédit Foncier, a liquid market including the requirement of two stock exchange listings, two credit ratings, the existence of market-making and fixed bid–ask spreads, and the functioning of active repurchase and spot markets. Lastly, jumbo OFs have appeared, the first ones with triple-A ratings.

Interestingly, French mortgage bonds were not legally defined until June, 1999, although the courts had allowed them special privileges. However, for most of their history they were more or less treated like ordinary securities. In particular, they cannot exist in bearer form; they must be registered. The French SEC, the *Commission des Opération de Bourse*, regulates the form of a prospectus and other details of public issuance. Beyond directly linking the rate on mortgage bonds to the coupon rate on the mortgages that they support, no further restrictions exist with regard to maturity, rates, redemption conditions, and so on. (In particular, matching mortgage bond maturity to mortgage maturity is not required.) The French have a cover principle in that the sums recovered from liens are allocated, by preference and as a guarantee, to the reimbursement of the mortgage bonds. This is not a one-to-one relationship between a particular lien and a bond, but rather a global coverage of a bank's portfolios of assets and liabilities. Therefore, the amount of mortgage loans was always at least equal to the amount of outstanding mortgage bonds.

French mortgages can be fixed-rate or floating-rate from 5 to 20 years maturity. One unusual aspect of adjustable-rate mortgages in France is that the monthly payment does not change; rather, the date of the final payment lengthens (shortens) with increasing (decreasing) interest rate. Thus, one trades uncertainty of maturity for interest rate risk. Life insurance sufficient to pay off the unpaid principal balance is also required, as are significant fees at closing, typically 6 to 10% (the *Frais de Garantie*, which is paid to a *Notaire*). Sometimes private unemployment insurance will be demanded as well. Finally, OFs are frequently overcollateralized to insure their credit worthiness.

6. The Spanish Mortgage Market

In Spain the mortgage bond security is known as a *Cédulas Hipotecarias*. This is the Spanish version of the German Pfandbrief and has a long history including a century without defaults. (A secondary security known as the *Bonos Hipotecarios* is also utilized.) It was introduced in 1861 and has primarily been a retail investment vehicle. It has served Spain well in that its homeownership rate is almost 80%. This instrument is backed by liens with an 80% loan-to-value ratio for residential housing and 70% otherwise. Only retail and savings banks with a mortgage portfolio can issue a Cédulas Hipotecarias (or CH). Unlike the Danish or German mortgage bond legislation, a strict matching principle is not required between assets and liabilities with respect to maturity, payment schedule, call option, or so on. Hence, there is a wider variety of securities in the Spanish market, with some carrying considerable interest rate risk.

Also different from the German model, assets and liabilities for mortgages are not segregated and mortgage-holders are not the most senior creditors of the issuing banks. This means that a CH issuance is fully on a balance sheet transaction and that investors in them do not enjoy the first claim of assets on the underlying mortgages. However, the entire asset pool of the bank is available to cover losses in the event of default. Therefore, one needs a high-quality portfolio to convince investors of the lack of credit risk. To compensate, there is a standard value of 11% overcollateralization of mortgage bonds. In addition, if assets are insufficient to provide this level of security, then the deficit must be offset by depositing cash or sovereign bonds with the Bank of Spain. Other alternatives to cure the problem are to redeem or repurchase mortgage certificates until the required limit is met or to add new mortgages to the pool of underlying collateral.

Cédulas Hipotecarias are similar to Pfandbrief in that bond holders have a claim on the parent company of the issuer. In the event of default bond holders have a preferential claim over the entire credit portfolio of the issuer (after deducting those mortgages held as collateral for mortgage bonds). In addition, an owner of a CH has a further special claim on revenues generated through the sale of other assets. Default rates have been relatively low in Spain, with nonperforming loans less than 1% of the total in terms of par value.

In 1999, after some major revisions in Spanish tax law, a jumbo mortgage-backed bond was issued by Argentaria, then Spain's third largest bank. This was designed to be a pan-European investment possibility rather than just limited to the domestic Spanish market. The face amount of this 5-year bond was euro 1.5 billion. Subsequent issues by Banco Bilbao Vizcaya and Caja Madrid were for euro 1 billion (each) and 10 years to maturity. These jumbo CH products typically sell at 10 bp over a German

Pfandbrief, mostly because of credit quality concerns. Finally, in Spain, there is nothing like the public Pfandbrief that so dominates the German mortgage market.

7. The Danish Mortgage Market

In 1795, a great fire destroyed 900 properties in Copenhagen and damaged many others. As part of the rebuilding effort, the first Danish mortgage bank was created in 1797. Danish mortgage banks use mortgage bonds as a source of funds rather than depositors' cash. In over 200 years there has not been a single mortgage-related default by an issuer of a mortgage-backed bond. In the Danish model the bonds are traded on the Copenhagen Stock Exchange where they represent about 60% of the total value of the Danish bond market (and about equal to their gross domestic product). Mortgage banks are restricted, by the Danish Mortgage Credit Act of 1989, to issuing mortgage bonds whose purpose is to finance the purchase of real property and other types of real fixed assets or *Realkreditobligation*. (Funds for the construction of property come from commercial banks.)

The largest investors in these securities are Danish life and nonlife insurance companies (about a third of the outstanding face value). Monetary institutions hold about 25% and the public sector about one-eighth. The remainder is more or less equally distributed over nonfinancial firms, individual households, and foreign investors. Homeownership is not especially widespread at just over 50%.

There are three principles backing the issuance of mortgage bonds in Denmark:

1. All lending is financed through the issuance of bonds on the Copenhagen Stock Exchange backed by real property accurately titled. (In Denmark **every** plot of land is specified by its title number rather than a lengthy word description of the property and its boundaries. A nationwide title register is kept and administered by the judicial system, usually electronically.)
2. The mortgage banks must observe what is known as the balance principle. This states that there will be a balance between the payments received from mortgagors and payments made to mortgage bondholders. In particular, the mortgage banks are generally issuing (callable) mortgage bonds with exactly the same nominal value and interest rate as the original principal amount and interest on the loans that the bonds will finance.
3. The lending rate on mortgages should be a market rate. Thus, mortgage banks act solely as intermediaries between borrowers seeking financing and investors seeking an investment opportunity. No direct connection exists between the individual borrowers and the investors except for the fact that their liens act as collateral for the bonds issued by the mortgage banks. Therefore, the risk of the mortgage banks is limited to the actual credit risk posed by the borrowers; there should be no interest rate risk nor foreign currency exchange risk. (The former is true also for the small amount of adjustable-rate lending funded by noncallable mortgage bonds, but not for the latter in the slowly growing euro-denominated segment of the market.)

The typical mortgage credit loan in Denmark, with mortgage credit defined as meaning granting loans against a registered mortgage on real property on the basis of issuing bonds, is a fixed-rate, fully amortizing, long-term loan just as in the U.S. The required down payment is usually 20% of the property value (i.e., an 80% loan-to-value ratio). Also, as in the U.S., a call option is embedded in the mortgage, which is why most mortgage bonds are callable. (In addition to the noncallable bonds issued in conjunction with adjustable-rate mortgages, there are some short-to-intermediate term bullet mortgage bonds.) Therefore, prepayment risk is a big factor in determining the price of a mortgage bond in Denmark.

The call option in the bonds is exercised at random (with respect to the owners of these bonds but within the same series that funded this repaid mortgage) and in monetary amount equal to the amount of prepayments. These are called repayments in Denmark; with electronic book entry registration of mortgage bonds, this system may be replaced by a strictly proportional one based on the *pro rata* share each bond holder owns. Recently ten different banks have been issuing mortgages and mortgage bonds to support the purchase of residential, agricultural, commercial, and industrial properties. The highest rated mortgage bonds are at the AA2 and AA3 level on Moody's scale.

8. The Swedish Mortgage Market

Sweden does not have uniform mortgage banking legislation and a relatively high permitted loan-to-value ratio of 85%, although 75% is the common practice for single-family housing and 60% for housing cooperatives and vacation homes. Swedish mortgage bond holders do not have explicit priority in the event of bankruptcy either. The Swedish mortgage bond market is the third largest in Europe (mainly because Italy has not had one until very recently). Its principal instrument, modeled after the German Pfandbrief, is known as the *Hypoteksobligation*. As usual, life insurance companies, pension funds, and institutional investors are the most active in the Swedish mortgage bond market, owning about 80% of the outstanding issues. Another peculiarity of the Swedish market is that yields are used as the basis for pricing. Thus, one typically sees bid–ask spreads of a few basis points. Sweden's laws also do not conform with Article 22/4 of the UCITS limiting other European investor's roles.

9. The Luxembourg Mortgage Market

In 1997 the Grand Duchy of Luxembourg passed a mortgage banking act very similar to the German *Hypothekenbankgesetz* of 1900, thereby creating their own version of a Pfandbrief. This is called the *lettres de gage*. It is to be issued by a new type of banking institution known as the *Banque d'Emission de Lettres de Gage* (translation seems to be superfluous). Moreover, the Luxembourg legislation allows mortgage banks to pursue a wider assortment of activities than those allowed the pure mortgage banks in Germany (and they are the majority in Germany). In particular, while German mortgage banks are restricted to lending with the European Economic Area plus Switzerland, banks in Luxembourg may lend to any member country of the Organization for Economic Development. Therefore, with the advent of the euro to eliminate foreign currency exchange rate risk, German mortgage banks can be expected to open branch offices in Luxembourg.

As in the German market there are two types of lettres de gage; public and private. The public sector loans are known as lettres de gage publiques and the private sector loans are known as lettres de gage hypothecaires. Bond holders have first claim on the cover assets for mortgage bonds and the German matching principle has also been copied. Hence, the nominal value of the lettres de gage outstanding must be covered by the value of the assets acting as collateral. Also, a collective effect is at work in that all the lettres de gage of a particular issuer are backed, in aggregate, by its pool of assets. No one-to-one correspondence exists between a particular mortgage and a specific mortgage bond.

C. OTHER WEST EUROPEAN MORTGAGE MARKETS

1. Belgium

In the small Belgium mortgage market, the home ownership rate of about 65% is comparable to that in the U.S.

2. Finland

In Finland the analog of the Pfandbrief is the *Hypoteekkilaina*. Their modern mortgage law was passed in December, 1999, and meets all the criteria of Article 22, Paragraph 4 of the UCITS Directive. They closely follow the German model by using specialist banks, mortgage Pfandbrief and public Pfandbrief, a maximum loan-to-value ratio of 60%, and so forth. The Finnish mortgage bond market dates back only to 1933.

3. Greece

The transliteration of the Greek mortgage instrument is known as the *Ktemateked omolgies.*

4. Italy

Italy has reintroduced an analog of the German Pfandbrief called the *obbligazione fondiaria.* It is used to support its relatively high rate of home ownership, approximately 75%.

5. The Netherlands

The Dutch mortgage market is fourth in size behind Germany, the U.K., and France, even though its homeownership rate is just below 50%. The Dutch use an instrument modeled after the Pfandbrief called a *Pandbrieven.* They have no special collateralization system of matching cover nor do they differentiate between public- and private-sector loans. An attempt to bring greater liquidity to the Dutch mortgage bond market and acquaint other European investors with it was begun by Achmea

Hypotheekbank, who issued a euro 500 million, 5-year floating-rate issue in March, 1999.

6. Norway

Norway has an instrument similar to the Pfandbrief known as the *panteobligasjon*.

7. Switzerland

There has been significant cross-border lending into Switzerland from Germany and Austria; therefore, it should not be surprising that the Swiss use a mortgage bond security called the Pfandbrief. The legal basis was a law passed in 1930 known as the Swiss Federal Pfandbrief Act (*Schweizer Pfandbriefgesetz*). There are separate Pfandbrief issuance facilities for the cantons and all others with names too long to repeat here. Swiss issuers can only lend against property in Switzerland. The security of Swiss Pfandbrief can be gleaned from the fact that cantonal law allows them to qualify for the trust portfolios of widows and orphans. (I did not make this up!) Because of the small population and geographic size of Switzerland, their mortgage bond market is relatively illiquid; they have not been aggressively marketed to foreign investors. Withholding tax concerns with all Swiss bonds make them unattractive to nondomestic investors.

D. EAST EUROPEAN MORTGAGE MARKETS

1. The Czech Republic

The Czechs have a mortgage bond, based on 70% loan-to-value liens, with a cover principle with respect to capital and interest. Mortgage bond creditors have a bankruptcy privilege of these assets. Their name for this instrument is the *hypotécní zástavní list*. There are no specialized mortgage banks in the Czech Republic; any bank may issue them.

2. Hungary

The Hungarians have a Mortgage Bank and Mortgage Bond Act that stipulates the permitted activities of a *jelzálog-hitelintézet*, or mortgage bank. These include raising capital, granting mortgages, making loans to public institutions not based on real property, and certain other operations. The name for their mortgage bond is *jelzálogkötvény*. Loan-to-value ratios may be up to 60%, with strict coverage for principal and interest in place. The mortgage banks have a cover register analogous to that of Denmark and all the assets entered into the cover register can be used to satisfy the claims of mortgage bondholders in the event of default.

3. Latvia

The Latvian mortgage bond, or *kilu zime,* must be covered by mortgage assets separately registered in a bond cover register. The maximum loan-to-value ratio is

60% of the property's market value. All banks may issue mortgages, but in the event of a bankruptcy, only nonmortgage assets can be used to satisfy the bank's creditors.

4. Poland

In Poland there are restrictions on the activities of mortgage banks as defined by their Act on Mortgage Bonds and Mortgage Banks. Basically, they can grant mortgages, grant loans not covered by real property to certain public borrowers, grant loans covered by real property to certain public borrowers, issue mortgage bonds to obtain the funds used for these three types of lending, and acquire loans of this nature issued by other mortgage banks. The public institutions to whom mortgage banks may lend are restricted to the Polish government, its central bank, the European Union and its member states, and some other specialized banks such as the World Bank, the European Investment Bank, and the European Bank for Reconstruction and Development.

The Polish mortgage bond is called a *list zastawny*; it is used to finance up to 60% of a mortgage bank's real estate portfolio. The Poles have a complete coverage principal for the unpaid principal balance and the interest owed. Separation of assets in different cover registers for public and private lending is required. There is preferential access to these assets in the event of default. Even though mortgage loans serving as collateral for mortgage bonds are limited to 60%, the full amount of the loan is recorded. Thus, a form of overcollateralization is built in as another level of protection for investors.

5. The Slovak Republic

In Slovakia the limit on lending is 60% of valuation and a cover principle applies. However, because of a public form of lending known as communal loans, the cover assets for each are separately registered. Mortgage and communal receivables serving as cover assets for mortgage bonds or public sector debentures have preferential treatment in the event of default. These two instruments are known as *hypotekárny zálozny list* and *komunála obligácia*, respectively.

E. OTHER FOREIGN MARKETS

1. The Argentinean Mortgage Market

Argentina uses the Spanish instrument, the Cédulas Hipotecarias, or CH, for its mortgage markets. In April of 1999, a jumbo international version of this was issued. Given the country's current economic problems, there will not be much international interest in this product.

2. The Australian Mortgage Market

The Australian mortgage markets offer a much wider variety of loan products than the American mortgage market does. Some of them are described here so that you can see the assortment from which an Australian homeowner can benefit. Also, the

Australian mortgage market has been totally reconfigured in the last few years, with hundreds of basis points of excess interest charges wrung out of it by nonbank financial firms that introduced mortgage-backed securities as a funding mechanism.

Standard variable loans are Australia's most popular type of home loan, comparable to the U.S. adjustable-rate mortgage. The term is usually 20 to 25 years. The option to make what the Australians refer to as additional repayments (i.e., curtailments) without incurring a penalty is frequently available.

Basic variable loans carry lower interest rates than standard variable home loans but with fewer features. For example, many basic variable loans cannot be used in combination with other loans and are not portable (meaning that the same loan can be used to purchase another property if the homeowner moves). As with floating-rate loans, the interest rate and repayments can vary over the term of the loan. The biggest advantage of this type of product is its price. Basic variable loans have a relatively low interest rates; consequently, the repayments are usually lower than for standard variable loans.

Fixed rate loans are very similar to U.S. hybrid mortgages, although they may have some of the features of a balloon re-set mortgage. Their typical maturity is usually between 1 and 5 years. Most fixed-rate loans will automatically default to a variable-rate loan at the end of the term but can be rolled over to another fixed-term lien. Fixed-rate loans either do not allow additional repayments without further charges or limit the amount of additional repayments that can be made without penalty. There can be penalties for changing from a fixed-rate loan to a variable-rate one or for changing lenders before the fixed-rate term is over (i.e., refinancing).

All-in-one loans are typically variable-rate home loans that allow one to deposit all of one's income into the loan account and then withdraw money from it for day-to-day purchases. The longer additional funds stay in the account, the greater the interest savings are. These instruments operate like a combined checking and savings account. Most all-in-one loans provide access to the loan account via a check book, have a debit card for ATM usage, and can perform electronic funds transfer via point-of-sale transactions. Using a home loan as the transaction account (the name in Australia for this type of account) can reduce the number of bank accounts one needs and simplify one's finances. The borrower may be required to pay a premium for the flexibility of an all-in-one loan such as a monthly fee or higher interest rate.

Introductory loans carry a lower interest rate to attract first-time borrowers. They normally have a period of 2 years or less; most are for 12 months. Introductory loans can have fixed, variable, or capped rates. After the initial period, most introductory loans revert to the standard variable rate, usually with the lowest interest rate available on the market. If payments are made at the interest rate applicable after the introductory period, then the unpaid principal balance can be quickly reduced. Some banks provide an offset account on these loans. Payments may increase when the initial period ends.

100% offset loans are a separate savings account run in conjunction with the home loan. The interest rate on this account is the same as the interest rate on the home loan. Any money put in the offset account is deducted from the home loan balance before interest is calculated. This account also operates like a transaction account. It will generally have a check facility and a cash card that allows one to make ATM and electronic funds transfers. The interest rates on 100% offset accounts are higher than other savings and transaction accounts. A 100% offset account may have a premium: either a monthly access fee or a higher interest rate. One may also need to have a minimum balance, such as $2,000, in the offset account for the offset effect to be calculated.

In *combination loans* the borrower takes a portion of the total amount borrowed under one loan product and the remainder under another. For example, half the amount borrowed could be under a variable interest rate and the other half under a fixed-rate vehicle. The homeowner chooses the proportion of the loan amount between fixed and variable.

A *line of credit* is secured by a mortgage on a residential property and therefore similar to a U.S. home-equity loan. With a line of credit it is possible to draw down to the set credit limit as needed or desired. Interest rates are usually lower than for credit cards or personal loans. Credit limits are usually higher than for credit cards or personal loans.

A *bridging facility* enables an existing homeowner to purchase another property prior to the sale of the existing home. One may borrow 100% of the purchase price without additional security. Surprisingly high loan amounts, up to $750,000, come with an equally surprisingly long term of up to 30 years. No payments are required for the first 6 months or until the sale of the existing home because interest will be capitalized (i.e., negative amortization) to the loan until the sale of the existing property or for a maximum of 6 months. After the sale of the property or 6 months (whichever occurs first), payments will be due monthly. If rates are fixed, then up to $20,000 per year above normal payments may be made without any fee. Redrawing of payments made over the required minimum is a special feature of this type of loan. Indeed, curtailments may be redrawn.

In Australia the common maximum lending amount is up to three times one's gross annual income. When more than one person is involved, for example, a married couple borrowing together or some other form of joint borrowing, both partners' incomes are normally considered. Income from a variety of other sources beyond salary, such as self-employed earnings, dividends, rental income, or any other source of regular and recurring income can be used to justify a lien. As for loan-to-value ratios, Australian banks will usually lend up to 90% of the valuation of the property.

In most cases, interest is calculated daily and debited monthly in arrears. When a bank account is attached, it is debited monthly. Just as the U.S. has bi-weekly payment options, so too does Australia have fortnightly and weekly repayment schedules available for some products. Most mortgage agreements allow curtailments (or extra repayments) at no charge. Redraw facilities are a feature not found in the U.S. This means that one can use the redraw facilities to take out any or all of additional repayments at a future date. Some products even allow redraws on fixed interest facilities.

One Australian bank even offers a *design-a-loan* feature that allows the mortgagor to design a loan best suited the circumstances. He may choose to split the loan into subaccounts or to choose a mixture of principal and interest and interest only repayments together with a choice of fixed and variable interest rates.

Finally, another feature about the Australian mortgage market is very different from that of the U.S. They have something called a mortgage manager. These individuals are responsible for originating and managing home loans, which means that they control the marketing, selling, and repayment management of the loan. They are not brokers because brokers usually sell mortgages and financial services but take no responsibility for the management of these facilities after the sale. The funds for mortgage managers usually come from commercial and investment banks or insurance companies that have excess monies to invest. Mortgage managers also typically use mortgage-backed securities to obtain financing. They are usually issued with A or higher ratings. The mortgage manager manages all aspects of a loan; he sends out periodic statements, can arrange curtailments, and so forth. Given that most loans have 20-year terms (or more), this means that the relationship with the borrower is likely to be long term.

References

Bartlett, W.W., *The Valuation of Mortgage-Backed Securities*, Irwin Professional Publishing, New York, 1994.

Carlson, S.J. and Tierney, J.F., Collaterized borrowing via dollar rolls, in *The Handbook of Mortgage-Backed Securities*, Fabozzi, F.J., ed., McGraw-Hill, Co., Inc., New York, 1995, chap. 6.

Copeland, T.E. and Weston, J.F., *Financial Theory and Corporate Policy*, 3rd Ed., Addison-Wesley Publishing. Co., Reading, MA, 1992, chap. 6.

Cox, J.C., Ingersoll, J.E., and Ross, S.A., A theory of the term structure of interest rates, *Econometrica*, 53, 385, 1985.

Heath, D., Jarrow, R., and Morton, A., Bond pricing and the term structure of interest rates; a new methodology, *Econometrica*, 60, 77, 1992.

Hull, J.C., *Options, Futures, and Other Derivatives*, 3rd Ed., Prentice Hall, Upper Saddle River, NJ, 1997, chap. 10.

Knez, P.J., Litterman, R., and Scheinkman, J., Explorations into factors explaining money market returns, *J. Finance*, 49, 1861, 1994.

Pilpel, S., Inverse floaters and inverse IOs, in *The Handbook of Mortgage-Backed Securities*, Fabozzi, F.J., ed., McGraw-Hill, Co., Inc., New York, 1995, chap. 21.

Stigum, M., *The Money Market*, 3rd Ed., McGraw-Hill Co., Inc., New York, 1990, Part I.

Index

D

E

F